THE CHARTER OF
RIGHTS AND FREEDOMS

FOURTH EDITION

Other books in the *Essentials of Canadian Law* Series

ESSENTIALS OF
CANADIAN LAW

THE CHARTER
OF RIGHTS
AND FREEDOMS

FOURTH EDITION

HON. ROBERT J. SHARPE
Court of Appeal for Ontario

KENT ROACH
Faculty of Law, University of Toronto

IRWIN
LAW

The Charter of Rights and Freedoms, fourth edition
© Irwin Law Inc., 2009

Published in 2009 by

Irwin Law Inc.
14 Duncan Street
Suite 206
Toronto, ON
M5H 3G8

www.irwinlaw.com

ISBN: 978-1-55221-175-5

Library and Archives Canada Cataloguing in Publication

Sharpe, Robert J.
    The Charter of Rights and Freedoms / Robert J. Sharpe, Kent Roach. —4th ed.

(Essentials of Canadian law)
Includes bibliographical references and index.
ISBN 978-1-55221-175-5

    1. Canada. Canadian Charter of Rights and Freedoms. 2. Civil rights—Canada. I. Roach, Kent, 1961– II. Title. III. Series: Essentials of Canadian law

KE4381.5.S54 2009   342.7108'5   C2009-904914-7
KF4483.C519S54 2009

The publisher acknowledges the financial support of the Government of Canada through the Book Publishing Industry Development Program (BPIDP) for its publishing activities.

We acknowledge the assistance of the OMDC Book Fund, an initiative of Ontario Media Development Corporation.

Printed and bound in Canada.

1 2 3 4 5   13 12 11 10 09

SUMMARY
TABLE OF CONTENTS

DETAILED
TABLE OF CONTENTS

CHAPTER 14:

CHARTER RIGHTS IN THE CRIMINAL PROCESS   259

PREFACE
To the Fourth Edition

The steady pace of *Charter* litigation has produced a long list of significant developments since the publication of the third edition four years ago. Notable among those developments are significant changes to the way the Supreme Court has approached the interpretation of equality rights and constitutional remedies including the exclusion of evidence under section 24(2) of the *Charter*. We have done our best to reflect those developments in the preparation of this edition and, where appropriate, to improve upon certain aspects of earlier editions. Although Katherine Swinton did not participate in the preparation of this edition or the third edition, we continue to benefit from her important contribution to the first and second editions and significant portions of the book continue to bear her mark. We thank James Renihan and Tom McConville for their excellent research assistance. We also thank our publishers, William Kaplan and Jeff Miller, for their confidence and support, and the staff at Irwin Law for all their help in the production of this edition.

INTRODUCTION

The amendment of the Canadian constitution in 1982 to include the *Charter of Rights and Freedoms* brought about a fundamental change in Canadian law and politics.[1] The *Charter* significantly increased the law-making power of Canadian courts. Decisions on many important public issues, formerly within the exclusive authority of Parliament and the provincial legislatures, are now subject to judicial review. *Charter* litigation has become an important tool used by interest groups to advance their political ends. Canadian courts now play a central role in deciding how the law should deal with such intractable issues as abortion,[2] mandatory retirement,[3] the legitimacy of laws restricting pornography[4] and hate propaganda,[5] the definition of what may properly constitute a criminal offence[6] and the treatment accorded minorities such as gays and lesbians.[7]

---

1   *Canadian Charter of Rights and Freedoms*, Part I of the *Constitution Act, 1982*, being Schedule B to the *Canada Act 1982*, (U.K.), 1982, c. 11 [*Charter*].
2   *R. v. Morgentaler*, [1988] 1 S.C.R. 30, 44 D.L.R. (4th) 385.
3   *McKinney v. University of Guelph*, [1990] 3 S.C.R. 229, 76 D.L.R. (4th) 545; *Stoffman v. Vancouver General Hospital*, [1990] 3 S.C.R. 483, 76 D.L.R. (4th) 700.
4   *R. v. Butler*, [1992] 1 S.C.R. 452, 70 C.C.C. (3d) 129; *R. v. Sharpe*, [2001] 1 S.C.R. 45, 194 D.L.R. (4th) 1.
5   *R. v. Keegstra*, [1990] 3 S.C.R. 697, 61 C.C.C. (3d) 1.
6   *R. v. Vaillancourt*, [1987] 2 S.C.R. 636, 47 D.L.R. (4th) 399.
7   *Vriend v. Alberta*, [1998] 1 S.C.R. 493, 156 D.L.R. (4th) 385; *M. v. H.*, [1999] 2 S.C.R. 3, 177 D.L.R. (4th) 577; *Little Sisters Book and Art Emporium v. Canada (Minister of Justice)*, [2000] 2 S.C.R. 1120, 193 D.L.R. (4th) 193; *Halpern v. Can-*

1

The *Charter* has unquestionably had a profound impact upon the role of the judiciary. The courts are now empowered to deal with issues that range far beyond what was seen as appropriate to the judicial function before 1982. In the pre-1982 era, to most Canadians the Supreme Court of Canada was a remote institution that had little, if any, real impact upon their lives. Since entrenchment, however, the Supreme Court has been recognized by the Canadian public as a seat of great power and influence. It has become the institution to which citizens may turn for protection of their fundamental rights and freedoms.

Media attention to legal issues has increased significantly, which is undoubtedly attributable in large part to the *Charter*. Decisions of the courts are routinely front-page news. The Supreme Court of Canada has developed a media-relations policy to ensure that its judgments are adequately reported, and the Canadian Judicial Council has suggested that provincial superior and appellate courts do the same.[8] Some judges have taken the view that they should become more visible and vocal. Interviews and profiles of judges in the daily news media are not uncommon as reporters try to demystify the judicial process and explain it in terms the ordinary citizen can understand. Judges contribute to scholarly journals, discussing their changed role under the *Charter*.[9]

This book attempts to explain the *Charter of Rights and Freedoms* to non-specialist readers interested in acquiring a basic understanding of the Canadian legal system and the Canadian constitution. We will survey the manner in which the Canadian courts have come to terms with a constitutionally entrenched bill of rights, focusing on the decisions of the Supreme Court of Canada. The purpose is to explain the *Charter*, its interpretation by the courts, and its practical application, rather than to present anything approaching a theoretical or philosophical account of *Charter* rights. It is, however, almost impossible to discuss the *Charter* without a theoretical framework. As will become apparent,

---

ada (Attorney General) (2003), 65 O.R. (3d) 161 (C.A.); *Reference Re Same-Sex Marriage*, [2004] 3 S.C.R. 698, 246 D.L.R. (4th) 193.

8   See R.J. Sharpe, "The Role of a Media Spokesperson for the Courts—The Supreme Court of Canada Experience" (1991) 1 Media & Comm. L. Rev. 271.

9   Chief Justice Beverley McLachlin, a former academic, has been particularly active in this regard. See the following by B.M. McLachlin: "The Role of the Court in the Post-*Charter* Era: Policy-Maker or Adjudicator?" (1990) 39 U.N.B.L.J. 43; "The *Charter of Rights and Freedoms*: A Judicial Perspective" (1989) 23 U.B.C. L. Rev. 579; "The *Charter*: A New Role for the Judiciary" (1991) 29 Alta. L. Rev. 540; "The Canadian *Charter* and the Democratic Process" (1991) 18 Melb. U. L. Rev. 350; "Equality: The Most Difficult Right" (2001) 14 Sup. Ct. L. Rev. (2d) 17; "The Supreme Court and the Public Interest" (2001) 64 Sask. L. Rev. 309; "*Charter* Myths" (1999) 33 U.B.C. L. Rev. 23.

we are believers in the *Charter* and in the important role it confers upon the courts. In our view, the courts are properly charged with the task of defining and protecting fundamental rights and freedoms in a modern liberal democracy. Furthermore, the Canadian experience to date suggests that an entrenched bill of rights enhances rather than detracts from fundamental democratic values.[10]

---

10 Further discussion is found in K. Roach, *The Supreme Court on Trial: Judicial Activism or Democratic Dialogue* (Toronto: Irwin Law, 2001).

CHAPTER 1

HISTORICAL CONTEXT

A. THE PRE-1982 CANADIAN CONSTITUTION

The *Charter of Rights and Freedoms* should be seen as one element in Canada's evolving constitution. While the *Charter* now occupies centre stage and has become the focus of public attention, its enactment in 1982 did not mark the beginning of rights protection in Canadian law. This introductory chapter will attempt to place the *Charter* in its proper constitutional context and will provide a brief survey of the protection of fundamental rights and freedoms in Canadian law before 1982.

Canada's primary constitutional document, the *British North America Act, 1867* (renamed the *Constitution Act, 1867* in 1982) contained two major features: a parliamentary system of government and federalism.

1) Parliamentary Supremacy

The first feature of our pre-1982 constitution was a parliamentary system of government modelled upon the principles of British parliamentary democracy. The preamble to the *Constitution Act, 1867*, states that Canada is to have "a Constitution similar in Principle to that of the United Kingdom." Apart from this very general reference, the basic principles of British constitutionalism are not spelled out in the written constitution. They are to be found in conventions, traditions, and practices that evolved over time and that continue to govern the structure of Canadian government.

The central concept of the British constitution is the supremacy of Parliament. The elected representatives of the people, assembled in Parliament, have unlimited power to make the law. The role of the courts is limited to deciding cases by interpreting the law as laid down by Parliament or as defined by the common law. In particular, judges do not have the authority to invalidate laws that have been duly enacted through the democratic process of Parliament. The one thing—perhaps the only thing—Parliament cannot do is to bind its successors. Whatever one Parliament has laid down as the law can be changed by the next.

The fundamental rights and freedoms of a liberal democracy (that is, freedom of expression, religion, association, and assembly) as well as basic legal rights (fair trial, freedom from arbitrary arrest, the presumption of innocence, and right to a jury trial) are, however, very much a part of our British parliamentary heritage. That tradition clearly recognizes and respects the importance of fundamental rights and freedoms but holds that Parliament is the proper institution to decide upon their meaning and scope. Courts are entitled to take fundamental rights into account when deciding cases and interpreting statutes, particularly where there is any ambiguity in the law, but the primary and final responsibility for achieving an appropriate balance between the rights of the individual and the general public interest remains with the elected representatives of the people sitting in Parliament.

Until 1982, the Canadian approach to the protection of fundamental rights and freedoms was strongly influenced by the principle of the supremacy of Parliament. As will be seen shortly, Canadian courts did exercise the power of judicial review in some cases to protect fundamental rights, but these cases were really exceptions rather than the rule. Canada's written constitution offered relatively little by way of rights protection until 1982.

2) Federalism

The second fundamental element of the Canadian constitution is federalism, that is, the division of legislative powers between the Parliament of Canada and the ten provincial legislatures. This division of powers is contained in Canada's original constitution, the *Constitution Act, 1867*. Canada is geographically, culturally, and linguistically diverse. The division of legislative power between a central national Parliament and ten provincial legislatures, defining the areas in which each level of government is entitled to act, represents an attempt to accommodate that diversity.

The federal structure itself contains a form of rights protection. When an ethnic or religious minority is concentrated in a geographical area, the grant of state or provincial status ensures a measure of self-government for that minority, especially if it constitutes a majority within that unit. Self-government allows the group to adopt laws that are informed by its distinctive culture or language. One of the reasons for adopting a federal state in Canada was to provide a measure of self-government for French Canadians who were and continue to be a majority in the province of Quebec.

While Canada's pre-1982 written constitution was silent on the power of judicial review, from the early years of Confederation, Canadian courts routinely acted as the referee in deciding whether legislative matters fell within federal or provincial jurisdiction, and they have invalidated those laws enacted without a proper constitutional basis. In this respect, the Canadian constitution has, almost from the very beginning, departed in one respect from the fundamental principle of parliamentary supremacy. Canadian judges have exercised the power of judicial review for well over one hundred years, striking down a significant number of statutes, both federal and provincial, on the ground that the law fell outside the authority assigned to the enacting body by the constitution.

The division of powers between the federal Parliament and the provincial legislatures and the role played by the courts in resolving jurisdictional conflicts is a complex subject that is dealt with in another volume in this series.[1] It is, however, appropriate here briefly to consider the manner in which the pre-*Charter* constitution protected certain fundamental rights.

B. RIGHTS PROTECTION THROUGH COMMON LAW AND STATUTORY INTERPRETATION

The legal protection of fundamental rights and freedoms does not rest entirely upon the explicit provisions of the constitution nor upon the *Charter of Rights and Freedoms*. Concern for civil liberties has always been an important feature of Canadian law. Throughout our history, judicial decisions have played an important role in the protection of fundamental rights,[2] and while Parliament may be supreme, our political culture has demanded that it pay heed to the basic rights of all citizens.

---

1   P. Monahan, *Constitutional Law*, 3d ed. (Toronto: Irwin Law, 2006).
2   See B. Laskin, "An Inquiry into the Diefenbaker *Bill of Rights*" (1959) 37 Can. Bar Rev. 77.

Most of our most important civil rights, such as *habeas corpus*, trial by jury, and the presumption of innocence, were creations of the common law. These rights are founded upon judicial decisions extending far back in the Anglo-American legal tradition. They are judge-made rights, often supplemented or bolstered by statutes, which formed an essential aspect of our legal system long before 1982 and the *Charter*.

Another important part of our legal tradition has been judicial review of administrative action. Judicial commitment to the rule of law has resulted in the nullification of decisions by officials or administrative tribunals when they have acted without jurisdiction, while the rules of natural justice have ensured fairness in administrative procedures. One of the most famous pre-*Charter* cases held that the Premier of Quebec could not arbitrarily revoke a person's liquor licence for reasons unrelated to the purpose of the legislation.[3]

In addition, in the interest of protecting liberal values, courts have imported certain presumptions when interpreting statutes.[4] For example, it is presumed that the state would not expropriate property without compensation. If property is taken, compensation must be given absent a clear signal from a legislature that it does not intend to provide it. Similarly, the courts presumed that criminal laws would only punish people who were at fault in the absence of a clear signal from the legislature. These presumptions played a role both in protecting fundamental values and requiring democratic debate and accountability for departures from those values.

Other rights and freedoms now enshrined in the *Charter* never crystallized as specific rights in the common law but did have force as basic principles that underlay the whole structure of the law, informing both political debate in Parliament and legal decision making in the courts. As the Supreme Court of Canada has said, rights and freedoms did not spring from a vacuum in 1982.[5] Freedom of expression and religion, for example, were well-known and well-respected principles of the Canadian constitution. These values were sometimes embodied in statutes to extend protection in specified circumstances.[6] They were vitally im-

---

3   *Roncarelli v. Duplessis* (1958), [1959] S.C.R. 121, 16 D.L.R. (2d) 689.

4   See J. Willis, "Statutory Interpretation in a Nutshell" (1938) 16 Can. Bar Rev. 1; K. Roach, "Common Law Bills of Rights as Dialogue between Courts and Legislatures" (2005) 55 U.T.L.J. 733.

5   See, for example, *R. v. Big M Drug Mart Ltd.*, [1985] 1 S.C.R. 295, 18 D.L.R. (4th) 321; *Reference Re Provincial Electoral Boundaries (Saskatchewan)*, [1991] 2 S.C.R. 158, 81 D.L.R. (4th) 16.

6   *Freedom of Worship Act*, (1850–51), 14 & 15 Vict., c. 175; *Constitution Act, 1867*, s. 93.

portant principles that the courts drew upon when interpreting and applying statutes or developing the common law. A leading example is the decision of the 1951 Supreme Court of Canada in *Boucher v. R.*,[7] where a Jehovah's Witness was charged with seditious libel because of a pamphlet that he distributed. The Supreme Court of Canada ordered a new trial because the trial judge had virtually ignored a defence of speaking in good faith.

C. THE *CONSTITUTION ACT, 1867,* AND THE PROTECTION OF FUNDAMENTAL RIGHTS

While the scope for judicial review under the 1867 constitution was essentially limited to questions of legislative jurisdiction as between the provinces and the federal Parliament, the courts did establish an element of rights protection through judicial review.

First, the *Constitution Act, 1867,* contains certain specific minority rights enforceable through the courts. The right to use English and French in Parliament, in the legislature of Quebec, and in the courts established by the federal Parliament (that is, the Supreme Court of Canada, the Federal Court, and the Tax Court) and by the province of Quebec is guaranteed by section 133.[8] Minority-religion education rights were secured for the Roman Catholic minority in Ontario and the Protestant minority in Quebec by section 93, and similar rights were accorded by the terms admitting some new provinces after 1867. Provisions relating to the appointment and tenure of judges (sections 96–100) have been interpreted to guarantee an independent judiciary and to secure the role of the courts as overseers of the legality of administrative and executive action. Although probably not judicially enforceable, the 1867 constitution also secures certain democratic rights relating to the length (section 50) and regularity (section 20) of sessions of Parliament.[9] As noted above, federalism itself may be seen as a form of minority-rights protection, particularly in the case of Quebec and the preservation of French language and culture and the civil law tradition.

---

7   *Boucher v. R.*, [1951] S.C.R. 265, [1951] 2 D.L.R. 369.

8   Similar rights with respect to the legislature and courts of Manitoba were specified in the *Manitoba Act, 1870,* and language rights have been expanded under the *Charter:* See chapter 16.

9   Section 20 was repealed by the *Charter* in 1982. For further discussion of democratic rights, see chapters 8 and 11.

Second, despite the limited nature of explicit rights protection under the 1867 constitution, civil liberties were protected in a number of cases through federalism review. The Supreme Court of Canada found that certain laws that limited fundamental rights could be attacked in the courts on the ground that authority to enact the law fell outside the scope of the powers accorded the enacting provincial legislature by the *Constitution Act, 1867*.

Perhaps the most notable example was the 1938 decision, *Reference Re Alberta Legislation*,[10] striking down Alberta legislation that interfered with the right of newspapers to report freely on the economic policies of the government. The law at issue was part of the package of measures put forth by the newly elected Social Credit government, which asserted that its economic and monetary policies would be effective only if media coverage was "accurate." While provinces normally have extensive authority to regulate businesses operating within the province, the Supreme Court of Canada held that the Alberta legislature lacked the legislative authority to enact a law that struck at the very foundation of our parliamentary democracy. Although freedom of expression and freedom of the press were not specifically protected by the constitution, the Court found that the right of every citizen to criticize government was a necessary and inherent element of Canada's constitution, and beyond the reach of a provincial legislature. Cannon J. reasoned as follows:

> Freedom of discussion is essential to enlighten public opinion in a democratic State; it cannot be curtailed without affecting the right of the people to be informed through sources independent of the Government concerning matters of public interest. There must be an untrammelled publication of the news and political opinions of the political parties contending for ascendancy. As stated in the preamble of the *British North America Act* [now the *Constitution Act, 1867*], our constitution is and will remain, unless radically changed, "similar in principle to that of the United Kingdom." At the time of Confederation, the United Kingdom was a democracy. Democracy cannot be maintained without its foundation: free public opinion and free discussion throughout the nation of all matters affecting the State within the limits set by the Criminal Code and the common law.[11]

Fifteen years later, in *Saumur v. Quebec (City)*,[12] the Supreme Court of Canada returned to the theme of the inherent rights of citizenship in

---

10   [1938] S.C.R. 100, [1938] 2 D.L.R. 81 [*Alberta Press*].
11   *Ibid.* at 145–46 (S.C.R.).
12   [1953] 2 S.C.R. 299, [1953] 4 D.L.R. 641.

a democracy, striking down a municipal bylaw that forbade the distribution of pamphlets without the permission of the chief of police. The action challenging the validity of the bylaw was brought by a member of the Jehovah's Witnesses. By a majority, the Court held that the bylaw was invalid. While the judges offered various reasons, Rand J., one of the majority of the Court that found in Saumur's favour, held that the effect of this measure was to confer on the police an unacceptably open-ended discretion amounting to a power of censorship. Like Cannon J. in the *Alberta Press* case, Rand J. drew upon the rights of citizenship inherent in democratic government to determine that the action was beyond the power of the provinces or the municipalities. He stated:

> [F]reedom of speech, religion and the inviolability of the person, are original freedoms which are at once the necessary attributes and modes of self-expression of human beings and the primary conditions of their community life within a legal order . . .. The Confederation Act recites the desire of the three Provinces to be federally united in one Dominion "with a constitution similar in principle to that of the United Kingdom." Under that constitution, Government is by parliamentary institutions, including popular assemblies elected by the people at large in both Provinces and Dominion: Government resting ultimately on public opinion reached by discussion and the interplay of ideas. If that discussion is placed under licence, its basic condition is destroyed: the Government, as licensor, becomes disjoined from the citizenry.[13]

Four years later, in *Switzman v. Elbling*,[14] another case from Quebec, the Supreme Court again adverted to the inherent rights of the citizen and the necessary conditions fundamental to democracy. At issue was the provincial "Padlock Act," which made it illegal for anyone to make use of a house for the propagation of communism or bolshevism. Rand J. again made an eloquent appeal to the fundamental rights of citizens in a democracy in finding the law to be beyond the powers of the provincial legislature:

> Parliamentary Government postulates a capacity in men, acting freely and under self-restraints, to govern themselves; and that advance is best served in the degree achieved of individual liberation from subjective as well as objective shackles. Under that Government, the freedom of discussion in Canada, as a subject-matter of legislation, has a unity of interest and significance extending equally to every part of

---

13   *Ibid.* at 329–30 (S.C.R.).
14   [1957] S.C.R. 285, 7 D.L.R. (2d) 337 [*Switzman*].

the Dominion . . . . This constitutional fact is the political expression of the primary condition of social life, thought and its communication by language. Liberty in this is little less vital to man's mind and spirit than breathing is to his physical existence. As such an inherence in the individual is embodied in his status of citizenship.[15]

These judicial pronouncements are significant. They identify a rationale for judicial review grounded in the principles of democracy so powerful that it can be exercised in the absence of an explicit bill of rights. Thus, even before the *Charter*, the courts were able to justify interference with legislative choices that were themselves inimical to the principles of democratic government. It has to be recognized, however, that the success of pre-*Charter* rights protection was limited. As noted, the cases and individual opinions referred to stand out as exceptions to the norm. More often, judges were unwilling to challenge the traditional conception of a strictly limited judicial role. Moreover, the cases cited all dealt with challenges to provincial authority, and the suggestion that there was an "unwritten bill of rights" in the 1867 constitution protecting fundamental freedoms from both levels of government garnered little support.[16] Constitutional protection of rights and freedoms based upon the division of powers between the federal and provincial governments, while significant in certain specific instances, was necessarily limited and subordinate to the basic rule of the pre-1982 approach to the protection of rights, namely, parliamentary supremacy. While the courts were prepared to protect fundamental democratic rights from provincial invasion, the general rule was that if the elected representatives of the people decided that the public interest required a law curtailing an individual right, there was little the courts could do.

D. THE *CONSTITUTION ACT, 1867,* AND PROTECTION AGAINST DISCRIMINATION

Another significant limitation of pre-*Charter* rights protection was the failure of the courts (and indeed, until the advent of human rights codes, discussed below, of the entire legal system) to protect minorities from discrimination. A series of cases coming before the Supreme

15   *Ibid.* at 358 (D.L.R.).
16   See the opinion of Abbott J. in *Switzman*, above note 14 at 371 (D.L.R.). For a post-*Charter* affirmation of this principle, see *O.P.S.E.U. v. Ontario (A.G.)*, [1987] 2 S.C.R. 2, 41 D.L.R. (4th) 1, Beetz J.; *Reference Re Public Sector Pay Reduction Act (P.E.I.), s. 10* (1997), 150 D.L.R. (4th) 577 at 623–28 (S.C.C.).

Court and the Judicial Committee of the Privy Council (then Canada's court of last resort) dealt with challenges to overtly racist legislation.[17] It was argued that the federal power with respect to "naturalization and aliens" in section 91(25) of the *Constitution Act, 1867* and Parliament's residual power to ensure "peace, order and good government" under section 91 included authority to ensure the enjoyment of ordinary legal rights without discrimination on the basis of race and national origin. These challenges proved unsuccessful.

Union Colliery Co. of British Columbia Ltd. v. Bryden,[18] the first case to raise these issues at the highest level, involved a challenge to British Columbia legislation forbidding the employment of "Chinamen" below ground in a coal mine. The prohibition was but one of a shockingly long list of legislative measures introduced in British Columbia attempting to prevent or restrict the settlement of Chinese immigrants in the province. The province asserted that the law was designed to ensure safety in the mines. The Privy Council rejected this characterization of the law and found that the law was unconstitutional: "[T]he whole pith and substance of the enactments . . . consists in establishing a statutory prohibition which affects aliens or naturalized subjects, and therefore trench upon the exclusive authority of the Parliament of Canada."[19] Although written in a formalistic style, with virtually no explicit appeal to the concept of equality, the Privy Council's opinion in *Bryden* gave some hope that despite the absence of any explicit anti-discrimination provision in the constitution, the courts might be prepared to protect racial minorities on the basis of the division of powers. The opinion provided a possible ground for the elaboration of an important branch of federal legislative power to ensure the rights and privileges attached to Canadian citizenship.

That hope proved short-lived. Shortly after *Bryden*, a naturalized Japanese resident of British Columbia challenged the constitutional validity of the province's electoral law, which denied the vote to all those of Japanese descent, whether naturalized or not. The plaintiff, Tomey

---

17   The discussion that follows is an abbreviated version of the first part of R.J. Sharpe, "Citizenship, the *Constitution Act, 1867*, and the *Charter*" in W. Kaplan, ed., *Belonging: The Meaning and Future of Canadian Citizenship* (Montreal: McGill-Queen's University Press, 1993) at 221. For further discussion, see B. Ryder, "Racism and the Constitution: The Constitutional Fate of British Columbia Anti-Asian Legislation, 1884–1909" (1991) 29 Osgoode Hall L.J. 619; J. St-G. Walker, *Race, Rights and the Law of the Supreme Court of Canada* (Waterloo, ON: Wilfrid Laurier University Press, 1997).

18   [1899] A.C. 580, 68 L.J.P.C. 118, 81 L.T. 277 (P.C.) [*Bryden*].

19   *Ibid.* at 587 (A.C.).

Homma, relied upon the expansive definition of the Dominion's power over naturalization in *Bryden* and upon the specific terms of the *Naturalization Act* of Canada, which provided that a naturalized alien was entitled to all political and other rights, powers, and privileges to which a natural-born British subject is entitled in Canada.[20] The province contended that section 92(1) of the *Constitution Act, 1867*, granting the power to legislate with respect to the constitution of the province, authorized it to decide which British subjects residing in the province should enjoy the franchise. The franchise was considered a privilege conferred by legislation rather than a right. Many subjects—women, those under the voting age, and certain office holders—did not have the vote. Tomey Homma succeeded in the British Columbia courts but the case was appealed to the Privy Council.[21] There, *Bryden* was abandoned and in its place was adopted an analysis that emphasized, to the exclusion of other values, the protection of provincial legislative authority. The franchise was seen as a privilege the province was entitled to grant or withhold as it saw fit. The constitution's grant of federal power was said to be too narrow to preclude discrimination on racial grounds. Race, like gender, was simply a category the province was entitled to adopt in determining who should have the "privilege" of the franchise.

For a time, the courts continued to follow *Bryden* with respect to legislative barriers to employment on racial lines. But even this suffered a setback with the decision of the Supreme Court of Canada in *Quong-Wing v. R.* in 1914.[22] At issue was the constitutional validity of a Saskatchewan law that created the following offence:

> No person shall employ in any capacity any white woman or girl or permit any white woman or girl to reside or lodge in or to work in or, save as a *bona fide* customer in a public apartment thereof only, to frequent any restaurant, laundry or other place of business or amusement owned, kept or managed by any Chinaman.

Quong-Wing, described in the decision of the Supreme Court of Canada as "a Chinaman and a naturalized Canadian citizen,"[23] was convicted of employing a white woman. He challenged the law, relying on *Bryden*. However, a majority of the Supreme Court of Canada saw the legislation as a valid exercise of the provincial legislative capacity to establish proper conditions of employment for women and thought that "[t]he difference between the restrictions imposed on all Canadians by

---

20   R.S.C. 1886, c. 113, s. 15, Fitzpatrick C.J.
21   *Cunningham v. Tomey Homma*, [1903] A.C. 151.
22   (1914), 49 S.C.R. 440.
23   *Ibid.* at 443.

such legislation and those resulting from the Act in question is one of degree, not of kind."[24]

The overt racism of the legislation challenged in these cases is shocking to the modern reader. Equally disturbing is the implicit acceptance of the racist assumptions underlying the legislation by many of the judges. Yet the failure of the courts to develop an expansive conception of basic rights of citizenship as implicit in the federal power with respect to "naturalization and aliens" is perhaps not surprising. The language of the constitution hardly led inexorably to that conclusion. It would have taken an exercise of judicial creativity and imagination of considerable magnitude to articulate a conception of citizenship that would embody at the federal level the authority to define and protect the essential attributes of citizenship, while at the same time respecting the legitimate claims of provincial power.

E. INTERNATIONAL HUMAN RIGHTS CHARTERS

The failure of the Canadian legal system to respond to the issue of racial and other forms of discrimination was not an isolated phenomenon. In the period immediately following the Second World War, there was an international trend towards the elaboration of human rights charters of various kinds. The horrors of war, the Holocaust, and the rise of totalitarianism created a climate in which it was increasingly felt that human rights values deserved enhanced recognition and protection. No nation was blameless — the fears of war had prompted Canada to perpetuate shameful discrimination against Japanese Canadians. There was an awakening to the evils of racism and a widespread feeling that new laws and legal techniques were required.

The adoption of formal charters proclaiming fundamental rights and freedoms occurred at both the national and international levels. The United Nations adopted the *Universal Declaration of Human Rights* in 1948. A large number of European states signed the European *Convention for the Protection of Human Rights and Fundamental Freedoms* in 1950. Other instruments came into being over the next two decades, to which Canada was a signatory — for example, the *International Covenant on Civil and Political Rights* in 1966. Some of the rights in these modern bills of rights could be subject to limits prescribed by law, limits that are necessary in a democratic society, and some of the rights

---

24   *Ibid.* at 445.

could be subject to formal derogation in times of officially proclaimed emergencies. These and other features of international human rights charters influenced the drafting of the *Charter*.

As colonialism collapsed, the constitutions of newly independent states almost invariably contained entrenched charters of rights and freedoms. Even in nations with established constitutional regimes, the protection of human rights and the struggle against discrimination and racism attracted unprecedented attention. The decision of the Supreme Court of the United States in its 1954 ruling, *Brown v. Board of Education*,[25] was a watershed. The Court found that racially segregated schools violated the guarantee of equal protection of the laws, and it overruled a late-nineteenth-century precedent that had implicitly sanctioned racial segregation by allowing states to establish "separate but equal" facilities.[26] In *Brown*, the Supreme Court proclaimed that separate schools were inherently unequal and thereby created an impetus for the dismantling of racial segregation in all areas. The focus of rights protection in American constitutional law shifted from property and traditional democratic rights to the struggle for equality, and the courts assumed an overtly activist role.

Both the *Canadian Bill of Rights*, enacted in 1960, and the Canadian *Charter* of 1982 were certainly influenced by these international developments and may be seen as a product of the same general trend. Canada's international human rights commitments also continue to play an important role in the interpretation of the *Charter* which will be examined in chapter three. As will be discussed in chapter 6, breach of Canada's international commitments when Canadian officials act outside of Canada can also trigger the extraterritorial application of the *Charter*.

F. HUMAN RIGHTS CODES

In domestic Canadian law, human rights codes emerged in the postwar period as important tools in the legal protection of the basic right to be free from discrimination. These codes, first enacted at the provincial level, initially provided protection against racial and religious discrimination. As awareness of other forms of discrimination has grown, so too has the list of forbidden grounds of discrimination. Age and gender followed race and religion, and eventually disability was added.

---

25   347 U.S. 483 (1954) [*Brown*].
26   *Plessy v. Ferguson*, 163 U.S. 537 (1895).

Other grounds found in different codes and applying to various activities include place of origin, marital status, receipt of public assistance, record of offence, and, most recently, sexual orientation.

A significant feature of human rights legislation is that, with some exceptions, anti-discrimination protection is achieved through an administrative process rather than through judges and courts. Typically, legislation creates a commission that is mandated to deal with individual complaints and to take appropriate educative and related remedial measures. Individual complaints are investigated by the commission at no cost to the complainant, and an attempt is made to resolve the matter by agreement or through mediation. Cases that cannot be resolved informally are referred to a judicial-style board of inquiry, which decides disputed questions of fact and law and which exercises broad remedial powers. In Ontario, human rights complaints are now made to a new human rights tribunal.

Human rights codes played an important role in the struggle against racism, sexism, and other forms of discrimination before the *Charter* and will continue to do so in light of the *Charter*'s limited application to private action.[27] Moreover, when interpreting and applying the equality guarantee of the *Charter*, the courts have paid close heed to the provisions of human rights codes and to the jurisprudence developed by human rights commissions.

G. THE *CANADIAN BILL OF RIGHTS, 1960*

While human rights legislation has been a success, another post-war, pre-*Charter* experiment in the statutory protection of fundamental freedoms was a disappointment. The 1960 *Canadian Bill of Rights*, an ordinary Act of Parliament, declared a list of important civil rights to be fundamental and provided that all laws should "be so construed and applied so as not to abrogate, abridge or infringe" any of the rights or freedoms so declared.[28] The list of rights and freedoms protected is similar, although not identical, to that found in the *Charter*. Although the *Bill of Rights* has been superseded in importance, it remains on the books and, as will be explained, should not be ignored, for it contains certain guarantees not found in the *Charter*.

---

27   See chapter 5. For further discussion of human rights codes, see W.S. Tarnopolsky & W.F. Pentney, *Discrimination and the Law* (Toronto: DeBoo, 1990).
28   R.S.C. 1985, App. III, s. 2.

The *Bill of Rights* suffered from two fundamental defects. First, it applied only to federal laws and thus did not reach the laws of the provinces. This meant that the actions of provincial legislatures and those acting under provincial authority were immune from its application. This feature of the *Bill of Rights* was seen by the future chief justice of Canada, Bora Laskin, then a law professor, as an inexcusable abdication of federal authority.[29]

Second, as the *Bill of Rights* was an ordinary Act of Parliament and did not form part of the constitution, the mandate it conferred upon the courts was suspect. Judges were reluctant to find that Parliament had, with one stroke of the legislative pen, authorized them to invalidate other duly enacted laws. The very notion seemed to run counter to the basic precepts of parliamentary supremacy.

Although the *Bill of Rights* acquired "*quasi*-constitutional" status in the view of Laskin C.J.C.,[30] with the notable exception of *R. v. Drybones*,[31] the courts did not consider that this enactment of the Parliament of Canada conferred upon the judiciary the authority to invalidate duly enacted laws. *Drybones* involved a provision of the federal *Indian Act* that made it an offence for an Indian to be intoxicated off a reserve, a harsher regime than that applied to others in the Northwest Territories, who were guilty of an offence only if found intoxicated in a public place. The Supreme Court of Canada struck down the offence on the ground that it violated the *Bill*'s guarantee of "equality before the law and the protection of the law." The ruling in *Drybones* suggested that the Court was prepared to give some weight to the *Bill of Rights*, but that promise proved short-lived. Instead, the Supreme Court made a hasty retreat. Although *Drybones* was never repudiated or overruled, its motivating spirit was abandoned. The rights and freedoms the *Bill* declared were almost invariably interpreted in a disappointingly formal and narrow fashion. In *Canada (Attorney General) v. Lavell*,[32] the Court refused to apply *Drybones* in the suit of an Aboriginal woman who lost her *Indian Act* status upon marrying a non-Aboriginal man. The same result did not apply where a man with *Indian Act* status married a non-status woman. Thus, the law created what seems to be an obvious form of sex discrimination. The Court adopted a purely formal definition of equality and dismissed the challenge on the ground that the law was applied equally to all women in Lavell's situation. This is but one of a long list of cases in which the courts adopted a narrow and restrictive

---

29   Laskin, above note 2.
30   *Hogan v. R.*, [1975] 2 S.C.R. 574 at 597, 48 D.L.R. (3d) 427.
31   (1969), [1970] S.C.R. 282, 9 D.L.R. (3d) 473 [*Drybones*].
32   [1974] S.C.R. 1349, 38 D.L.R. (3d) 481.

interpretation of the *Bill of Rights*, thereby rendering much of its authority nugatory.

Despite its limited success, there are two provisions of the *Bill of Rights* that have to be kept in mind since they have no counterpart in the *Charter*. The right of property is protected by section 1(a), and section 2(e) guarantees everyone "the right to a fair hearing in accordance with the principles of fundamental justice for the determination of his rights and obligations." The *Charter* does not protect property rights, and its guarantee of a fair hearing is arguably narrower, applying only in the criminal process under section 11(d) or, under section 7, where one's "life, liberty and security of the person" are implicated. Both of the above provisions were relied upon by war veterans to challenge legislation that limited the federal government's liability for mismanagement of their pensions. The Supreme Court rejected this challenge in *Authorson v. Canada (Attorney General)*[33] on the basis that the *Bill of Rights* does not protect against expropriation of property without compensation by the passage of unambiguous legislation or require Parliament to give property holders notice and a hearing before their property is expropriated. Although the Court acknowledged that federal legislation that is inconsistent with the *Bill of Rights* will be inoperative unless the legislation expressly declares that it operates notwithstanding the *Bill of Rights*, the Supreme Court also stressed that the *Bill of Rights* only protects rights as they existed in 1960 prior to its passage.[34] This decision may well dissuade litigants from relying on the *Bill of Rights* as a means to protect property rights from legislative encroachment.

The *Bill of Rights* experience was very much in the minds of the political actors who enacted the *Charter*. The courts were given a deliberate push away from the cautious and highly deferential posture they exhibited in the *Bill of Rights* caselaw. As the Supreme Court of Canada has observed,[35] the judges of Canada did not seek a mandate for judicial review: that choice was consciously and deliberately made by the political leaders of the day.

H. THE DRAFTING OF THE *CHARTER*

The drafting of the *Charter* was a difficult affair involving initial opposition by most provinces to the very idea of a charter; challenges by

---

33   [2003] 2 S.C.R. 40, 227 D.L.R. (4th) 385.

34   *Ibid.* at para. 33.

35   *Reference Re s. 94(2) of the Motor Vehicle Act (B.C.)*, [1985] 2 S.C.R. 486 at 497, 24 D.L.R. (4th) 536.

the provinces to the constitutionality of asking the British Parliament to amend the constitution without unanimous provincial consent; and the eventual refusal of one province, Quebec, to agree to the enactment of the *Charter*. What is most significant in terms of understanding the *Charter* are a number of changes made between October 1980 and the eventual agreement that was reached in November of 1981 among all governments except Quebec to enact the *Charter*, as well as a domestic amending formula to govern future changes to the constitution. During this time, a Joint Committee of Parliament heard from many witnesses representing civil liberties and women's groups, defence lawyers and prosecutors, the police, and others. Many of these groups were critical of the October 1980 version of the *Charter*. That draft had been weakened in an unsuccessful attempt to win provincial consent. The critics feared that the October 1980 version of the *Charter* would produce weak protection of rights and freedoms, as had the *Canadian Bill of Rights*. The federal government accepted many of these criticisms and introduced some fundamental changes to strengthen the *Charter*.

Section 1 of the *Charter* is perhaps its most important provision. In October 1980, it provided that the rights and freedoms would be "subject only to such reasonable limits as are generally acceptable in a free and democratic society with a parliamentary system of government." Some critics coined this the "Mack Truck clause" on the basis that the traditions of Parliamentary supremacy, examined above, would allow governments to drive a truck through guaranteed rights and freedoms.[36] The federal government accepted this argument, and section 1 was changed to provide new requirements that any reasonable limit on *Charter* rights be "prescribed by law" and be "demonstrably justified in a free and democratic society."

Many of the legal rights of the *Charter* were also strengthened. For example, the October 1980 draft provided that "everyone has the right not to be subjected to search or seizure except on grounds, and in accordance with procedures, established by law." This guarantee that searches and seizures would be conducted in accordance with laws was changed to the more substantive guarantee now found in section 8 of the *Charter* of "the right to be secure against unreasonable search or seizure." Section 9 of the *Charter* was similarly changed from the right "not to be detained or imprisoned except on grounds, and in accordance with procedures, established by law" to the present right "not to be arbitrarily detained or imprisoned," as was section 11(e), which now

---

36   See L. Weinrib, "Canada's *Charter* of Rights: Paradigm Lost?" (2002) 6 Rev. of Constitutional Studies 119 at 132–46.

provides a right "not to be denied reasonable bail without just cause," as opposed to the more limited right not to be denied reasonable bail "except on grounds and in accordance with procedures, established by law." The effects of these changes were to limit Parliamentary supremacy in defining the rules to govern search and seizure and detention. Section 10(b) was changed to provide not only the right to retain and instruct counsel without delay, but also the right to be informed of that right. Legal rights were also strengthened by replacing a provision of the October 1980 draft, which preserved legislative supremacy over the laws of evidence, with section 24(2) of the *Charter*, which requires the exclusion of unconstitutionally obtained evidence "if it is established that, having regard to all the circumstances, the admission of it would bring the administration of justice into disrepute."[37]

The *Canadian Bill of Rights* had been criticized for its lack of effective remedies, but the October 1980 draft provided no specific provision for remedies. The general remedial provision in what is now section 24(1) was added at the suggestion of civil liberties groups. It allows anyone whose rights and freedoms have been infringed to apply to a court of competent jurisdiction "to obtain such remedy as the court considers appropriate and just in the circumstances."

In addition to some strengthening of voting rights in section 3 of the *Charter* and minority language education rights in section 23, equality rights also were strengthened in part to avoid the restrictive interpretation that equality rights had received under the *Canadian Bill of Rights*. The October 1980 draft provided that "Everyone has the right to equality before the law and to the equal protection of the law without discrimination because of race, national or ethnic origin, colour, religion, age or sex." This was changed to the more open-ended and expansive provision contained now in section 15(1) of the *Charter*, "Every individual is equal before and under the law and has the right to the equal protection and equal benefit of the law without discrimination and, in particular, without discrimination based on race, national or ethnic origin, colour, religion, sex, age, or mental or physical disability." Section 28 was subsequently added to underline the importance of gender equality by providing "Notwithstanding anything in this *Charter*, the rights and freedoms referred to in it are guaranteed equally to male and female persons." Section 27 was also added, providing that the *Charter* "shall be interpreted in a manner consistent with the preservation and enhancement of the multicultural heritage of Canada."

---

37   See K. Roach, *Due Process and Victims' Rights: The New Law and Politics of Criminal Justice* (Toronto: University of Toronto Press, 1999) at 42–50.

Not all the changes made in the drafting of the *Charter* expanded its rights and freedoms. Section 29 was added providing that nothing in the *Charter* takes away from denominational school rights. Section 33 was added, as a result of the agreement between the federal government and all provinces except Quebec in November of 1981, allowing provincial and federal legislatures to enact legislation notwithstanding the fundamental freedoms, legal rights, or equality rights for renewable five-year periods.

I. THE *SECESSION REFERENCE* AND THE UNWRITTEN STRUCTURAL PRINCIPLES OF THE CONSTITUTION

In 1998, the Supreme Court of Canada was asked to decide whether Quebec had the right to secede from Canada unilaterally.[38] The Court's answer to this difficult and politically loaded question represents a significant statement of the basic principles underlying the Canadian constitution. The Court ruled that a constitutional amendment would be required in order for a province to legally secede from Confederation. However, the Court also stated that considerable weight would have to be given to a clear expression of the will of the people of Quebec to secede. The other provinces and the federal government would have to respect that democratically expressed choice and enter into negotiations with Quebec. In those negotiations, "four fundamental and organizing principles of the Constitution"[39] would have to be respected. These principles are "not expressly dealt with by the text of the Constitution"[40] but they nonetheless have normative force as operative instruments of our constitutional order. The four principles are federalism, constitutionalism and the rule of law, respect for minorities, and democracy. The Court stated that these principles "inform and sustain the constitutional text: they are the vital unstated assumptions upon which the text is based."[41] The unwritten principles represent the "major elements of the architecture of the Constitution itself and are as such its lifeblood." They "infuse our Constitution and breathe life into it."[42]

The first unwritten principle—federalism—has already been discussed. In the *Quebec Secession Reference*, the Court explained that

---

38   *Reference Re Secession of Quebec*, [1998] 2 S.C.R. 217, 161 D.L.R. (4th) 385 [*Quebec Secession Reference*].

39   *Ibid.* at 240 (S.C.R.).

40   *Ibid.* at 240.

41   *Ibid.* at 247.

42   *Ibid.* at 248.

federalism is "a legal response to the underlying political and cultural realities that existed at Confederation and continue to exist today."[43] Federalism is what the Court described as "the political mechanism by which diversity could be reconciled with unity."[44]

The second unwritten principle—constitutionalism and the rule of law—reflects the values of an orderly and civil society in which the constitution is the supreme source of law and authority. The Court identified three essential elements of the rule of law. First, "[t]here is . . . one law for all"[45] and the law is supreme over both public officials and private actors. Second, the normative basis for civil society is the creation and maintenance of a positive legal order. Third, the law governs the relationship between the state and the individual, and the exercise of public power must be based on law.

Closely related to the rule of law is constitutionalism, the idea that all government action must comply with the constitution as Canada's supreme source of law. Constitutionalism constrains power, even the power of the elected representatives of the majority. Constitutionally entrenched individual and minority rights are protected against the will of the majority. The constitution may, the Court explained, "seek to ensure that vulnerable minority groups are endowed with the institutions and rights necessary to maintain and promote their identities against the assimilative pressures of the majority."[46]

The third unwritten or structural principle is "respect for minorities" or "protection of minorities." As the Supreme Court explained, "There are linguistic and cultural minorities, including aboriginal peoples, unevenly distributed across the country who look to the Constitution of Canada for the protection of their rights."[47] The protection of minority rights has always been a feature of Canada's constitution and was significantly enhanced by the *Charter* and other 1982 amendments. The guarantee of equality rights in section 15, the enhancement of minority language rights, and the provisions requiring respect for and protection of Aboriginal rights are particularly notable. As the Supreme Court of Canada explained, respect for and protection of minorities transcend the specific guarantees and "[a] superficial reading of selected provisions of the written constitutional enactment, without more, may be misleading."[48]

---

43   *Ibid.* at 244.
44   *Ibid.* at 245.
45   *Ibid.* at 258.
46   *Ibid.* at 259.
47   *Ibid.* at 269.
48   *Ibid.* at 292.

The fourth unwritten structural principle is democracy, "a fundamental value in our constitutional law and political culture"[49] and a "baseline against which the framers of our Constitution, and subsequently, our elected representatives under it, have always operated."[50] Although democracy is not mentioned in the text of the *Constitution Act, 1867*, it has always been a fundamental feature of our constitutional structure.

Aspects of the democratic principle have already been discussed above. Democracy was the foundation for the principle of parliamentary supremacy. As will be discussed in chapter 2, many argue that the *Charter* is anti-democratic as it allows unelected judges to strike down the laws Parliament and the legislatures have enacted. In this regard, there may appear to be a tension between democracy and the other three unwritten principles, each of which posits significant power in the courts to ensure that those elected by the majority respect the constitutionally imposed limits on their power. However, as the Supreme Court pointed out, the principle of democracy may be reconciled with the other three principles. Democracy can only operate under the rule of law and within a constitutional and legal framework upon which democratic institutions depend for their legitimacy. Through federalism, Canada's constitution recognizes that there can be "different and equally legitimate majorities in different provinces and territories and at the federal level." Federalism offers a richer form of democracy by enabling citizens "to participate concurrently in different collectivities and to pursue goals at both a federal and provincial level."[51] A properly functioning democracy "requires a continuous process of discussion"[52] and the opportunity for full participation by all. By limiting the power of the majority to infringe upon the rights of individuals and by allowing vulnerable minorities to fully participate in Canadian society, the constitution reinforces rather than weakens the democratic principle.

J. USE OF UNWRITTEN CONSTITUTIONAL PRINCIPLES IN SUBSEQUENT LITIGATION

As discussed above, the rule of law was recognized in the *Quebec Secession Reference*[53] as one of four unwritten constitutional principles

---

49   *Ibid.* at 252.
50   *Ibid.* at 253.
51   *Ibid.* at 255–56.
52   *Ibid.* at 256.
53   *Ibid.*

that are fundamental to the Canadian constitutional order. The rule of law is also mentioned in the preamble of the *Charter* and is promoted by the requirement under section 1 of the *Charter* that all limits on *Charter* rights must be "prescribed by law." The rule of law requires that the law apply to governmental officials as well as private citizens; that there be a positive legal order and that relationship between the state and the individual be regulated by law.[54] This understanding of the rule of law has been said by the Court to focus on the existence and application of the law and not on its content. "So understood, it is difficult to conceive of how the rule of law could be used as a basis for invalidating legislation such as the Act based on its content."[55]

The Court has made reference to the unwritten principle of the rule of law in a number of cases. In a series of references involving the setting of judicial salaries, the Court has cited the unwritten principle of the rule of law in support of its conclusion that a commission independent of the judiciary and the state should be able to make recommendations to the legislature about judicial salaries.[56] This decision resulted in strong criticism by some including Justice La Forest who argued in dissent that the court should not resort to unwritten constitutional principles.[57] The Court also relied on unwritten constitutional principles in the *Quebec Secession Reference* discussed above.

In recent years, the Court has been more hesitant to rely on unwritten constitutional principles. The court has rejected a claim made by tobacco companies that provincial legislation that allowed the government to bring actions against them related to health care costs infringed the rule of law because it retroactively targeted them. The Court concluded that the appeal to unwritten principles of the rule of law relating to the desirability of general and prospective legislation "fail to recognize that in a constitutional democracy such as ours, protection from legislation that some might view as unjust or unfair properly lies not in the amorphous underlying principles of our Constitution, but in its text and the ballot box."[58] The Court has also held that "general access to legal services is not a currently recognized aspect of the rule of law" and as such could not be a basis for invalidating a tax on legal services.[59]

---

54   *British Columbia v. Imperial Tobacco Canada Ltd.*, [2005] 2 S.C.R. 473 at para. 58; *British Columbia (Attorney General) v. Christie*, [2007] 1 S.C.R. 873 at para. 20.
55   *British Columbia v. Imperial Tobacco Canada Ltd.*, ibid. at para. 59.
56   *Reference re Remuneration of Judges of the Provincial Court of P.E.I.*, [1997] 3 S.C.R. 3.
57   *Ibid.* at paras. 296-325.
58   *British Columbia v. Imperial Tobacco Canada Ltd.*, above note 54 at para. 66.
59   *British Columbia (Attorney General) v. Christie*, above note 54 at para. 21.

The Court in that judgment paid attention to the text of the *Charter* in noting that the right to counsel under section 10(b) did not include a general right to legal assistance and that section 7 of the *Charter* had only been interpreted to require legal assistance in specific situations.[60] The Court has also held that the absence of any appeal rights from a finding that a security certificate issued under immigration law was reasonable or a requirement of automatic detention once the executive had issued a certificate also did not offend unwritten principles of the rule of law.[61]

The recognition of federalism, constitutionalism and the rule of law, respect for minorities and democracy as fundamental unwritten principles of the Canadian constitution is an important recognition of the basic values that pervade and influence the constitution including the *Charter*. In most respects the values are mutually re-enforcing. For example, respect for the rule of law can support democracy by requiring the legislature to make clear statements that authorize limits on rights and freedoms. At the same time, these foundational principles can be in tension for example when rulings about federalism, the rule of law or the rights of minorities overturn legislation that has been enacted by elected governments.

All four principles and especially those relating to the rule of law, the rights of minorities and democracy will play a role in the interpretation of various sections of the *Charter*. At the same time, the Supreme Court has in recent years demonstrated more caution about relying on unwritten constitutional principles as a direct source of authority and these principles are at their strongest when they can be supported by the text of the constitution.

FURTHER READINGS

DICKSON, B., "The *Canadian Charter of Rights and Freedoms*: Context and Evolution" in G.A. Beaudoin & E. Mendes, eds., *The Canadian Charter of Rights and Freedoms*, 4th ed. (Markham, ON: LexisNexis Butterworths, 2005)

ELLIOT, R., "Interpreting the *Charter*: Use of the Earlier Version as an Aid" (1982) (*Charter* Edition) U.B.C. L. Rev. 11

---

60 *Ibid.* at para. 24-26.
61 *Charkaoui v. Canada*, [2007] 1 S.C.R. 350 at paras. 133-137.

ELLIOT, R., "References, Structural Argumentation and the Organizing Principles of Canada's Constitution" (2001) 80 Can. Bar Rev. 67

HOGG, P.W., *Constitutional Law of Canada*, 5th ed. (Toronto: Carswell, 2007) cc. 31 and 32

LYSYK, K.M., "The *Canadian Charter of Rights and Freedoms*: General Principles" (1994) 16 Advocates' Q. 1

MCLACHLIN, B.M., "The *Charter*: A New Role for the Judiciary" (1991) 29 Alta. L. Rev. 540

MCMURTRY R.R. "The Creation of an Entrenched *Charter of Rights and Freedoms*" (2006) 31 Queens L.J. 456.

ROACH, K., "Common Law Bills of Rights as Dialogue between Courts and Legislatures" (2005) 55 U.T.L.J. 733

ROMANOW, R., J. WHYTE, & H. LEESON, *Canada . . . Notwithstanding: The Making of the Constitution 1976–1982*, 25th anniversary ed. (Toronto: Carswell, 2007)

RUSSELL, P.H., "The Political Purposes of the *Canadian Charter of Rights and Freedoms*" (1983) 61 Can. Bar Rev. 30

TARNOPOLSKY, W., *The Canadian Bill of Rights*, 2d rev. ed. (Toronto: McClelland and Stewart, 1975)

TARNOPOLSKY, W.S., & W.F. PENTNEY, *Discrimination and the Law* (Toronto: DeBoo, 1990)

CHAPTER 2

THE LEGITIMACY OF JUDICIAL REVIEW

There has been a lively debate in Canada, particularly since the enactment of the *Charter of Rights and Freedoms* in 1982, regarding the legitimacy of judicial review. Although judicial review on federalism grounds has been a feature of the Canadian constitution since the early days of Confederation, the tradition of parliamentary supremacy remained strong until the advent of the *Charter*. In that tradition, there are no constraints upon what Parliament can do, and it is thought that Parliament is the best place to achieve an appropriate balance between individual rights and freedoms and the broader public interest. This principle had always been qualified in Canada by the practice of judicial review on federalism grounds, but the *Charter of Rights and Freedoms* added significantly to the judiciary's power.

Under the *Charter*, the questions put to judges involve issues of value and moral choice, which are not only more open-ended and apparently less constrained by strict legal principles, but also of greater significance to the average citizen than those relating to federalism. For example, does the right to life, liberty, and security of the person in section 7 include a woman's right to choose whether to have an abortion? Does the right to freedom of expression include the right to spread hatred against particular racial or religious groups? Can the government deny benefits or marital status to couples who are of the same sex?

The result of a *Charter* decision can also be more significant than one made on federalism grounds. Because the Canadian constitution exhaustively grants legislative power to either the federal Parliament or the provincial legislatures, the result of a decision holding that, say, a province cannot enact a certain law will almost inevitably be that the federal government can. On the other hand, the result of a *Charter* decision striking down a law is that, unless resort is had to the "override" clause, neither level of government can enact exactly the same law. Hence, a *Charter* decision can have a much more telling impact upon the scope for legislative choice.

The debate over the legitimacy of judicial review is fuelled by the fact that the Canadian judicial system in general, and the adjudication of constitutional cases in particular, are premised on the assumption that questions coming before the courts are legal rather than political and as such are to be decided strictly upon legal grounds. As will be noted later in chapter 7, the procedure for a constitutional case is more or less the same as that used for a property or contracts dispute between two private parties. The same judges decide the constitutional issue as decide the private dispute, and in theory they decide the constitutional issue on grounds similar to those that apply to the private dispute. It has become increasingly obvious, however, that many, if not most, *Charter* issues involve matters of value and public policy quite different in nature from the questions formerly posed to the courts. It is not surprising to find many observers asking whether it is legitimate to give unelected and unaccountable judges a definitive say on these vitally important and highly controversial matters. In particular, some have questioned the qualifications of the lawyers who sit on the bench to decide political, moral, and philosophical controversies.

From a formal perspective, there is a clear answer. As the Supreme Court itself has pointed out, the judges did not ask for the *Charter of Rights and Freedoms* nor for the powers it confers upon them.[1] The enactment of the *Charter* and the decision to confer a broader mandate upon the courts was the conscious choice of the elected representatives of the people. In 1982 the constitution was amended to include an ex-

---

1   In *Reference Re s. 94(2) of the Motor Vehicle Act (B.C.)*, [1985] 2 S.C.R. 486, 24 D.L.R. (4th) 536, Lamer J. states at 497 (S.C.R.):

> It ought not to be forgotten that the historic decision to entrench the *Charter* in our Constitution was taken not by the courts but by the elected representatives of the people of Canada. It was those representatives who extended the scope of constitutional adjudication and entrusted the courts with this new and onerous responsibility. Adjudication under the *Charter* must be approached free of any lingering doubts as to its legitimacy.

See also *Vriend v. Alberta*, [1998] 1 S.C.R. 493, 156 D.L.R. (4th) 385 at paras. 131–32 [*Vriend*], *per* Iacobucci J.

plicit supremacy clause that provides that the constitution, including the *Charter*, "is the supreme law of Canada, and any law that is inconsistent is, to the extent of the inconsistency, of no force and effect."[2] Individuals were also expressly given the right, under section 24(1) of the *Charter*, "to obtain such remedy as the court considers appropriate and just in the circumstances." Accordingly, the text of the constitution reflects the conscious political choice to grant judges extensive power to interfere with decisions of the democratically elected representatives of the people.[3] At the same time, the framers of the *Charter* did not necessarily grant courts the last word on matters affected by the *Charter*. Legislatures can enact laws and justify them to the courts under section 1 of the *Charter* as "reasonable limits prescribed by law as can be demonstrably justified in a free and democratic society." Legislatures also retain the ability under section 33 of the *Charter* to enact laws notwithstanding the *Charter*'s fundamental freedoms, legal rights, and equality rights for a renewable five-year period.

While it is clear that the power of judicial review is legally legitimate, one may still ask whether this power is legitimate in a more fundamental sense. Is it consistent with the most fundamental values of the constitution—the principles of democracy and the right of the citizens of Canada to elect and remove those who exercise political power?

A. JUSTIFICATION FOR JUDICIAL REVIEW— FEDERALISM

The legitimacy of judicial review on federalism grounds has been challenged, but this practice is perhaps more readily justified than is judicial review under the *Charter*. A federal system needs a referee to resolve jurisdictional disputes that cannot be sorted out through the ordinary political process. The federal structure of government represents a conscious decision to allocate functions between national and regional governments and to divide responsibility for certain legisla-

---

2   Section 52(1) of the *Constitution Act, 1982*.

3   As Justice Bertha Wilson has written: "we should keep in mind that by a widely accepted constitutional process Canadians decided to charge the courts with the onerous responsibility of reviewing legislative and executive action for compliance with the constitution, and they did so with full knowledge of the American experience and the criticism of the role of the courts in that society by some of its most eminent judges." Hon. B. Wilson, "We Didn't Volunteer" in P. Howe & P. Russell, eds., *Judicial Power and Canadian Democracy* (Montreal: McGill-Queen's University Press, 2001) at 75.

tive subject matters accordingly. Situations are bound to arise where the political actors will not be able to resolve their differences about jurisdiction — hence the need for some specified body to settle the matter according to the principles established by the constitution. Canadian courts have not hesitated to wield the power of judicial review on federalism grounds, striking down many laws, both federal and provincial. While some scholars have argued that the resolution of jurisdictional disputes could be the responsibility of a non-judicial political authority,[4] their arguments have been unpersuasive.[5]

Nevertheless controversy has, at times, surrounded particular decisions of the courts on the division of powers between the federal and provincial authorities. For example, judicial invalidation of federal attempts to implement a "New Deal" to regulate the economy during the Great Depression of the 1930s produced widespread criticism. Unlike the *Charter*, the division of powers is not subject to legislative override, and the eventual response to judicial decisions holding that the federal government could not implement the New Deal was a constitutional amendment to give it jurisdiction to legislate in relation to unemployment insurance, as well as the commencement of a process that abolished appeals to the highest court at the time — the Judicial Committee of the Privy Council. In the 1980s, there was also controversy over natural resources, which again resulted in constitutional amendments. Despite these controversies, the appropriateness of the courts exercising the power of judicial review is generally well accepted.[6]

An important factor contributing to the acceptance of judicial review in the area of federalism has been the development of interpretative doctrines designed to minimize intrusion into legislative decision making. The emphasis upon purpose over effects limits judicial review significantly, avoiding a situation where the courts would be called upon to review the impact of all manner of legislation. It reflects the modern judicial tolerance for overlapping powers, and this deferential judicial stance has produced many areas where both levels of government act concurrently. The courts have not insisted upon excessively sharp distinctions being drawn or upon jurisdictional categories being viewed as watertight compartments.

---

4   P. Weiler, *In the Last Resort: A Critical Study of the Supreme Court of Canada* (Toronto: Carswell Methuen, 1974).

5   K.E. Swinton, *The Supreme Court and Canadian Federalism: The Laskin-Dickson Years* (Toronto: Carswell, 1990), c. 2, refutes the arguments made by Weiler, above.

6   Compare, however, H. Brun & G. Tremblay, *Droit constitutionnel*, 2e ed. (Montreal: Yvon Blais, 1990) at 453–54 and 490–92.

Another element of judicial deference has been the adoption of a traditionally narrow view of paramountcy. While the rule is that, in the event of conflict, federal law prevails, the courts have, in the past, defined conflict narrowly, as being a situation where one law requires one thing and the other law requires precisely the opposite.[7] Recent cases suggest the acceptance of a broader test in some circumstances, which leads to a finding of paramountcy when the provincial law seriously interferes with the underlying policy objectives of the federal legislation.[8] However, there are still many policy areas in which federal and provincial laws overlap and in which federal paramountcy does not lead to dismantling of the provincial scheme in the absence of conflict in the strict sense. These techniques of functional concurrency are important because once a court has held that a particular type of law is clearly beyond the jurisdictional capacity of one level of government, the options for that government are extremely limited. As will be seen, a government faced with an adverse *Charter* decision frequently has less drastic options than changing the constitution or the court's mind.

B. CONCERNS ABOUT JUDICIAL POWER UNDER THE *CHARTER*

More controversial is judicial review under the *Charter*, which clearly puts the courts in the position of overruling the democratically elected representatives of the people on value-laden questions of public policy. Many critics argue that an entrenched bill of rights undermines democratic debate and decision making. In Peter Russell's words, "The principal impact of a charter on the process of government can be neatly summarized as a tendency to judicialize politics and politicize the judiciary."[9] He goes on to say:

> The danger here is not so much that non-elected judges will impose their will on a democratic majority, but that questions of social and political justice will be transformed into technical legal questions and the great bulk of the citizenry who are not judges and lawyers

---

7   *Multiple Access Ltd. v. McCutcheon*, [1982] 2 S.C.R. 161, 138 D.L.R. (3d) 1.

8   *Bank of Montreal v. Hall*, [1990] 1 S.C.R. 121, 65 D.L.R. (4th) 361; *Husky Oil Operations Ltd. v. M.N.R.*, [1995] 3 S.C.R. 453, 128 D.L.R. (4th) 1 (S.C.C.).

9   P. Russell, "The Political Purposes of the *Canadian Charter of Rights and Freedoms*" (1983) 61 Can. Bar Rev. 30 at 51–52.

will abdicate their responsibility for working out reasonable and mutually acceptable resolutions of the issues which divide them.[10]

The fear is that litigation in the courts will replace open public debate on important issues of public policy.

Other critics add a concern about the lack of judicial expertise in many of the areas litigated. In view of the relative resources and expertise of judges vis-à-vis legislatures and bureaucracies in making decisions on complex issues, these critics denounce the use of *Charter* litigation to make determinations affecting important policy matters involving difficult trade-offs between competing interests.

Still other critics point to the vagueness and indeterminacy of constitutional language as a reason for concern about judicial review. Words such as "liberty," "equality," and "reasonable limits" are so open-ended, it is argued, that judges cannot help but infuse the constitution with their own values. Concerns are expressed that judges will use the open-ended nature of the *Charter* to increase their own power and impose their own views.[11] Why, it is asked, should we trust nine Supreme Court judges with the task of delineating the meaning of those phrases for a diverse society, rather than leave such issues to be resolved through open legislative debate?

This criticism of judicial review is shared by those from the left, who worry that judicial decisions will tend to favour liberal values hostile to an interventionist state, especially where the state intervenes to promote greater equality among groups and classes. For example, Andrew Petter has written:

> First, we must bear in mind what has just been said about a charter of rights: it gives to citizens only insofar as it takes from government. For example, the guarantee of equality rights in the *Charter* does not give people a guarantee of social equality; it does not even commit the government to guaranteeing social equality. Its role is much more limited. What it does is inhibit government from implementing measures that would bring about or perpetuate inequality.[12]

In effect, the fear is that the individual-rights focus of the *Charter* will undermine a more communitarian spirit expressed through legislative

---

10   *Ibid.* at 52.

11   C. Manfredi, *Judicial Power and the Charter: Canada and the Paradox of Liberal Constitutionalism*, 2d ed. (Toronto: Oxford University Press, 2001) at 33–35.

12   A.J. Petter, "The Politics of the *Charter*" (1986) 8 Supreme Court L.R. 473 at 476. Another critic from this perspective, who examines the Supreme Court's performance in some detail, is M. Mandel, *The Charter of Rights and the Legalization of Politics in Canada*, 2d ed. (Toronto: Thompson, 1994).

action. Inevitably, those on the left invoke the ghost of the *Lochner* case from the turn-of-the-century United States, where the Supreme Court struck down protective labour legislation limiting the hours of bakery workers to ten in a day and sixty in a week as an unjustifiable limitation on liberty.[13] These critics fear that powerful forces will be able to use the *Charter*'s framework of individual rights to protect their own self-interest at the expense of the less advantaged. Even if the *Charter* does not always harm progressive state activity, many critics fear that it only provides limited and "blunt tools for redressing social injustice."[14]

The legitimacy of judicial review under the *Charter* has also been challenged by critics on the political right.[15] They are concerned that courts have too much freedom to impose their own views under the *Charter* and that they have decided issues that could have been avoided and left to legislators and administrators. These scholars argue that unelected judges have assumed an unacceptable law-making role under the *Charter* and that a "Court Party" made up of interest groups such as women's and civil liberties groups has been able to exploit this new-found judicial power to achieve policies that would not otherwise attract majority support.[16] Abortion, equality rights for minorities, especially gays and lesbians, and rights for those accused of crime have attracted particular attention. F.L. Morton and Rainer Knopff have argued:

> Our primary objection to the *Charter* Revolution is that it is deeply and fundamentally undemocratic, not just in the simple and obvious sense of being anti-majoritarian, but also in the more serious sense of erod-ing the habits and temperament of representative democracy . . . . The kind of courtroom politics promoted by the Court Party, in short, is authoritarian, not just in process but, more dangerously, in spirit.[17]

Although their politics differ, critics of judicial power on both the left and the right share some common concerns. They are both con-cerned that judges will have discretion to read their own personal pref-

---

13 *Lochner v. New York*, 198 U.S. 45 (1905).

14 J. Bakan, *Just Words: Constitutional Rights and Social Wrongs* (Toronto: University of Toronto Press, 1997) at 152.

15 See R. Knopff & F.L. Morton, *Charter Politics* (Scarborough, ON: Nelson Can-ada, 1992) and F.L. Morton & R. Knopff, *The Charter Revolution and the Court Party* (Peterborough, ON: Broadview Press, 2000).

16 Robert Bork endorses the "Court Party" thesis and argues that "the courts are enacting the agenda of the cultural left" and that "the same liberal intelligentsia dominates the jurisprudence" of Canada and the United States. R. Bork, *Coer-cing Virtue: The Worldwide Rule of Judges* (Toronto: Vintage, 2002) at 3, 58, 68.

17 F.L. Morton & R. Knopff, *The Charter Revolution and the Court Party* (Peterbor-ough, ON: Broadview Press, 2000) at 149.

erences into the vague words of the *Charter*. They are concerned that the *Charter* will give some groups too much power in our democracy. The left is troubled about corporations and other advantaged interests using the *Charter*, while the right is troubled about minorities and accused persons using the *Charter*.[18]

Critics are also uneasy with the rights guaranteed in the *Charter*. The left believes that these rights are too individualistic and negative, while the right is concerned about group, positive, and inflated rights. Critics of judicial activism on both the left and the right also share the view that elected legislatures are the best vehicle to promote democracy. They both worry that unelected courts under the *Charter* will frequently have the last word over elected legislatures.

C. JUSTIFICATIONS FOR JUDICIAL REVIEW—*CHARTER OF RIGHTS AND FREEDOMS*

There are a variety of defences of judicial review. These include the ideas that judicial review is necessary to protect the fundamental principles of democracy; that judicial review is necessary to protect rights; and that judicial review can be justified on the basis of the intent of the democratically enacted framers of the constitution. Finally, there has been support for the idea that judicial review is part of a democratic dialogue that involves not only the courts but also legislatures and society.

1) Judicial Review to Protect Democracy

One of the best defences of judicial review is the argument that the entrenchment of constitutional rights is consistent with the fundamental principles of democracy. There is a strong argument that democracy cannot be explained simply in terms of majority rule and that adherence to certain fundamental values and principles is necessary for democracy to flourish.[19] An obvious example would be judicial review to protect the right to vote, a right that "underpins the legitimacy of Canadian democracy and Parliament's claim to power." The right to

---

18   This paragraph is adapted from K. Roach, *The Supreme Court on Trial: Judicial Activism or Democratic Dialogue* (Toronto: Irwin Law, 2001) c. 5.

19   J.H. Ely is a strong proponent of this view in *Democracy and Distrust: A Theory of Judicial Review* (Cambridge: Harvard University Press, 1980). Patrick Monahan echoes this view, with his own refinements, in *Politics and the Constitution: The Charter, Federalism and the Supreme Court of Canada* (Toronto: Carswell, 1987).

vote has been robustly defended by the courts "unaffected by the shift-ing winds of public opinion and electoral interests" against legislative curtailment.[20] Should majorities be entitled to deny that right to certain members of society, without having to justify the decision other than by the force of their numbers? Surely the power of judicial review, re-quiring demonstrable justification for the decision, enhances, rather than detracts from, democratic values. Similarly, free and open debate of public issues is essential to democracy, and the exercise of the power of judicial review to protect the fundamental freedoms of expression, opinion, and the press can be seen as enhancing and reinforcing dem-ocracy. Majorities of the day have a tendency to try to suppress the expression of unpopular views that threaten the status quo. Judicial review serves to bolster democratic values by requiring reasoned justi-fication for laws that limit the rights of those who hold views diverging from the prevailing wisdom of the day. As noted in the previous chap-ter, even before the introduction of the *Charter*, the Supreme Court, at times, protected freedom of expression on the basis that it was neces-sary for democracy.

Other fundamental freedoms, less directly implicated in the demo-cratic process, are nonetheless essential if democracy is to flourish. The values of individual dignity, autonomy, and freedom of choice, reflected in the freedom of religion and equality and in the protection of life, liberty, and security of the person, are preconditions to individuals being capable of making independent, intelligent, and informed deci-sions. Judicial intervention to protect these values against incursions by majoritarian actors may be seen as enhancing and protecting dem-ocracy rather than undermining it. Chief Justice Dickson made this point when striking down a law that infringed on freedom of religion: "The ability of each citizen to make free and informed decisions is the absolute prerequisite for the legitimacy, acceptability, and efficacy of our system of self-government."[21]

In a similar vein, decisions of the courts protecting minorities or other vulnerable groups may be defended on the basis of democratic principle.[22] Judicial review, from this perspective, is justified to protect those whose voices are not adequately heard in political debate because they are too few or too unpopular. It is argued that judicial review strengthens democracy by ensuring that the rights and interests of all citizens are protected. The Supreme Court of Canada has been particu-

---

20 *Sauvé v. Canada (Chief Electoral Officer)*, [2002] 3 S.C.R. 519 at paras. 34 and 13 [*Sauvé*]. See further discussion in chapter 11.

21 *R. v. Big M Drug Mart Ltd.*, [1985] 1 S.C.R. 295, 18 D.L.R. (4th) 321 at 361.

22 *Vriend*, above note 1.

larly active in defending the legal rights of those accused of crimes, as well as the equality rights of minorities under section 15 of the *Charter*. This aspect of judicial review is also reflected in the manner in which the Court has interpreted existing Aboriginal and treaty rights, which are guaranteed in section 35 of the *Constitution Act, 1982*.[23] The minority-language education rights in the *Charter* have also been interpreted liberally by the Court.[24]

Perhaps even more significant was the Court's initial interpretation of the equality guarantee, section 15 of the *Charter*. It stressed that the focus for equality review must be upon historic patterns of discrimination and disadvantage, an interpretation that included explicit reference to the need to protect those vulnerable groups who lack an effective voice in majoritarian politics. In the leading decision, the Court held that a law prohibiting non-citizens from being admitted to the legal profession was contrary to the guarantee of equality and justified interfering with the majoritarian decision to exclude non-citizens by an appeal to basic democratic principles:

> Non-citizens, to take only the most obvious example, do not have the right to vote. Their vulnerability to becoming a disadvantaged group in our society is captured by John Stuart Mill's observation in Book III of *On Liberty and Considerations of Representative Government* that "in the absence of its natural defenders, the interests of the excluded is always in danger of being overlooked . . ."[25]

The Court reiterated this theme in a 1998 decision holding that Alberta's human rights legislation, which failed to protect gays and lesbians, violated the guarantee of equality:

> Democratic values and principles under the *Charter* demand that legislators and the executive take these [democratic attributes] into account; and if they fail to do so, courts should stand ready to intervene to protect these democratic values as appropriate. As others have so forcefully stated, judges are not acting undemocratically by intervening when there are indications that a legislative or executive decision was not reached in accordance with the democratic principles mandated by the *Charter*.[26]

---

23 *R. v. Sparrow*, [1990] 1 S.C.R. 1075, 70 D.L.R. (4th) 385.
24 *Mahé v. Alberta*, [1990] 1 S.C.R. 342, 68 D.L.R. (4th) 69.
25 *Andrews v. Law Society (British Columbia)*, [1989] 1 S.C.R. 143 at 152, 56 D.L.R. (4th) 1, Wilson J. This approach is further described in chapter 15.
26 *Vriend*, above note 1 at para. 142, Iacobucci J.

The above justification for judicial review is sometimes called a "process-based" approach, since the main function of the *Charter* is seen to be the checking of malfunctions in the operation of the democratic process. The underlying assumption is that Parliament and the legislatures should be left with considerable scope to make determinations about the shape of public policy, but that the *Charter* allows the courts to intervene where the political process is deficient in some way.[27]

2) Judicial Review and Rights Protection

Another justification offered for judicial enforcement of a charter of rights emphasizes the central importance of rights protection to individual self-development. As with the process model, this theory is based on a perception that majoritarian politics may have deficiencies that require correction. But this model can take the courts much further in curtailing government action and, in the abstract, is based upon an unwavering and unqualified commitment to the protection of individual autonomy. This justification for judicial review is sometimes based on the idea of rights as trumps over the policy preferences of governments.[28] Consider, for example, the following quotation from Lorraine Weinrib advocating a "constitutional rights" model of judicial review:

> This model welcomes judicial protection of individual rights and their value structure to continuously correct for the perceived inadequacies of majoritarian politics. Underlying this model is respect for the dignity, equality and autonomy of each member of the community. The individual must be able to espouse, and follow, and modify his or her own conception of the good. Whatever the sources and trajectories of these commitments, the aim of collective political life is to create and preserve a structure in which each of us, to an equal extent, may pursue and act upon these commitments, either alone or in a given or chosen community.[29]

An exclusive focus on rights protection may be in conflict with the ability of legislatures to justify limitations on rights under section

---

27 Ely, above note 19. For a similar defence of the role of the *Charter*, from the perspective of the left, see R. Penner, "The Canadian Experience with the *Charter of Rights*: Are There Lessons for the United Kingdom?" [1996] Pub. L. 104 at 113.

28 Ronald Dworkin is a strong proponent of this view. See, for example, R. Dworkin, *Taking Rights Seriously* (Cambridge: Harvard University Press, 1977).

29 L. Weinrib, "Limitations on Rights in a Constitutional Democracy" (1996) 6 Caribbean L. Rev. 428 at 439.

1 of the *Charter*. Another robust approach to judicial review is that advocated by David Beatty, who argues that courts should not impose definitional limits on rights and only accept limits on rights under section 1 if "there is no other, less drastic policy available that would interfere less with people's rights and freedoms."[30] As will be seen, however, the courts have resisted a mechanical approach to the justification of reasonable limits under section 1, which would invalidate legislation simply because a less drastic alternative could be imagined. They have stressed that a contextual approach is required under section 1 with attention to the competing policies at stake in many *Charter* cases.

3) Judicial Review and Framers' Intent

Another theory of judicial review that has had little influence under the *Charter* is the idea that courts only act legitimately to the extent that they implement the intent of the framers of the constitution. This theory assumes that following the framers' intent is more democratic than relying on a judge's interpretation of the text of the constitution and that judges should only constrain democratically elected legislatures if they have a clear mandate in the constitution to do so. Robert Bork, for example, has argued that because both the *Charter* and the American *Bill of Rights* "are silent" on the issue of abortion, "the Supreme Court should have stated that neither provision was enacted with abortion in mind, and that the *Charter*, having deliberately avoided the issue, had nothing to say and so the issue must remain with the legislature."[31]

There are many problems with the framers' intent approach. One problem is that the *Charter*, like other bills of rights, is generally framed in terms that are "vague and open" and whose meaning "cannot be determined by recourse to a dictionary, nor for that matter, by reference to the rules of statutory interpretation."[32] Another problem is the difficulty of determining the intent of the framers: the Supreme Court has rejected being bound by the expectations of senior civil servants who helped draft the *Charter*, in part, on the basis that "the intention of the legislative bodies which adopted the *Charter*" is a "fact which is nearly impossible of proof."[33]

The *Charter* is also a part of the constitution that can only be amended with the consent of the federal government and all provinces.

---

30   D. Beatty, *Constitutional Law in Theory and Practice* (Toronto: University of Toronto Press, 1995) at 70.
31   R. Bork, above note 16 at 87.
32   *Hunter v. Southam*, [1984] 2 S.C.R. 145, 11 D.L.R. (4th) 641 at 649.
33   *Reference Re s. 94(2) of the Motor Vehicle Act*, above note 1 at para. 51.

This makes amending the *Charter* very difficult. If the *Charter* is to remain relevant to the needs of a rapidly evolving society, it must be interpreted in a manner that allows for growth over the years. The Supreme Court has held that limiting its interpretation of the *Charter* on the basis of the drafters' expectations would create a danger of *Charter* rights becoming

> frozen in time to the moment of adoption with little or no possibility of growth, development and adjustment to changing societal needs . . . If the newly planted "living tree" which is the *Charter* is to have the possibility of growth and adjustment over time, care must be taken to ensure that historical materials . . . do not stunt its growth.[34]

The issue of the intent of the framers is also not very helpful in resolving whether the government has justified reasonable limits on *Charter* rights under section 1 of the *Charter* in a particular case. As we shall see in chapter 4, the reasonable limits clause gives both Parliament and the courts considerable scope to adapt the *Charter* to changing social needs. Finally, the existence of the section 33 override suggests that the framers of the *Charter* recognized that courts might interpret the *Charter* in unexpected ways.

4) Judicial Review as Part of a Democratic Dialogue

Another approach to the justification of judicial review is to situate judicial review in the context of an ongoing dialogue between courts and legislatures in which there is neither legislative or judicial supremacy.[35] A judicial decision invalidating a law or an administrative action under the *Charter* need not be the final word as legislatures can reformulate laws and authorize administrative actions. Such reply legislation can be defended under section 1 of the *Charter* as a reasonable limit on *Charter* rights as interpreted by the courts. In exceptional cases, the legislature can override a *Charter* decision with legislation that is enacted notwithstanding the fundamental freedoms, legal rights, and equality rights of the *Charter*. One of the strengths of dialogue theory is its abil-

---

34 *Ibid.* at para. 52.

35 Alexander Bickel argued for a form of dialogue in which "the Court placed itself in position to engage in a continual colloquy with the political institutions, leaving it to them to tell the Court what expedients of accommodation and compromise they deemed necessary. The Court would reply in the negative . . . only when a suggested expedient amounted to the abandonment of principle." A. Bickel, *The Least Dangerous Branch: The Supreme Court at the Bar of Politics*, 2d ed. (New Haven: Yale University Press, 1986) at 254.

ity to account for the power of legislatures under the *Charter* to place explicit limits and overrides on rights as interpreted by the courts. Another strength of dialogue theory is its ability to account for the frequent interplay between courts and legislatures on matters affected by the *Charter*. There is evidence that legislatures have frequently enacted new legislation after the courts have invalidated legislation under the *Charter*.[36] For example, Parliament has enacted new laws in response to some of the Supreme Court's more unpopular criminal law judgments concerning the right of the accused to introduce and have access to evidence affecting the privacy of complainants in sexual assault cases, rights against unreasonable search and seizures, and the defence of extreme intoxication. Parliament has also responded legislatively to judgments dealing with the voting rights of prisoners and the right of tobacco companies to advertise their product.[37]

The Supreme Court appears to accept the idea that judicial review under the *Charter* is part of a dialogue between courts and legislatures. In its 1998 decision, holding that protection for gays and lesbians against discrimination should be read into Alberta's human rights legislation, the Court observed that "the work of the legislature is reviewed by the courts and the work of the court in its decisions can be reacted to by the legislature in the passing of new legislation (or even overarching laws under section 33 of the *Charter*). This dialogue between and accountability of each of the branches have the effect of enhancing the democratic process, not denying it."[38] Alberta decided not to respond to the Court's decision in that case, but it did later enact legislation using the section 33 override that reserved marriage to opposite-sex couples. In a 2007 decision,[39] the Court again expressly referred to the dialogue metaphor when considering tobacco advertising legislation enacted in

---

36   There are some disputes about the exact number of such legislative replies with Peter Hogg and Allison Bushell arguing that there have been legislative replies in about two-thirds of cases and Professors Manfredi and Kelly arguing that the number of true replies is closer to one-third. See P. Hogg & A. Bushell, "The *Charter* Dialogue between Courts and Legislatures (Or Perhaps The *Charter of Rights* Isn't Such a Bad Thing After All)" (1997) 35 Osgoode Hall L.J. 75 and C. Manfredi & J. Kelly, "Six Degrees of Dialogue: A Response to Hogg and Bushell" (1999) 37 Osgoode Hall L.J. 513, arguing that only one-third of cases result in genuine dialogue. But see P. Hogg, A. Bushell Thornton, & W. Wright, "*Charter* Dialogue Revisited" (2007) 45 Osgoode Hall L.J. 1.

37   These legislative replies are examined in K. Roach, *The Supreme Court on Trial*, above note 18, cc. 10 and 14 and J. Hiebert, *Charter Conflicts: What Is Parliament's Role?* (Montreal: McGill-Queen's University Press, 2002).

38   *Vriend*, above note 1 at para. 139.

39   *Canada (Attorney General v. JTI-Macdonald Corp.*, [2007] 2 S.C.R. 610.

response to the Court's earlier decision striking down an earlier version of the same law.[40]

It may well be that courts could adopt a more vigorous approach to judicial review knowing that their decisions will not necessarily be the last word.

The implications of dialogue theory are less clear when the courts are reviewing legislation that has been enacted in response to a court's decision under the *Charter*. In *R. v. Mills*, the Supreme Court upheld legislation passed in response to an earlier decision by the Court, concerning the accused's right of access to the private records of complainants in sexual assault cases. Noting that dialogue between courts and legislatures occurs under the common law as well as the *Charter*, the Court observed that "if the common law were to be taken as establishing the only possible constitutional regime, then we could not speak of a dialogue with the legislature. Such a situation could only undermine rather than enhance democracy." In upholding Parliament's reply legislation, which not only emphasized the privacy rights of complainants and the equality rights of women and children, but also took into account the accused's right to full answer and defence, the Court observed that "courts do not hold a monopoly on the protection and promotion of rights and freedoms."[41] However, the majority's decision to uphold a limitation on the right to bail enacted in response to a decision striking down a very similar law provoked a sharp dissent from Iacobucci J., who complained that upholding the law "transformed dialogue into abdication."[42] *Sauvé v. Canada (Chief Electoral Officer)*[43] represents a strong reassertion of the Court's determination to subject responsive legislation to careful *Charter* scrutiny. In *Sauvé*, the Supreme Court struck down legislation denying the vote to prisoners serving sentences longer than two years, a law that had been enacted in response to the Court's earlier decision striking down a blanket prohibition on inmate voting.[44] McLachlin C.J.C. rejected any suggestion that "the fact that the challenged denial of the right to vote followed judicial rejection of an even more comprehensive denial" means "that the Court should defer to Parliament as part of a 'dialogue.'" She insisted that conformity to the demands of the constitution must be ensured "at whatever stage of the process" and that "[t]he healthy and important promotion of a

---

40   *RJR-MacDonald Inc. v. Canada (Attorney General)*, [1995] 3 S.C.R. 199. These cases are discussed in greater detail in chapter 9.

41   *R. v. Mills*, [1999] 3 S.C.R. 668, 180 D.L.R. (4th) 1 at paras. 56–58.

42   *R. v. Hall*, [2002] 3 S.C.R. 309 at para. 127.

43   *Sauvé*, above note 20.

44   *Sauvé v. Canada (Attorney General)*, [1993] 2 S.C.R. 438.

dialogue between the legislature and the courts should not be debased to a rule of 'if at first you don't succeed, try, try again.'"[45]

The metaphor of judicial review as dialogue is likely to continue to evolve. It remains to be seen in what direction. Courts and legislatures could play distinct and complementary roles with dialogue being conducted under section 1 of the *Charter* about the objectives of the legislation and the alternatives that the legislature has considered. Another possibility is that both institutions will see fit to act on their own interpretations of the constitution. Yet another is that both institutions will hold each other accountable.[46] Whatever precise direction is taken, the metaphor of dialogue and the recognition it accords to the distinct but related roles played by courts and legislatures reflects a fundamental aspect of the Canadian approach to judicial review under the *Charter*.

D. THE ROLE OF THE COURTS UNDER THE *CHARTER*

Assessing the relative merits of the arguments for and against judicial review requires looking at what the courts do not do, as well as what they do. While the critics of the left assert that the courts will import conservative values, it is important to put in perspective the outcomes of some of the so-called "bad cases" that they decry. In some of these cases, the failure to adopt the view of the left does not automatically translate into a victory for the right. For example, when the Supreme Court of Canada refused to find that collective bargaining was a constitutional right under the guarantee of freedom of association, that did not mean an end to collective bargaining; rather, it pushed the debate about the nature and scope of labour powers into the political arena.[47]

Similarly, when the courts refuse to recognize positive rights—for example, to welfare as an element of security of the person—that does not prevent political debate and action with respect to welfare policy; instead, it leaves the difficult policy choices to the political process. There will only be a danger to continued democracy if the legislature confuses the court's decision that some measure is consistent with the

---

45   *Sauvé*, above note 20 at para. 17.
46   K. Roach, "Constitutional and Common Law Dialogues Between the Supreme Court and Canadian Legislatures" (2001) 80 Can. Bar Rev. 481.
47   *Reference Re Public Service Employee Relations Act (Alberta)*, [1987] 1 S.C.R. 313, 38 D.L.R. (4th) 161; *P.S.A.C. v. Canada (A.G.)*, [1987] 1 S.C.R. 424, 38 D.L.R. (4th) 249; *R.W.D.S.U., Locals 544, 496, 635, 955 v. Saskatchewan*, [1987] 1 S.C.R. 460, 38 D.L.R. (4th) 277, discussed in chapter 10.

Charter with the separate question of whether it is wise and necessary policy.[48]

Finally, in other areas, while the result in a given case may provide a victory to a powerful economic interest, the decision often has implications throughout the legal system in ways that may also benefit the less advantaged. For instance, when a powerful corporation wins protection against unreasonable searches and seizures in the criminal process, it will not be the only beneficiary. As discussed above, many *Charter* decisions on controversial topics, such as the rights of tobacco companies to advertise, have not proven to be the final word on the subject. Legislatures still retain the right to enact new legislation that can be justified under section 1 of the *Charter* or subject to the section 33 override.

In the chapters that follow, we will see that Canadian courts have demonstrated a marked deference in certain areas which, it may be argued, results from their recognition of the limits of the judicial function. The Canadian Supreme Court has been unsympathetic to claims of pure economic rights and has refused to become embroiled in most distributional issues.[49] This has been manifested by the Court's refusal to imply a right of property in the constitution and its rejection of overtures to protect rights of contract. This cautious and deferential stance contrasts sharply with the Court's willingness to engage its power to protect freedom of expression and the rights of criminally accused. While the Court has expressed a commitment to vigilance in the protection of minorities from prejudice and stereotypes, it has also insisted that governments be given some leeway in making difficult social-policy decisions — for example, with respect to mandatory retirement and the criminalization of marijuana.

The Court's refusal to intervene in the areas of property and contract reflects its view that economic and social-policy questions are best left to the legislative arenas.[50] Similarly, the Court has respected and

---

48   Some theorists have expressed a concern that legislatures will "fall into a habit of assuming that whatever they could constitutionally do they may do" so that the people "lose the political experience, and the moral education and stimulus that comes from fighting the question out in the ordinary way, and correcting their own errors." A. Bickel, *The Least Dangerous Branch*, above note 35 at 21–22, quoting James Bradley Thayer.

49   See, for example, *Irwin Toy Ltd. v. Quebec (A.G.)*, [1989] 1 S.C.R. 927, 58 D.L.R. (4th) 577, holding that commercial expression is protected by s. 2(b) of the *Charter*, but making it clear that purely economic rights are not protected.

50   Peter Russell has observed that "[t]here is not much empirical evidence to support" the concerns of the left or the right about judicial activism because "none of the key economic and social policy interests of government — monet-

upheld legislative initiatives to protect vulnerable groups when these initiatives have been challenged as violating the fundamental freedoms of more powerful interests in society.[51] The Court recognizes that Parliament and the legislatures have an important role in enhancing and protecting these very same values that inform judicial review, wisely refusing to claim the exclusive authority to determine when those rights should be protected.

In sum, it can be argued that the purpose of constitutionalizing rights is to facilitate, not frustrate, democracy. The *Charter* protects the values of individual dignity, autonomy, and respect, which are essential for free and open democratic debate, and it gives a voice to many in our society who are effectively excluded from the political process. A true democracy is surely one in which the exercise of power by the many is conditional on respect for the rights of the few. Majorities may fail to respect individual dignity and conscience and may be inclined to shut out annoying and unpopular views. Constitutionalizing rights empowers the courts to check these unworthy inclinations by requiring those who exercise power to justify their actions through evidence and reasoned argument when the bedrock values of our democratic tradition are impinged. The Canadian experience to date indicates that the judiciary is capable of exercising the powers of judicial review to protect such fundamental rights as freedom of religion and expression and the right to equality without unduly inhibiting the capacity of the elected representatives to develop social policy.

E. CONCLUSION

Overall, we suggest that the *Charter* has had a beneficial impact upon democratic life in Canada. Fundamental human rights are now properly at the forefront of public debate, and the claims of those often

---

ary and fiscal policy, international trade, resource development, social welfare, education, labour relations, environmental protection — have been significantly encroached by judicial enforcement of the *Charter*." P. Russell, "Canadian Constraints on Judicialization from Without" (1994) 15 International Political Science Rev. 165 at 168, 169.

51 See *Edwards Books & Art Ltd. v. R.*, [1986] 2 S.C.R. 713, 35 D.L.R. (4th) 1 at 49, where Dickson C.J.C. stated that care had to be taken so that the *Charter* "does not simply become an instrument of better situated individuals to roll back legislation that has as its object the improvement of the condition of less advantaged persons." See also *R. v. Kapp*, [2008] 2 S.C.R. 483, upholding affirmative action programs under s. 15(2) of the *Charter*.

drowned out in the cut and thrust of day-to-day politics can no longer be ignored. Indeed, the *Charter* has made an important contribution to Canadian political life by creating what Roland Penner calls a "culture of liberty."[52] Legislators cannot enact laws without consideration of their impact on individual rights, and government legal officers play an important role in encouraging their political masters to justify any limitations on *Charter* rights.

The *Charter* has the potential to strengthen the Canadian democratic tradition and commitment to toleration and equal respect for all, and judges have an appropriate part to play in protecting those values. As interpreted by the courts to date, the *Charter* neither precludes nor entrenches particular socio-economic outcomes but rather enriches the democratic process.

FURTHER READINGS

BAKAN, J., *Just Words: Constitutional Rights and Social Wrongs* (Toronto: University of Toronto Press, 1997)

BEATTY, D.M., *Constitutional Law in Theory and Practice* (Toronto: University of Toronto Press, 1995)

BEATTY, D.M., *The Ultimate Rule of Law* (Oxford: Oxford University Press, 2004)

BOGART, W.A., *Courts and Country: The Limits of Litigation and the Social and Political Life of Canada* (Toronto: Oxford University Press, 1994)

BRUDNER, A., *Constitutional Goods* (Oxford: Oxford University Press, 2004)

CONKLIN, W.E., *Images of a Constitution* (Toronto: University of Toronto Press, 1989)

DICKSON, B., ed., *Judicial Activism in Common Law Supreme Courts* (Oxford: Oxford University Press, 2007).

ELY, J.H., *Democracy and Distrust: A Theory of Judicial Review* (Cambridge: Harvard University Press, 1980)

HIEBERT, J., *Charter Conflicts? What is Parliament's Role?* (Montreal: McGill-Queen's University Press, 2002)

---

52   Penner, above note 27 at 114–15.

HOGG, P., & A. THORNTON, "The *Charter* Dialogue between Courts and Legislatures" (1997) 35 Osgoode Hall L.J. 75

HUTCHINSON, A.C., *Waiting for CORAF: A Critique of Law and Rights* (Toronto: University of Toronto Press, 1995)

KELLY, JAMES, & C. MANFREDI, eds., *Contested Constitutionalisms: Reflections on the Canadian Charter of Rights and Freedoms* (Vancouver: University of British Columbia Press, 2009).

KNOPFF, R., & F.L. MORTON, *Charter Politics* (Scarborough, ON: Nelson Canada, 1992)

MANDEL, M., *The Charter of Rights and the Legalization of Politics in Canada*, 2d ed. (Toronto: Thompson, 1994)

MANFREDI, C., *Judicial Power and the Charter: Canada and the Paradox of Liberal Constitutionalism*, 2d ed. (Toronto: Oxford University Press, 2001)

McLACHLAN, B.," The *Charter* 25 Years Later: The Good, the Bad, and the Challenges" (2007) 45 Osgoode Hall L.J. 365.

MONAHAN, P., *Politics and the Constitution: The Charter, Federalism and the Supreme Court of Canada* (Toronto: Carswell, 1987)

MORTON, F.L., & R. KNOPFF, *The Charter Revolution and the Court Party* (Peterborough, ON: Broadview Press, 2000)

PENNER, R., "The Canadian Experience with the *Charter of Rights*: Are There Lessons for the United Kingdom?" [1996] Pub. L. 104

ROACH, K., *The Supreme Court on Trial: Judicial Activism or Democratic Dialogue* (Toronto: Irwin Law, 2001)

SLATTERY, B., "A Theory of the *Charter*" (1987) 25 Osgoode Hall L.J. 701

SYMPOSIUM, "*Charter* Dialogue: Ten Years Later" (2007) 45 Osgoode Hall L.J. 1–202

CHAPTER 3

INTERPRETATION OF THE *CHARTER OF RIGHTS AND FREEDOMS*

Entrenching rights in the constitution does not end the debate about the legitimacy of judicial review. Rather, the debate takes on a different form, revolving around the justification for various approaches to constitutional interpretation. Some argue for a strict reading of the constitutional text, often maintaining that the words of the document should be understood in light of their meaning at the time of drafting. Others argue for a more "progressive" approach that will allow the content to adapt to new societal needs and values. Those who take this latter position turn to moral philosophy, international human rights norms, or evolving community values for help in the interpretive process.

In this chapter, we outline the structure of the *Canadian Charter of Rights and Freedoms* and then canvass some of the debates about its interpretation.

A. THE NATURE OF *CHARTER* RIGHTS

The Canadian *Charter* identifies and enshrines six broad categories of rights:

- the "fundamental freedoms" of conscience, religion, thought, belief, opinion, expression, assembly, and association;[1]

---

1   Section 2.

- democratic rights, including the right to vote, the guarantee of regular elections, and annual parliamentary sessions;[2]
- mobility rights to enter and leave the country and the right to reside in and gain a livelihood in any province;[3]
- legal rights, particularly those pertaining to the criminal process, such as the rights to counsel, protection against unreasonable search and seizure, *habeas corpus*, trial within a reasonable time, and the presumption of innocence until proven guilty, as well as a more general right to life, liberty, and security of the person, and the right not to be deprived thereof except in accordance with principles of fundamental justice;[4]
- the right to equality before and under the law and to the equal protection and equal benefit of the law;[5] and
- language rights.[6]

These rights are both guaranteed and made subject to limitations in section 1 of the *Charter*, which states that the *Charter* "guarantees the rights and freedoms set out in it subject to such reasonable limits prescribed by law as can be demonstrably justified in a free and democratic society." Thus, the Canadian *Charter* follows the model of international human rights documents rather than the American constitution. While the American document sets out the rights as if they are absolute, international documents, such as the *International Covenant on Civil and Political Rights*, expressly acknowledge that rights can be limited to protect other individual rights or broader community interests.

The *Charter* also includes a number of distinctive interpretive provisions, including a clause ensuring that there will be no derogation from Aboriginal rights by the *Charter* in section 25,[7] a commitment to preserve and enhance our multicultural heritage in section 27, and a further guarantee of gender equality in section 28. Also significant to interpretive issues is the specific remedial clause in section 24, discussed in chapter 17, as well as a mechanism to override certain *Charter* rights, found in section 33, which is discussed in chapter 5.

The rights included in a constitutional document reflect the concerns prevalent at the time of drafting. To the extent that the goal of the constitution is to curtail majority tyranny and government excesses,

---

2   Sections 3–5.
3   Section 6.
4   Sections 7–14.
5   Section 15.
6   Sections 16–23.
7   Aboriginal rights are recognized and affirmed in s. 35 of the *Constitution Act, 1982*, which does not form part of the *Charter*.

the rights protected will tend to lie in those areas where there has been evidence of problems—for example, government measures against unpopular expression or the practices of some religions. Similarly, to the extent that the constitution expresses an aspiration to greater equality in society, the listed grounds of discrimination may reflect historical or contemporary bases for unfair treatment against individuals and groups. The Canadian *Charter*, for example, was one of the world's first to include disability, while South Africa's new constitution, in force since December 1996, goes further to include sexual orientation in its equality guarantee.[8]

The emphasis in many countries has been on a liberal approach that protects the individual *from* certain state actions. There is, however, pressure in many countries today for the inclusion of positive rights—that is, rights to make governments act in order to provide greater equality or human dignity. While the Canadian *Charter* does include the positive right to minority-language schools in section 23, it does not contain the range of positive rights found, for example, in the new South African constitution, which includes the right to a healthy environment, the right to have access to adequate housing, health-care services, sufficient food and water, and social security, and the right to a basic education.[9] Efforts were made to add a "social charter" to the Canadian constitution during the constitutional-reform discussions occurring between 1990 and 1992, but serious opposition from a wide range of opinion undermined the project.[10]

In sum, the Canadian catalogue of rights and freedoms in the *Charter* looks essentially liberal in nature, in the sense that its language of rights and freedoms seems to define a zone of autonomy for the individual within which the state may not intrude. This feature of the *Charter* has been a cause for concern on the part of those who fear that its emphasis upon traditional liberal values will have an Americanizing influence on a Canadian legal and political culture, which emphasizes the communitarian values of "peace, order, and good government" rather

---

8   South African Constitution, s. 9.

9   *Ibid.*, ss. 24, 26, 27, 29. These rights often contain qualifications—for example, the right to access to adequate housing states in subs. (2) that "[t]he state must take reasonable legislative and other measures, within its available resources, to achieve the progressive realisation of this right."

10   Some of the arguments pro and con are found in W. Kymlicka & W.J. Norman, "The Social *Charter* Debate: Should Social Justice be Constitutionalized?" (Ottawa: Network on the Constitution, 1992); J. Bakan & D. Schneiderman, *Social Justice and the Constitution: Perspectives on the Social Union for Canada* (Ottawa: Carleton University Press, 1992).

than the American ideal of the "right to life, liberty, and the pursuit of happiness." Instead of seeing government as a positive force because of its capacity to create greater equality or help the vulnerable, the *Charter* may foster the view that the state is the enemy of individual freedom.[11]

In looking at the experience under the *Charter*, one would have to conclude that the Canadian legal system has moved closer to the American model. However, this conclusion should be tempered by a realization that both the text and the interpretation of the *Charter* reflect an attitude more receptive to affirmative state measures designed to advance certain collective interests than that found in American constitutional law. For instance, "affirmative action" measures that have as their object the amelioration of conditions of disadvantaged individuals or groups are explicitly protected from claims of "reverse discrimination" and, thus, denials of equality.[12] The promise of equality itself has been found to require affirmative measures by the state.[13] Also significant is the Supreme Court's pronouncement that even rights that are cast in negative terms may impose positive obligations in some situations.[14] Unless the *Charter* right is cast in positive terms, ordinarily a claimant cannot assert the *Charter* right against the government to insist upon statutory protection.[15] Likewise, an existing statutorily created platform, such as collective bargaining legislation, that relates to a *Charter* right will not by itself ground a claim advanced by individuals excluded from the statutory regime. However, where the claimant can demonstrate that exclusion from a statutory regime permits a substantial interference with a *Charter* right, and the state is thereby accountable for the claimant's inability to exercise a protected right or freedom, the *Charter* requires that affirmative measures be taken. While there are few cases where the Court has been prepared to interpret one of the negative rights against government interference as giving rise to positive obligations, a notable example is the decision requiring a provincial legislature to enact legislation to protect the right of vulnerable

---

11   This passage echoes the criticisms of Andrew Petter, among others, discussed in chapter 2.

12   Section 15(2). In addition, s. 6(4) protects discriminatory labour practices against out-of-province workers in provinces with unemployment rates above the national average.

13   *Eldridge v. British Columbia (A.G.)*, [1997] 3 S.C.R. 624, 151 D.L.R. (4th) 577; *Vriend v. Alberta*, [1998] 1 S.C.R. 493, 156 D.L.R. (4th) 385 [*Vriend*].

14   *Dunmore v. Ontario (Attorney General)*, [2001] 3 S.C.R. 1016, 207 D.L.R. (4th) 193 [*Dunmore*]; *Baier v. Alberta*, [2007] 2 S.C.R. 673 at paras. 21–30.

15   *Haig v. Canada (Chief Electoral Officer)*, [1993] 2 S.C.R. 995, 105 D.L.R. (4th) 577 at 607; *Native Women's Association of Canada v. Canada* (1994), 119 D.L.R. (4th) 224 at 245 (S.C.C.); *Vriend*, above note 13 at para. 64.

agricultural workers to engage in associational activities necessary to protect their interests as employees.[16]

Most important, section 1 of the *Charter*, the "reasonable limits" clause discussed in chapter 4, has been interpreted to permit legislative measures designed to enhance the values underlying the fundamental rights and freedoms and to acknowledge that the liberty of the individual is sometimes justifiably limited in the interests of broader community interests and values.

Especially in the early years, American jurisprudence was frequently cited in *Charter* litigation and treated as relevant and sometimes persuasive. But American approaches have also been flatly rejected in some areas and American jurisprudence is certainly not determinative, as the Supreme Court of Canada has frequently stated, given the differences in Canadian and American political and legal traditions.[17]

B. INTERPRETATION OF *CHARTER* RIGHTS

The Canadian courts have adopted a two-step process of interpretation and justification to give the general language of the *Charter* concrete meaning. First, the courts interpret the meaning of the right or freedom at issue to determine whether the matter complained of constitutes an infringement. Often, at this first stage, the courts have avoided narrow definitional limitations on rights that take into account the general social interest. It has been held, for example, that commercial advertising,[18] hate propaganda,[19] and pornography[20] are, subject to limitations justifiable under section 1, forms of expression protected by section 2(b). Only violence has been held to be excluded from the definition of expression.

With respect to some other rights, however, the courts have taken a more restrictive approach and defined certain limits to their scope. In interpreting the right to vote in section 3, for example, the courts

---

16 *Dunmore*, above note 14.

17 See J. Cameron, "The Motor Vehicle Reference and the Relevance of American Doctrine in *Charter* Adjudication" in R.J. Sharpe, ed., *Charter Litigation* (Toronto: Butterworths, 1987) c. 4. Indeed, the Canadian Court has embarked on jurisprudence that is quite distinctive from the American in areas such as hate propaganda and pornography, equality rights, and the drawing of electoral boundaries.

18 *Irwin Toy Ltd. v. Quebec (A.G.)*, [1989] 1 S.C.R. 927, 58 D.L.R. (4th) 577.

19 *R. v. Keegstra*, [1990] 3 S.C.R. 697, 61 C.C.C. (3d) 1 [*Keegstra*].

20 *R. v. Butler*, [1992] 1 S.C.R. 452, 70 C.C.C. (3d) 129.

have held that this provision gives a right to effective representation, not a guarantee of "one person, one vote."[21] Freedom of association was initially limited by excluding some group activities, such as the right to strike.[22] Section 15, the equality guarantee, can be invoked only by those discriminated against on the basis of the enumerated (for example, race, sex, or disability) or analogous grounds.[23] Certain rights are defined in a contextual manner. For example, the section 8 right to be protected against unreasonable search and seizure requires the courts to take into account the context in which the right is claimed when defining what searches and seizures are "unreasonable."[24]

A claimant can demonstrate that a right has been infringed either by looking at the government's purpose or at the effects of the government's actions. In some cases, the legislature's purpose will directly interfere with the exercise of the right — for example, a state-imposed compulsory religion for all would violate freedom of religion in section 2(a). In most cases, while the underlying objective of state action is not to interfere with a protected freedom, the legislation being challenged has that effect. For example, when a government prohibits individuals from fastening anything to telephone poles, the objective may be to prevent unsightly displays or even obstructions that may interfere with traffic safety. However, the effect of such a rule is to prevent the putting up of posters, which can be seen as an interference with freedom of expression.[25]

Once a right is infringed, the case is not over. The *Charter* recognizes that rights are not absolute; there are many situations when the interests of society at large or the rights of other individuals will require that the claimant's rights be limited. The consideration of whether these limits are justified under section 1 of the *Charter*, as reasonable limits prescribed by law in a free and democratic society, is left to the second step of a rights case — justification pursuant to section 1. The balance of this chapter discusses the initial interpretive stage, leaving the limitation of rights to the following chapter.

1) The Purposive Method

From the earliest *Charter* cases, the Supreme Court of Canada clearly recognized that *Charter* adjudication should be different from the

---

21   See chapter 11.
22   See chapter 10.
23   See chapter 15.
24   See chapter 14.
25   *Peterborough (City) v. Ramsden*, [1993] 2 S.C.R. 1084, 106 D.L.R. (4th) 233.

traditional work of the courts. In *Law Society of Upper Canada v. Skapinker*,[26] the first *Charter* case to reach the Court, the judges indicated that they were prepared to assume responsibility for interpreting this "new yardstick of reconciliation between the individual and the community and their respective rights." Mindful that the "*Charter* is designed and adopted to guide and serve the Canadian community for a long time," Estey J. added that "narrow and technical interpretation" that could "stunt the growth of the law and hence the community it serves"[27] would be avoided.

In another early case, *Hunter v. Southam*,[28] the Supreme Court distinguished the method of statutory construction from that of constitutional interpretation. Insisting that the *Charter* must "be capable of growth and development over time to meet new social, political, and historical realities often unimagined by its framers," Dickson C.J.C. repeated Professor Paul Freund's plea that courts should not "read the provisions of the Constitution like a last will and testament lest it become one."[29] A similar note was struck by Beetz J. in *Manitoba (A.G.) v. Metropolitan Stores (MTS) Ltd.*[30] when he dismissed the contention that the "presumption of constitutionality" should be weighed in the scales of *Charter* adjudication: "[T]he innovative and evolutive character of the Canadian *Charter of Rights and Freedoms* conflicts with the idea that a legislative provision can be presumed to be consistent with the *Charter*."[31] The rights and freedoms set out were not "frozen" in content and had to "remain susceptible to evolve in the future."[32]

These passages harken back to earlier decisions of the Privy Council and the Supreme Court of Canada interpreting the *Constitution Act, 1867*, in which the judges advocated an "organic" or "progressive" theory of interpretation with respect to the constitution. The judges rejected an approach advocated by some American scholars and judges, which emphasizes the original intent of the framers of the constitution and interprets the document in light of the meaning of its terms at the time it was created. The "original intent" approach was soundly rejected by the Privy Council as being inconsistent with the idea of an enduring constitution that, if it is to last, must be capable of growth and expansion. In the *Edwards* case, the Privy Council determined

---

26   [1984] 1 S.C.R. 357, 9 D.L.R. (4th) 161.
27   *Ibid.* at 366 (S.C.R.).
28   [1984] 2 S.C.R. 145, 11 D.L.R. (4th) 641.
29   *Ibid.* at 649 (D.L.R.).
30   [1987] 1 S.C.R. 110, 38 D.L.R. (4th) 321.
31   *Ibid.* at 122 (S.C.R.).
32   *Ibid.* at 124 (S.C.R.).

that, in the twentieth century, women were qualified "persons" for the purposes of eligibility for Senate appointments, even though in 1867, at the time the constitution was adopted, women were not eligible to hold public office. Viscount Sankey's words from that case have been frequently quoted:

> The *B.N.A. Act* planted in Canada a living tree capable of growth and expansion within its natural limits. The object of the Act was to grant a Constitution to Canada . . .
>
>   Their Lordships do not conceive it to be the duty of this Board — it is certainly not their desire — to cut down the provisions of the Act by a narrow and technical construction, but rather to give it a large and liberal interpretation . . .[33]

The Supreme Court reaffirmed the vitality of the "living tree" approach to constitutional interpretation in *Reference Re Same-Sex Marriage*[34] when it unanimously rejected the idea that Parliament's jurisdiction over marriage under section 91(26) of the *Constitution Act, 1867* was limited to marriages as understood at the time of Confederation.

The Supreme Court of Canada has specifically held that the supposed "original intent" of those who drafted the *Charter* will not be conclusive in its interpretation for two reasons.[35] First, statements of the intent of particular individuals are an unreliable guide to discerning the intent of many others who took an active role in the creation of the *Charter*. Furthermore, it is doubtful that there was a single or identifiable intent shared by all, given the number of federal and provincial politicians and bureaucrats involved. Second, adoption of a strict interpretivist approach would freeze the meaning of the *Charter* at a particular time "with little or no possibility of growth, development and adjustment to changing societal needs."[36] Even if there were concrete evidence to help in determining the original understanding of the right, it would be wrong to fasten on to that meaning without question, for the original drafters themselves in all likelihood considered this to be an inappropriate method of interpretation. Constitutions are deliberately phrased in general, open-ended terms in order to let them adapt to changing circumstances and needs over the years. In the words of Ronald Dworkin, constitutions are meant to set out concepts,

---

33   *Edwards v. R.*, [1930] A.C. 124 at 136–37 [*Edwards*].
34   [2004] 3 S.C.R. 698 at paras. 22–30.
35   *Reference Re s. 94(2) of the Motor Vehicle Act (B.C.)*, [1985] 2 S.C.R. 486 at 508–9, 24 D.L.R. (4th) 536.
36   *Ibid.* at 554 (D.L.R.), Lamer J.

not conceptions, and thus, their content necessarily varies over time and place.[37]

Given the rejection of "original intent" to guide interpretation, how should a court proceed? In *Hunter v. Southam*, the Supreme Court of Canada first enunciated and applied the "purposive" method that has served as the standard approach in the elaboration of *Charter* rights and freedoms. This is a complex, value-laden exercise that draws upon a range of sources in the innovative spirit that the *Charter* demands. It calls upon the judge to reflect upon the purpose of and rationale for the *Charter* right at issue in the light of the overall structure of the *Charter*, our legal and political tradition, our history, and the changing needs and demands of modern society.

Perhaps the most often cited passage describing the nature of this exercise of purposive interpretation is from the judgment of Dickson J. in *R. v. Big M Drug Mart Ltd.*:

> In my view, this analysis is to be undertaken, and the purpose of the right or freedom in question is to be sought by reference to the character and the larger objects of the *Charter* itself, to the language chosen to articulate the specific right or freedom, to the historical origins of the concepts enshrined, and where applicable, to the meaning and purpose of the other specific rights and freedoms with which it is associated within the text of the *Charter*. The interpretation should be, as the judgment in *Southam* emphasizes, a generous rather than a legalistic one, aimed at fulfilling the purpose of the guarantee and securing for individuals the full benefit of the *Charter*'s protection. At the same time it is important not to overshoot the actual purpose of the right or freedom in question, but to recall that the *Charter* was not enacted in a vacuum, and must therefore, as this Court's decision in *Law Society of Upper Canada v. Skapinker* illustrates, be placed in its proper linguistic, philosophic and historical contexts.[38]

The purposive method of interpretation is indicative of the most significant effect of the *Charter* upon the role of the judiciary. *Charter* adjudication is anything but the mechanical application of pre-established rules. The judges are called upon to delve deeply into the very foundations of our legal system and political culture to answer questions of the most fundamental nature, and many of these questions cannot be answered adequately by reference only to traditional legal sources.

---

37   R. Dworkin, *Taking Rights Seriously* (Cambridge: Harvard University Press, 1977) at 134.

38   [1985] 1 S.C.R. 295 at 344, 18 D.L.R. (4th) 321 [*Big M Drug Mart*].

2) The Contextual Method

Although the purposive approach to interpretation remains the dominant approach to the interpretation of the *Charter*, a growing number of cases emphasize the need to take a contextual approach to the interpretation of *Charter* rights. A contextual approach will most often be used to impose some definitional limits on *Charter* rights and when the court assesses whether a limit on a *Charter* right is reasonable under section 1 of the *Charter*.

One example of a contextual approach to the interpretation of a *Charter* right is the emphasis given to the context of Canadian democracy when interpreting section 3 of the *Charter* to require effective representation as opposed to a strict one person one vote standard for electoral districts. The Supreme Court's interpretation of the right to vote was influenced by contextual factors such as Canadian history and geography.[39] A contextual approach is also often taken when the courts interpret section 7 of the *Charter* which provides that "everyone has the right to life, liberty and security of the person and the right not to be deprived thereof except in accordance with the principles of fundamental justice."[40] When interpreting section 7 of the *Charter*, the Court has drawn a distinction between matters of public policy or philosophy and matters that fall "squarely within 'the inherent domain of the judiciary as a guardian of the justice system.'"[41] Thus the Court ruled that extradition of a fugitive without assurances that the death penalty would not be imposed would generally violate section 7 not because of any conclusion about the morality or efficacy of the death penalty, but because of the contextual factors of Canadian and foreign experience of wrongful convictions and a growing international movement towards abolition of the death penalty and Canada's participation in that movement. The Court has also rejected concepts such as that the criminal law should only be used to protect others from harm,[42] or that criminal law should reflect the best interests of the child,[43] on the basis that there was not a sufficient societal consensus that such principles were essential to the administration of justice. The Court has also taken a contextual approach in determining the extent of *Charter* rights in the

---

39   *Reference Re Provincial Electoral Boundaries (Saskatchewan)*, [1991] 2 S.C.R. 158, 81 D.L.R. (4th) 16. For further discussion, see chapter 11.

40   Discussed in chapter 13.

41   *United States of America v. Burns*, [2001] 1 S.C.R. 283, 195 D.L.R. (4th) 1 at para. 38.

42   *R. v. Malmo-Levine, R. v. Caine*, [2003] 3 S.C.R. 571 at para. 103. For further discussion, see chapter 13.

43   *Canadian Foundation for Children, Youth and the Law v. Canada (Attorney General)*, [2004] 1 S.C.R. 76 at para. 8. For further discussion, see chapter 13.

regulatory or criminal context. The accused will generally have diminished *Charter* rights when operating in a regulated or licensed field, but will have access to full *Charter* rights when the predominant purpose of the state is to determine penal liability.[44]

Contextual factors also play a crucial role in the interpretation of equality rights.[45] From the start, the Supreme Court has rejected the idea that every inequality in the law will violate the *Charter* and has called for an examination of whether a particular inequality will result in discrimination when viewed in a larger political and social context.[46] A feature of the test for determining when equality rights in section 15 of the *Charter* are violated is an open-ended list of "contextual factors" that includes whether there is pre-existing disadvantage and whether the government is attempting to ameliorate disadvantage. The current test also endorses a contextual approach to interpretation by suggesting that the relevant point of view for determining whether an inequality in the law results in substantive discrimination "is that of a reasonable person, in circumstances similar to those of the claimant."[47]

A contextual approach that judges the *Charter* claim in a larger social context is also very important for determining whether a limitation on a *Charter* right is justified and reasonable under section 1 of the *Charter*. In an early *Charter* case holding that Sunday closing laws enacted for the secular purpose of providing a common day of rest were a reasonable limit on religious freedom, Chief Justice Dickson observed that the courts should be cautious about allowing the *Charter* to "become an instrument of better situated individuals to roll back legislation that has as its object the improvement of the conditions of less advantaged persons."[48] As discussed in the next chapter, the Supreme Court has also taken into account the context of social and economic policy and legislative attempts to mediate between competing groups when determining whether particular limits on rights are reasonable. Indeed, the Court has even viewed the context of a severe financial crisis in a province as an important factor in determining whether legislation that deferred and extinguished part of a pay equity scheme for female

---

44 *R. v. Jarvis*, [2002] 3 S.C.R. 757 at paras. 63–65. For further discussion, see chapter 14.

45 Discussed in chapter 15.

46 *Andrews v. Law Society (British Columbia)*, [1989] 1 S.C.R. 143, 56 D.L.R. (4th) 1 [*Andrews*].

47 *Law v. Canada*, [1999] 1 S.C.R. 497 at para. 88. For further discussion see chapter 15.

48 *Edwards Books & Art Ltd. v. R.* (1986), 35 D.L.R. (4th) 1 at 49 (S.C.C.), discussed in chapter 4.

health care workers was justified under section 1 of the *Charter*.[49] Both in determining the ambit of some *Charter* rights and the justification for limiting *Charter* rights, the courts pay attention to the wider social and political context of the *Charter* claim.

3) The Reconciliation of Competing Rights

One of the most difficult dilemmas for courts in interpreting *Charter* rights is how to deal with claims of competing and potentially conflicting rights. For example, what should be done when a person's right to freedom of expression in the context of hate speech or pornography could affect the right of a disadvantaged group to enjoy the equal protection of the law? What should happen when the accused's right to full answer and defence and disclosure of the state's case could conflict with a complainant's right to privacy and equality with respect to confidential documents? What should happen when freedom of religion competes with equality rights on issues such as same-sex marriage?

The Supreme Court has rejected a hierarchical approach to rights that places some *Charter* rights above others. For example, it has rejected pre-*Charter* common law that placed the accused's right to a fair trial before freedom of expression and has urged courts to balance and reconcile fair trial and free expression rights. Thus courts should restrict expression by ordering publication bans only when necessary to prevent a real and substantial risk to the accused's right to a fair trial and only after considering the adequacy of reasonable alternatives that are more respectful of freedom of expression. In the final analysis, the court must determine that the benefits of any proposed publication ban outweigh its harms after considering all of the relevant rights, including the accused's right to a fair trial and the public's right to freedom of expression.[50]

The Supreme Court has indicated that courts must attempt to reconcile equality rights with religious freedom as much as possible. For example, religious freedom should protect a Christian college from being refused certification as a teachers college even though the college teaches that homosexuality is a sin, but it may not protect individual teachers who act on such beliefs.[51] In most cases, freedom of religion would protect religious officials from being required to perform same-

---

49 *Newfoundland (Treasury Board) v. N.A.P.E.*, [2004] 3 S.C.R. 381.

50 *R. v. Mentuck*, [2001] 3 S.C.R. 442; *Dagenais v. Canadian Broadcasting Corp.*, [1994] 3 S.C.R. 835. For further discussion see chapter 9.

51 *Trinity Western University v. British Columbia College of Teachers*, [2001] 1 S.C.R. 772.

sex marriages, but freedom of religion would not prevent the recognition of same-sex marriage as a matter of secular law.[52]

In a case dealing with the controversial issue of whether courts and judges should have access to the private therapeutic documents of complainants in sexual assault cases, the Supreme Court has indicated that the accused's right to full answer and defence should be defined in a manner that reconciles that right with the competing privacy and equality rights of the complainant in sexual assault cases. This reconciliation of rights takes place outside of the section 1 justification process under which the state bears the burden of demonstrating that limits on *Charter* rights are demonstrably justifiable.[53] At the same time, however, the internal reconciliation process draws on factors such as reasonable alternatives that are quite important under section 1 of the *Charter*.

Another manifestation of the Supreme Court's commitment to reconciling competing rights is its refusal to allow one *Charter* right to nullify another constitutional right. For example, the Court has rejected arguments that denominational schools that were constitutionally protected before the enactment of the *Charter*[54] or specific minority language rights[55] are inconsistent with equality rights because they single out particular minorities for preferential treatment. One constitutional right should not be allowed to nullify another.

The courts also confront the problems of competing rights under section 1 of the *Charter*. This issue has frequently arisen in the context of freedom of expression claims. The courts have interpreted the right to freedom of expression in a broad and purposive manner to include speech such as hate speech and pornography that may cause harms to others. At the same time, however, the courts have recognized that competing rights such as equality rights are at stake and constitute governmental objectives that are important enough to justify restrictions on freedom of expression.[56]

4) Interpretive Sources

The task of *Charter* interpretation has structure and discipline. The first source is obvious — the language of the *Charter* itself. For example, the

---

52 *Reference Re Same-Sex Marriage*, above note 34; *EGALE Canada Inc. v. Canada (Attorney General)* (2003), 225 D.L.R. (4th) 472 (B.C.C.A.); *Halpern v. Canada (Attorney General)* (2003), 65 O.R. (3d) 161 (C.A.).

53 *R. v. Mills*, [1999] 3 S.C.R. 668 at para. 66.

54 *Reference Re Bill 30*, [1987] 1 S.C.R. 1148; *Adler v. Ontario*, [1996] 3 S.C.R. 609.

55 *Gosselin (Tutor of) v. Quebec (Attorney General)* 2005 SCC 15.

56 *Keegstra*, above note 19.

recognition of Aboriginal rights, commitment to multiculturalism, and protection of affirmative action in section 15(2) all helped the Supreme Court to determine that the meaning of equality in section 15(1) did not require that all must be treated in the same way, and that equality sometimes requires different treatment for different individuals and groups.[57]

Although the Supreme Court has avoided an overtly philosophical approach, many of its opinions are sprinkled with references to philosophical writings. In *Dolphin Delivery*, the first case to interpret the meaning of freedom of expression, reference was made to the writings of John Stuart Mill and John Milton in elaborating the meaning of freedom of expression.[58] In fact, Mill has been cited with some frequency in a range of cases,[59] as has Ronald Dworkin.[60] Justice Wilson was probably the most frequent user of philosophical materials in her years on the bench as she strove to give meaning to the rights and freedoms in the early days of *Charter* interpretation.[61]

While the Supreme Court rejected appeals to original intent, the judges have nevertheless looked to historical material and traditions to inform the meaning of the rights. In *Big M Drug Mart*, the first major case on freedom of religion, Dickson J. looked back in history to determine the rationale for protecting individuals' choice of religion, noting the many excesses of governments in the past to suppress religions with which they did not agree.[62] McLachlin J., in the first case on electoral boundaries under section 3, looked closer to home to determine the

---

57   *Andrews*, above note 46.

58   *R.W.D.S.U., Local 580 v. Dolphin Delivery Ltd.*, [1986] 2 S.C.R. 573 at 583, 33 D.L.R. (4th) 174 [*Dolphin Delivery*].

59   *Reference Re Public Service Employee Relations Act (Alberta)*, [1987] 1 S.C.R. 313 at 365, 38 D.L.R. (4th) 161, Dickson C.J.C.; *Jones v. R.*, [1986] 2 S.C.R. 284 at 318, 31 D.L.R. (4th) 569 [*Jones*], Wilson J.

60   *Edwards Books & Art Ltd. v. R.*, [1986] 2 S.C.R. 713 at 809, 35 D.L.R. (4th) 1, Wilson J.; *Operation Dismantle Inc. v. R.*, [1985] 1 S.C.R. 441 at 481, 18 D.L.R. (4th) 481, Wilson J.; *R. v. Therens*, [1985] 1 S.C.R. 613 at 638, 18 D.L.R. (4th) 655, LeDain J.

61   For example, in an opinion in a case dealing with language rights under s. 133 of the *Constitution Act, 1867*, she includes an extensive discussion of the views of various legal philosophers—Hohfeld, Austin, Hart, Stone, and Salmond—on the meaning of rights: *MacDonald v. Montreal (City)*, [1986] 1 S.C.R. 460 at 515–18, 27 D.L.R. (4th) 321. She also cites the writings of various philosophers when elaborating the meaning of "liberty" in s. 7: *R. v. Morgentaler*, [1988] 1 S.C.R. 30 at 178–79, 44 D.L.R. (4th) 385; *Jones*, above note 59 at 318–19 (S.C.R.); *Reference Re ss. 193 and 195.1(1)(c) of the Criminal Code (Canada)*, [1990] 1 S.C.R. 1123, 56 C.C.C. (3d) 65 at 135.

62   *Big M Drug Mart*, above note 38.

meaning of the right to vote within Canadian history. In rejecting an interpretation that guaranteed "one person, one vote," as in the United States, she drew on Canada's history (and geography) to explain why the right in Canada should aspire towards equality of voters in various electoral constituencies while at the same time emphasizing a right to effective representation. With quotes from our first prime minister, Sir John A. Macdonald, and other references to tradition, she concluded:

> [T]he history of our right to vote and the context in which it existed at the time the *Charter* was adopted support the conclusion that the purpose of the guarantee of the right to vote is not to effect perfect voter equality, in so far as that can be done, but the broader goal of guaranteeing effective representation . . . [D]emocracy in Canada is rooted in a different history than in the United States . . .[63]

McLachlin J. made it clear that she did not accept history or tradition as definitive. However, she did insist that the *Charter* should be seen as a Canadian document rooted in certain cultural and historical traditions that courts should take into consideration.[64]

The Supreme Court has also been asked to look outside Canada's borders to assist in the interpretation of rights. In some cases, the meaning of a right in other countries is discussed. Often but not always, American sources are used. The Court takes this information into consideration, but in no case has it been determinative. Increasingly, reference is made to norms of international law, such as Canada's commitments under the *International Covenant on Economic, Social and Cultural Rights*, the *International Covenant on Civil and Political Rights*, conventions of the International Labour Organization, and the *Convention on the Elimination of Racial Discrimination*.[65] The use of international norms is a reflection of the fact that the rights and freedoms guaranteed

---

63 *Reference Re Provincial Electoral Boundaries (Saskatchewan)*, above note 39 at 184 (S.C.R.).

64 *Ibid*. For example, she stated at 187 (S.C.R.):

> This is not to suggest, however, that inequities in our voting system are to be accepted merely because they have historical precedent. History is important in so far as it suggests that the philosophy underlying the development of the right to vote in this country is the broad goal of effective representation. It has nothing to do with the specious argument that historical anomalies and abuses can be used to justify continued anomalies and abuses, or to suggest that the right to vote should not be interpreted broadly and remedially as befits *Charter* rights.

65 For example, in *Keegstra*, above note 19 and *Health Services and Support—Facilities Subsector Bargaining Assn. v. British Columbia*, [2007] 2 S.C.R. 391 [*Health Services*].

by the *Charter* are specific emanations of internationally recognized human rights. While international treaties are not directly enforceable in Canadian courts, the Supreme Court does see international commitments as a valid consideration, concluding that the *Charter* should be interpreted, where possible, in a manner consistent with Canada's international obligations.[66] In a recent case concerning section 7, the Court stated: "our concern is not with Canada's international obligations *qua* obligations; rather our concern is with the principles of fundamental justice. We look to international law as evidence of these principles and not as controlling in itself."[67] Similarly, in a case involving collective bargaining rights, the Court held that "Canada's current international law commitments and the current state of international thought on human rights provide a persuasive source for interpreting the scope of the *Charter*."[68] As noted in Chapter 13, the decision in *Canada v. Khadr*[69] reflects the importance of Canada's international human rights obligations in the interpretation of section 7 rights. That decision suggests that a violation of Canada's international human rights obligations may also constitute a violation of the principles of fundamental justice in section 7 that requires application of the *Charter* to activities of Canadian officials outside of Canada. These cases reflect a shift from the traditional "dualist" tradition according to which Canada's international commitment had to be specifically incorporated into domestic law and towards a position where international obligations have more immediate impact.

C. CONCLUSION

Judges are subject to significant restraints when interpreting the *Charter*. They must pay heed to its language, to past decisions under the doctrine of precedent, and to the respective institutional roles of the courts and the legislatures, albeit redefined by the *Charter*. Yet it is apparent that judicial interpretation of the rights and freedoms guaranteed by the *Charter* has proved to be a complex and controversial task that at times involves the difficult burden of reconciling competing rights. Our legal regime does not provide judges with precise rules to guide them in this

---

66   For example, see the reasons of Dickson C.J.C. in *Slaight Communications Inc. v. Davidson*, [1989] 1 S.C.R. 1038 at 1056–57, 59 D.L.R. (4th) 416.
67   *Suresh v. Minister of Citizenship and Immigration and Attorney General of Canada*, 2002 SCC 1, 208 D.L.R. (4th) 1 at 32.
68   *Health Services*, above note 66, at para. 78.
69   2008 SCC 28.

exercise. Indeed, our constitutional tradition directs the courts to resist the argument that the language of the constitution has a rigid and fixed meaning. The constitution is seen as an organic document that must grow with the times and remain capable of responding to the demands of a changing society. The debate about the *Charter's* meaning is legal in structure, but the purposive and contextual approaches adopted by the Supreme Court to *Charter* interpretation require the judges to consider a rich array of historical, philosophical, and comparative sources.

FURTHER READINGS

ARBOUR, L., & F. LAFONTAINE, "Beyond Self-congratulation: The *Charter* at 25 in an International Perspective" (2007) 45 Osgoode Hall L.J. 239.

BAKAN, J., *Just Words: Constitutional Rights and Social Wrongs* (Toronto: University of Toronto Press, 1997)

BASTARACHE, M., "The *Canadian Charter of Rights and Freedoms*: Domestic Application of Universal Values" (2003) 19 Sup. Ct. L. Rev. (2d) 371

BAYEFSKY, A., *International Human Rights Law: Use in Canadian Charter of Rights and Freedoms Litigation* (Toronto: Butterworths, 1992)

BEATTY, D.M., *Talking Heads and the Supremes: The Canadian Production of Constitutional Review* (Toronto: Carswell, 1990)

GOLDSWORTHY, J., *Interpreting Constitutions: A Comparative Study* (Oxford: Oxford University Press, 2007)

HOGG, P.W., "The *Charter of Rights* and American Theories of Interpretation" (1987) 15 Osgoode Hall L.J. 87

HOGG, P.W., "Interpreting the *Charter of Rights*: Generosity and Justification" (1990) 28 Osgoode Hall L.J. 817

HUSCROFT, G., "A Constitutional 'Work in Progress': The *Charter* and the Limits of Progressive Interpretation" (2004) 25 Sup. Ct. L. Rev. 241

LEBEL, L., "The Rise of International Law in Canadian Constitutional Litigation: Fugue or Fusion?" (2002) 16 Sup. Ct. L. Rev. (2d) 23

ROACH, K., "Dialogic Judicial Review and Its Critics" (2004) 23 Sup. Ct. L. Rev. (2d) 49

SCHABAS, W., & S. BEAULAC, *International Human Rights and Canadian Law: Legal Commitment, Implementation and the Charter*, 3d ed. (Toronto: Thomson, 2007)

TRAKMAN, L.E., *Reasoning with the Charter* (Toronto: Butterworths, 1991)

WEINRIB, L., "Canada's *Charter of Rights*: Paradigm Lost?" (2002) 6 Rev. of Constitutional Studies 119

WEINRIB, L., "A Primer on International Law and the *Charter*" (2007) 21 National Journal of Constitutional Law 313

CHAPTER 4

LIMITATION OF *CHARTER* RIGHTS

A central task in the interpretation of any instrument guaranteeing fundamental rights and freedoms is to reconcile the rights of the individual with the interests of the community at large. The effect of the *Charter* is to shift an important share of responsibility for this task from the elected representatives of the people to the judiciary. In light of the Supreme Court's generous definition of most enumerated rights through the purposive method of interpretation described in chapter 3, it is not surprising to find that the Court places heavy reliance on the second stage of *Charter* adjudication, defining the limitation of rights. This is mandated by section 1, which provides that the rights and freedoms guaranteed are "subject only to such reasonable limits prescribed by law as can be demonstrably justified in a free and democratic society." The Supreme Court has interpreted that provision as encompassing both a formal and a substantive element—the formal element is caught by the words "prescribed by law" and the substantive element is contained in an examination of the state's justification for limiting the right and its chosen means for doing so.

A. LIMITS PRESCRIBED BY LAW

The first requirement for a justifiable limit is that it be, in the words of section 1, "prescribed by law." Initially, the courts refused to uphold laws that conferred an open-ended or vaguely defined discretion to limit protected freedoms. Thus, for example, the courts struck down as too ill-defined a customs regulation that allowed officials to restrict entry into Canada of materials that they considered to be "immoral."[1] Similarly, a provincial scheme conferring the power of censorship on a film board without setting out the criteria by which such powers were to be exercised was struck down as a violation of freedom of expression that was not prescribed by law.[2]

In the words of LeDain J., "the requirement that the limit be prescribed by law is chiefly concerned with the distinction between a limit imposed by law and one that is arbitrary."[3] In that case, a *Charter* violation could not be justified under section 1 because the legislation authorizing the police to require a driver to provide a breath sample did not clearly authorize a denial or limitation of the detainee's right to counsel. Following this approach, section 1 does not play a role in many *Charter* challenges to the exercise of police powers, where the police officer's actions in limiting the *Charter* right are not specifically authorized or prescribed by law. This was reaffirmed in *Little Sisters*, where the Supreme Court stated: "Violative conduct by government officials that is not authorized by statute is not 'prescribed by law' and cannot therefore be justified under section 1." In such cases, courts must "therefore proceed directly to the remedy phase of the analysis."[4] On the other hand, the Supreme Court held that a public transit authority's policy, adopted pursuant to a statutory power, on what advertising it would accept for display on the sides of buses, is a form of "law" that satisfies the "prescribed by law" requirement.[5]

There are important justifications for a rigorous approach to the "prescribed by law" requirement under section 1 of the *Charter*. Government actions that infringe *Charter* rights should be accompanied by notice to citizens of the conduct that is permitted and prohibited so that they can regulate their activities accordingly. Similarly, the law should set adequate limits on officials who exercise discretion in applying and enforcing the law, and limits on *Charter* rights should be clearly stated to encourage democratic debate and accountability about such limitations.

---

1   *Luscher v. Deputy Minister of National Revenue (Customs & Excise)*, [1985] 1 F.C. 85, 17 D.L.R. (4th) 503.

2   *Re Ontario Film & Video Appreciation Society and Ontario Board of Censors* (1984), 5 D.L.R. (4th) 766 (Ont. C.A.).

3   *R. v. Therens*, [1985] 1 S.C.R. 613, 18 D.L.R. (4th) 655 at 680.

4   *Little Sisters Book and Art Emporium v. Canada (Minister of Justice)*, [2000] 2 S.C.R. 1120, 193 D.L.R. (4th) 193 at para. 141 [*Little Sisters*].

5   *Greater Vancouver Transportation Authority v. Canadian Federation of Students — British Columbia Component*, 2009 SCC 31.

Despite these concerns about vagueness, courts have tended to apply a relatively relaxed standard under the "prescribed by law" requirement. A common law rule or a regulation, in addition to legislation, can constitute a limit "prescribed by law."[6] A limitation on freedom of expression was held to be "prescribed by law" even though the labour relations adjudicator made the restriction in the exercise of a general remedial discretion that did not specifically contemplate remedial orders that would restrict *Charter* rights.[7]

Limitations can be implicitly prescribed by law. For example, a *Criminal Code* provision providing for a roadside breathalyser test implicitly authorizes a limitation on the right to counsel by requiring that the sample be provided "forthwith" without access to counsel.[8] The Supreme Court has also accepted that an open-ended legislative provision allowing police to stop drivers is a "prescribed by law" limit on the right against arbitrary detention in section 9 of the *Charter*.[9] Finally, a majority of the Court in *Little Sisters* upheld customs legislation despite evidence that custom officials had frequently erred in applying the standard of detaining obscene material. The Court stated: "While there is evidence of actual abuse here, there is the potential for abuse in many areas, and a rule requiring Parliament to enact in each case special procedures for the protection of *Charter* rights would be unnecessarily rigid."[10]

The issue of whether a limit on a *Charter* right is "prescribed by law" is also connected with the issue of vagueness. Excessively vague laws that do not define powers in a precise manner do not provide effective limitations on the exercise of those powers. Here again, the trend is towards a more relaxed approach that leaves the legislature room to limit *Charter* rights by the use of vague terms. The Supreme Court has stated that merely because a law is subject to various shadings of interpretation does not render it unacceptably vague.[11] In some

---

6   *Irwin Toy Ltd. v. Quebec*, [1989] 1 S.C.R. 927 (regulation); *R. v. Swain*, [1991] 1 S.C.R. 933 (common law rule). At the same time, administrative guidelines cannot constitute a limit that is prescribed by law or a source of law that can be directly challenged under the *Charter* because "it is simply not feasible for the courts to review for *Charter* compliance the vast array of manuals and guides prepared by the public service for the internal guidance of officials." *Little Sisters, ibid.* at para. 85.

7   *Slaight Communications Inc. v. Davidson*, [1989] 1 S.C.R. 1038, 59 D.L.R. (4th) 416.

8   *R. v. Thomsen*, [1988] 1 S.C.R. 640. See also *R. v. Orbanski* 2005 SCC 37 at para. 52.

9   *R. v. Hufsky*, [1999] 1 S.C.R. 621; *R. v. Ladouceur*, [1990] 1 S.C.R. 1257. Note, however, that a stop that is not conducted for valid reasons related to traffic safety will not constitute a reasonable limit on the right against arbitrary detention and the *Charter* analysis will proceed directly from the rights violation to the remedy phase: *R. v. Mellenthin*, [1992] 3 S.C.R. 615.

10   *Little Sisters*, above note 4 at para. 137.

11   *R. v. Lucas*, [1998] 1 S.C.R. 439, 157 D.L.R. (4th) 423 [*Lucas*].

instances, laws that appear more than unusually vague and uncertain have been upheld.[12] The cases that have considered the vagueness point in most detail have arisen under the fundamental-justice guarantee in section 7 and are discussed in chapter 13. As will be seen there, the Supreme Court has said that, since laws define standards of general application, there is an inherent element of uncertainty in all laws. While there must be some limit to open-ended and ill-defined standards, the vagueness argument is not one that has found favour with the Supreme Court in recent years.

B. PROPORTIONALITY

The text of the *Charter* says little about how limitations on rights are to be justified, but the Supreme Court of Canada, employing the purposive approach, established the basic framework for analysis in *R. v. Oakes*.[13] It is at the justification stage that a court must consider the interest in limiting a right or freedom and weigh collective interests or the competing rights of other individuals against the right of the claimant. The reconciliation of the competing interests against individual rights is achieved by focusing on the legitimacy of the government's objective and the "proportionality" between the means chosen to achieve that objective and the burden on the rights claimant.

In addition to the "prescribed by law" requirement discussed above, there are four steps to the section 1 analysis:

1) the objective of the measure must be important enough to warrant overriding a *Charter* right;
2) there must be a rational connection between the limit on the *Charter* right and the legislative objective;
3) the limit should impair the *Charter* right as little as possible; and
4) there should be an overall balance or proportionality between the benefits of the limit and its deleterious effects.

---

12 *Suresh v. Canada*, [2002] 1 S.C.R. 3, 208 D.L.R. (4th) 1 [*Suresh*] (undefined reference to "terrorism" and "national security" in immigration legislation not unconstitutionally vague); *Little Sisters*, above note 4 at para. 145 (undefined reference to the prohibition of "obscene" material not unconstitutionally vague and satisfying "prescribed by law" requirement for a limitation on freedom of expression).

13 [1986] 1 S.C.R. 103, 26 D.L.R. (4th) 200 [*Oakes*]. For a good discussion of the evolution of s. 1, see P.W. Hogg, "Section 1 Revisited" (1991) 1 N.J.C.L. 1; E. Mendes, "The Crucible of the *Charter*: Judicial Principles v. Judicial Deference in the Context of Section 1" in G.A. Beaudoin & E. Mendes, eds., *The Canadian Charter of Rights and Freedoms*, 4th ed. (Markham, ON: LexisNexis Butterworths, 2005).

1) Sufficiently Important Objective

First, it must be established that there is an objective "of sufficient importance to warrant overriding a constitutionally protected right or freedom."[14] In *Oakes*, the Supreme Court of Canada said that the objective must "relate to concerns which are pressing and substantial in a free and democratic society." The courts have been relatively deferential to legislative judgment of the importance of the objective. However, the government has failed on a number of occasions to satisfy this requirement. In one case, the Supreme Court held that Quebec legislation limiting the rights of English-speaking parents to have their children attend English-language schools unless the parents had been educated in English in Quebec constituted a direct attack on the very right enshrined in section 23 of the *Charter*, and hence the law was not motivated by a proper objective.[15] In another early *Charter* case, the Supreme Court indicated that compelling the observance of the Christian Sabbath was not a satisfactory objective for limiting the rights of non-Christians by requiring stores to close on Sundays. This objective was not satisfactory because "it would justify the law upon the very basis upon which it is attacked for violating s. 2(a)," namely the protection of freedom of all religions and not just the religion of Christians.[16] Similarly, in an Ontario case, the Court of Appeal held that legislation requiring the recital of the Lord's Prayer in non-denominational public schools constituted an attempt to impose a form of religious observance and that such an objective was not permitted by the guarantee of freedom of religion.[17] In all these cases, the stated objective denied rather than limited or qualified the right. As McLachlin C.J.C. put it in a right-

---

14   *R. v. Big M Drug Mart Ltd.*, [1985] 1 S.C.R. 295 at 352, 18 D.L.R. (4th) 321 [*Big M Drug Mart*], Dickson C.J.C.

15   *Quebec (A.G.) v. Quebec Association of Protestant School Boards*, [1984] 2 S.C.R. 66, 10 D.L.R. (4th) 321. The language of s. 23, discussed further in chapter 16, grants the right to the children of parents educated anywhere in Canada in English.

16   *Big M Drug Mart*, above note 14. The Court indicated that a secular justification for a common day of rest was acceptable, but not available in this case because the impugned *Lord's Day Act* had been enacted by Parliament as a criminal law for religious reasons and legislation in relation to a common day of rest for workers could only be enacted by the provinces. The Court subsequently accepted the secular justification for provincial Sunday closing laws and found them to be a justified restriction on freedom of religion. See *Edwards Books & Art Ltd. v. R.*, [1986] 2 S.C.R. 713, 35 D.L.R. (4th) 1 [*Edwards Books*]. See chapter 8, section A for further discussion.

17   *Zylberberg v. Sudbury Board of Education (Director)* (1988), 52 D.L.R. (4th) 577 (Ont. C.A.).

to-vote case, "a simple majoritarian political preference for abolishing a right altogether would not be a constitutionally valid objective."[18] In another case, the Supreme Court dealt with a challenge to a vague law prohibiting the spreading of "false news."[19] Given the ancient origin of the law, it was unclear what its objective was at the time it was enacted. While the law was now used to deal with hate propaganda, it had not been designed for that purpose, and the majority of the Court held that it was not acceptable for the government to advance a new objective or shifting purpose not in the mind of Parliament when the law was enacted.

In *Vriend v. Alberta*,[20] the Supreme Court found that Alberta had failed to articulate any objective or purpose that would be achieved by denying the protection of its human rights law to gays and lesbians. As Iacobucci J. stated, to sustain a limit on a protected freedom, a government must offer more than an explanation why it chose to deny the right—it must be pursuing some objective: "An 'objective', being a goal or an 'explanation' which makes plain that which is not immediately obvious."[21] The Court also hinted that the "legislative omission is on its face the very antithesis of the principles involved in the legislation as a whole" which, like the *Charter*, was concerned with preventing discrimination and protecting the equal dignity of all persons.

On the other hand, the state has not been held to a strict standard of proof of the harm at which challenged legislation is aimed.[22] Indeed, in most cases, the Court has accepted the objective once asserted without the need for evidence.[23] Cases in which the government fails to satisfy this first branch of the section 1 test are the exception rather than the rule. One study has concluded that in 97 percent of cases, the state is readily able to satisfy the court that the law being challenged is motivated by a permissible objective of sufficient weight.[24]

Although courts will accept most articulated and non-discriminatory legislative objectives as sufficiently important to limit *Charter*

---

18   *Sauvé v. Canada (Chief Electoral Officer)*, [2002] 3 S.C.R. 519 at para. 20 (denying federal inmates the right to vote) [*Sauvé*].

19   *R. v. Zundel*, [1992] 2 S.C.R. 731, 95 D.L.R. (4th) 202.

20   [1998] 1 S.C.R. 493, 156 D.L.R. (4th) 385.

21   *Ibid.* at para. 114. See also *Canada (Attorney General) v. Hislop*, [2007] 1 S.C.R. 429 (no pressing and substantial objective to justify denial of spousal benefits to gay couple.)

22   *Harper v. Canada (Attorney General)*, [2004] 1 S.C.R. 827 at para. 90 [*Harper*]. See also discussion below in section B(2).

23   *R. v. Bryan*, [2007] 1 S.C.R. 527 at paras. 32–34.

24   L. Trakman *et al.*, "*R. v. Oakes* 1986–1987: Back to the Drawing Board" (1998) 36 Osgoode Hall L.J. 83 at 95.

rights, this first step in proportionality analysis can have a crucial effect on subsequent stages of the analysis. If the court defines the legislative objective broadly, it may be more difficult for the government to demonstrate that there has been minimal impairment of the right and that there is no less restrictive means to advance the legislative objective. On the other hand, if the objective is defined more narrowly, it may be easier to justify the limitation as a proportionate means of advancing the particular objective. Indeed, if the objective is defined too narrowly, there is a danger that the rest of the proportionality analysis may become "no more than a pair of tautologies"[25] that are self-fulfilling. The Supreme Court has indicated that under section 1 of the *Charter* "it is desirable to state the purpose of the limiting provision as precisely and specifically as possible so as to provide a clear framework for evaluating its importance, and the precision with which the means have been crafted to fulfil that objective."[26] "Vague and symbolic objectives" render proportionality analysis hollow and "almost guarantee a positive answer."[27] One exception to this general preference for a fairly narrow definition of the objective is in the case of underinclusive legislation, in which case the courts will examine not only the purposes of the unconstitutional omission, but also of the legislation as a whole.[28]

2) Rational Connection between Limit and Objective

The next phase in proportionality review is to consider whether there is a rational, non-arbitrary, non-capricious connection between the legislative objective and the law that is challenged.

At this second stage, the courts again have been deferential, and it is rare to find that there is no rational connection between the legislative objective and the law that is subject to scrutiny. As Iacobucci J. remarked in a freedom of expression case, "[t]his test is not particularly onerous."[29] In the *Oakes* case itself, however, the Supreme Court held that there was no rational connection between the objective of curbing traffic in drugs and a law that reversed the usual onus of proof in criminal cases and required anyone found in possession of any amount of drugs to prove that he or she did not have the intent to traffic. In the

---

25 P.W. Hogg, *Constitutional Law of Canada*, 4th ed. (Toronto: Carswell, 1997) at 35.9(a).

26 *Thomson Newspapers Co. v. Canada (Attorney General)*, [1998] 1 S.C.R. 877 at para. 98 [*Thomson Newspapers*].

27 *Sauvé*, above note 18 at para. 22.

28 *M. v. H.*, [1999] 2 S.C.R. 3, 171 D.L.R. (4th) 577.

29 *Little Sisters*, above note 4 at para. 228.

Court's view, there was a lack of internal rationality in the legislation, because the reverse-onus provision assumed that an individual in possession of even a very small amount of a drug would be likely to traffic. In the words of Dickson C.J.C.:

> [P]ossession of a small or negligible quantity of narcotics does not support the inference of trafficking. In other words, it would be irrational to infer that a person had an intent to traffic on the basis of his or her possession of a very small quantity of narcotics. The presumption required under s. 8 of the *Narcotic Control Act* is overinclusive and could lead to results in certain cases which would defy both rationality and fairness.[30]

Most commentators suggest that the Court might more readily have justified striking down the law under the minimal impairment test, discussed below. Some have argued that there is a rational connection between the objective of suppressing drug trafficking and making convictions easier for the state by a reverse-onus clause.[31] However, the Court in *Oakes* not only looked at the rationality of the means to meet the objective from the state's point of view, but also considered the arbitrariness of the law with respect to the rights claimant, a consideration now more likely to be addressed under the minimal impairment and overall balance components.[32]

The rational connection test can be used to prevent the justification of laws based on arbitrary or discriminatory assumptions and a choice of discriminatory means to implement a standard will be vulnerable under the rational connection requirement. For example, the Supreme Court has indicated that requiring a security check for those born of Canadian mothers, but not of Canadian fathers, was not rationally connected to the legitimate objective of screening citizenship applicants.[33] Similarly, the exclusion of same-sex couples from support provisions was held not to be rationally connected to the objective of assisting women to deal with the financial hardships of the breakdown of marriages and common law partnerships.[34]

---

30   *Oakes*, above note 13 at 142 (S.C.R.).
31   See, for example, P.J. Monahan & A.J. Petter, "Developments in Constitutional Law (The 1986–87 Term)" (1988) 10 Sup. Ct. L. Rev. 61.
32   The way in which Dickson C.J.C. phrased this stage of inquiry in *Oakes* is as follows: "[The measures] must not be arbitrary, unfair or based on irrational considerations. In short, they must be rationally connected to the objective." *Oakes*, above note 13 at 227 (D.L.R.).
33   *Benner v. Canada*, [1997] 1 S.C.R. 358 at para. 95, 143 D.L.R. (4th) 577.
34   *M. v. H.*, above note 28 at para. 108.

The rational connection test can be decisive,[35] but this remains the exception rather than the rule. In the case of violations of the presumption of innocence subsequent to *Oakes*, the Supreme Court has held, contrary to *Oakes*, that there need not be internal rationality between the proven and the presumed facts.[36] In other words, all that has to be established is that there is a rational connection between the limitation and the legislative objective of facilitating the detection and conviction of crime.

In *Chaoulli v. Quebec (Attorney General)*,[37] McLachlin C.J.C. and Major J. (Bastarache J. concurring) took a much more demanding approach to the rational connection requirement. They concluded that Quebec had failed to demonstrate that its prohibition on private health insurance was rationally connected to the objective of preserving the integrity of the health system because of "the absence of evidence that the prohibition on the purchase and sale of private health insurance protects the health care system." They also questioned "whether an arbitrary provision, which by reason of its arbitrariness cannot further its stated objective, will ever meet the rational connection test under *R. v. Oakes*."[38] This latter statement may suggest that three judges are willing to reconsider the post-*Oakes* jurisprudence that suggests that lack of internal rationality within a law that produces a violation of a *Charter* right is not necessarily fatal to a section 1 justification. Binnie and LeBel JJ. (Fish J. concurring) in dissent concluded that there was a rational connection between the prohibition of private medical insurance and the protection of the public health system on the basis of royal commission reports and other policy statements.[39] As discussed in chapter 13, they also rejected the argument that Quebec's prohibition on private insurance violated section 7 of the *Charter* because it was arbitrary.

Rational connection between the limit on the *Charter* right and the legislative objective does not require scientific proof.[40] The Supreme Court has recognized that "[w]hile some matters can be proved with empirical or mathematical precision, others, involving philosophical, political and social considerations, cannot."[41] For example, the Court has held that there was a rational connection between prohibiting ob-

---

35   See *Figueroa v. Canada (Attorney General)*, [2003] 1 S.C.R. 912 [*Figueroa*].
36   *R. v. Laba*, [1994] 3 S.C.R. 965, 94 C.C.C. (3d) 385 at 417.
37   2005 SCC 35 [*Chaoulli*].
38   *Ibid.* at para. 155.
39   *Ibid.* at para. 276.
40   *Harper*, above note 22 at para. 104.
41   *Sauvé*, above note 18 at para. 18.

scene materials and the objective of protecting women and children from violence, even though the social science data about causal connections between pornography and violence was far from conclusive.[42] Similarly, the Court has found a rational connection between limiting freedom of expression by restricting tobacco advertising and the legislative objective of curbing the use of tobacco, even though, again, the evidence was inconclusive.[43] At the same time, the majority in *Chaoulli* concluded that evidence of the health care experience in other provinces and in other countries did not demonstrate that Quebec's prohibition on private medical insurance was rationally connected to the objective of protecting the public health care system. McLachlin C.J.C. and Major J. (Bastarache J. concurring) stressed that the courts should evaluate the relevant issues "in the light, not just of common sense or theory, but of the evidence."[44] Deschamps J. similarly reviewed the evidence in support of the prohibition and found it wanting in light of the combination of public and private health care in many other countries. Given that this case was decided by a 4 to 3 majority, it remains to be seen whether the Court in the future will demand evidential proof of rational connection between an impugned measure and the government's objective under section 1. Courts should be cautious about demanding an unrealistically high level of proof or requiring that the government demonstrate success or effectiveness in pursuing its objective at this stage of section 1 analysis. The effectiveness of the government's measure can be evaluated at a later stage in section 1 analysis when the court assesses the overall balance of the harms and benefits of the impugned measure.

3) Minimal Impairment

The core element of proportionality review is the minimal impairment test. While *Oakes* described this as the principle of "least intrusive means," later cases, discussed below, seemed to relax the test, asking whether there was some other reasonable way for the legislature to satisfy the objective that would not impair the right or freedom at issue, or that would have less impact on the right or freedom than does the law under review.[45] In one of the most notable cases to be decided by the Su-

---

42 *R. v. Butler*, [1992] 1 S.C.R. 452, 89 D.L.R. (4th) 449 [*Butler*].

43 *RJR–MacDonald v. Canada*, [1995] 3 S.C.R. 199, 127 D.L.R. (4th) 1 [*RJR*].

44 *Chaoulli*, above note 37 at para. 150.

45 Specifically, in *Edwards Books*, above note 16, Dickson C.J.C. reformulated the test to ask whether the right was impaired "as little as reasonably possible," which suggested that the limitation need not be the least intrusive, but the least intrusive

preme Court in this area, it was held that a Quebec law prohibiting the display of commercial signs in English could not survive scrutiny under the minimal impairment test.[46] The Court was prepared to find that the preservation and enhancement of the French language was a sufficiently important objective in the province of Quebec to justify limiting the guarantee of freedom of expression, and that a law that required such signs to be in French and forbade signs in English was rationally connected to this objective. However, the Court found that the law went too far in prohibiting English altogether. The province could, in the Court's view, have satisfied the legitimate objective of preserving and enhancing French by requiring that commercial signs display a marked predominance of French. Such a law would achieve the goal of enhancing the aim of a *visage linguistique* appropriate to a predominantly French society but at the same time would respect, to the extent possible consistent with the attainment of that goal, the right of non-francophones to use their language. The Court was not persuaded that a total ban on English was necessary, and the law therefore failed, since it was not the least intrusive means of satisfying the legislative objective.

A violation that is characterized as a total denial of the right in question will often be struck down on the basis that it does not minimally impair the right in question. Thus the complete denial of the right of Indian Band members, not residing on their Band's reserve, to vote in their Band's elections[47] has been held not to be justified, as has a complete ban on all forms of secondary picketing including peaceful leafleting,[48] and the failure to provide for any association of farm workers.[49]

The minimal impairment test remains the core of the section 1 proportionality analysis, but there has been a trend away from a rigorous or mechanical approach to the question of minimal impairment towards a more contextual approach. The reasons for this will be examined below in section C. Evidence of the use of less restrictive means in other Canadian jurisdictions and in other countries may be relevant, but will rarely be determinative given the value placed on federalism[50]

given the legislature's objective and other competing interests—that is, the test more openly balanced the interests of the state and the rights claimant.

46   *Ford v. Quebec (A.G.)*, [1988] 2 S.C.R. 712, 54 D.L.R. (4th) 577. The case was decided under the Quebec *Charter of Human Rights and Freedoms*, but the Supreme Court made it clear that the same principles applied as under the Canadian *Charter*.

47   *Corbiere v. Canada*, [1999] 2 S.C.R. 202, 172 D.L.R. (4th) 1.

48   *UFCW v. KMart*, [1999] 2 S.C.R. 1083, 176 D.L.R. (4th) 607.

49   *Dunmore v. Ontario*, [2001] 3 S.C.R. 1016, 207 D.L.R. (4th) 193.

50   *R. v. Advance Cutting and Coring Ltd.*, [2001] 3 S.C.R. 209, 205 D.L.R. (4th) 385 [*Advance Cutting*].

and the particular context of Canada.[51] If there is evidence of a less restrictive alternative, however, the government would be well advised to demonstrate why that alternative would not be as effective in advancing the government's objective as the impugned legislation.

4) Overall Balance

The final step in proportionality review, in the words of *Oakes*, requires that there "be a proportionality between the *effects* of the measure which are responsible for limiting the *Charter* right or freedom, and the objective which has been identified as of 'sufficient importance.'"[52] This final step applies when all the other aspects of proportionality have been satisfied. It engages the court in a balancing exercise, weighing the significance of the infringement of the right against the importance of attaining the objective of the legislation. In a later case, Lamer C.J.C. refined this test by saying that this step requires "both that the underlying *objective* of a measure and the *salutary effects* that actually result from its implementation be proportional to the deleterious effects the measure has on fundamental rights and freedoms."[53] What matters in the overall balance is not simply the objective of the legislation but its effectiveness in achieving that objective.

Until recently, this final balancing step has not been decisive and was thought by many to be redundant. It appeared unlikely that the Supreme Court would ever find that the objective was of sufficient importance to justify overriding a protected freedom, and that the least intrusive means had been employed, but nevertheless conclude that on balance the effects on the right were disproportionate. In cases like *Keegstra* (upholding the federal hate-propaganda offence in the *Criminal Code*) and *McKinney* (upholding mandatory retirement), the Court fairly quickly concluded that the respective legislation passed the balancing test, having found that each was justified under the minimal impairment stage.[54] More recently, however, this final stage has taken on more importance. In *Thomson Newspapers v. Canada*, the Court struck down a ban on the publication of opinion polls within seventy-two hours of an election as an unjustified violation of freedom of expression. Although the Court accepted the objective of preventing inaccurate polls

51   *Thomson Newspapers*, above note 26 at para. 121.
52   *Oakes*, above note 13 at 139 (S.C.R.).
53   *Dagenais v. Canadian Broadcasting Corp.*, [1994] 3 S.C.R. 835 at 887, 120 D.L.R. (4th) 12.
54   *R. v. Keegstra*, [1990] 3 S.C.R. 697, 61 C.C.C. (3d) 1 [*Keegstra*]; *McKinney v. University of Guelph*, [1990] 3 S.C.R. 229, 76 D.L.R. (4th) 545 [*McKinney*].

from influencing the last days of an election campaign as pressing and substantial under the first part of the test, it held under the fourth part of the test that the benefits of pursuing this objective were "marginal" because "the postulated harm will seldom occur." On the other hand, the deleterious effects of the ban were "substantial" because the ban interfered with press reporting of an election and deprived voters of information about the election.[55] Similarly, the Court was prepared to take a closer look at the effectiveness of a *Charter* violation in achieving the government's objective, when it refused to find that a denial of legal aid in violation of section 7 of the *Charter* was justified under section 1, on the basis that the budgetary savings achieved by the violation were minimal, especially when compared to the harmful effects of an unfair hearing.[56]

If the fourth part of the proportionality review continues to assume increasing importance, governments will bear a greater obligation to demonstrate that impugned legislation is not only rationally connected to its objectives, but also effective in achieving the objectives. This stage will further require the courts to balance the effectiveness of the violation in achieving the government's objective against the harms of denying the *Charter* right. In cases in which the harms of the *Charter* violations are great and the benefits are slight, the courts may strike down a law under this last stage of the section 1 test, even though there is not an obviously less restrictive means to pursue the government's objective.

C. THE *OAKES* TEST: STRICT RULES OR GUIDING PRINCIPLES?

The key issue is really how strictly the *Oakes* test is applied. The decided cases indicate that the stringency of review and particularly the application of the minimal impairment tests are both controversial and variable. Indeed, some judges quarrel with the term the *Oakes* "test." For example, La Forest J. rejected the term, stating that *Oakes* did no more than establish some principles or guidelines to help in making a decision and insisted that these principles should be applied "flexibly, having regard to the specific factual and social context of each case."[57]

---

55 *Thomson Newspapers*, above note 26 at para. 129.

56 *New Brunswick (Minister of Health and Community Services) v. G.(J.)*, [1999] 3 S.C.R. 46, 177 D.L.R. (4th) 124 at para. 100 [*New Brunswick v. G.(J.)*].

57 *RJR*, above note 43 at 46 (D.L.R.) (dissenting judgment).

However, the majority view is that the *Oakes* approach remains help-ful, provided it is applied flexibly, with sensitivity to the context of the particular law at issue.[58]

The central element in the application of section 1 is the principle of least intrusive means. It is this aspect of the *Oakes* test that is the focus of most litigation under the *Charter*. The least-intrusive-means prin-ciple is significant in assessing the impact the *Charter* has upon the role of the judiciary. Proportionality review, especially the minimal impair-ment test, requires judges to weigh and assess the choices made by the legislature and the other policy options that were available. This is not an exercise considered to fall within the realm of judicial competence in non-constitutional cases, yet it is very often the central question in *Charter* litigation. It is now clear that the Supreme Court will not apply the minimal impairment test mechanically or literally to strike down a law simply because it is possible to conceive of another measure that might be less intrusive on a protected freedom. As Gonthier J. put it, "it is not sufficient that a judge, freed from all such constraints, could im-agine a less restrictive alternative."[59] Even Wilson J., a staunch defender of the minimal impairment test, held that it is only where there are measures "clearly superior to the measures currently in use" that a law will fail on this ground.[60] A unanimous judgment of the Court adopted the following formulation of the test by McLachlin J.:

> The impairment must be "minimal," that is, the law must be carefully tailored so that the rights are impaired no more than necessary. The tailoring process seldom admits of perfection and the courts must accord some leeway to the legislator. If the law falls within a range of reasonable alternatives, the courts will not find it overbroad merely because they can conceive of an alternative which might better tailor objective to infringment . . . .[61]

---

58   *Ibid.* at 88–90 (D.L.R.), McLachlin J; *Libman v. Quebec (A.G.)*, [1997] 3 S.C.R. 569, 151 D.L.R. (4th) 385 at 407 [*Libman*].

59   *Nova Scotia (Workers' Compensation Board) v. Martin; Nova Scotia (Workers' Compensation Board) v. Laseur*, [2003] 2 S.C.R. 504 at para. 112.

60   *Lavigne v. Ontario Public Service Employees Union*, [1991] 2 S.C.R. 211 at 296, 81 D.L.R. (4th) 545.

61   *Libman*, above note 58 at 415 (D.L.R.), adopting McLachlin J.'s statement from *RJR*, above note 43. See also *Montreal (City) v. 2952-1366 Québec Inc.*, [2005] 3 S.C.R. 141 at para. 94: "The Court will not interfere simply because it can think of a better, less intrusive way to manage the problem. What is required is that the [government concerned] establish that it has tailored the limit to the exi-gencies of the problem in a reasonable way."

Although the Supreme Court has rejected the idea that "there is one category of cases in which a low standard of justification under section 1 is applied, and another category in which a higher standard is applied,"[62] it would seem that the standard of review is influenced by several factors.[63]

1) Broad Issues of Social and Economic Policy

The Supreme Court has demonstrated a marked tendency to defer to legislative judgment and apply a relatively deferential standard of review in cases involving broad issues of social and economic policy, especially where the problem is complex and the implications of various solutions are not fully understood. Courts are experts in the matter of liberty, but not in the realm of social policy, and the Supreme Court has stated that "the role of the legislature demands deference from the courts to those types of policy decisions that the legislature is best placed to make."[64] The Court has recognized that the making of social policy "is a role properly assigned to the elected representatives of the people, who have at their disposal the necessary institutional resources to enable them to compile and assess social science evidence, to mediate between competing social interests and to reach out to protect vulnerable groups."[65] The Court has also indicated that deference to the legislature will usually be warranted on matters such as labour relations policy that involve complex issues of social and economic policy[66] and in relation to "environmental issues, where views and interests often conflict and precision is elusive."[67]

One of the most striking examples of a relaxed standard of section 1 review is the case dealing with mandatory retirement.[68] The Supreme Court found that mandatory retirement at age sixty-five violated

---

62 *Thomson Newspapers*, above note 26 at para. 88.

63 The American Supreme Court has developed different standards of review depending on the particular right at issue or, in the case of the equal-protection clause, the basis for differential treatment. For example, differential treatment on the basis of race triggers "strict scrutiny," while differential treatment on the basis of a characteristic such as veteran's status leads to a much more deferential "rationality" review.

64 *M. v. H.*, above note 28 at para. 78; *Newfoundland (Treasury Board) v. N.A.P.E.*, [2004] 3 S.C.R. 381 at paras. 83–84 [*Newfoundland*].

65 *Libman*, above note 58 at 416 (D.L.R.), adopting a passage from the dissenting judgment of La Forest J. in *RJR*, above note 43.

66 *Advance Cutting*, above note 50 at paras. 256, 257, 267.

67 *Montreal (City) v. 2952-1366*, above note 61 at para. 94.

68 *McKinney*, above note 54.

the right conferred by section 15 not to be discriminated against on grounds of age, but it held that the legislation permitting this form of discrimination should be upheld under section 1. In the view of the majority of the Court, the issue was "whether the government had a reasonable basis, on the evidence tendered, for concluding that the legislation interferes as little as possible with a guaranteed right, given the government's pressing and substantial objectives."[69] This is plainly a much more relaxed standard of review than that applied in cases dealing with those rights or freedoms that do not pose complex social-policy questions.

Chaoulli marks a dramatic break from the Supreme Court's previous deferential approach to broad issues of social and economic policy. The case involved a challenge to Quebec's prohibition of private medical insurance for procedures covered by the public health care system. All seven judges[70] who heard the case agreed that the government's objective was to preserve the integrity of the public health system and that this objective was pressing and substantial.[71] A majority of four judges took a strict approach to proportionality and stressed the government's obligation under section 1 to justify any limitation on the basis of evidence. "The fact that the matter is complex, contentious or laden with social values does not mean that the courts can abdicate the responsibility vested in them by our Constitution to review legislation for Charter compliance when citizens challenge it."[72] The majority found that the prohibition on private health care was disproportionate in all respects. McLachlin C.J.C. and Major J. (Bastarache J. concurring) concluded that there was no rational connection between the prohibition and the protection of the public health care system. In addition, the "denial of access to timely and effective medical care to those who need it is not proportionate to the beneficial effects of the prohibition on private insurance to the health system as a whole."[73] Finally they also concluded that "the physical and psychological suffering and risk

---

69   Ibid. at 666 (D.L.R.), La Forest J.

70   Deschamps J. dealt with the question under s. 9.1 of the Quebec Charter of Rights and Freedoms which she concluded should be interpreted in accordance with the Oakes test. Chaoulli, above note 37 at para. 48.

71   Ibid. at para. 55, Deschamps J.; at para. 155, McLachlin C.J.C and Major J.; at para. 239, Binnie and LeBel JJ.

72   Ibid. at para. 107, McLachlin C.J.C. and Major J. (Bastarache J. concurring). Deschamps J. similarly concluded that although legislatures create social policies, "when such social policies infringe rights that are protected by charters, the courts cannot shy away from considering them." Ibid. at para. 89, Deschamps J.

73   Ibid. at para. 156.

of death that may result outweigh whatever benefit (and none has been demonstrated to us here) there may be to the system as a whole."[74]

In their dissent, Binnie and LeBel JJ. (Fish J. concurring) stated that "the decision boils down to an application of the minimal impairment test. In respect of questions of social and economic policy, this test leaves a substantial margin of appreciation to the Quebec legislature."[75] In their view, difficult choices in the rationing of scarce medical resources and attempts to ensure equal access to medical care to all should be left to the legislature. They also warned that

> those who seek private health insurance are those who can afford it and can qualify for it. They are differentiated from the general population, not by their health problems, which are found in every group in society, but by their income status. We share the view of Dickson C.J. that the *Charter* should not become an instrument to be used by the wealthy to 'roll back' the benefits of a legislative scheme that helps protect the poorer members of society.[76]

It remains to be seen whether this 4 to 3 decision signals a permanent willingness of the Court to enter into complex, distributional and multi-faceted aspects of public policy such as the design of the health care system.

2) Reconciling Competing Claims and Protecting Vulnerable Groups

The Supreme Court has explicitly stated that a more relaxed standard of scrutiny is called for where the legislation challenged represents an attempt by the legislature to reconcile competing claims or protect vulnerable groups. In these cases, the majority judges in *Irwin Toy* indicated:

> If the legislature has made a reasonable assessment as to where the line is most properly drawn, especially if that assessment involves weighing conflicting scientific evidence and allocating scarce resources on this basis, it is not for the court to second guess. That would only be to substitute one estimate for another.[77]

---

74 *Ibid.* at para. 157.
75 *Ibid.* at para. 276.
76 *Ibid.* at para. 274, citing *Edwards Books*, above note 16, discussed below.
77 *Irwin Toy Ltd. v. Quebec (A.G.)*, [1989] 1 S.C.R. 927, 58 D.L.R. (4th) 577 at 623 [*Irwin Toy*].

In a case dealing with a Sunday closing law,[78] the Court noted that the legislature had been motivated by a secular purpose, namely, to provide workers with a common day of rest. The legislation did attempt to accommodate non-Sunday observers, but those exemptions were drafted with a view to protecting retail-sales workers, a particularly vulnerable group, from being forced to work. The exemptions were less than perfect from the perspective of non-Sunday observers. However, the majority held that, in such circumstances, the legislature had to be given a certain latitude to ensure that the *Charter* "does not simply become an instrument of better situated individuals to roll back legislation that has as its object the improvement of the condition of less advantaged persons."[79]

This line of analysis was later expanded when the Court indicated that a distinction should be drawn between cases where "the government is best characterized as the singular antagonist of the individual whose right has been infringed" and those where the government is "mediating between the claims of competing groups" and attempting to strike a balance that will protect the vulnerable, while impinging as little as possible upon protected freedoms "without the benefit of absolute certainty concerning how that balance is best struck."[80] In the former case, a rigorous standard of review should be applied under section 1, while in the latter, the legislature will not be held to such a strict test. In practical terms, the line between these two types of laws cannot be sharply drawn, for many laws affecting the criminal process, while placing the state in opposition to the individual, also implicate the interests of other groups. The Court has held, for example, that hate-crimes laws, obscenity and child pornography laws, provisions limiting access to the medical records of sexual assault victims, or rules about the prior sexual conduct of a sexual assault victim all raise equality issues and affect the interests of competing groups.[81] The Court has also distinguished between defining competing rights in a non-hierarchical manner that minimizes conflict, and considering competing rights and interests as part of the section 1 process. As will be discussed below, the government only bears the onus with respect to the latter process of justifying a limit on a *Charter* right under section 1.[82]

---

78   *Edwards Books*, above note 16.
79   *Ibid.* at 49 (D.L.R.), Dickson C.J.C.
80   *Irwin Toy*, above note 77 at 993, 994 (S.C.R.).
81   See, for example, *R. v. Seaboyer*, [1991] 2 S.C.R. 577, 83 D.L.R. (4th) 193 (rape-shield case).
82   *R. v. Mills*, [1999] 3 S.C.R. 668, 180 D.L.R. (4th) 1.

3) Definitional Elements

Definitional elements may affect proportionality review. As noted above, the Supreme Court has often avoided definitional limitations and given *Charter* rights a liberal and generous meaning. For example, both commercial expression and hate propaganda have been found to fall within the definition of "expression" and accordingly are *prima facie* protected by section 2(b).[83] Any limits imposed upon those forms of expression must be justified under section 1 to survive *Charter* scrutiny. However, definitional considerations seem to affect the strictness of review under section 1, especially with respect to expression cases. The Court has spoken of a "core" meaning of freedom of expression, leading to a strict application of section 1 when a form of expression lies at or near that "core" — for example, political speech.[84] But when the form of expression at issue is peripheral to the core, legislation imposing limitations is much more likely to survive.

While neither commercial speech nor hate propaganda are excluded at the stage of defining *Charter* rights, it is equally the case that neither lies at or near the "core" meaning of freedom of expression and, as a result, a relatively relaxed level of *Charter* scrutiny is applied.

Again, the motivation is to avoid an unduly burdensome standard of *Charter* review when the legislature is acting to protect vulnerable groups. In the children's advertising case, *Irwin Toy*,[85] the law at issue was designed to protect children from exploitative commercial messages, and the Supreme Court felt that the government had struck a reasonable balance in limiting advertising directed at children under thirteen years of age. In upholding the hate-propaganda law designed to protect ethnic minorities[86] and obscenity laws aimed at protecting women from degrading portrayals and children from child pornography, the Court noted that the expression at issue was far from the core.[87] In upholding offences of defamatory libel, the Court also noted that intentional defamations were far from the core value of freedom of expression.[88] The Court makes distinctions based on the value of expression under section 1 of the *Charter* that it does not make in determining whether expression is protected under section 2(b).

---

83 *Irwin Toy*, above note 77; *Keegstra*, above note 54.
84 *Thomson Newspapers*, above note 26 at para. 91.
85 *Irwin Toy*, above note 77.
86 *Keegstra*, above note 54.
87 *Butler*, above note 42; *R. v. Sharpe*, [2001] 1 S.C.R. 45, 194 D.L.R. (4th) 1.
88 *Lucas*, above note 11.

The distinction between different forms of expression under section 1 does not mean, however, that speech further from the core is without *Charter* protection. For example, challenges to legislation in some commercial-speech cases have succeeded because the bans—advertising dentists' services and tobacco products—did not pass the minimal-impairment test.[89] At the same time, however, the Supreme Court's generous approach to defining freedom of expression to include matters such as obscenity, child pornography, hate speech, and even deliberate lies has influenced the section 1 analysis and led to many cases in which violations of section 2(b) have been held to be justified under section 1 of the *Charter*.

The strict definitional limitations imposed in determining violations of section 7 of the *Charter* also influence section 1 analysis. In *Reference Re s. 94(2) of the Motor Vehicle Act (B.C.)*, the Court stated:

> Section 1 may, for reasons of administrative expediency, successfully come to the rescue of an otherwise violation of s. 7, but only in cases arising out of exceptional conditions, such as natural disasters, the outbreak of war, epidemics, and the like.[90]

The Supreme Court has reaffirmed this dictum noting that "the rights protected by section 7—life, liberty, and security of the person—are very significant and cannot ordinarily be overridden by competing social interests. Second, rarely will a violation of the principles of fundamental justice, specifically the right to a fair hearing, be upheld as a reasonable limit demonstrably justified in a free and democratic society."[91] Section 1 justifications for violations of section 7 will be "rare," albeit possible.[92] In more than one case the Court had held that "[o]verbroad legislation which infringes s. 7 of the *Charter* would appear to be incapable of passing the minimal impairment branch of the s. 1 analysis."[93] The Court has also been reluctant to hold the violations of the right against unreasonable search and seizure in section 8[94] of

---

89   *Rocket v. Royal College of Dental Surgeons of Ontario*, [1990] 2 S.C.R. 232, 71 D.L.R. (4th) 68; *RJR*, above note 43.

90   [1985] 2 S.C.R. 486 at 518, 24 D.L.R. (4th) 536.

91   *New Brunswick v. G.(J.)*, above note 56 at para. 99; *Suresh*, above note 12 at para. 78 (S.C.R.); *Charkaoui v. Canada (Citizenship and Immigration)*, [2007] 1 S.C.R. 350.

92   *United States of America v. Burns*, [2001] 1 S.C.R. 283, 195 D.L.R. (4th) 1 at para. 133.

93   *R. v. Heywood*, [1994] 3 S.C.R. 761 at 802–3 [*Heywood*]; *R. v. Demers*, [2004] 2 S.C.R. 489 at para. 46.

94   *Heywood*, *ibid.*; *Lavallee, Rackel & Heintz v. Canada (Attorney General)*; *White, Ottenheimer & Baker v. Canada (Attorney General)*; *R. v. Fink*, [2002] 3 S.C.R. 209.

the *Charter* or the right against cruel and unusual punishment in section 12 of the *Charter* are justified under section 1, in part because of the definitional limits placed on those rights.

On the other hand, violations of the equality rights in section 15 of the *Charter* have been held to be justified under section 1 despite the definitional limitations on what constitutes a violation of equality rights. Bastarache J. (Gonthier, Iacobucci and Major JJ. concurring) recently stated that he rejects the suggestion:

> that section 15(1) rights are all but absolute, in that their violation should only be justifiable in rare circumstances. This Court has often applied section 1 to breaches of section 15(1) . . . This is not indicative of undue deference, but of the need for a flexible approach to section 1 justification and, more broadly, the recognition that any balancing between individual rights and societal needs occurs in section 1, not section 15(1).[95]

A number of judges at different times have expressed concerns that an overly generous approach to finding violations of the section 15 equality rights will place unhealthy pressures to dilute the requirement that the state establish that limits on the right are reasonable and demonstrably justified under section 1 of the *Charter*.[96]

4) Relationship to Section 33

The Supreme Court has stated that an attempt to justify limits rights not subject to the section 33 override will be subjected to "careful examination" rather than "deference."[97] The case dealt with the right to vote, said by the Court to be "fundamental to our system of democracy." It followed that "great care must be exercised in determining whether or not the government has justified a violation of s. 3"[98] and in the result, the Court rejected the government's argument that denying the vote to inmates of federal penitentiaries could be justified as a reasonable limit on the right to vote.

---

95 *Lavoie v. Canada*, [2002] 1 S.C.R. 769, 210 D.L.R. (4th) 193 at para. 49 [*Lavoie*].
96 *Andrews v. Law Society of British Columbia*, [1989] 1 S.C.R. 143, 56 D.L.R. (4th) 1, Wilson J.; *Lavoie*, *ibid.*, Arbour J. (in dissent).
97 *Figueroa*, above note 35 at para. 60.
98 *Ibid.*

5) Cost

Should the government be able to justify limitations on *Charter* rights because the cost of compliance is too high? Rights are often expensive to implement. Respecting *Charter* rights represents a drain on the public purse and thereby limits the capacity of the state to carry out other worthy objectives. On the other hand, the very notion of a right is that it must be given priority over other claims and not made subject to utilitarian concerns such as cost and administrative inconvenience.

In several cases, the Supreme Court appeared to exclude the possibility that protecting the public purse could ever justify limiting a *Charter* right.[99] However, the decision in *Newfoundland (Treasury Board) v. N.A.P.E.* holds that while cost arguments should be viewed with "strong scepticism,"[100] there is no absolute rule barring section 1 justification on grounds of cost. The Newfoundland government enacted legislation to avoid implementation of a pay equity scheme for female health care workers. The legislation violated section 15 of the *Charter*, but the Supreme Court accepted the province's argument that a "severe" financial crisis justified denying the equality rights of this vulnerable group of workers. Writing for the Court, Binnie J. stated that in a case of financial crisis "elected governments must be accorded significant scope to take remedial measures, even if the measures taken have an adverse effect on a *Charter* right, subject, of course, to the measures being proportional both to the fiscal crisis and to their impact on the affected *Charter* interests."[101]

6) Consultation

While legislators are not required to consult with affected parties before acting,[102] the Supreme Court has held that in some cases it may be useful to consider "whether the government considered other options or engaged in consultations with the affected parties, in choosing to adopt

---

99 *Schachter v. Canada*, [1992] 2 S.C.R. 679 at 709: "budgetary considerations can-not be used to justify a violation under s. 1"; *Egan v. Canada*, [1995] 2 S.C.R. 513 at para. 99; *Reference Re Remuneration of Judges of the Provincial Court of Prince Edward Island*, [1997] 3 S.C.R. 3 at para. 281; *Nova Scotia (Workers' Compensation Board) v. Martin*, above note 59 at para. 109.

100 *Newfoundland*, above note 64 at para. 72.

101 *Ibid.* at para. 64.

102 Compare the situation of aboriginal rights where the Court has found the right to include a duty to consult: see, e.g., *Haida Nation v. British Columbia (Minister of Forests)*, [2004] 3 S.C.R. 511.

its preferred approach."[103] That statement was made in a case involving drastic changes to collective bargaining rights, an environment characterized by consultation, negotiation, and give and take bargaining. The government's failure to consult obviously influenced the Court's decision that it had failed to adopt a law that minimally impaired the employees' collective bargaining rights.

D. BURDEN OF PROOF AND SECTION 1 EVIDENCE

The initial burden of proving a violation of rights rests with the individual asserting a *Charter* violation. In light of the generous definition accorded *Charter* rights such as freedom of expression, this burden can, in some cases, be relatively easy to discharge. In other cases, it will be more difficult to establish a violation. Once a *prima facie* violation is proved, the burden shifts to the party attempting to justify the infringement as a reasonable limit. This means that the government has the burden of proof of establishing that limits on *Charter* rights are reasonable. Support for giving the government such a burden is found in the reference to limits that are "demonstrably justified" as well as the superior ability and resources of governments in establishing the need for limiting *Charter* rights. The standard of proof is the standard used in civil trial: proof on a balance of probabilities or preponderance of evidence.

The Supreme Court in *Oakes* indicated that governments seeking to justify limitations on rights will generally be required to present evidence in support of their argument. The result has been a significant expansion in the kind of materials coming before the courts. Historical, philosophical, and economic data, as well as government reports (both domestic and international), are presented, sometimes through expert witnesses, sometimes by way of judicial notice.[104] Occasionally, however, the Court seems demanding with respect to evidence—for example, in the tobacco advertising case, the majority judges commented on the failure of the federal government to show why an alternative to a total ban on advertising would undermine the government's objective. Not only had the government failed to show that it was necessary to have a complete ban, it had also refused to disclose a study of alterna-

---

103 *Health Services and Support – Facilities Subsector Bargaining Assn. v. British Columbia*, [2007] 2 S.C.R. 391 at para. 157.
104 *Ibid.* at paras. 56–57.

tives to a total ban, despite the request by the party challenging the law to have the information.[105] In other cases, the Court seems to have taken a relaxed approach to the evidence. In an earlier case, for example, the Court relied on government data justifying Sunday closing legislation that was imprecise and over fifteen years old.[106]

E. CONCLUSION

Much of the debate about the Supreme Court's treatment of section 1 of the *Charter* revolves around the issue of deference. When should the courts intervene to protect rights and when should they leave decisions about rights and limits to the legislatures? There is no easy answer. Too much deference can easily undermine the purpose of the *Charter* — to protect individual rights against the majority. Yet a court that demands an extensive factual record and the least intrusive means for rights impairment in all cases could unduly constrain the legislature's efforts to govern in the broad public interest. In the end, while the *Oakes* test provides the basic framework for analysis, the courts have not adhered to a single test that serves in all cases to determine where to draw the line between protection of rights and respect for the legislative role and competing rights and claims. As the Supreme Court has made clear,[107] the context of a particular case is of fundamental importance in the application of section 1 of the *Charter*.

FURTHER READINGS

BEATTY, D., *Constitutional Law* (Toronto: University of Toronto Press, 1995)

BREDT, C., & A. DODEK, "The Increasing Irrelevance of Section One" (2001) 14 Sup. Ct. L. Rev. (2d) 175

CHOUDHRY, S., "So What Is the Real Legacy of *Oakes*? Two Decades of Proportionality Analysis under the Canadian *Charter's* Section 1" (2006) 34 Sup. Ct. L. Rev. (2d) 501

COLKER, R., "Section 1, Contextuality and the Anti-Disadvantage Principle" (1992) 42 U.T.L.J. 77

---

105 *RJR*, above note 43 at 101, 108 (D.L.R.).
106 *Edwards Books*, above note 16.
107 *Edmonton Journal v. Alberta (A.G.)*, [1989] 2 S.C.R. 1326, 64 D.L.R. (4th) 577.

HIEBERT, J., *Limiting Rights: The Dilemmas of Judicial Review* (Montreal: McGill-Queen's University Press, 1996)

HOGG, P.W., "Section 1 Revisited" (1991) 1 N.J.C.L. 1

JACKMAN, M., "Protecting Rights and Promoting Democracy: Judicial Review under Section 1 of the *Charter*" (1996) 34 Osgoode Hall L.J. 661

LECKEY, R., "Prescribed by Law" (2007) 45 Osgoode Hall L.J. 571

MENDES, E., "The Crucible of the *Charter*: Judicial Principles v. Judicial Deference in the Context of Section 1" in G.A. Beaudoin & E. Mendes, eds., *The Canadian Charter of Rights and Freedoms*, 4th ed. (Markham, ON: LexisNexis Butterworths, 2005)

TRAKMAN, L., *et al.*, "*R. v. Oakes* 1986–1997: Back to the Drawing Board" (1998) 36 Osgoode Hall L.J. 83

CHAPTER 5

THE LEGISLATIVE OVERRIDE

There is a significant qualification in the Canadian constitution on the power of judicial review under the *Charter of Rights and Freedoms*, namely, the legislative override or notwithstanding clause found in section 33. This provision represents an important compromise reached at the time of the entrenchment of the *Charter* to meet concerns about the enhanced power of judicial review. It reflects the judgment that, while a strong element of judicial review is justifiable in a democracy, judicial power also needs to be constrained. Although the override has been rarely used, it is a fundamental structural feature of the *Charter* that shapes the respective responsibilities of the courts on the one hand and Parliament and the legislatures on the other.

Section 33 of the *Charter* permits Parliament or a provincial legislature to declare that a law shall operate "notwithstanding a provision included in section 2 or sections 7 to 15" of the *Charter*. In other words, a law containing a simple declaration from Parliament or a legislature that it is to have effect "notwithstanding" one of these sections will be protected from judicial review, and the law will remain in effect despite violating a *Charter* guaranteed right or freedom. This means that the fundamental freedoms (expression, religion, association, and assembly) are subject to being overridden by legislative decision, as are the legal rights and, subject to section 28, the right to equality. The reach of the legislative override does not extend to democratic rights (the right to vote and the requirement of regular sessions of Parliament and the legislatures), mobility rights (the right of citizens to enter, leave, and move about the country), minority or language rights. It also does not apply to the constitutional division of powers.

Override declarations can be in effect for a maximum period of five years, which is roughly tied to the life of a Parliament. As a result, the decision to renew an override will come before a newly elected Parliament or legislature and will have to be debated again by another group of elected legislators.

There is, as might be expected, enormous controversy concerning the wisdom of including the override clause in the constitution but it was a fundamental compromise without which Canada probably would have no *Charter*. The notwithstanding clause was modelled on similar clauses in human rights codes and a provision in the *Canadian Bill of Rights*.[1] Other countries, notably the United Kingdom, have included an override clause in human rights instruments drafted after the *Charter*.[2]

The Supreme Court of Canada has clearly stated that it will not engage in reviewing the legitimacy of a legislative decision to invoke the override clause.[3] The Court made this pronouncement in a case involving the Quebec government's decision to enact an omnibus override clause shortly after the enactment of the *Charter*. Through one stroke of the legislative pen, all Quebec statutes were exempted from the *Charter* by a blanket repeal and then re-enacted with the inclusion of a standard override clause. In addition, all new Quebec statutes were enacted with an override clause. The result was to protect all Quebec statutes from judicial review under the *Charter*. The decision to enact the override was taken by the separatist Parti Québécois government, which had opposed the 1982 amendments to the constitution including the *Charter*. Maintaining that the government of Quebec should have a veto over any such fundamental constitutional changes, the Quebec National Assembly refused to recognize the legitimacy of the *Charter*.

These override measures were challenged. The Quebec Court of Appeal held that such a sweeping and general declaration of override was invalid and that a much more specific approach was called for.[4] The Supreme Court of Canada disagreed, holding that, so long as the form of section 33 was observed, the courts had no business second-guessing or reviewing the exercise of the override power by a legislature. According to the Supreme Court, section 33 requires only a formal declaration

---

1   See, for example, Ontario *Human Rights Code*, R.S.O. 1990, c. H.19, s. 47(2); *Canadian Bill of Rights*, S.C. 1960, c. 44, s. 2.

2   *Human Rights Act 1998*, (U.K.), s. 14.

3   *Ford v. Quebec (A.G.)*, [1988] 2 S.C.R. 712, 54 D.L.R. (4th) 577 [*Ford*].

4   *Alliance des professeurs de Montréal v. Quebec (A.G.)* (1985), 21 D.L.R. (4th) 354 (Que. C.A.).

expressly referring to the sections of the *Charter* being overridden. The Court did, however, impose one significant limitation—a declaration under the override power could not have retroactive effect.

The override clause has been resorted to infrequently and the federal government under both Prime Ministers Mulroney and Chretien has stated that its government would never use it. The most dramatic invocation of the override clause, apart from the general declaration exempting Quebec from the reach of the *Charter*, was the decision to override the Supreme Court of Canada's decision that the Quebec "signs law" was contrary to freedom of expression.[5] As noted in chapter 4, the Court recognized Quebec's right to act to preserve and enhance the French language, but held that it had failed to justify the virtual total prohibition of the use of English and other languages on such signs. The Quebec National Assembly immediately resorted to the override clause in enacting a new signs law (the general override enactment having expired after five years), thereby provoking an enormously negative reaction in the rest of Canada that significantly eroded support for the package of constitutional amendments known as the Meech Lake Accord.[6] Quebec did not renew its use of the override when it expired in 1993 and the language law now generally allows the use of languages other than French in commercial signs so long as French remains the predominant language. Alberta used the override in 2000 to declare that the limitation of marriage to opposite-sex partners would operate notwithstanding the *Charter* and particularly section 15 of the *Charter*. In addition, there have been other uses of the override that have attracted no attention from the media and the public.[7]

There are many who argue that the override clause represents a significant defect in the Canadian constitution, since fundamental rights should never have to yield to majoritarian decisions regarding the general welfare.[8] It is argued that the courts should have the exclusive and final say in matters of fundamental rights and that the majority must forever comply with their interpretations of the *Charter*.

---

5   *Ford*, above note 3.

6   While the Accord was much favoured in Quebec, it did not generate enough support in the rest of Canada to be enacted within the three-year timeframe necessary under the amendment process. As a result, it died in June 1990.

7   A recent study has concluded that there have been sixteen uses of the override since 1982. T. Kahana, "The Notwithstanding Mechanism and Public Discussion: Lessons from the Ignored Practice of Section 33 of the *Charter*" (2001) 44 Can. Public Admin. 255.

8   See especially J.D. Whyte, "On Not Standing for Notwithstanding" (1990) 28 Alta. L. Rev. 347.

Another school of thought is more accepting of the override clause.[9] The override is seen as a useful safety valve, which can be invoked to escape significant errors or departures by the courts in the interpretation of constitutional guarantees. But for the override clause, nothing short of a subsequent case reversing the earlier decision or a constitutional amendment will correct the error.

Defenders of section 33 also argue that the override is deeply rooted in the Canadian political and constitutional tradition, which accepts that Parliament itself has an important role in the protection of rights.[10] Rather than seeing Parliament and the legislatures as being inevitably at odds with the courts in this sphere, the override clause recognizes the legitimate role of legislators in defining an appropriate balance between the rights of individuals and the interests of society at large.

Finally, the override clause may be seen as creating a check on the power of both legislatures and the courts. On the one hand, the *Charter* confers a broad mandate upon the judiciary to act to protect fundamental rights and freedoms, thereby significantly curtailing legislative power. On the other hand, the override clause ensures that the courts' power is not unlimited. Taken as a whole, section 33 ensures that no one has the last word. Even if the clause is invoked to overcome judicial review, the five-year limitation period on any use of the override ensures that the issue will have to be revisited after another election in which the people can hold accountable their democratically elected representatives. The net effect of the section is to achieve a subtle and effective check on both legislative and judicial power.[11]

It is impossible to know whether the override clause has had an impact on the Supreme Court of Canada's interpretation of the *Charter*. Some commentators have speculated that the availability of the override has made the judges more willing to engage in a rigorous protection of rights.[12] At the same time, the Court has accepted legislative replies to its decisions, replies that some commentators have argued

---

9   See especially P.H. Russell, "Standing Up for Notwithstanding" (1991) 29 Alta. L. Rev. 293.

10   See B. Slattery, "A Theory of the *Charter*" (1987) 25 Osgoode Hall L.J. 701.

11   The theme of dialogue between the courts and the legislature is developed by Slattery, *ibid.*, and by P.W. Hogg & A.A. Bushell, "The *Charter* Dialogue between Courts and Legislatures" (1997) 35 Osgoode Hall L.J. 75. It is also discussed by Iacobucci J. in *Vriend v. Alberta*, [1998] 1 S.C.R. 493, 156 D.L.R. (4th) 385 at para. 138 [*Vriend*], and in chapter 2, section C(4).

12   Russell, above note 9, and above in chapter 2.

should have been accompanied by the override because the legislation essentially reversed the Court's earlier *Charter* decision.[13]

Saskatchewan invoked the override in an effort to protect back-to-work legislation introduced during a labour dispute. Its concern was with a Court of Appeal decision that had not been appealed to the Supreme Court. The Supreme Court of Canada subsequently upheld the constitutionality of the legislation, thereby removing any need for the override. Some observers have argued that the override should only be used in response to a Supreme Court decision,[14] but the override can and has been used to pre-empt *Charter* challenges.

The suggestion by the Alberta government in 1998 that it intended to use the override to protect legislation limiting compensation for victims of forced sterilization provoked an outcry. Shortly thereafter, the same government refused to employ the override to reverse the decision of the Supreme Court extending the protection of the human-rights legislation to gays and lesbians.[15] Premier Klein suggested that the override should not be used unless authorized by the public in a referendum.[16] In 2000, however, a private member's bill invoking the override to prevent *Charter* challenges to restrictions on marriage to opposite-sex couples was passed by the Alberta legislature. There was little public discussion of this use of the override and there was no referendum authorizing its use. Some commentators have suggested that Alberta's use of the override would be vulnerable to challenge on the basis of the division of powers because Parliament, not the provincial legislature, has the exclusive jurisdiction to legislate in relation to marriage.[17] In any event, Alberta's use of the override lapsed when it was not renewed after five years.

The override gives the majority a legal mechanism to have its way, but it may well be that the people will rarely, if ever, assume the moral

---

13   *R. v. Mills*, [1999] 3 S.C.R. 668, as discussed in K. Roach, "Constitutional and Common Law Dialogues Between the Supreme Court and Canadian Legislatures" (2001) 80 Can. Bar Rev. 481 at 528–30.

14   C. Manfredi, *Judicial Power and the Charter*, 2d ed. (Toronto: Oxford University Press, 2001) at 192; T. Kahana, "Understanding the Notwithstanding Mechanism" (2002) 52 U.T.L.J. 221.

15   *Vriend*, above note 11.

16   See also S. Reid, "Penumbras for the People: Placing Judicial Supremacy under Popular Control" in A. Peacock, ed., *Rethinking the Constitution: Perspectives on Canadian Constitutional Reform* (Toronto: Oxford University Press, 1996).

17   T. Kahana, "The Notwithstanding Mechanism and Public Discussion: Lessons from the Ignored Practice of Section 33 of the *Charter*" (2001) 44 Can. Public Admin. 255 at 268–69.

and political burden of overriding protected rights and freedoms. At the same time, a vigilant democracy is essential to ensure that the public closely examines and re-examines a legislature's decision to enact legislation notwithstanding the fundamental freedoms, legal rights, and equality rights of the *Charter*.

FURTHER READINGS

CAMERON, J., "The *Charter*'s Legislative Override: Feat or Figment of the Constitutional Imagination?" (2004) 23 Sup. Ct. L. Rev. 135

GRESCHNER, D., & K. NORMAN, "The Courts and Section 33" (1987) 12 Queen's L.J. 155

HIEBERT, J., "Is It Too Late to Rehabilitate Canada's Notwithstanding Clause?" (2004) 23 Sup. Ct. L. Rev. (2d) 169

KAHANA, T., "The Notwithstanding Mechanism and Public Discussion: Lessons from the Ignored Practice of Section 33" (2001) 43 Can. Public Admin. 255

KAHANA, T., "Understanding the Notwithstanding Mechanism" (2002) 52 U.T.L.J. 221

LESSON, H., "Section 33, The Notwithstanding Clause: A Paper Tiger?" in P. Howe & P.H. Russell, eds., *Judicial Power and Canadian Democracy* (Montreal: McGill-Queen's University Press, 2001)

MANFREDI, C., *Judicial Power and the Charter*, 2d ed. (Toronto: Oxford University Press, 2001) c. 7

REID, S., "Penumbras for the People: Placing Judicial Supremacy under Popular Control" in A. Peacock, ed., *Rethinking the Constitution: Perspectives on Canadian Constitutional Reform* (Toronto: Oxford University Press, 1996)

ROACH, K., "When Should the Section 33 Override Be Used?" (1999) 42 Crim. L.Q. 1

RUSSELL, P.H., "Standing Up for Notwithstanding" (1991) 29 Alta. L. Rev. 293

SLATTERY, B., "A Theory of the *Charter*" (1987) 25 Osgoode Hall L.J. 701

WEILER, P., "Rights and Judge in a Democracy: A New Canadian Version" (1984) U. Mich. J.L. Ref. 51

WEINRIB, L.E., "Learning to Live with the Override" (1990) 35 McGill L.J. 541

WHYTE, J.D., "On Not Standing for Notwithstanding" (1990) 28 Alta. L. Rev. 347

CHAPTER 6

APPLICATION

Section 32 of the *Canadian Charter of Rights and Freedoms* states that the *Charter* applies to "the Parliament and government of Canada in respect of all matters within the authority of Parliament" and "to the legislature and government of each province in respect of all matters within the authority of the legislature of each province." In the early years of the *Charter*, there was considerable debate and uncertainty as to the appropriate interpretation of this section. It was not clear whether all legal relationships were subject to *Charter* scrutiny. In all provinces except Quebec, the residual source of law is the common law, which does not depend upon any explicit legislative enactment. Common law rules of contract, property, and tort govern an enormous range of social and economic activity. Does the *Charter* apply to the common law? Another aspect of the common law tradition is the concept that individuals are free to do as they please in the absence of some specific legal measure restraining their freedom. Does the *Charter* reach areas of human activity that are not subject to any specific legislation?

Despite the importance of these issues, the text of the *Charter* was ambiguous. Some commentators thought that the purpose of section 32 was to limit the application of the *Charter* to *government* action. They argued that it would be wrong to subject the entire legal regime to *Charter* review, and that the essence of a constitutional charter of rights was to deal with the relationship between the individual and the state, not all relationships between individuals. Others argued that the supremacy clause in section 52 of the *Constitution Act, 1982*, made the *Charter* applicable to all action, public and private, and that section 32 was included simply as a precautionary measure to ensure that all levels of governments were bound.

A. *DOLPHIN DELIVERY*—LIMITING THE APPLICATION OF THE *CHARTER*

This debate was largely put to rest in *Dolphin Delivery*, a case involving unlawful secondary picketing by a union.[1] The employer sought an injunction to prevent the picketing. While most provincial labour codes regulate secondary picketing, this dispute was governed by the *Canada Labour Code*, which was silent on the issue. The employer argued that the union's activity was unlawful on the basis that it amounted to a tort, or civil wrong, recognized by the common law. The union argued that an injunction would violate the guarantee of freedom of expression under section 2(b) of the *Charter*, and the issue arose as to whether the *Charter* had any application to the activities of non-governmental private actors and to the judge-made common law in areas such as tort, contract, and property.

The Supreme Court of Canada concluded that the *Charter* applies only to government. The Court determined that "government" includes the legislative, executive, and administrative branches. Therefore, all laws and regulations are subject to *Charter* scrutiny, as are the actions of the police or other governmental officials in their treatment of individuals. The Court also concluded that the *Charter* must apply to the common law, but only to the extent that the government relies upon it. For example, had the picketers been protesting some public matter and faced a suit by the government, the *Charter* would apply to any common law rules relied upon by the government.[2]

Some commentators have argued that the judicial branch and the judge-made common law should be included within the definition of "government." McIntyre J., writing for the majority, rejected the argument that a court order constitutes government action.[3] In McIntyre J.'s words:

> The courts are, of course, bound by the *Charter* as they are bound by all law. It is their duty to apply the law, but in so doing they act as

---

1   R.W.D.S.U., *Local 580* v. *Dolphin Delivery Ltd.*, [1986] 2 S.C.R. 573, 33 D.L.R. (4th) 174 [*Dolphin Delivery*].
2   *Ibid.* at 194–95 (D.L.R.).
3   This had been the holding in the leading American case on the point, *Shelley* v. *Kraemer*, 334 U.S. 1 (1948).

neutral arbiters, not as contending parties in a dispute. To regard a court order as an element of governmental intervention necessary to invoke the *Charter* would, it seems to me, widen the scope of *Charter* application to virtually all private litigation.[4]

The Supreme Court's decision in *Dolphin Delivery* generated a great deal of criticism. Many argued that the *Charter* should apply to the common law, since it is an important source of law in Canada.[5] Others were critical of the public/private distinction drawn, which would subject the government—but not other actors—to the *Charter*. In the view of some critics, the Court's decision ignored the fact that private power, often exercised by corporate entities, could just as easily undermine individual liberty and equality as could government action.[6]

Yet there are countervailing arguments to an expansive application of the *Charter*. Was the *Charter* really meant to govern all aspects of individual relationships? For example, should parents' constraints on children's expression or the refusal of a women's bridge group to include male members be subject to *Charter* review?[7] To invite the courts to scrutinize all private as well as public action would greatly extend the reach of the *Charter*, the scope of *Charter* litigation, and the power of the courts. Ironically, many of those who criticize *Dolphin Delivery* for restricting the reach of the *Charter* also contend that the *Charter* represents an unjustifiable expansion of judicial power.

Despite the academic invitation to rethink its approach, the Supreme Court of Canada affirmed its holding in *Dolphin Delivery* in later cases. The explanation for the Court's conclusion lies in its particular vision of the role of the *Charter*. La Forest J. developed this conception in the mandatory-retirement case. He wrote: "[T]he *Charter* is essentially an instrument for checking the powers of government over the individual . . . . To open up all private and public action to judicial review could strangle the operation of society and . . . could seriously interfere with

---

4   *Dolphin Delivery*, above note 1 at 196 (D.L.R.).

5   B. Slattery, "The *Charter's* Relevance to Private Litigation: Does *Dolphin* Deliver?" (1987) 32 McGill L.J. 905; D.M. Beatty, "Constitutional Conceits: The Coercive Authority of Courts" (1987) 37 U.T.L.J. 183. Slattery, for example, pointed out the irrationality of having the *Charter* apply to the *Civil Code* in Quebec, which is found in statute, but not to common law.

6   A.C. Hutchinson & A.J. Petter, "Private Wrongs/Public Wrongs: The Liberal Lie of the *Charter*" (1988) 38 U.T.L.J. 278.

7   See, for example, J. Whyte, "Is the Private Sector Affected by the *Charter*?" in L. Smith *et al.*, eds., *Righting the Balance: Canada's New Equality Rights* (Saskatoon: Canadian Human Rights Reporter, 1986) at 145; R. Elliot & R. Grant, "The *Charter's* Application in Private Litigation" (1989) 23 U.B.C. L. Rev. 459.

freedom of contract."[8] In other words, the Supreme Court of Canada sees the exclusive focus of the *Charter* as a judicially enforceable check on government, necessary to protect fundamental rights from the unreasonable actions of politicians and public officials. Absent the Court's intervention, the excesses of government could be curbed only by political action. As noted in chapter 2, the philosophy underlying the constitutional guarantee of rights is that ordinary politics may not always be adequate to protect individuals and minorities from abuse by majorities. With respect to non-governmental action, this argument for the need for judicial oversight has no application. The legislature has the power to decide the appropriate scope of individual liberty or the balance between equality and liberty, as well as the power to intervene where necessary to check abuses of private authority that undermine individual rights.[9] To say that the *Charter* does not apply to private actors is not to ignore the potential for abuse of private power. Rather, it is to say that the locus of authority for legal controls is best left with the legislature and that it would be inappropriate for the courts to assume responsibility for all issues of social justice for all elements of society.[10]

B. WHAT IS GOVERNMENT?

In the cases following *Dolphin Delivery*, the task for the courts has been to determine what constitutes governmental action for the purposes of the *Charter*. The Supreme Court has held that the *Charter* applies to Cabinet decisions[11] but not to actions of legislative assemblies protected by parliamentary privilege.[12] The Court has found that professional bodies exercising regulatory power delegated by the government, such as law societies, are subject to the *Charter*.[13] An adjudicator, appointed under the federal labour code to determine whether an employee was

---

8 *McKinney v. University of Guelph*, [1990] 3 S.C.R. 229, 76 D.L.R. (4th) 545 at 633–44 [*McKinney*].

9 In *Dolphin Delivery*, above note 1, McIntyre J. noted that there are instruments such as human rights codes available to check private abuses.

10 Compare J. Bakan, *Just Words: Constitutional Rights and Social Wrongs* (Toronto: University of Toronto Press, 1997).

11 *Operation Dismantle Inc. v. R.*, [1985] 1 S.C.R. 441, 18 D.L.R. (4th) 481, a case involving a Cabinet decision to allow missile testing.

12 *New Brunswick Broadcasting Co. v. Nova Scotia (Speaker of the House of Assembly)*, [1993] 1 S.C.R. 319, 100 D.L.R. (4th) 212, which refused to subject to *Charter* scrutiny a decision to ban television proceedings in the legislative assembly.

13 *Black v. Law Society of Alberta*, [1989] 1 S.C.R. 591, 58 D.L.R. (4th) 317; *Rocket v. Royal College of Dental Surgeons of Ontario*, [1990] 2 S.C.R. 232, 71 D.L.R. (4th) 68.

unjustly dismissed, was held to have issued a remedial order contrary to the *Charter* when he ordered the former employer to issue a specific letter of reference. The fact that the statute was the source of the authority for the order made the exercise of the adjudicator's discretion subject to *Charter* principles.[14] Similarly, a provincial human rights commission derives its powers from statute and is subject to the *Charter*, despite the fact that it is not subject to direct government control but exercises independent judicial powers when dealing with particular cases.[15]

Cases have also considered, with varying results, the application of the *Charter* to a number of institutions in the broader public sector. In *McKinney* and *Harrison*, the Supreme Court of Canada held that the *Charter* does not apply to universities, even though they receive government funding, are created by statute, and may have government appointees on their governing bodies.[16] Despite these close links to government, the Court focused on the independence of universities from government control in their day-to-day operations and academic decision making, and it concluded that the *Charter* did not apply to the mandatory-retirement policies of these institutions. Similarly, in *Stoffman*, a hospital was held not to be subject to the *Charter*, despite government funding and some degree of oversight, since here as well there was a sufficient element of day-to-day independence.[17]

In contrast, school boards[18] and community colleges[19] have been held to be part of government for purposes of the *Charter*. In a British Columbia case involving a community college, the Supreme Court found that the college was an agent of the Crown. In both cases it was noted that there was greater control of college operations and programs by governmental officials than with universities. The result in an Ontario case was to find not only that the college was part of government, but also that the collective agreement signed with a union was subject to the *Charter*. The Court concluded that government, through the college, was bound by the *Charter* not only with respect to its legislative function, but also when making a contract or engaging in commercial activity. As a result, public-sector employment rules are subject to *Charter* scrutiny.

---

14   *Slaight Communications Inc. v. Davidson*, [1989] 1 S.C.R. 1038, 59 D.L.R. (4th) 416.

15   *Blencoe v. British Columbia (Human Rights Commission)*, [2000] 2 S.C.R. 307.

16   *McKinney*, above note 8; *Harrison v. University of British Columbia*, [1990] 3 S.C.R. 451, [1991] 77 D.L.R. (4th) 55 [*Harrison*].

17   *Stoffman v. Vancouver General Hospital*, [1990] 3 S.C.R. 483, 76 D.L.R. (4th) 700 [*Stoffman*].

18   *Chamberlain v. Surrey School District No. 36*, [2002] 4 S.C.R. 710.

19   *Douglas/Kwantlen Faculty Assn. v. Douglas College*, [1990] 3 S.C.R. 570,; *Lavigne v. Ontario Public Service Employees Union*, [1991] 2 S.C.R. 211.

Institutions such as hospitals, regarded as private for certain purposes, may still be subject to the *Charter* where they act on behalf of the government or in furtherance of some specific governmental policy or program. In *Eldridge v. British Columbia (A.G.)*,[20] a hospital's failure to provide an interpreter for hearing-impaired patients was found to be contrary to section 15 of the *Charter*. Although a hospital is not a "government" for *Charter* purposes, its decisions regarding the provision of medically necessary services carried out the specific government objectives of the provincial *Hospital Insurance Act*. The government cannot, in effect, shield such decisions from *Charter* scrutiny by delegating a discretionary power to a private entity. As governments increasingly "contract out" the provision of public services, the issue of *Charter* application to private actors is likely to arise. The Supreme Court has held that, absent specific direction from the police, the actions of private security officers will not be subject to the *Charter*, but warned: "It may be that if the state were to abandon in whole or in part an essential public function to the private sector, even without an express delegation, the private activity could be assimilated to that of a state actor for *Charter* purposes."[21] In *Greater Vancouver Transportation Authority v. Canadian Federation of Students — British Columbia Component*,[22] the Supreme Court held that a public transit authority designated by statute to be an "agent of the government" and that was subject to substantial control in its day-to-day activities by means of regulations, was "government" for the purposes of section 32 and therefore subject to the *Charter*.

In sum, the test for determining whether entities such as hospitals, public broadcasters, or the post office are "government" for purposes of the *Charter* turns on the degree to which there is significant control by government ministers or their officials in their day-to-day operations and on the extent to which the entity acts on the government's behalf or furthers some specific governmental policy or program.[23]

C. INDIRECT APPLICATION OF THE *CHARTER*

The *Charter* may also apply to non-governmental actors indirectly, where the courts find that a law fails to go far enough in protecting

---

20   [1997] 3 S.C.R. 624, 151 D.L.R. (4th) 577.

21   *R. v. Buhay*, [2003] 1 S.C.R. 631 at para. 31.

22   2009 SCC 31.

23   Just as the Canadian test for what is government is developed on a case-by-case basis, so, too, do the American courts struggle with what constitutes "state action." See, for example, the discussion in K.E. Swinton, "Application of the *Canadian Charter of Rights and Freedoms*" in W.S. Tarnopolsky & G.A. Beaudoin, eds., *The Canadian Charter of Rights and Freedoms: Commentary* (Toronto: Carswell, 1982) at 41.

Charter rights. In *Vriend v. Alberta*,[24] the issue was whether a private school could refuse to hire teachers because of their sexual orientation. The school was not subject to the *Charter* but did have to comply with Alberta's *Individual's Rights Protection Act*, a statute created to combat discrimination in the private sector. The *Individual's Rights Protection Act* dealt with various forms of discrimination but did not prohibit discrimination on grounds of sexual orientation. The Supreme Court held that the Act violated the gay teacher's *Charter* right to equality by failing to protect him from discrimination. The Court added sexual orientation as a prohibited ground of discrimination under the Act. The practical effect of this ruling was to extend the application of the *Charter*'s equality guarantee to the private sector. Similarly, in *Dunmore v. Ontario (Attorney General)*,[25] the Court held that the freedom of association right of agricultural workers was denied by a law that excluded them from the reach of provincial labour laws. The law did nothing to prohibit agricultural workers from forming an association, but without the protection of the law, agricultural workers were impeded from organizing by the economic power of their private-sector employers. The Supreme Court held that this failure to protect *Charter* rights against private power amounted to a *Charter* violation and that the province was required to take the necessary steps to afford agricultural workers the protections enjoyed by other workers. Again, the practical effect of the ruling is indirectly to apply the *Charter* to private action.

D. APPLYING THE *CHARTER* TO THE COMMON LAW

In *Dolphin Delivery*, the Supreme Court concluded that the *Charter* did not apply to the common law unless government relied on it. Nevertheless, the Court went on to say that, although the *Charter* did not apply to disputes between private parties, this was "a distinct issue from the question whether the judiciary ought to apply and develop the principles of the common law in a manner consistent with the fundamental values enshrined in the Constitution. The answer to this question must be in the affirmative."[26] Accordingly, the courts are to consider *Charter* principles when developing the common law. This is potentially a significant exception to the otherwise restrictive view of the *Charter*'s application reflected by the *Dolphin Delivery* decision.

---

24   [1998] 1 S.C.R. 493, 156 D.L.R. (4th) 385 (also discussed in chapter 17).
25   [2001] 3 S.C.R. 1016, 207 D.L.R. (4th) 193.
26   *Dolphin Delivery*, above note 1 at 198 (D.L.R.).

In a decision rendered shortly after *Dolphin Delivery*, the Supreme Court of Canada held that the *Charter* applied in a proceeding involving an *ex parte* injunction.[27] The injunction was issued to restrain picketing of a courthouse during a lawful strike, on the basis that this constituted criminal contempt of court. The rules about contempt of court were found in the common law, but the Supreme Court held that the *Charter* nevertheless applied because the judge, in issuing the injunction, acted in a public capacity and invoked criminal law powers: "The criminal law is being applied to vindicate the rule of law and the fundamental freedoms protected by the *Charter*. At the same time, however, this branch of the criminal law, like any other, must comply with the fundamental standards established by the *Charter*."[28]

The *Charter* was similarly invoked in proceedings challenging a judge's order restraining the broadcast of a docudrama while a criminal trial on similar issues was ongoing or about to start.[29] The accused feared that the program might influence jurors and thereby affect the fairness of their criminal trials. On that basis, they obtained an order from a superior court judge prohibiting the broadcast until the completion of the criminal trials. The media then challenged the publication ban under section 2(b) of the *Charter*. Lamer C.J.C. stated that the discretion at common law to order a publication ban in criminal proceedings must be exercised so as to conform to the *Charter*. In his view, the pre-*Charter* common law rule emphasized the right to a fair trial over the right to freedom of expression. The enhanced protection accorded by the *Charter* to freedom of expression called for a reformulation of the common law rule.[30] Applying the new rule to the facts in the case, Lamer C.J.C. concluded that the initial ban was not justified, since there were alternative measures to safeguard the trial process.[31]

---

27   *B.C.G.E.U. v. British Columbia (A.G.)*, [1988] 2 S.C.R. 214, 53 D.L.R. (4th) 1, also discussed in chapter 9.

28   *Ibid.* at 244 (S.C.R.).

29   *Dagenais v. Canadian Broadcasting Corp.*, [1994] 3 S.C.R. 835, 120 D.L.R. (4th) 12, also discussed in chapter 9.

30   *Ibid.* at 38 (D.L.R.):

A publication ban should only be ordered when:
  (a)   Such a ban is *necessary* in order to prevent a real and substantial risk to the fairness of the trial, because reasonably available alternative measures will not prevent the risk; and
  (b)   The salutary effects of the publication ban outweigh the deleterious effects to the free expression of those affected by the ban. [emphasis added]

31   *Ibid.* at 40 (D.L.R.). The *Charter* was also used to modify the common law rules allowing the Crown prosecutor to introduce evidence of an accused's insanity in *R. v. Swain*, [1991] 1 S.C.R. 933, 63 C.C.C. (3d) 481.

In both these cases, the application of the common law arose in the context of the administration of the criminal law by the courts. In *Hill v. Church of Scientology*,[32] the Supreme Court considered the interaction of the *Charter* and the common law in a purely private context. Hill, then a Crown prosecutor, sued the Church of Scientology and its counsel for libel because of various statements made about his conduct. The defendants challenged the validity of the common law of libel, claiming that it violated their right to freedom of expression. Speaking for the Court, Cory J. explained why it was necessary to interpret the common law in a manner consistent with *Charter* principles:

> Historically, the common law evolved as a result of the courts making those incremental changes which were necessary in order to make the law comply with current societal values. The *Charter* represents a restatement of the fundamental values which guide and shape our democratic society and our legal system. It follows that it is appropriate for the courts to make such incremental revisions to the common law as may be necessary to have it comply with the values enunciated in the *Charter*.[33]

Cory J. was careful to insist that the *Charter* does not apply directly to private activity, and that it cannot be applied in the same manner as when government action is involved. Judicial law-making is constrained. The courts will effect only incremental changes to the common law; more far-reaching change should be left to the legislature. The limitations clause in section 1 and the *Oakes* test do not apply to the modification of the common law in private litigation. Rather, said Cory J., a more flexible balancing of interests is required, with *Charter* values weighed against the principles underlying the common law. While the Court refused to make significant changes to the common law of libel, the Court did alter the common law rule relating to the reporting of court proceedings as being inconsistent with the *Charter* value of freedom of expression.

More recently, in *WIC Radio Ltd. v. Simpson*,[34] the Supreme Court was prepared to take a more aggressive approach. Binnie J., for the majority, signalled that the tort of defamation "may require modification to provide

---

32   *Hill v. Church of Scientology of Toronto*, [1995] 2 S.C.R. 1130, 126 D.L.R. (4th) 129, also discussed in chapter 9. The Court rejected the argument that there was government action here because Hill was a government employee, concluding that the defamation had been made against him personally, not against the government.

33   *Ibid.* at 1169 (S.C.R.).

34   [2008] 2 S.C.R. 420 at para. 2.

broader accommodation to the value of freedom of expression" and that rules that chill "debate on matters of legitimate public interest" ought to be re-examined[35]and "will necessarily evolve in ways that are consistent with *Charter* values."[36] While those values include "the worth and dignity of each individual, including reputation,"[37] the direction is clearly to ac-commodate freedom of expression and to move away from common law rules that strongly favoured the protection of reputation.[38] In *WIC Radio*, the Court found the common law defence of fair comment to be unduly restrictive and adopted the approach taken by Dickson J. in a pre-*Charter* dissenting opinion. The defence is made out, held the Court, where the comment was on a matter of public interest, is based on fact but is recog-nizable as comment and satisfies the following objective test: could any person honestly express that opinion on the proven facts?

In *Retail, Wholesale and Department Store Union, Local 558 v. Pepsi-Cola Canada Beverages (West) Ltd.*,[39] the Supreme Court returned to the issue of secondary picketing, the same issue raised in *Dolphin Delivery*. While the Court did not depart from its earlier ruling on *Charter* appli-cation, it overruled the result in *Dolphin Delivery* by changing the com-mon law rule on secondary picketing. The Court stressed the importance of freedom of expression in the labour context and the need to modify common law rules that impinge upon *Charter* values. The Court found that the common law rule that secondary picketing was in and of itself unlawful conflicted with the fundamental rights of striking workers. The Court ruled that the common law should be modified to allow secondary picketing unless it involved tortious or criminal conduct.

The Court's recognition of the application of *Charter* values to the common law in a private context is significant. By expanding the pow-ers of the courts to modify common law rules, the Supreme Court has softened the impact of the strict public/private distinction drawn in *Dolphin Delivery*.

E. EXTRATERRITORIAL APPLICATION

The *Charter* does not, as a general rule, apply to control the conduct of foreign officials acting outside Canada. Ordinarily, the laws of one state

---

35   *Ibid.* at para. 15.
36   *Ibid.* at para. 24.
37   *Ibid.* at para. 2.
38   See, for example, *Cusson v.Quan* (2007), 87 O.R. (3d) 241 (C.A.)
39   [2002] 1 S.C.R. 156, 208 D.L.R. (4th) 385.

do not have extraterritorial effect nor do they interfere with the sovereignty of another state, and foreign states are not mentioned in section 32. In extradition matters, the Canadian courts have no authority to limit or control the manner in which criminal proceedings are conducted elsewhere.[40] However, where it would "shock the conscience" of Canadians to send an accused person to face treatment that would amount to a violation of fundamental human rights, extradition may be refused on the grounds that the individual's section 7 rights would be violated.[41]

A person facing charges in Canada cannot complain that foreign police gathered evidence in a way that would not be permitted under the *Charter* if the investigation had taken place in Canada.[42] The situation is more complicated where Canadian government officials, such as police, exercise their authority extraterritorially. In *R. v. Cook*,[43] the appellant, suspected in a murder that had taken place in Vancouver, was arrested in New Orleans by a United States Marshal pursuant to a Canadian extradition request. Two days after the arrest, two Canadian police officers interviewed the appellant in custody New Orleans. The officers did not properly advise the appellant of his section 10(b) rights, and the appellant proceeded to make a statement to the officers. At trial, the appellant sought to have the statement excluded from the evidence, and argued that it was taken in violation of his *Charter* rights. The Crown argued that the *Charter* did not apply to the officers' actions in New Orleans. The Supreme Court of Canada held that the *Charter* applied to the officers while they were interviewing the appellant, and excluded the evidence. The majority recognized that the extraterritorial application of the *Charter* could possibly infringe on the sovereignty of the United States, but found that this did not totally preclude the *Charter* from applying. They held that the *Charter* would apply outside of Canada only when two factors were met: the impugned act fell within section 32(1) of the *Charter* and the application of the *Charter* would not generate "an objectionable extraterritorial effect" by interfering with the sovereign authority of the foreign state.[44]

This Court took a more restrictive approach in *R. v. Hape*.[45] The RCMP suspected that the appellant, a Canadian citizen, was using his investment company, based in Turks and Caicos, to launder money. The

40   *Canada v. Schmidt*, [1987] 1 S.C.R. 500, 39 D.L.R. (4th) 18.

41   *United States of America v. Burns*, [2001] 1 S.C.R. 283, 195 D.L.R. (4th) 1.

42   *R. v. Harrer*, [1995] 3 S.C.R. 562, 128 D.L.R. (4th) 98; *R. v. Terry*, [1996] 2 S.C.R. 207, 135 D.L.R. (4th) 214.

43   *R. v. Cook*, [1998] 2 S.C.R. 597, 164 D.L.R. (4th) 1.

44   *Ibid.* at para. 25.

45   *R. v. Hape*, [2007] 2 S.C.R. 292 [*Hape*].

RCMP received permission from the Detective Superintendent of the Turks and Caicos Police Force to conduct an investigation in Turks and Caicos, subject to the condition that the RCMP would work under the Detective Superintendent's authority. On several occasions, the Detective Superintendent and the RCMP surreptitiously searched the company's premises and seized a large number of documents. The appellant was subsequently charged in Canada for money laundering, and he claimed that the searches and seizures violated his rights under section 8 of the *Charter*. A majority of the Supreme Court found that the international legal norm of the sovereign equality of states prevents Canada from enforcing its laws within the territory of other nations. Application of section 8 of the *Charter* in favour of the appellant would involve enforcing the *Charter* in the foreign country and thus was held to be prohibited by the norms of public international law.

However, application of the *Charter* is not excluded where the norm of sovereign equality of states does not apply. The Court identified two situations where this may occur. The first is where the foreign state consents to Canada enforcing its laws within the foreign state, a situation which, the Court conceded, "may be rare."[46] The second is where Canada's actions in the foreign state have involved it in activities which violate international law. In such a situation, the principle of comity does not require that Canada respect the sovereign equality of the foreign state to breach international law, and thus there is no obstacle to the *Charter's* application. It was on this basis that the Supreme Court held in *Canada (Justice) v. Khadr*[47] that a prisoner at Guantanamo Bay was entitled to disclosure of interviews conducted by Canadian authorities at Guantanamo Bay because the process of indefinite detention subject to possible trial as unlawful combatants by military commission at Guantanamo Bay had been found by the Supreme Court of the United States to violate international norms, namely the Geneva Conventions. Omar Khadr's right to disclosure, however, did not follow domestic standards accorded to those in Canada. Khadr was only entitled to disclosure of material that was directly related to Canadian participation in the violation of international human rights. The Court did not specify the exact nature of the *Charter* violation in this case, but it possible that Canadian conduct that violates Canada's international human rights obligations will violate section 7 of the *Charter*.[48] In addition, the Court in *Khadr* made reference to Omar Khadr's Canadian

---

46   *Ibid.* at para. 106.
47   [2008] 2 S.C.R. 125.
48   See discussion below in chapter 13.

citizenship and lower courts have rejected similar claims for disclosure of material collected by Canadian officials about non-citizens held at Guantanamo Bay.[49] *Khadr* has also been distinguished by the Federal Court of Appeal in holding that the *Charter* does not apply with respect to the detention of Canadian captives in Afghanistan.[50]

Even in cases where the *Charter* is found to be inapplicable to extra-territorial activities of the Canadian authorities, claimants may not be without a remedy. In situations where an accused being tried in Canada claims that evidence was gathered in a foreign jurisdiction in breach of their *Charter* rights but the *Charter* does not apply, the accused may still seek to have the evidence excluded pursuant to sections 7 or 11(d) of the *Charter* where admitting the evidence would render the trial unfair.[51] Application of the *Charter* in this manner to protect fair trial rights in Canada does not violate the international legal norm as it does not involve the enforcement of Canadian law in a foreign state.

F. CLAIMING *CHARTER* RIGHTS

To this point, the focus has been on whether the *Charter* applies to particular actions or entities. There is another important application issue that should also be mentioned: namely, who can invoke *Charter* rights? Some of the rights are framed as "everyone has the right" (for example, the fundamental freedoms of expression and religion in section 2 and the right to life, liberty, and security of the person in section 7). Others are available to "any person," as in the legal rights in section 11, or to an "individual," as in the equality rights in section 15. Some are available to citizens or permanent residents (for example, mobility rights in section 6 and minority-language education rights in section 23).

Some *Charter* rights have been held to be unavailable to corporations. For example, the equality rights in section 15 and the right to life, liberty, and security of the person in section 7 have been deemed to be rights that can be exercised only by human beings.[52] Corporations can, however, invoke certain rights that have been seen as appropriate for a corporate entity—for example, freedom of expression.[53]

---

49   *Slahi and Zemiri v. Canada*, 2009 FC 160.
50   *Amnesty International v. Canada*, 2008 FCA 401.
51   *Hape*, above note 45 at paras. 107–9.
52   *Irwin Toy v. Quebec (Attorney General)*, [1989] 1 S.C.R. 927 at 1001-3.
53   *Ibid.*

Even if a corporation cannot directly claim that its rights have been violated, it may have standing to raise a *Charter* issue in criminal or regulatory proceedings, where a law under which it is being prosecuted is alleged to be in violation of others' *Charter* rights. For example, if a corporation is prosecuted under a law prohibiting Sunday shopping, it can challenge the law as a denial of freedom of religion even though section 2(a), the guarantee of freedom of religion, does not apply directly to a corporation.[54] The reason for this lies in the concept of the rule of law: that no one should be subject to prosecution under an unconstitutional law.[55]

G. CONCLUSION

Dolphin Delivery determined that the basic principle of *Charter* application is that the purpose of the constitution is to check the power of government over the individual. There is no question but that this represents a significant constraint on the reach of the *Charter*, especially in an age of shrinking government. The sharp distinction between the public and private domains and the immunity of powerful private interests from *Charter* scrutiny is thought by many to be unduly restrictive. On the other hand, the courts have also been criticized for assuming too much power under the *Charter* and, indeed, the reach of the *Charter* would be unlimited were it not for *Dolphin Delivery*. In the end, the question is an institutional one: which body is best able to deal with the power of private interests, the courts or the legislatures? The Supreme Court has determined that it is simply not prepared to assume responsibility for all issues of social justice, and that it should focus its efforts under the *Charter* to resolving conflicts between the individual and the state. On the other hand, *Dolphin Delivery* leaves considerable scope for extending the *Charter*'s reach into the common law. While not directly subject to the *Charter*, the common law is a form of judge-made law, and the courts are directed to pay heed to *Charter* values in its development. This has produced some significant changes and represents an important gloss on the principle that limits the *Charter*'s application to government action.

---

54   *R. v. Big M Drug Mart Ltd.*, [1985] 1 S.C.R. 295, 18 D.L.R. (4th) 321.
55   Further discussion of constitutional litigation is found in chapter 7.

FURTHER READINGS

BEATTY, D.M., "Constitutional Conceits: The Coercive Authority of Courts" (1987) 37 U.T.L.J. 183

BERGER, B., "The Reach of the Security State" (2008) 56 C.R. (6th) 268.

DE MESTRAL, A., & E. FOX-DECENT, "Rethinking the Relationship between International and Domestic Law" (2008) 53 McGill L.J. 573

ELLIOT, R., & R. GRANT, "The *Charter's* Application in Private Litigation" (1989) 23 U.B.C. L. Rev. 459

FAIRLEY, H.S., "International Law Comes of Age: *R. v. Hape*" (2008) 87 Can. Bar Rev. 229

REICHMAN, A., "A *Charter*-Free Domain: In Defence of *Dolphin Delivery*" (2002) 35 U.B.C. L. Rev. 329

ROACH, K., "*R. v. Hape* Creates *Charter* Free Zone for Canadian Officials Abroad" (2007) 53 Crim. L.Q. 1

SLATTERY, B., "The *Charter's* Relevance to Private Litigation: Does *Dolphin* Deliver?" (1987) 32 McGill L.J. 905

SWINTON, K.E., "Application of the Canadian *Charter of Rights and Freedoms*" in W.S. Tarnopolsky & G.A. Beaudoin, eds., *The Canadian Charter of Rights and Freedoms: Commentary* (Toronto: Carswell, 1982)

WALDMAN, L., "The *Charter* in an International Context" (2007) 23 N.J.C.L. 85

WHYTE, J., "Is the Private Sector Affected by the *Charter*?" in L. Smith *et al.*, eds., *Righting the Balance: Canada's New Equality Rights* (Saskatoon: Canadian Human Rights Reporter, 1986)

CHAPTER 7

CHARTER LITIGATION

Charter issues are decided in the ordinary course of litigation.[1] Any citizen whose rights are affected is entitled to raise a constitutional issue in a civil proceeding or by way of defence to a criminal prosecution. Canadian law follows the Anglo-American legal tradition and does not assign particular responsibility to a specialized court for the adjudication of constitutional disputes. The court that has jurisdiction over the dispute has, by virtue of that jurisdiction, authority to decide the constitutional issue.

This method of dealing with constitutional cases has important implications for the manner in which constitutional issues are decided. It means that *Charter* issues will almost always arise in a fact-specific context and be decided in the course of a concrete dispute between two parties. The primary task of the court is to decide the case before it, not to pronounce at large upon the constitution or its meaning. It is an established practice in Canadian law that, if a judge can decide a case without dealing with a constitutional issue, he or she should do so. Moreover, because proceedings in Canadian courts are strictly adversarial, a judge will not ordinarily comment upon a constitutional issue unless one is raised by the parties. Even if there is believed to be a constitutional issue that may arise on the facts, it would be unusual for

---

1   Both this chapter and chapter 17 draw freely on a contribution to a collection on Canadian constitutional law published in Italian: R.J. Sharpe, "Ordinamento giudiziario e giustizia costituzionale" in *L'ordinamento costituzionale del Canada* (Torino, G. Giappichelli Editore, 1997).

a judge to deal with the issue if the parties do not raise it. It is for the parties to the dispute to define the issues before the court. Similarly, the parties control the presentation of evidence and argument.

A. INTERVENTION BY THE ATTORNEY GENERAL AND PUBLIC-INTEREST GROUPS

While constitutional cases generally follow the same procedural path as other cases, there are some important exceptions and special procedural rules to reflect the wide range of interests implicated and the importance of any decision for the future. The first concerns the representation of the public and other interests. A party who challenges the constitutional validity of a statute is required to give notice to the attorney general, provincial, federal, or both, as appropriate.[2] The attorney general has the right to intervene in the proceeding and to present whatever evidence or argument he or she deems necessary to defend the constitutionality of the law. This may seem to depart from the adversarial system by allowing for non-party participation, but, in fact, interventions by the attorney general reflect the underlying values of the adversarial system. A constitutional case implicates the public interest and it is a basic tenet of the adversarial system that rights should not be affected without affording the right-holder a hearing. The intervention of the attorney general ensures that the public interest will be represented before the courts when the constitutionality of a statute is attacked.

A second important development in constitutional litigation, particularly at the level of the Supreme Court of Canada, is the generous allowance for public-interest groups to appear as intervenors.[3] While the courts were initially cautious in this area,[4] the discretion to permit public-interest groups to intervene has been frequently exercised. Once again, this is a reflection of the fact that the decision of the court on a constitutional matter will have broad public ramifications. Those who have particular interests that are affected and who can assist the court should be heard.

---

2   See B.L. Strayer, *The Canadian Constitution and the Courts: The Function and Scope of Judicial Review*, 3d ed. (Toronto: Butterworths, 1988) at 73–86.

3   P.R. Muldoon, *Law of Intervention: Status and Practice* (Aurora, ON: Canada Law Book, 1989).

4   K. Swan, "Intervention and Amicus Curiae Status in *Charter* Litigation" in R.J. Sharpe, ed., *Charter Litigation* (Toronto: Butterworths, 1987).

Certain public-interest groups have appeared regularly before the Supreme Court of Canada in *Charter* litigation and they have had a significant influence. Notable are the interventions of the Canadian Civil Liberties Association, a body that exists to defend the interests of civil liberties, and the Women's Legal Education and Action Fund, or LEAF, a feminist group concerned with equality rights. There can be little question but that the reasoning of certain Supreme Court judgments has been influenced by, or even based upon, arguments presented by these groups. At the same time, it should be noted that these two groups have opposed each other on issues such as hate propaganda and obscenity and that attorneys general remain the most frequent intervenors in *Charter* cases. To be accepted as an intervenor, a group must apply to the court before the case is heard and demonstrate both that it has a serious interest in the issues to be litigated and that it has a distinctive perspective to bring to bear upon those issues. If given intervenor status, the group will have the opportunity to file written argument and will often be permitted to make brief oral submissions. Intervenors are bound by the evidence heard at trial, but they can call the attention of the court to published articles and reports.

B. REFERENCES

There is one significant exception to the general rule that constitutional disputes are decided in the course of ordinary litigation. The *Supreme Court Act* provides that the federal government may refer directly to the Court questions of law or fact concerning the interpretation of the constitution or the constitutionality or interpretation of any federal or provincial legislation.[5] There is similar legislation in each province permitting provincial governments to refer questions to the provincial Court of Appeal.[6] References have become a familiar and distinctive feature of Canadian constitutional law.[7] Most countries that follow the common law tradition do not permit references, and the device has been rejected as unconstitutional in both the United States[8] and Australia[9]

---

5   R.S.C. 1985, c. S-26, s. 53.

6   See, for example, *Courts of Justice Act*, R.S.O. 1990, c. C-43, s. 8.

7   See Strayer, above note 2 at 315–18.

8   L. Tribe, *American Constitutional Law*, 2d ed. (Mineola: Foundation Press, 1988) at 73–77.

9   *Re Judiciary and Navigation Acts* (1921), 29 C.L.R. 257.

and exists only in a very different and modified form in England.[10] Technically, a reference asks the court for an advisory opinion and, accordingly, the answer given by the court lacks the formal quality of a judgment for purposes of the doctrine of precedent. However, in practice, opinions rendered on references are almost invariably followed in subsequent litigation and treated in the same way as a judgment given in an ordinary case.

References have often been used when a government considers it to be in the public interest to have an immediate resolution by the appellate court of a constitutional issue. The procedure circumvents the normal process of trial, appeal, and further appeal to the Supreme Court of Canada and allows the government to obtain a relatively quick answer to a constitutional issue. It is also possible for one government to direct a reference as to the constitutionality of another government's law or proposed course of action. There are important examples of this being done by the federal government,[11] and the technique has also been used by provincial governments.

The most notable instance of a provincial reference with regard to a proposed federal course of action arose in connection with the patriation of the constitution in 1981.[12] The federal government had indicated that it would proceed to request the United Kingdom Parliament to amend the Canadian constitution, although it had the consent of only two of the ten provinces. Three provincial governments referred the question to their courts of appeal and those cases were then appealed to the Supreme Court of Canada, which ruled that constitutional convention precluded the federal government from proceeding in the manner proposed. The result was that all governments were sent back to the bargaining table for a further round of talks and negotiation and significant changes were made to the constitutional amendments that were eventually enacted.[13]

The most notable instance of a federal reference in relation to possible provincial action was the 1998 reference on the constitutionality of unilateral separation of a province. The reference, known as the

---

10   See J. Jaconelli, "Hypothetical Disputes, Moot Points of Law, and Advisory Opinions" (1985) 101 L.Q.R. 587.

11   *Reference Re Alberta Legislation*, [1938] S.C.R. 100, [1938] 2 D.L.R. 81.

12   *Reference Re Amendment to the Constitution of Canada*, [1981] 1 S.C.R. 753, 125 D.L.R. (3d) 1 [*Patriation Reference*].

13   For an account of the process and negotiations, see R.J. Romanow, J. Whyte, & H.A. Leeson, *Canada . . . Notwithstanding: The Making of the Constitution, 1976–1982* (Toronto: Carswell Methuen, 1984).

Quebec Secession Reference,[14] posed a hypothetical question because the province was not proposing to separate from Canada. The Quebec government refused to participate in the reference and the Court appointed an *amicus curaie* or friend of the court to argue that Quebec had a right under domestic and international law to unilateral separation from Canada. The Court concluded that there was no right to unilateral separation. It indicated, however, that there would be an obligation for Canada to negotiate separation should a province receive a sufficient popular mandate, on a sufficiently clear question, to separate from Canada. The Court, however, refused to decide what would be a sufficiently clear question or mandate. As with the earlier *Patriation Reference*, the ultimate effect of this reference may be to send the parties to the bargaining table should a province ever decide to vote to separate from Canada.

One of the shortcomings of the reference procedure is that the court lacks the usual factual foundation because it is presented with an abstract question. Canadian judges are often troubled by this, since it is out of keeping with the fact-specific manner in which constitutional issues are ordinarily presented. On occasion, the Supreme Court has complained of being asked to answer a constitutional question without a specific factual context.[15] The Court has even said that it is not obliged to answer a reference if there is an insufficient basis for adjudication,[16] but the right to decline has been exercised infrequently. The most significant case in which the Supreme Court has refused to answer a reference question was *Reference Re Same-Sex Marriage*.[17] In that high-profile reference, the Court exercised its discretion to refuse to answer one of four questions placed before it by the federal government. The question, which had been added by the government after the reference was originally posed, was whether restricting marriages to unions of men with women was consistent with the *Charter*. Courts in five provinces and one territory had already decided that the opposite-sex requirement violated equality rights under section 15 of the *Charter* and could not be justified under section 1. The Supreme Court concluded that an answer to this question was not advisable given that a ruling might undermine the government's stated goal of legislating

---

14   *Reference Re Secession of Quebec*, [1998] 2 S.C.R. 217, 161 D.L.R. (4th) 385, also discussed in chapter 1.

15   *Manitoba (A.G.) v. Manitoba Egg and Poultry Association*, [1971] S.C.R. 689 at 704–5, 19 D.L.R. (3d) 169.

16   *Reference Re Legislative Authority of Parliament to Alter or Replace the Senate*, [1980] 1 S.C.R. 54, 102 D.L.R. (3d) 1.

17   [2004] 3 S.C.R. 698, 246 D.L.R. (4th) 193.

to recognize same-sex marriages and achieving uniformity in the law. The Court also noted that perhaps thousands of same-sex couples had relied on the finality of the lower court judgments and that their vested rights outweighed the benefits of answering the question. At the same time, the Court answered three other questions relating to Parliament's exclusive legislative authority to legislate in relation to marriage, the consistency of proposed legislation extending the right to marry to same-sex couples with the *Charter*, and the protection that freedom of religion provided religious officials from being compelled to perform a same-sex marriage.

References have been used to resolve pressing *Charter* issues. In Ontario, the provincial government employed the reference proced-ure when it decided to extend full funding to Roman Catholic separate schools. A variety of interests, including private and religious schools, which did not enjoy like support, attacked this measure as being con-trary to the section 15 guarantee of equality. Prolonged litigation could have disrupted the administration of Ontario schools for years and the government decided that it would be in the public interest to have the matter resolved quickly. A reference was directed to the Ontario Court of Appeal,[18] and an appeal was then taken to the Supreme Court of Canada.[19] Both courts upheld the constitutionality of the scheme. With a few exceptions, however, there has been little use of the reference pro-cedure with almost all *Charter* cases being decided through ordinary litigation between parties in adversarial disputes and most frequently in cases in which the state prosecuted an individual.

C. DECLARATORY PROCEEDINGS, STANDING, ADVANCE COSTS AND MOOTNESS

A private citizen is not entitled to direct a reference but may, in certain specific situations, bring what is known as a declaratory action in which no relief or remedy is sought other than an order of a court that a statute is contrary to the constitution. Canadian courts, like other common law courts, are wary of declaratory proceedings and have established certain rules of standing that must be met. Rules of standing are thought to be necessary to avoid a flood of litigation, to conserve judicial resources

---

18   *Reference Re Bill 30, An Act to Amend the Education Act (Ontario)* (1986), 53 O.R. (2d) 513 (C.A.).

19   *Reference Re Bill 30, An Act to Amend the Education Act (Ontario)*, [1987] 1 S.C.R. 1148, 40 D.L.R. (4th) 18.

and limit judicial power, and to ensure that constitutional disputes arise in the usual adversarial setting where only interested parties motivated to present strong arguments are represented. Ordinarily, a citizen must indicate a specific legal interest or right that is threatened by the statute challenged. However, the Canadian courts have also carved out generous exceptions to the rules of standing and have said that the courts have a discretion to permit a declaratory suit to proceed even where the plaintiff does not present the usual specific legal right or interest.[20] First, the citizen must demonstrate that the case raises a serious legal issue. Second, it must be shown that the citizen has some genuine interest in bringing the proceeding. Third, there must be no other reasonable or effective way to bring the issue before the court. Certain statutes do not specify penalties or other sanctions, or, if they do, it is unlikely that those who are subjected to such penalties or sanctions would challenge the statute. In these situations, a private citizen who lacks the usual special interest will be permitted to bring a declaratory proceeding. The underlying rationale to this exception to the standing rules is that no statute should be immune from judicial review. Despite this relaxed approach, the Supreme Court denied public-interest standing to an interest group to challenge the constitutionality of refugee procedures on the basis that individual refugee applicants were in a better position to bring challenges in individual cases.[21]

More recently, the Supreme Court held that an opponent of medical waiting lists, who had received operations in the public system, and a doctor who wanted to open a private hospital, had public interest standing to challenge a Quebec restriction on private health insurance. It was not reasonable to expect a person who was actually denied treatment because of a waiting list to bring the case because "the material, physical and emotional resources of individuals who are ill, and quite possibly dying, are likely to be focused on their own circumstances."[22]

Section 24(1) of the *Charter* has its own test for standing, which requires that "anyone whose rights or freedoms guaranteed by this *Char-*

---

20   *Thorson v. Canada (A.G.)*, [1975] 1 S.C.R. 138, 43 D.L.R. (3d) 1; *Nova Scotia Board of Censors v. McNeil*, [1976] 2 S.C.R. 265, 55 D.L.R. (3d) 632; *Borowski v. Canada (Minister of Justice)*, [1981] 2 S.C.R. 575, 130 D.L.R. (3d) 588; *Canadian Council of Churches v. Canada*, [1992] 1 S.C.R. 236, 88 D.L.R. (4th) 193 [*Canadian Council of Churches*]; *Hy and Zel's Inc. v. Ontario (Attorney General)*, [1993] 3 S.C.R. 675, 107 D.L.R. (4th) 634. For a general account of standing in Canadian law, see T.A. Cromwell, *Locus Standi* (Toronto: Carswell, 1986).

21   *Canadian Council of Churches*, ibid.

22   *Chaoulli v. Quebec (Attorney General)*, 2005 SCC 35 at para. 189, Binnie and LeBel JJ., in dissent but not on this point. See also para. 35, Deschamps J.

ter, have been infringed or denied" may apply for an appropriate and just remedy. The Supreme Court has interpreted this section to apply to apprehended violations of the *Charter* so that a person does not have to wait until his or her rights have been violated before obtaining a remedy.[23] At the same time, however, the Court has required that the person's own rights be at stake and have not granted an accused standing under section 24(1) to argue that police seizure of evidence violated the rights of a third party.[24]

Even if a person has been granted public interest standing or standing under section 24(1) of the *Charter*, *Charter* litigation is expensive. The majority of *Charter* cases that are decided by the Supreme Court arise in criminal cases. In such cases, the accused has every incentive to litigate a *Charter* issue and can generally obtain legal aid funding if he or she cannot afford to defend serious criminal charges and faces the risk of imprisonment. It may be more difficult to finance civil litigation, and a litigant who commences an action against the government also faces the downside risk of being liable for a portion of the successful party's costs should the litigant not prevail. The courts, however, have a discretion not to require an unsuccessful *Charter* litigant to pay the government's costs. The courts also have a discretion to award advance costs but have restricted this discretion to rare and exceptional cases where the party cannot afford to pay for litigation, where the claim is meritorious, and when the issues transcend the individual interests of the litigants and are of public importance. [25] Even when those conditions are satisfied, advance costs are only ordered as a "last resort"[26] and are not intended "to create a parallel system of legal-aid."[27]

Another issue that arises with some frequency in *Charter* litigation is whether the courts should decide a *Charter* issue that is "moot" because there is no longer a concrete dispute between the parties. The courts have a discretion to decide moot cases and the exercise of that discretion is influenced by factors similar to those used to decide whether to grant public-interest standing. These factors include the question of whether the case has been presented in an adversarial man-

---

23   *New Brunswick (Minister of Health and Community Services) v. G.(J.)*, [1999] 3 S.C.R. 46, 177 D.L.R. (4th) 124 at para. 51; *United States of America v. Kwok* (2001), 197 D.L.R. (4th) 1 at para. 66.

24   *R. v. Edwards*, [1996] 1 S.C.R. 128, 132 D.L.R. (4th) 31; *Benner v. Canada (Secretary of State)* (1997), 143 D.L.R. (4th) 577 at 604.

25   *Little Sisters Book and Art Emporium v Canada (Commissioner of Customs and Revenue)*, [2007] 1 S.C.R. 38 at para 37.

26   *Ibid.* at paras 73, 105.

27   *Ibid.* at para 5.

ner, judicial economy, relations with the executive and legislature, and the dangers of immunizing actions from review.[28] The last factor especially has been held to justify deciding a *Charter* issue that is moot, but that is "evasive of review" because the same issue is unlikely to come before the courts in a concrete form.[29]

D. THE SYSTEM OF COURTS AND JURISDICTION IN *CHARTER* CASES

As noted above, the general rule is that *Charter* issues are resolved in the ordinary course of litigation. The Supreme Court of Canada has rejected the proposition that the *Charter* itself confers jurisdiction to decide cases under either section 24(1) of the *Charter*, which contemplates courts awarding appropriate and just remedies, or section 52(1) of the *Constitution Act, 1982*, which provides that laws inconsistent with the *Charter* are of no force and effect. Accordingly, authority to decide a *Charter* issue turns on the pre-1982 court structure. In order to award a remedy under section 24(1) of the *Charter*, the court or administrative tribunal must have jurisdiction independent of the *Charter* over the parties, the subject matter, and the remedy.[30] In order to apply the *Charter*, an administrative body must generally have the power to decide questions of law.[31] The Supreme Court has recently taken a more generous approach to the ability of administrative bodies to apply the *Charter* and has indicated that a body with the explicit or implicit authority to decide questions of law should be able to apply the *Charter* in its decisions and decide whether its enabling legislation is consistent with the *Charter*. At the same time, all *Charter* decisions made by administrative bodies are reviewed by the superior courts on a correctness standard and only the superior courts have the power to

---

28 *Borowski v. Canada (Attorney General)*, [1989] 1 S.C.R. 342, 57 D.L.R. (4th) 231.

29 *New Brunswick (Minister of Health and Community Services) v. G.(J.)*, above note 23 at para. 45; *Doucet-Boudreau v. Nova Scotia (Minister of Education)*, [2003] 3 S.C.R. 3 at para. 20.

30 *R. v. Mills*, [1986] 1 S.C.R. 863, 29 D.L.R. (4th) 161 [*Mills*]; *R. v. 974649 Ontario Inc.*, [2001] 3 S.C.R. 575, 206 D.L.R. (4th) 444 [*Ontario Inc.*].

31 For decisions holding that various administrative bodies could not apply the *Charter*, see *Canada (Employment and Immigration Commission) v. Tétreault-Gadoury*, [1991] 2 S.C.R. 22, 81 D.L.R. (4th) 121 and *Cooper v. Canada (Human Rights Commission)*, [1996] 3 S.C.R. 854, 140 D.L.R. (4th) 193. For a general account of jurisdiction under s. 24(1) of the *Charter* and s. 52(1) of the *Constitution Act, 1982*, see K. Roach, *Constitutional Remedies in Canada* (Aurora, ON: Canada Law Book, 1994) c. 6.

make general declarations of constitutional invalidity that are binding on others.[32]

1) Provincial Courts

Each of the ten provinces has its own judicial system with trial courts and a Court of Appeal. At the trial level, provincial courts deal with minor criminal offences and also have jurisdiction over more serious offences with the consent of the accused. In addition, provincial courts deal with small civil claims and some family matters. The judges of these courts are appointed by the provincial governments. As many *Charter* issues arise in criminal cases, the provincial courts are often the court of first instance for a *Charter* challenge. However, because these courts are statutory and exercise only the jurisdiction that is specifically assigned to them, there are limits upon their authority to resolve *Charter* issues. For example, provincial court judges hearing preliminary inquiries, as opposed to trials, do not have jurisdiction to exclude unconstitutionally obtained evidence.[33] Provincial court judges in criminal courts also do not have jurisdiction to award damages as a section 24(1) *Charter* remedy, but they have been held to have jurisdiction to award costs as such a remedy.[34]

2) Superior Courts

The superior courts of each province exercise general and "inherent," or residual, jurisdiction over civil and criminal matters and play a special and constitutionally guaranteed role under the Canadian constitution. The judges of these courts are appointed by the federal government. Superior courts also possess the authority of judicial review with respect to administrative agencies and have some appellate jurisdiction over the provincial courts. The provincial superior courts have authority to apply both federal and provincial laws. They have "constant, complete and concurrent jurisdiction"[35] to hear requests for *Charter* remedies under section 24(1) of the *Charter*, as well as to hear challenges to the constitutional validity of all laws. Thus, it follows that the provincial

---

32 *Nova Scotia (Workers' Compensation Board) v. Martin*, [2003] 2 S.C.R. 504; *Okwuobi v. Lester Pearson School Board*, 2005 SCC 16; *Multani v. Commission scolaire Marguerite-Bourgeoys*, [2006] 1 S.C.R. 256.

33 *Mills*, above note 30; *R. v. Hynes*, [2001] 3 S.C.R. 623.

34 *Ontario Inc.*, above note 30.

35 *R. v. Rahey*, [1987] 1 S.C.R. 588, 39 D.L.R. (4th) 481 at 491.

superior courts have the broadest possible authority to decide *Charter* issues in the first instance.

3) Federal Court

The Federal Court of Canada has specific jurisdiction over certain matters that fall within federal legislative competence as enumerated by the division of powers. Yet it does not have inherent jurisdiction and there are strict limits on its jurisdiction.[36] The Federal Court has authority over federal administrative law as well as certain special subjects such as admiralty, intellectual property, and suits against the federal government. Given its jurisdiction over federal administrative law and suits against the federal government, many *Charter* issues are decided by the Federal Court. However, the provincial superior courts also have full jurisdiction with respect to the constitutionality of federal laws, including declaratory suits brought against the federal Crown.[37] Hence, the provincial superior courts retain a much broader jurisdiction than the Federal Court and play a more important role in the adjudication of *Charter* issues.

4) The Supreme Court of Canada

Appeals from judgments from the provincial courts and the provincial superior courts are taken to the provincial Court of Appeal, and from there to the Supreme Court of Canada. Appeals from the Federal Court, Trial Division, are taken to the Federal Court of Appeal, and then to the Supreme Court of Canada.

The Supreme Court of Canada, sitting at the top of the judicial hierarchy, is Canada's most important court. The common law doctrine of precedent or *stare decisis* makes its decisions binding upon all other courts. Accordingly, the Supreme Court exercises a considerable lawmaking role both in constitutional and in non-constitutional matters. The Supreme Court is seen, not only by lawyers and judges but also by the public at large, as one of our most important national institutions.

The high public profile of the Supreme Court is, however, a relatively recent phenomenon. The Court is not mentioned in the original 1867 constitution; indeed, despite an obscure and confusing reference to the

---

36   P.W. Hogg, "Comment" (1977) 55 Can. Bar Rev. 550; P.W. Hogg, "Federalism and the Jurisdiction of Canadian Courts" (1981) 30 U.N.B.L.J. 9; J.M. Evans, "Comment" (1981) 59 Can. Bar Rev. 124; B. Laskin & R.J. Sharpe, "Constricting Federal Court Jurisdiction" (1980) 30 U.T.L.J. 283.

37   *Jabour v. Law Society of British Columbia*, [1982] 2 S.C.R. 307, 137 D.L.R. (3d) 1; *Kourtessis v. M.N.R.*, [1993] 2 S.C.R. 53, 102 D.L.R. (4th) 456 at 496.

Court in the amending formula enacted in 1982,[38] the Court lacks formal status in the written constitution to this day. The Court was created by an Act of Parliament in 1875 pursuant to the power conferred upon Parliament by section 101 of the *Constitution Act, 1867*, to establish a general court of appeal for Canada.[39] At the time of the Court's establishment, there were many who thought it unnecessary since there already existed a supreme appellate authority for constitutional as well as non-constitutional issues, namely, the Judicial Committee of the Privy Council in England.[40] This body, consisting essentially of members of the English House of Lords, heard appeals from the colonial courts and, after the creation of the Dominion of Canada in 1867, entertained cases directly from the provincial courts of appeal. In the early years of Canada's history, it was thought that the establishment of the Supreme Court of Canada would merely add another costly and unnecessary level of appeal.

For a long time, the Supreme Court of Canada was supreme in name only: the Judicial Committee of the Privy Council functioned as Canada's highest appellate court until 1949 when appeals to the Privy Council were abolished. This body of English judges had an important influence upon the evolution of the Canadian constitution, and its judgments remain significant today. The Privy Council established the principles of interpretation of Canada's federal structure and, throughout Canadian history, many have argued that its judgments unduly favoured provincial interests to the detriment of a strong and effective central government.[41]

---

38   The *Constitution Act, 1982*, s. 41(d) provides that amendments to the constitution in relation to "the composition of the Supreme Court of Canada" require the unanimous consent of the federal Parliament and the provincial legislatures, while s. 42(1)(d) provides that other amendments in relation to the Court fall under the usual formula (federal Parliament and at least seven provinces having at least 50 percent of the population of all the provinces). For varying views as to the effect of these provisions, see P.W. Hogg, *Canada Act 1982 Annotated* (Toronto: Carswell, 1982) at 92–94; Strayer, above note 2 at 30–31; R.I. Cheffins, "The *Constitution Act, 1982* and the Amending Formula: Political and Legal Implications" (1982) 4 Sup. Ct. L. Rev. 43 at 53; W.R. Lederman, "Constitutional Procedure and Reform of the Supreme Court of Canada" (1985) 26 Cahiers de Droit 195.

39   For the history of the Supreme Court, see J.G. Snell & F. Vaughan, *The Supreme Court of Canada: History of the Institution* (Toronto: University of Toronto Press, 1985).

40   See G. Bale, *Chief Justice William Johnstone Ritchie: Responsible Government and Judicial Review* (Ottawa: Carleton University Press, 1990).

41   See, for example, B. Laskin, "Peace, Order and Good Government Re-Examined" (1947) 25 Can. Bar Rev. 1054. Compare, however, A.C. Cairns, "The Judicial Committee and Its Critics" (1971) 4 Can. J. Pol. Sci. 301.

An important step in the evolution of the Supreme Court of Canada to its present status occurred in 1975 when an amendment to the *Supreme Court Act* gave the Court control over the cases it hears. Most appeals as of right to the Court were abolished, and a leave-to-appeal procedure was introduced whereby the Court is able to screen cases and permit only those cases with national importance to proceed. This change has permitted the Court to focus its efforts on those cases that have the most legal and public significance. It has altered the role of the Supreme Court from that of error correction to one of law making.[42]

The final significant step in the evolution of the Supreme Court of Canada occurred in 1982 with the enactment of the *Charter of Rights and Freedoms*. As noted in chapter 1, the *Charter* significantly increased the scope for judicial review and brought the Supreme Court of Canada into public prominence.

a) Composition of the Court and Appointment of Judges

The composition of the Supreme Court is fixed by the *Supreme Court Act*. The Court consists of nine judges. The *Supreme Court Act*, section 6, requires that three of the nine judges be appointed from the judges or bar of the province of Quebec. This provision is designed to ensure that there are at least three judges trained in Quebec's distinctive civil law tradition. By practice or convention, there are ordinarily three judges from Ontario, as it is Canada's most populous province, one judge from the eastern provinces, and two judges from the western provinces. A quorum of the Court is five judges but it is usual for the Court to have all nine judges sit on important cases.

The office of chief justice usually, but not invariably, alternates between an English- and French-speaking judge. The chief justice has important public and administrative responsibilities, including the assignment of judges to each case. However, in terms of the Court's decisions, the chief justice has no special authority and exercises the usual functions of a justice of the Court, sitting on cases and voting as any other judge.

The qualifications for appointment to the Court are specified in section 5 of the *Supreme Court Act*. One must be a judge of a superior court or a barrister of ten years' standing. The same qualification is specified by the *Judges Act* for appointment to the superior and provincial appellate courts.[43] Most Supreme Court judges have had prior judicial

---

42   See R. J. Sharpe & K. Roach, *Brian Dickson: A Judge's Journey* (Toronto: University of Toronto Press, 2003) cc. 7 & 8.

43   *Judges Act*, R.S.C. 1985, c. J-1, s. 3.

experience. It is not unusual, however, for one or more of the judges to have been appointed directly from the bar and to have no prior judicial experience. In recent years, academics have frequently been appointed to the Court. The *Supreme Court Act* also provides (section 9) that judges of the Court hold office until reaching the age of seventy-five.

Judges of the Supreme Court of Canada and of the superior courts are appointed by the federal cabinet on the advice of the minister of justice. In the case of Supreme Court appointments, it has become the practice for the prime minister to make the appointments. Most observers recognize that the quality of individuals appointed to the Court has been high, but the secretive nature of Supreme Court appointments has come under increasing criticism.[44] It is felt by many critics that the public should have some prior knowledge of the background and abilities of the candidates. Provincial governments have long complained that it is unfair for the federal government to have the exclusive decision with respect to appointments since the Supreme Court acts as the referee in disputes between the federal government and the provinces. Had constitutional amendments proposed in the Meech Lake and Charlottetown packages been enacted, the federal government would have been obliged to select Supreme Court justices from lists supplied by the provinces.

While it is unlikely that Canada would ever adopt the American practice of confirmation hearings whereby nominees to the Court are subjected to lengthy partisan questioning, it seems inevitable that demands for a less secretive and more open process will grow.[45] The federal government has also come under increasing pressure to appoint more women and members of cultural and ethnic minorities to the bench, an experience shared by provincial governments in their sphere of judicial appointments. Though this pressure stems partly from changing demographics and social attitudes, it is undoubtedly tied as well to the enhanced power of the courts in the *Charter* era. Since the *Charter* requires the courts to decide important public-policy issues, it is thought

---

44 See D.M. Beatty, *Talking Heads and the Supremes: The Canadian Production of Constitutional Review* (Toronto: Carswell, 1990).

45 For an interesting proposal, see M.L. Friedland, *A Place Apart: Judicial Independence and Accountability in Canada* (Ottawa: Canadian Judicial Council, 1995) at 256–57. Appointments to the provincial superior courts are now made after candidates have been privately reviewed by committees of senior judges, lawyers, and lay people. In some provinces, appointments to the provincial bench are made after a similar process that involves lay participation. For discussion, see Ontario Law Reform Commission, *Appointing Judges: Philosophy, Politics and Practice* (Toronto, 1991).

in many quarters that a diversity of backgrounds among judges is necessary to ensure that judicial decisions reflect a wide range of values.

In 2004, the minister of justice appeared before an *ad hoc* committee of members of Parliament, one representative of the Canadian Judicial Council, and one representative of the relevant provincial law society to discuss the qualifications of two appointments to the Supreme Court. He has subsequently proposed a four-stage process for appointments to the Supreme Court. First, the minister of justice would compile an initial list of candidates after consulting with the relevant provincial attorney general, chief justices, and law societies. Next, an advisory committee with members of Parliament from various parties, a retired judge, a provincial representative, a representative of the relevant law society, and two lay members would prepare an unranked short list of three candidates. The advisory committee would consult widely, but not interview the candidates. Third, the prime minister would make a selection that would, in all but exceptional circumstances, come from the short list. Finally, the minister of justice would appear before the parliamentary justice committee to explain the process and qualifications of the appointee.[46]

In 2006, the government accepted a three-person short list prepared by a committee initiated under the previous government. The prime minister selected Justice Rothstein from that list and Justice Rothstein was subject to a public three-hour interview by an *ad hoc* committee chaired by the minister of justice and including members of Parliament from all major parties. The hearing was generally viewed as successful with parliamentarians understanding that it would not be appropriate to ask Justice Rothstein how he would decide particular cases. A few days after this process in which Justice Rothstein was asked about sixty questions, the prime minister appointed him to join the Court.[47] A different process was used with respect to the appointment of the next justice. The government proposed to submit a initial list of candidates to a five-person selection panel composed of two government members of Parliament and three from each of the opposition parties. This process was, however, halted because of opposition objections to the composition of the selection panel. The government announced that Justice Cromwell would be the nominee. It was proposed that Justice Cromwell, like Justice Rothstein, would answer questions from an ad hoc all party committee of members of the House of Commons before his official appointment. This public hearing was not held,

---

46   Minister of Justice, *Proposal to Reform the Supreme Court of Canada Appointments Process* (Ottawa: Department of Justice Canada, April 2005).

47   Peter Hogg "Appointment of Justice Rothstein to the Supreme Court of Canada" (2006) 44 Osgoode Hall L.J. 527.

however, because of the prorogation of Parliament. Justice Cromwell was appointed by the prime minister to the Court in January, 2009, six months after the retirement of Justice Bastarache.[48] The new appointment process remains in a state of flux and it remains to be seen whether the appropriate balance has been struck among parliamentary input, provincial input, transparency, merit, diversity, non-partisanship, and judicial independence in selecting members of the Supreme Court.

b) The Hearing of Appeals

The Supreme Court of Canada hears about eighty appeals each year.[49] In addition, it receives about 600 applications for leave to appeal. Approximately thirty-five percent of the cases heard by the Court are criminal, while the remaining sixty-five percent are civil. The Court exercises important jurisdiction in private law, but it has become predominantly a public law court with *Charter* and constitutional cases constituting a significant portion of the civil or private law appeals.

The Supreme Court receives the full record of the proceedings in the lower courts, including all of the evidence led at trial and all judgments rendered in the case. The parties present written argument, ordinarily limited to forty pages, and they are afforded one hour each for oral argument. The procedure is adversarial, in keeping with the common law tradition.

After the presentation of oral arguments, all deliberations of the Court are confidential until the judgment is released. Following the oral argument, the Court retires to a conference of all the judges sitting on the case. Each judge presents his or her view of the case, until recently commencing with the most junior judge. The chief justice assigns the task of preparing the first opinion to one of the judges who is in the majority. The first opinion is circulated among the judges sitting on the case and each judge either agrees with the opinion as drafted or prepares concurring or dissenting reasons. It has become increasingly apparent that law clerks, recent law school graduates who serve for a period of one year with the justices, play an important role in doing background research and assisting in the preparation of the final opinions. The Court publishes all opinions, including dissents, and dissenting opinions not infrequently provide the foundation for future developments in the jurisprudence. When all judges sitting on the case

---

48 Peter Hogg, "The Appointment of Justice Cromwell to the Supreme Court of Canada" (2009) Sup. Ct. L. Rev. (2d) (forthcoming).

49 Statistics on the work of the Court are published regularly in the Supreme Court *Bulletin*.

have signed an opinion, the judgment of the Court is released to the parties and to the public in both English and French.

E. CONCLUSION

Charter cases are essentially dealt with in the same manner as any other litigation. It is apparent, however, that *Charter* issues pose special challenges for our courts. Special procedural rules relating to standing and intervention by attorneys general and interested groups reflect the public significance of *Charter* rulings.

The role of judges in dealing with complex social issues under the *Charter* has altered the mandate of our courts and resulted in increased public scrutiny of the judicial process. The method of appointing judges has come under particular criticism. Many observers have asked whether the traditional approach is adequate, especially for the selection of those who sit on our highest court. Though rarely, if ever, is exception taken to particular appointments, it may be expected that there will be continuing pressure to have a more open appointments process.

FURTHER READINGS

HOGG, P.W., *Constitutional Law of Canada*, 5th ed. (Toronto: Carswell, 2007) Part IV cc. 55–57

LAMBERT, N., "The *Charter* in the Administrative Process: Statutory Remedy or Refounding of Administrative Jurisdiction?" (2007) 13 Rev. Const. Stud. 21–65

MULLAN, D., "Administrative Tribunals and Judicial Review of *Charter* Issues after *Multani*" (2006–2007) 21 N.J.C.L. 127–49

PILKINGTON, M., "Enforcing the *Charter*: The Supervisory Role of Superior Courts and the Responsibility of Legislatures for Remedial Systems" (2004) 25 Sup. Ct. L. Rev. (2d) 77

ROACH, K., *Constitutional Remedies in Canada* (Aurora, ON: Canada Law Book, 1994)

SHARPE, R.J., ed., *Charter Litigation* (Toronto: Butterworths, 1986)

STRAYER, B.L., *The Canadian Constitution and the Courts: The Function and Scope of Judicial Review*, 3d ed. (Toronto: Butterworths, 1988)

CHAPTER 8

FREEDOM OF CONSCIENCE AND RELIGION

Freedom of religion was recognized by the courts as an important value of Canadian society long before the enactment of the *Charter of Rights and Freedoms*, but it could only be protected indirectly through the interpretation of statutes and the enforcement of the division of powers. In particular, the inability of provinces to enact criminal laws led to the striking down of some laws that had discriminatory effects against religious minorities.[1] The Supreme Court has recognized that "an important feature of our constitutional democracy is respect for minorities, which includes, of course, religious minorities. Indeed respect for and tolerance of the rights and practices of religious minorities is one of the hallmarks of an enlightened democracy."[2]

Section 2(a) of the *Charter* now provides that "freedom of conscience and religion" is a fundamental right of all Canadians. Although the *Charter* respects every individual's freedom of conscience and religion as a necessary element of personal dignity, autonomy, and self-development, this does not mean that it offers protection to all actions dictated by religious belief. Can the state prevent religious practices, such as female circumcision, which are regarded by the majority as harmful? Does the state have a positive duty to provide funding for religious schools or to make special allowances for the construction of places of worship? Does section 2(a) protect only the right to hold beliefs, or does it include

---

1   *Saumur v. Quebec*, [1953] 2 S.C.R. 299, [1953] 4 D.L.R. 641, discussed in chapter 1.
2   *Syndicat Northcrest v. Amselem*, [2004] 2 S.C.R. 551 at para. 1 [*Syndicat Northcrest*].

the right to express those beliefs, free from state interference? What should be done when religious beliefs clash with other *Charter* values, for example, equality and freedom from discrimination on issues such as same-sex marriage? As with the other *Charter* rights, the courts have had to determine the scope of the right to freedom of conscience and religion guaranteed by section 2(a), the proper approach to reconciling freedom of conscience and religion with other *Charter* rights, and the range of acceptable limitations under section 1.

Freedom of religion protects individual autonomy, freedom, and dignity. The Supreme Court has articulated the purpose of freedom of religion as related to the ability of every individual to "be free to hold and to manifest whatever beliefs and opinions his or her conscience dictates, provided *inter alia* only that such manifestations do not injure his or her neighbours or their parallel rights to hold and manifest beliefs and opinions of their own."[3] It has elaborated that "the purpose of section 2(a) is to ensure that society does not interfere with profoundly personal beliefs that govern one's perception of oneself, humankind, nature, and in some cases, a higher or different order of being. These beliefs, in turn, govern one's conduct and practices."[4]

The Supreme Court has recently endorsed "a personal or subjective conception of freedom of religion, one that is integrally linked with an individual's self-definition and fulfillment and is a function of personal autonomy and choice, elements which undergird the right."[5] The subjective approach to freedom of religion means that the emphasis is on the sincerity of a person's subjective claim of belief and not whether a particular practice objectively fits into an official religion. In other words,

> Freedom of religion consists of the freedom to undertake practices and harbour beliefs, having a nexus with religion, in which an individual demonstrates that he or she sincerely believes or is sincerely undertaking in order to connect with the divine or as a function of his or her spiritual faith, irrespective of whether a particular practice or belief is required by official religious dogma or is in conformity with the position of religious officials.[6]

At the same time, freedom of religion also applies to "the right to manifest religious belief by worship, teaching, dissemination and religious

---

3   *R. v. Big M Drug Mart Ltd.*, [1985] 1 S.C.R. 295, 18 D.L.R. (4th) 321 at 346 (S.C.R.) [*Big M Drug Mart*].

4   *Edwards Books & Art Ltd. v. R.*, [1986] 2 S.C.R. 713, 35 D.L.R. (4th) 1 at 759 (S.C.R.) [*Edwards Books*].

5   *Syndicat Northcrest*, above note 2 at para. 42.

6   *Ibid.* at para. 46.

practice . . . . The practice of religious rites is a fundamental aspect of religious practice."[7]

As an initial matter, the *Charter* applicant must establish a sincere practice or belief that, for the applicant, is subjectively connected with the divine or his or her spiritual faith and that the impugned action interferes with his or her ability to act in accordance with his or her religious beliefs in a manner that is more than trivial or insubstantial. Once such a violation is established, the onus is on the state under section 1 of the *Charter* to justify the limitation on freedom of religion as reasonable and demonstrably justifiable. The Court has added that "no right, including freedom of religion is absolute . . . This is so because we live in a society of individuals in which we must always take the rights of others into account."[8]

A. SUNDAY CLOSING LAWS

Sunday closing laws may be characterized as having a religious purpose. Their origins lie, at least in part, in the desire to protect against the profanation of the Christian Sabbath and to maintain Sunday as a holy day. Over time, however, Sunday closing laws have also taken on a secular purpose, that of providing workers with a day of rest or a "pause day." From this perspective, Sunday was chosen not because of its religious significance but because it historically has been a day without work. On the other hand, even if there is a secular purpose behind Sunday closing laws, they do impose burdens on those who observe another day of rest for religious reasons.

R. v. Big M Drug Mart,[9] a case dealing with the constitutionality of the federal *Lord's Day Act* prohibition of Sunday shopping, was the Supreme Court's first decision on the *Charter* guarantee of freedom of religion. As a corporate entity, the drug store could not claim a right to freedom of religion for itself, but, since it had been prosecuted, it was allowed to challenge the constitutionality of the *Lord's Day Act* on the theory that no one should be prosecuted under an unconstitutional law.

The distribution of powers between federal and provincial governments in the Canadian federal system allows the federal Parliament to enact laws designed to protect religion and to prevent profanation of the Sabbath. The *Lord's Day Act* was enacted pursuant to this authority to legislate with respect to the criminal law under section 91(27) of the

---

7 *Reference Re Same-Sex Marriage,* [2004] 3 S.C.R. 698 at para. 57.
8 *Syndicat Northcrest,* above note 2 at para. 61.
9 *Big M Drug Mart,* above note 3.

Constitution Act, 1867. The federal Parliament does not, however, have jurisdiction to enact Sunday closing laws with a secular purpose. Legislation of that kind falls within the general provincial jurisdiction under section 92(13) over "property and civil rights," which includes labour relations and regulation of business within the province. Accordingly, any attempt to justify the *Lord's Day Act* as having a secular "day of rest" purpose would make it vulnerable to a finding of invalidity on federalism grounds. As a result, the federal *Lord's Day Act* was held to have the purpose of promoting observance of the Christian Sabbath.

Writing for the majority, Dickson J. took the opportunity to interpret the guarantee broadly, as protecting not only the right to hold religious beliefs but also the right to express beliefs through observance, teaching, and practice. The state would violate an individual's freedom if it coerced religious observance. In his words,

> [F]reedom means that, subject to such limitations as are necessary to protect public safety, order, health, or morals or the fundamental rights and freedoms of others, no one is to be forced to act in a way contrary to his beliefs or his conscience.[10]

Dickson J. concluded that the *Lord's Day Act* was coercive in nature because its purpose was to compel universal observance of the Christian Sabbath:

> Non-Christians are prohibited for religious reasons from carrying out activities which are otherwise lawful, moral and normal. The arm of the State requires all to remember the Lord's day of the Christians and to keep it holy. The protection of one religion and the concomitant non-protection of others imports disparate impact destructive of the religious freedom of the collectivity.[11]

In reaching this conclusion, Dickson J. referred to section 27 of the *Charter,* which requires that the document be interpreted in a manner "consistent with the preservation and enhancement of the multicultural heritage of Canadians." The preferred position of the Christian religion under the *Lord's Day Act* was seen as undermining respect for the religions of other groups in Canadian society.

The government's attempt to defend the legislation as a reasonable limit under section 1 of the *Charter* was unsuccessful. Given that the law was enacted under the federal power over the criminal law in order to enforce the Christian Sabbath, it was impossible for the federal government to establish a valid legislative objective. The result was a di-

---

10   *Ibid.* at 337 (S.C.R.).
11   *Ibid.*

lemma fatal to the law. Its purpose for the division-of-powers analysis, the protection of the majority's religion, was repugnant to the *Charter*'s protection of religious freedom for the minority. The law could not be defended as a worker-protection law, since that purpose would render it invalid on federalism grounds.

In light of the religious foundation of the law, *Big M Drug Mart* was not a particularly difficult case. More troublesome for the Supreme Court was the next Sunday closing case, *Edwards Books*.[12] This case involved Ontario legislation, secular in purpose, which was enacted to give retail workers a day of rest. The law made a concession to those who, for religious reasons, observed a different day of rest. It contained an exemption from the requirement that retail businesses close on Sundays if a store had closed the previous Saturday, had seven or fewer employees, and was smaller than 5,000 square feet.

On its face, the legislation did not require religious observance. However, in *Big M Drug Mart*, the Supreme Court had stated that rights could be infringed under the *Charter* not only by legislation whose purpose was to infringe the right but also by laws that had the effect of interfering with the right. Not every burden on the practice of religion will constitute a *Charter* violation. The Court had said that a *Charter* breach will be made out only where the burden is more than trivial and insubstantial.[13] However, many apparently "neutral" laws—that is, laws enacted for a perfectly proper reason unrelated to religion—may run afoul of the *Charter* guarantee because of their impact on religious practice.

In *Edwards Books*, five judges concluded that the effect of the closing law interfered with freedom of religion. For Dickson C.J.C. and the majority of the Supreme Court, the problem was the impact of Sunday closing on those whose day of worship was Saturday (for example, those of the Jewish or Seventh Day Adventist faiths). Retailers whose holy day was Sunday were able to close their establishments and observe that day without any financial disadvantage. Saturday observers were faced with a dilemma: they could close Saturday, as required by their religion, but they would suffer a financial loss as a result. Alternatively, faced with the burden imposed by the law requiring them to close on Sunday, they might feel pressured to open on their holy day. Dickson C.J.C. found that the Sunday closing law was not neutral in its effect. It put Saturday observers at a disadvantage compared to Sunday observers who enjoyed statutory protection for their holy day. This financial burden was found to violate freedom of religion.

---

12 *Edwards Books*, above note 4.
13 *Jones v. R.*, [1986] 2 S.C.R. 284, 31 D.L.R. (4th) 569 [*Jones*], discussed below.

In dissent, Beetz J. concluded that there was no interference with freedom of religion. In his view, when an individual closed a store on Saturdays to observe his or her faith, the cause of the closure was the individual's religious beliefs, not any action by the state. The fact that Sunday observers might get a financial advantage from the Sunday closing law did not affect the *Charter* claim. For Beetz J., it was telling that, if the Sunday closing law was repealed, the Saturday observers (as well as the Sunday observers) would still be at a business disadvantage in relation to the non-observant retailer who could open any day, while religious individuals would choose not to work. This, he thought, proved that it was religious belief that caused the decision to close and the consequent loss of income on Saturday, and that the Sunday closing law did not interfere with freedom of religion.

While the majority concluded that the section 2(a) guarantee of freedom of religion was violated, the law was upheld under section 1 of the *Charter*, Wilson J. dissenting.[14] The judges were split as to why the law was justified. In Dickson C.J.C.'s view (supported by two other judges), the exemption given to small retailers who observed Saturday was necessary to sustain the validity of the Act under section 1. He found that the state was justified in trying to protect a pause day for vulnerable workers in the retail industry. Further, he found that it was not necessary, under the *Oakes* minimal-impairment test, to require that all retailers close. Small retailers could be allowed to open, without undue interference with their employees' interests or the general nature of the pause day. La Forest J. held that no exemption was needed, since any effort to provide an exemption would create problems in enforcing the legislation and could undermine the protection of employees. He concluded that the courts should defer to the legislatures of the various provinces and allow them to determine whether they wanted to provide an exemption or not, and, if so, how to structure it.

Wilson J. dissented on the basis that the exemption for only some Saturday observers and not others was an unprincipled decision that did not satisfy the *Oakes* test. If religious freedom was important and deserving of *Charter* protection for some members of a religious group, there was no reason, in her view, that it should not be provided for all members of that group.

The debate in *Edwards Books* may seem dated today, given the current widespread adoption of Sunday shopping in Canada. However, the issues remain significant for challenges to statutory holidays such as Christmas Day, Good Friday, and Easter Sunday. The requirement of re-

---

14   The importance of the *Edwards Books* s. 1 analysis is considered in chapter 4.

tail closure on such days seems rooted in Christian tradition, although the argument will be made that these holidays now have a largely secular basis in the minds of many.

B. ACCOMMODATION OF RELIGION

In *Syndicat Northcrest v. Amselem*,[15] the Supreme Court dealt with whether Orthodox Jews could construct a succah, a temporary structure on their balconies, in order to observe the nine-day festival of Succot even though they had signed a contract prohibiting constructions on their balconies and they were offered an alternative of a communal succah. They relied on freedom of religion under the Quebec *Charter of Human Rights and Freedoms*,[16] which, unlike the Canadian *Charter*, applies to private conduct. The Supreme Court nevertheless indicated that its analysis of freedom of religion would also apply to the Canadian *Charter*.

The Court divided 5 to 4 on whether freedom of religion had been violated by the prohibition on balcony constructions and on whether any violation was justified. Iacobucci J. held for the majority that, assuming that freedom of religion could be waived, there had not been a voluntary or clear and express waiver of rights when the applicants signed the co-ownership agreement prohibiting constructions on balconies. He also concluded that there was a violation of freedom of religion and that it had not been justified. He held that a trial judge who had granted a permanent injunction against the construction of the succahs had erred in finding no violation of freedom of religion on the basis of the testimony of one Rabbi over another Rabbi about the objective and mandatory requirements of the Jewish religion. Iacobucci J. warned that the proper focus was on the subjective, personal, and sincere beliefs of the applicants and that courts should not adjudicate questions of religious doctrine or obligations. He also indicated that "beliefs and observances evolve and change over time" for individuals and that their subjective distress at having to use a communal succah should be considered as it made the violation of freedom of religion more than trivial or insubstantial.[17]

The Court then found that the limitation of freedom of religion in order to protect the property interests of other residents in the balconies was not justified, especially given that the succahs were only con-

---

15   Above note 2.
16   R.S.Q., c. C-12.
17   *Syndicat Northcrest*, above note 2 at para. 71.

structed for nine days each year. It recognized that "security concerns, if soundly established would require appropriate recognition in ascertaining any limit on the exercise of the appellants' religious freedom."[18] The majority indicated that in this case the succahs could and should be constructed not to block any doors or fire lanes. The majority's decision in this case indicates that the courts will take a broad and generous approach to the protection of religious freedom that focuses on the subjective beliefs of adherents and that the state will have to satisfy a demanding and rigorous test for justifying limits on religion freedom.

Four judges dissented from the majority's finding of an unjustified violation of freedom of religion. Bastarache J., with the concurrence of LeBel and Deschamps JJ., concluded that there was no violation of freedom of religion. He did not accept that the appellants had a sincere belief, one based on religious precepts, that they were required to erect their own succahs and found that "it is their practice of eating or celebrating Succot that is protected by the guarantee of freedom of religion .... The declaration of co-ownership does not hinder this practice, as it does not bar the appellants from celebrating Succot in a succah, whether at the homes of friends or family or even in a communal succah, as proposed by the respondent."[19] Even if one of the appellants did sincerely believe that he was required to construct his own succah, Bastarache J. held that the compromise of a communal succah was reasonable given the need to respect the property and safety rights of others. Binnie J. also dissented, but on the more limited basis that the appellants had contractually committed themselves to a neutral restriction on all changes to the exterior of the units and that there was "a vast difference . . . between using freedom of religion as a shield against interference with religious freedom by the State and as a sword against co-contractors in a private building."[20]

In *Congrégation des témoins de Jéhovah de St.-Jérôme-Lafontaine v. Lafontaine (Village)*,[21] the Supreme Court dealt with a municipality's repeated refusal to amend zoning bylaws to allow the Jehovah's Witnesses to construct a place of worship. The majority of the Court decided the case in the favour of the Jehovah's Witnesses on non-*Charter* grounds by ruling that the municipality had acted unfairly by providing no reasons for its refusal to amend the zoning bylaw. LeBel J., with the concurrence of Major, Bastarache, and Deschamps JJ., dissented and would have upheld the municipality's decision. The dissent raises, but does not resolve,

18   *Ibid.* at para. 88.
19   *Ibid.* at para. 162.
20   *Ibid.* at para. 185.
21   [2004] 2 S.C.R. 650.

the issue of whether and when the state has a positive obligation under the *Charter* to accommodate the exercise of religion. LeBel J. concluded that there was no infringement of freedom of religion because the by-laws allowed at least one lot for the construction of a place of worship in the municipality, and freedom of religion did not include an absolute freedom to select the location for a place of worship. Moreover, a zoning bylaw amendment to allow the Jehovah's Witnesses to construct a place of worship might have been incompatible with the municipality's duty "to be neutral in matters of religion."[22] LeBel J. added, "for the sake of discussion only,"[23] that freedom of religion would have been violated had no lots whatsoever been available in the municipality for the construction of a Kingdom Hall by the Jehovah's Witnesses. In such a hypothetical case, it would have been impossible for the Jehovah's Witnesses to practise their religion and the zoning bylaws would have directly interfered with freedom of religion, requiring the municipality to take positive action by amending its zoning bylaws.

In *Alberta v. Hutterian Brethren of Wilson Colony*,[24] the Supreme Court indicated that there are clear limits on the extent to which laws will be struck down for imposing indirect costs or burdens on religious beliefs. At issue was an Alberta regulation requiring all holders of a driver's licence to be digitally photographed. It was conceded that the photo requirement interfered with the Hutterian sincerely held religious belief against being photographed. The Supreme Court held, however, that the regulation was justified under section 1. The Court accepted that the purpose of the photo requirement — to protect the integrity of the licensing scheme and to guard against identity theft — was an objective of sufficient importance to warrant overriding a *Charter* right. The Court also agreed that the government had demonstrated that the regulation was rationally connected to that objective. The claimants argued that given their small numbers, the government should have exempted them from the scheme and that failure to do so failed the minimal impairment test. Writing for the majority, McLachlin C.J.C. rejected that contention on the ground that allowing for exemptions would destroy the one-to-one correspondence between issued licences and photos in the data bank and that this would significantly undermine the government's objective of guarding against the use of drivers' licences as a tool for identity theft. Where the validity of a law is at stake and accommodating a religious belief would significantly compromise the govern-

---

22   *Ibid.* at para. 71.
23   *Ibid.* at para. 72.
24   2009 SCC 37.

ment's objective, the majority held that accommodation is not required. The crucial phase of the proportionality test was the third stage, weighing the proportionality of effects: were the overall effects of the law on the claimants' rights disproportionate to the government's objective? The impugned law did not force Hutterites to be photographed or compel any religious practice or observance, but rather indirectly imposed a cost or burden on the claimants who had to choose between following the dictates of their religion and holding a driver's licence. McLachlin C.J.C. held that while the *Charter* guarantees freedom of religion, it "does not indemnify practitioners against all costs incident to the practice of religion."[25] In a multicultural, multi-religious society, "the duty of state authorities to legislate for the general good inevitably produces conflicts with individual beliefs"[26] and the resulting cost or burden on those who chose to follow the dictates of their religion will not always outweigh the salutary effect of the impugned law. Here, those who refused to be photographed for religious reasons could arrange alternate means of transportation and, as the salutary effect of the law would be significantly undermined by granting exemptions, the majority found that Alberta had satisfied the third stage of proportionality review.

C. PARENTAL RIGHTS

Freedom of religion has been an issue in a number of cases involving the family and parental rights. For example, in *B.(R.)*,[27] parents of the Jehovah's Witness religion refused to allow their infant child to undergo a blood transfusion thought by doctors to be required to save the child's life. When the Children's Aid Society brought an application to take the child into care to ensure that she could be given necessary treatment, the parents argued that this application violated their freedom of religion. The Supreme Court of Canada upheld the order placing the child under the protection of the Society. Five of the judges agreed that the parents' right to freedom of religion was violated, concluding that the guarantee protected religious beliefs even if those beliefs could harm another. However, the limitation on the parents' rights was justified under section 1 in order to protect the child. In contrast, four judges argued that the guarantee of freedom of religion should not extend to conduct endangering the life or seriously endangering the health of the child.

---

25   *Ibid.* at para. 95.
26   *Ibid.* at para. 90.
27   *B.(R.) v. Children's Aid Society of Metropolitan Toronto*, [1995] 1 S.C.R. 315, 122 D.L.R. (4th) 1 [*B.(R.)*].

Similarly, in *A.C. v. Manitoba (Director of Child and Family Services)*[28] the Court upheld legislation authorizing a court to order treatment of a child under sixteen years old where the treatment is in the best interests of the child. Properly interpreted, the "best interests" standard reflected the adolescent's maturity and developing autonomy interest and, where the court is satisfied that the adolescent is capable of making a mature and independent decision, greater weight must be given to the adolescent's views when deciding whether or not to order treatment.

This case followed an earlier pair of decisions dealing with restrictions on parents' rights to discuss religion with their children as a condition of access to their children following marriage breakdown. In *Young v. Young*,[29] the trial judge had given custody of the children to the mother and permitted access to the father. However, the order had forbidden the father, a Jehovah's Witness, from taking his children to religious services or on his proselytizing activities or from commenting unfavourably on the mother's religion. This restriction was overturned by the British Columbia Court of Appeal as violating section 2(a). The Supreme Court of Canada, by a narrow majority, agreed that the father should not be forbidden from discussing his religion with his children. By this time, he had promised not to take them to services or to involve them in proselytizing. The majority reasoning noted that custody and access decisions are made on the basis of the "best interests of the child." Where a parent's religious beliefs are harmful to a child, the best-interests test will apply to protect the child from those beliefs. In the Court's view, there would be no *Charter* violation associated with such a determination, since the right to freedom of religion does not permit one to harm another. In light of the father's promises with respect to services and proselytizing, it was found that the children would not be harmed by discussions about his religious beliefs.

D. RELIGION AND EDUCATION

Another area of controversy under section 2(a) has been with respect to religion and education. There are a number of issues that arise: the extent to which there is room for religious instruction and practice in the public school system, the right of parents to withdraw their children

---

28   2009 SCC 30, also discussed in chapter 13.
29   [1993] 4 S.C.R. 3, 108 D.L.R. (4th) 193. In *P.(D.) v. S.(C.)*, [1993] 4 S.C.R. 141, 108 D.L.R. (4th) 287, the majority upheld a condition of access forbidding the father to indoctrinate the child in the Jehovah's Witness religion, although he was allowed to teach her about religion.

from public schools for religious reasons, the extent of the state's obligation to fund independent religious schools, and the reconciliation of freedom of religion with other *Charter* rights and freedoms.

1) School Prayer and Religious Instruction

The Supreme Court of Canada has not dealt directly with the issue of the role of religion in the public school system. However, two important decisions of the Ontario Court of Appeal struck down provincial laws and regulations requiring school prayer and religious education in public schools. In *Zylberberg*,[30] the Court dealt with a requirement that public schools open with religious exercises consisting of the reading of scripture or other suitable works and the repeating of the Lord's Prayer or other suitable prayers. The regulations provided that a pupil could be excused from participating if his or her parent requested this. The province defended the legislation on the basis that there was no denial of freedom of religion, given the right to claim an exemption. The majority of the Court of Appeal disagreed. It found that the requirement of prayers and scripture reading violated the rights of both Christians and non-Christians by compelling religious observance. The right to claim an exemption did not negate the coercive quality of the regime, for the reality was that members of minority religions or those opposed to the practices felt pressured to conform. Indeed, the exemption provisions were described as imposing a penalty on religious minorities, "stigmatizing them as non-conforming."[31]

A similar result was reached in a subsequent case involving religious education.[32] Ontario legislation and regulations required two one-half-hour periods of religious instruction in each week in public schools, although, again, children could be exempted. While the regulations provided that issues of a controversial or sectarian nature were to be avoided, the curriculum in Elgin County was delivered by members of a local Bible club and clergy, with the result that the instruction had a strong evangelical Christian tone. Again, the Ontario Court of Appeal concluded that the curriculum was a form of religious indoctrination,

---

30   *Zylberberg v. Sudbury Board of Education (Director)* (1988), 52 D.L.R. (4th) 577 (Ont. C.A.).

31   *Ibid.* at 592. See also at 591: "The peer pressure and the class-room norms to which children are acutely sensitive, in our opinion, are real and pervasive and operate to compel members of religious minorities to conform with majority religious practices."

32   *Canadian Civil Liberties Assn. v. Ontario (Minister of Education)* (1990), 65 D.L.R. (4th) 1 (Ont. C.A.).

which placed a burden on both religious minorities and non-observers. The court held that, while teaching children about religious perspectives is permissible under section 2(a), indoctrination is not.

It might be noted that the result of these cases does not necessarily draw a strict line between church and state. Unlike the language of the First Amendment to the American constitution, which guarantees the free exercise of religion and prohibits the establishment of religion, section 2(a) of the *Charter* does not prohibit government support for religion nor does it require state neutrality with respect to religion.

2) School Safety and Religious Requirements

When school policy conflicts with the freedom of religion, it is not always because the school has introduced religious elements into its curriculum. Instead, school policies may prevent students from freely practicing their religion while at school. In *Multani v. Commission scolaire Marguerite-Bourgeoys*,[33] the Supreme Court dealt with a Sikh student who had been prohibited from bringing his kirpan to school. A kirpan is a religious object which resembles a dagger, and is made of metal. The prohibition on the kirpan was imposed after the school's governing board refused to ratify an agreement reached with the student and the school board, which would have allowed the student to bring the kirpan to school provided that it was kept in its sheath, sewn securely into a sturdy cloth envelope, and worn under his clothes. The student and his father challenged the prohibition, arguing that the student believed that his religion required him to keep the kirpan on his person at all times, even while sleeping.

A majority of the Court found that the prohibition violated the student's freedom of religion.[34] Writing for the majority, Charron J. held that, in determining whether the ban violated the student's freedom of religion, it was inappropriate to view the kirpan as a weapon, since the student held a genuine belief that he was required to wear the kirpan to comply with the demands of his religion. The fact that the kirpan is a bladed weapon that could be used to seriously injure another per-

---

33   [2006] 1 S.C.R. 256.
34   In a concurring judgment, Deschamps and Abella JJ. found that the matter was more appropriately resolved on principles of administrative law, rather than the *Charter*. They held that the board's decision was unreasonable, as it had failed to consider the student's freedom to practice his religion. In a further, brief concurring judgment, LeBel J. dealt both with both administrative law principles and *Charter* jurisprudence, and found that the board's decision violated s. 2(a) and could not be saved under s. 1.

son was relevant to the section 1 inquiry but irrelevant for the purposes of determining whether the student's religious freedoms had been breached. Charron J. further held that the fact that other Sikhs had been willing to accept compromises that the student in this case had refused, such as substituting the metal kirpan with a plastic or wooden one, was not relevant to the section 2(a) analysis. Instead, concerns such as the dangerousness of the kirpan and possible compromises to the dispute were left for the section 1 analysis.

In conducting her section 1 analysis, Charron J. held that the prohibition on the kirpan could not be justified, as it failed to minimally impair the rights of the student. She stated that in cases such as this, the minimal impairment prong of the *Oakes* test was analogous to the concept of reasonable accommodation. If there was a reasonable accommodation that the school board could make so as to allow the student to safely bring the kirpan to school, the prohibition could not be minimally impairing. Noting that the student in question had never exhibited any behavioural problems at school, and that the evidence suggested that there had not been a single incident in Canada of kirpan-related violence in school, Charron J. found that the original compromise reached between the student and the school board, in which the kirpan would be sewn into its sheath and kept under the his clothes, was such a reasonable accommodation. Accordingly, the prohibition was deemed unconstitutional.

3) Sectarian Schools

Because of the secular nature of public schools, some parents refuse to send their children to the public system for religious reasons. Section 2(a) clearly affords parents the right to provide their children with alternative schooling if their religious beliefs require them to do so. However, the state may validly require that the child be provided with an education that meets minimum standards. Thus, in *Jones*,[35] the Supreme Court of Canada found no violation of section 2(a) because a father, educating his children and others at a church school, had to obtain an exemption from the school board on the basis that he was providing "efficient instruction." In Wilson J.'s view, Jones had failed to show "any substantial impact of this legislation on his belief that God and not the State is the true source of authority over the education of his children."[36]

---

35   *Jones*, above note 13.
36   *Ibid.* at 315 (S.C.R.). However, Wilson J., in dissent, did find a s. 7 violation.

Again, as in *Edwards Books*, the Court indicated that burdens on the practice of religion are not always in violation of the *Charter*.

While the *Jones* case indicated that members of religious groups could avoid public school attendance, the case did not deal with the question whether the state was required to fund independent religious schools. In a number of provinces, constitutional guarantees ensure funding for certain denominational schools.[37] Schools operated by other religious groups argue that they, too, should be included—either on the basis of the equality guarantee in section 15 of the *Charter* (which includes protection against discrimination on the ground of religion) or on the basis of section 2(a). Under section 2(a), the argument is that the secular program of the public school system may be considered inappropriate by adherents of certain religions. Though such parents have the right to send their children to religious schools, the cost of private education may be burdensome. Many may be unable to afford the tuition at independent religious schools. Such individuals, who still pay taxes to support the public system, argue that their religious beliefs are burdened and that the state should fund their religious schools, to ensure that those whose religion requires distinctive teaching may effectively enjoy their rights.

The specific guarantees for religious schools found in the earlier constitutional documents have to be taken into account in relation to these claims. The *Constitution Act, 1867*, section 93, guaranteed that the rights of certain religious denominations to schools possessed by law at the time of Confederation will be maintained. This provision gave constitutional protection to the Roman Catholic schools in Ontario and both the Catholic and Protestant schools in Quebec. Some of the other provinces were made subject to similar guarantees when they joined Confederation. Recently, constitutional amendments have altered these rights in Newfoundland and Labrador and Quebec.

Supporters of non-Catholic religious schools in Ontario contend that they, too, should be given public financial support for their schools. This argument was first raised in the *Bill 30 Reference*, a case arising when Ontario extended funding for the Roman Catholic school system to Grade 13.[38] Until that time, funding had stopped at Grade 10. The Supreme Court of Canada interpreted section 93 to require full funding to Grade 13 but dismissed the argument that sections 2(a) and 15 of the *Charter* required equal funding for other religious schools. The government had relied on section 29 of the *Charter* to defend its decision not to fund other religious schools:

---

37 *Constitution Act, 1867*, s. 93.

38 *Reference Re Bill 30, An Act to Amend the Education Act (Ontario)*, [1987] 1 S.C.R. 1148, 40 D.L.R. (4th) 18 [*Bill 30 Reference*].

> Nothing in this *Charter* abrogates or derogates from any rights or privileges guaranteed by or under the Constitution of Canada in respect of denominational, separate or dissentient schools.

The Court held that, even without this "non-derogation" clause, the rights enjoyed by Roman Catholic school supporters in Ontario were specially protected. The denominational school guarantees in section 93 of the *Constitution Act, 1867*, were described as a "fundamental part of the Confederation compromise" immune from review under the *Charter*. The Court held that the general right to freedom of religion conferred by the *Charter* could not be used to qualify the specific rights conferred on religious minorities by the 1867 constitution.

Despite this ruling, adherents of independent religious schools tried again in the *Adler* case to seek public funding. As they were precluded by the *Bill 30 Reference* decision from basing their claim on the rights of the Roman Catholic schools in Ontario, they focused on the effect of a secular school education on their freedom of religion and equality rights. They argued that the compulsion to support a secular public school system, coupled with mandatory schooling, imposed a financial burden on those who believe in religion as part of education. This burden both interfered with their freedom of religion and meant that they were being treated unequally.

The Supreme Court of Canada again rejected these arguments.[39] Writing for the majority, Iacobucci J. held that section 93 of the *Constitution Act, 1867*, was conclusive. Like Wilson J. in the *Bill 30 Reference*, he emphasized that section 93 was part of a historical compromise leading to Confederation. Not only did it guarantee funding for Roman Catholic schools in Ontario, it also implicitly contemplated public, secular schools. The constitution entrenched a power in the provincial legislature to legislate with respect to non-denominational schools. The province had the power to fund other denominational schools, but its decision not to do so was protected from *Charter* review.

While other judges found that section 93 was not conclusive, none found a violation of the section 2(a) guarantee of freedom of religion.[40] Four members of the Court held that the legislative decision not to fund independent religious schools was subject to *Charter* review. However,

---

39   *Adler v. Ontario*, [1996] 3 S.C.R. 609, 140 D.L.R. (4th) 385 [*Adler*].

40   In the case, all nine judges found no violation of s. 2(a); McLachlin J. found a violation of s. 15 that was justified under s. 1, although she dissented on the issue of funding for school health services: the failure to provide them to independent religious schools violated s. 15 in her view. L'Heureux-Dubé J. dissented on both the broad funding issue and the health services issue, arguing that both decisions were unjustified violations of s. 15.

there was, in their view, no violation of section 2(a). According to Sopinka J., although parents have the constitutional right to educate their children in the religion of their choice, there was no state obligation to fund religious schools. In his view, the state's failure to act in order to facilitate the practice of an individual's religion did not constitute state interference with freedom of religion. Any disadvantage flowing from a decision to send a child to a religious school rather than a public school flowed from the tenets of the religion, not state action.

The result is that in certain provinces, including Ontario, there is an apparently anomalous situation in which Roman Catholic schools are guaranteed public funding but other religious schools get none. Implicit in the decision of the Supreme Court in *Adler* is a belief that secular education is important to Canadian society. Indeed, McLachlin J., dissenting on other grounds, would have upheld the decision not to fund independent religious schools under section 1, even though she found it to be a violation of the equality guarantee. In her view, the preservation of an education system designed to encourage tolerance and harmony in a multicultural society was an important objective, reasonably achieved by funding only the public system.

While the issue of religious school funding seems to have been resolved under the *Charter*, this is not likely to be the end of the issue. Advocates of religious school funding are now turning to the arena of international law. They claim that the failure to fund their schools, especially in light of the funding for the Catholic schools, is a violation of the right against religious discrimination in the *International Covenant on Civil and Political Rights*. The United Nations Human Rights Committee has found that Canada has breached that right by deciding to fund some religious schools, but not others. The Committee indicated that the fact that the religious distinction was enshrined in the *Constitution Act, 1867* did not make it reasonable or objective.[41]

E. RECONCILING FREEDOM OF RELIGION WITH OTHER VALUES

A number of cases have raised the issue of reconciling freedom of religion with other *Charter* rights and freedoms, particularly the right to equality. In *Ross v. New Brunswick School District No. 15*,[42] the Su-

---

41   *Waldman v. Canada*, Canada Communication No. #694/1996, United Nations Document CCPR/C/67/D/694/1996 at 10.5–10.6.
42   [1996] 1 S.C.R. 825.

preme Court of Canada held that the decision of a provincial human rights tribunal, ordering a school board to remove from the classroom a teacher who had expressed anti-Semitic views about Jews, violated the teacher's freedom of religion, as well as his freedom of expression. The Court stressed the need to interpret freedom of religion broadly to include all sincere religious belief and to leave the justifications for restricting freedom of religion to section 1 of the *Charter*. The Court then held that the removal order was justified under section 1 because

> any religious belief that denigrates and defames the religious beliefs of others erodes the very basis of the guarantee in s. 2(*a*)—a basis that guarantees that every individual is free to hold and to manifest the beliefs dictated by one's conscience.[43]

Trinity Western University v. British Columbia College of Teachers[44] involved the reconciliation of freedom of religion and equality rights. A private institution in British Columbia offered baccalaureate degrees in education and applied to the British Columbia College of Teachers (the College) for permission to assume full responsibility for its program. One of the institution's reasons for applying was its desire to have the full program reflect its Christian worldview. The College denied the application because it was concerned that the institution appeared to follow discriminatory practices against homosexuals; in particular, it was concerned that members were asked to sign a document agreeing to refrain from engaging in "sexual sins" including "homosexual behaviour." The majority of the Supreme Court held that the College had erred in not considering the freedom of religion of the institution's members and in not reconciling that freedom with British Columbia public school students' freedom from discrimination on the basis of sexual orientation. The majority held that neither freedom is absolute and that the appropriate place to draw the line is generally between belief and conduct. The freedom to hold beliefs is broader than the freedom to act on those beliefs. There was no evidence that training teachers at the institution fostered discrimination in British Columbia's public schools. Therefore, the freedom of members to hold certain religious beliefs while at the institution should be respected.

In dissent, L'Heureux-Dubé J. held that the College was not required to reconcile freedom of religion with equality rights in considering the institution's application to assume full responsibility for its program. In her view, that was not the statutory mandate of the College and the

---

43   *Ibid.* at para. 94.
44   [2001] 1 S.C.R. 772, 199 D.L.R. (4th) 1.

balancing and interpretation of human rights values was beyond the College's expertise. The College's decision only engaged one *Charter* right—equality—and only did so in the limited context of assessing the impact of the institution's proposal on the province's classrooms. Accordingly, the College was not required to consider other *Charter* rights, including freedom of religion.

In *Chamberlain v. Surrey School District No. 36*,[45] the Supreme Court considered a decision by a school board not to approve books about same-sex families for use in kindergarten and grade one. The trial judge found that the school board had not approved the books in large part because of a concern about controversy involving some parents' religious objections to same-sex relationships. The majority of the Court overturned the board's decision on the basis that it conflicted with a statutory obligation that public schools in British Columbia be conducted "on strictly secular and non-sectarian principles."[46] The Court decided the case on statutory grounds and not under the *Charter*, but it did note that the statutory policy

> reflects the fact that Canada is a diverse and multicultural society, bound together by the values of accommodation, tolerance and respect for diversity. These values are reflected in our Constitution's commitments to equality rights and minority rights.[47]

Gonthier J. dissented (Bastarache J. concurring) and would have upheld the school board's decision not to allow use of books about same-sex families. He stressed the need to reconcile and balance freedom of religion, including some religious beliefs about the immorality of same-sex relationships, with equality rights. He concluded that the board's decision struck a reasonable balance given that same-sex relationships would be discussed in the higher grades.

The proper reconciliation between freedom of religion and equality rights was also considered in a number of cases dealing with same-sex marriage. The Supreme Court rejected arguments that a draft bill recognizing same-sex marriage would violate freedom of religion or the equality rights of those who believed on religious grounds that same-sex marriages were immoral. The Court stated:

> The mere recognition of the equality rights of one group cannot, in itself, constitute a violation of the rights of another. The promotion of *Charter* rights and values enriches our society as a whole and the

---

45   [2002] 4 S.C.R. 710 [*Chamberlain*].
46   *School Act*, R.S.B.C. 1996, c. 412, s. 76.
47   *Chamberlain*, above note 45 at para. 21.

furtherance of those rights cannot undermine the very principles that the *Charter* was meant to foster.[48]

The Court indicated that any conflict between the right to same-sex marriage and freedom of religion would be resolved within the *Charter* through an interpretation of the scope of the respective rights. It also stated that it

> seems clear that state compulsion on religious officials to perform same-sex marriages contrary to their religious beliefs would violate the guarantee of freedom of religion under s. 2(a) of the *Charter*. It also seems apparent that, absent exceptional circumstances which we cannot at present foresee, such a violation could not be justified under s. 1 of the *Charter*.[49]

F. CONCLUSION

Freedom of religion and conscience lies at the heart of a free and democratic society. While the principle of religious freedom is taken for granted, difficult issues arise when deeply held religious views and practices collide with other important state interests. The courts have been asked to pronounce on a number of controversial issues involving religious freedom. A dominant theme is the judicial tendency to protect vulnerable minorities in this area. Sunday closing laws imposing the religious values of the majority have been found to offend the *Charter* guarantee, as have policies involving school prayer, religious instruction and the prohibition of wearing religious objects. As with other *Charter* guarantees, however, difficult questions arise when the state is asked to take positive measures to ensure the better enjoyment of a protected freedom. For certain religious groups, religious education is fundamental. While there seems to be little question that the *Charter* protects the right of religious minorities to educate their children as they see fit, the courts have been unsympathetic to the claims that religious freedom requires state support for religious schools in the absence of a specific constitutional right to denominational schooling.

---

48   *Reference Re Same-Sex Marriage*, above note 7 at para. 46.
49   *Ibid.* at para. 58.

FURTHER READINGS

BERGER, B., "Law's Religion: Rendering Culture" (2007) 45 Osgoode Hall L.J. 277

BROWN, D.M., "Freedom From or Freedom For? Religion as a Case Study in Defining the Content of *Charter* Rights" (2000) 33 U.B.C. L. Rev. 551

BROWN, D.M., "Where Can I Pray? Sacred Space in a Secular Land" (2004) 14 N.J.C.L. 121

BUCKINGHAM, J.E., "Caesar and God: Limits to Religious Freedom in Canada and South Africa" (2001) 15 Sup. Ct. L. Rev. (2d) 461

BUCKINGHAM, J.E., "The Fundamentals of Religious Freedoms: The Case for Recognizing the Collective Aspects of Religion" (2007) 36 Sup. Ct. L. Rev. (2d) 251

ELBERG, B. & M. POWER, "Freedom of Conscience and Religion" in G.A. Beaudoin & E. Mendes, eds., *The Canadian Charter of Rights and Freedoms*, 4th ed. (Markham, ON: LexisNexis Butterworths, 2005)

HORWITZ, P., "The Sources and Limits of Freedom of Religion in a Liberal Democracy: Section 2(a) and Beyond" (1996) 54 U.T. Fac. L. Rev. 1

MACKLEM, T., "Faith as a Secular Value" (2000) 45 McGill L.J. 1

MOON, R., ed., *Law and Religious Pluralism in Canada* (Vancouver: University of British Columbia Press, 2008)

WOEHRLING, J., "L'obligation d'accommodement raisonnable et l'adaptation de la société à la diversité religieuse" (1998) 43 McGill L.J. 325

CHAPTER 9

FREEDOM
OF EXPRESSION

Even before the *Charter of Rights and Freedoms*, freedom of expression was recognized by the Supreme Court of Canada as inherent in our system of government.[1] Democracy rests on the premise that public issues be freely and openly debated. Indeed, the freedom to criticize those who exercise power in our society is the very lifeblood of our democratic tradition. Political debate is often heated and intemperate. Criticism of public institutions and officials will not always be respectful and measured: those who challenge established authority often have to resort to strong language and exaggeration in order to gain attention. "If these exchanges are stifled, democratic government itself is threatened."[2]

Freedom of expression is also vital in other areas of human activity outside the realm of politics. Artists and writers often push the limits of conventional values. Scholars question "sacred cows" and accepted wisdom. Freedom of expression represents society's commitment to tolerate the annoyance of being confronted by unacceptable views. As stated by the Ontario Court of Appeal in an early *Charter* case:[3] "[T]he constitutional guarantee extends not only to that which is pleasing, but also to that which to many may be aesthetically distasteful or morally

---

1   *Reference Re Alberta Legislation*, [1938] S.C.R. 100, [1938] 2 D.L.R. 81.
2   *R. v. Kopyto* (1987), 62 O.R. (2d) 449 at 462, 47 D.L.R. (4th) 213 (C.A.) [*Kopyto*], Cory J.A.
3   *Re Information Retailers Association and Metropolitan Toronto* (1985), 22 D.L.R. (4th) 161 at 180 (Ont. C.A.), Robins J.A.

offensive: it is indeed often true that 'one man's vulgarity is another's lyric.'" More recently, the Supreme Court of Canada emphasized that freedom of expression must include the "right to express outrageous and ridiculous opinions" and that as "[p]ublic controversy can be a rough trade . . . the law needs to accommodate its requirements." [4]

There are two rationales for extending the guarantee this widely. The first is instrumental in nature and is reflected by the metaphor of the "marketplace in ideas." The great American judge Oliver Wendell Holmes, echoing the thoughts of John Milton and John Stuart Mill, said that "the best test of truth is the power of the thought to get itself accepted in the competition of the market." [5] Suppression of ideas in the name of truth is notoriously dangerous. The rationale of the marketplace of ideas posits that the free flow of ideas is the best way to get at the truth.

The second important rationale values expression less for the results it produces than for its intrinsic worth to the individual. Expression is seen as a vital element of individual autonomy, personal growth, and self-realization. The ability to say what one thinks and to follow whatever lines of inquiry that occur to one's imagination is an essential attribute of a free society.

In a 2002 decision,[6] the Supreme Court of Canada summarized the values protected by freedom of expression in these terms:

> The core values which free expression promotes include self-fulfil-ment, participation in social and political decision-making, and the communal exchange of ideas. Free speech protects human dignity and the right to think and reflect freely on one's circumstances and condition. It allows a person to speak not only for the sake of expression itself, but also to advocate change, attempting to persuade others in the hope of improving one's life and perhaps the wider social, political, and economic environment.[7]

A. RECONCILING FREEDOM OF EXPRESSION WITH OTHER VALUES

Does freedom of expression preclude any law limiting what individuals can say or publish? The answer is surely no. To take a familiar example,

---

4   *WIC Radio Ltd. v. Simpson*, [2008] 2 S.C.R. 420 at paras. 4 and 15.

5   *Abrams v. United States*, 250 U.S. 616 at 630 (1919).

6   *Retail, Wholesale and Department Store Union, Local 558 v. Pepsi-Cola Canada Beverages (West) Ltd.*, [2002] 1 SC.R. 156, 208 D.L.R. (4th) 385.

7   *Ibid.* at 399 (D.L.R.).

freedom of expression does not protect the right, falsely, to shout "Fire!" in a crowded theatre.[8] As with the other rights and freedoms guaranteed by the *Charter*, freedom of expression is not absolute. There are situations in which the freedom of one individual must be curtailed so that other important social values may be respected and protected.

How should these competing claims be reconciled? The American approach has been to accord near-absolute respect to expression deemed worthy of the constitutional guarantee; however, the American courts define freedom of expression narrowly so as not to include forms of speech that do not qualify for protection. The Supreme Court of Canada has adopted a different method to reconcile respect for this vital freedom with competing claims. Our Court has said that the structure of the *Charter*, and in particular section 1, requires that freedom of expression be given a broad definition with virtually no limitations, and that any curtailment of expression be justified under section 1 as a limit that is reasonable in a free and democratic society.

In 1988 the Supreme Court heard two cases from Quebec in which it charted the course to be followed. *Ford v. Quebec (A.G.)*[9] involved a challenge to the Quebec "signs law," which prohibited, with virtually no exception, the display of commercial signs not written in French. *Ford* was argued at the same time as *Irwin Toy Ltd. v. Quebec (A.G.)*,[10] which involved a challenge to a Quebec statute that limited the right to broadcast advertising aimed at children. In both cases, the Attorney General of Quebec argued that the law did not limit freedom of expression. In *Ford*, Quebec contended that the "signs law" did not limit in any way the message that could be conveyed. The language of the speaker was merely the medium for expression. It was contended in both cases that commercial expression is not worthy of constitutional protection and that the Court should adhere to a core definition of freedom of expression, limiting the right to the most vital areas of political speech and artistic expression. The Supreme Court rejected these arguments, holding that freedom of expression should be given a wide and generous definition admitting few exceptions. Yet at the same time the Court recognized that expression may be curtailed if the standard of section 1 is met.

In *Ford* the Court stated that language was an essential component of expression:

> Language is so intimately related to the form and content of expression that there cannot be true freedom of expression by means of

8   *Schenk v. United States*, 249 U.S. 47 at 52 (1919), Holmes J.
9   [1988] 2 S.C.R. 712, 54 D.L.R. (4th) 577 [*Ford*].
10   [1989] 1 S.C.R. 927, 58 D.L.R. (4th) 577 [*Irwin Toy*].

language if one is prohibited from using the language of one's choice. Language is not merely a means or medium of expression; it colours the content and meaning of expression.[11]

The Court was also unsympathetic to the argument that expression should be limited to political speech, thereby excluding advertising. The Court found that the purpose of protecting freedom of expression was not limited to political speech and the enhancement of democratic self-government. Other values were also involved. The Court accepted as a valid rationale for protecting expression the concept of a "market-place of ideas." It also recognized the important element of individual autonomy and self-development inherent in expression. Informed by these purposes, the Court found that freedom of expression embraced expressive conduct extending to most areas of human activity, including commerce and the arts.

The Supreme Court has recognized that freedom of expression should be defined generously in other ways as well. Although we usually regard the right as that of the speaker, meaningful expression assumes an audience. The purposes underlying the guarantee contemplate a recipient of the message, and the Court has said that the right extends to the listener as well as to the speaker.[12] Cases of freedom of expression typically involve a restraint on speech. The Court has acknowledged, however, that the freedom also protects the individual from being required to express one particular view.[13]

In *Irwin Toy*, the Supreme Court described in a formal manner the framework for interpretative analysis to be followed in a freedom of expression case. The first stage is definitional. Here, the Court said, a broad approach is called for. Expression includes any activity that conveys or attempts to convey a meaning. The use of the word "activity" is significant as the Court recognized that, in some situations, actions without words may have expressive content. For example, parking a car ordinarily has no expressive feature, but, as the Supreme Court explained, if an unmarried person, as a protest, were to park in a space reserved for spouses, that action would have expressive content. The only restriction the Court placed on conduct of an expressive nature was for acts of violence. Violence is often used by terrorists as a means to convey a message, but, said the Supreme Court, it is obvious that the perpetrator

---

11   *Ford*, above note 9 at 748 (S.C.R.).
12   *Rocket v. Royal College of Dental Surgeons of Ontario*, [1990] 2 S.C.R. 232, 71 D.L.R. (4th) 68 [*Rocket*].
13   *RJR-MacDonald Inc. v. Canada (Attorney General)*, [1995] 3 S.C.R. 199, 127 D.L.R. (4th) 1 [*RJR*].

of an act of violence for an expressive purpose cannot gain constitutional protection from the ordinary law of the land.[14] In *Montreal (City) v. 2952-1366 Québec Inc.*,[15] the Court added another definitional filter, namely that there are some otherwise public places that must remain outside the protected sphere of section 2(b). The historical or actual function of the place may require a degree of privacy that would be undermined if anyone could intrude to offer his or her opinion. Likewise, where allowing free expression in a place would undermine the very values the guarantee is designed to promote, the constitutional right is excluded. Certain government functions—cabinet meetings for example—can only be conducted effectively if accorded a level of privacy. Other highly public and political activities—such as sittings of Parliament—require a level of order and decorum that is incompatible with according any member of the public the right to intrude with the expression of his or her views.

The second stage of the analysis is to determine whether there has been a violation. Here, the Supreme Court distinguished content-based restraints from those that merely have the effect of limiting expression. The former category includes laws or practices that have as their purpose the restriction of the actual type of speech as well as restraints on a form of expression tied to content. Content-based restraints are the most familiar: examples include the law of defamation, the prohibition of pornography, and restrictions on advertising. An example of a restraint on a form of expression tied to content is a law that prohibits the handing out of pamphlets. While such a law is indifferent to the content of the pamphlet, it inevitably bans whatever content the pamphlet has and thus necessarily constitutes a restraint on expression. An effects-based restraint is one that is aimed at some other aspect of the activity but that may nevertheless have an impact on expression. A prohibition against littering has a valid purpose and is not aimed at expression. Yet it may have the effect of limiting expression depending upon the circumstances. If enforced against someone handing out pamphlets, it would have that effect, but if applied to someone carelessly discarding a candy wrapper, it would not. In the case of an effects-based restraint, the Supreme Court held, the party claiming the protection of the *Charter* must be able to show that the activity in question promotes one of

---

14   In *Suresh v. Canada (Minister of Citizenship and Immigration)*, 2002 SCC 1, 208 D.L.R. (4th) 1 and in *Ahani v. Canada (Minister of Citizenship and Immigration)*, 2002 SCC 2, 208 D.L.R. (4th) 57, the Supreme Court of Canada held that anti-terrorism legislation did not violate s. 2(b) or s. 2(d) as it is aimed at violent conduct.

15   [2005] 3 S.C.R. 141.

the three principles underlying freedom of expression: political debate, the marketplace of ideas, or autonomy and self-fulfilment.

Given the generous scope of this definition of expression, most claims for *Charter* protection will survive these first two stages. The Supreme Court has found, for example, that in addition to commercial expression, pornography,[16] hate speech,[17] and even deliberate falsehoods[18] qualify as expression. The purpose of these activities is to convey a message, however unpleasant, and the purpose of the *Criminal Code* provisions criminalizing pornography and hate speech is to restrict the very content of the messages being conveyed.

There remains, however, the third stage of analysis under section 1 of the *Charter*. Here, as seen in chapter 4, the burden is on the state to justify the limit it seeks to impose as being reasonable in a free and democratic society. In virtually all of the freedom of expression cases to reach the Supreme Court of Canada, the crucial analysis has been under section 1. The most significant decisions are discussed in the pages that follow.

B. COMMERCIAL EXPRESSION

The Supreme Court has decided a number of cases involving restraints on commercial speech, with mixed results. In *Ford*,[19] the case involving the Quebec "signs law," the issues extended well beyond what constitutes the permissible regulation of advertising. The Court struck down the "signs law" on the ground that Quebec had failed to justify it as a reasonable limit. While the Supreme Court was prepared to accept as a legitimate purpose the protection and enhancement of the French language in Quebec, it held that the virtual total ban on public signs in any other language went too far. Quebec had failed to introduce evidence to show that such an extreme measure was necessary and the Court held that the law failed to meet the minimal-impairment test. In making the minimal-impairment assessment, the Court considered alternative measures that might satisfy the goal of protecting and enhancing the French language. It suggested that a law that required the use of French in commercial signs but that did not ban other languages might be ac-

---

16   R. v. Butler, [1992] 1 S.C.R. 452, 70 C.C.C. (3d) 129 [Butler].

17   R. v. Keegstra, [1990] 3 S.C.R. 697, 61 C.C.C. (3d) 1 [Keegstra].

18   R. v. Zundel, [1992] 2 S.C.R. 731, 95 D.L.R. (4th) 202 [Zundel]; R. v. Lucas, [1998] 1 S.C.R. 439, 157 D.L.R. (4th) 425 [Lucas].

19   Ford, above note 9.

ceptable, even if such a measure called for a marked predominance of French. A law along these lines would meet the aim of protecting and enhancing the French language while at the same time respecting the rights of non-French speakers.

In the companion case, *Irwin Toy*,[20] the Supreme Court was faced with a more typical case of commercial speech. At issue was the right of a toy manufacturer to advertise its products for commercial purposes. Quebec legislation prohibited commercial advertising directed at persons under thirteen years of age. The statute established certain criteria to determine whether the advertising was directed at children. A majority of the Court found that the Quebec law could be justified as a reasonable limit on the right of freedom of expression. As noted in chapter 4, the decision in *Irwin Toy* represents a significant statement by the Court on the application of section 1 where a law has been enacted to protect a vulnerable group. In the Court's view, the legislature had acted reasonably in protecting children who it deemed less than fully capable of making informed judgments on the basis of advertising. As in *Ford*, the law imposed a total ban, but in *Irwin Toy* there was some evidence that such a measure was required. The evidence, it must be said, fell well short of proving with certainty that the law enacted by Quebec was the only or even the least drastic way to achieve the goal of protecting children from advertising. However, the Supreme Court accepted that the evidence was sufficient to support Quebec's claim. The Court recognized that, in this area, the facts were not susceptible of clear proof and that the legislature had to be given some latitude:

> If the legislature has made a reasonable assessment as to where the line is most properly drawn, especially if that assessment involves weighing conflicting scientific evidence and allocating scarce resources on this basis, it is not for the court to second guess. That would only be to substitute one estimate for another.[21]

There is much to be said for the view that, while commercial expression does qualify for constitutional protection, Parliament and the legislatures are entitled to some latitude when enacting protective measures in the public interest. Commercial expression has only tenuous connection to the underlying values of democratic self-government and individual autonomy and self-development. There is an obvious connection with the rationale of the marketplace of ideas, although here the search for the truth is surely less elusive than in other areas of

---

20   *Irwin Toy*, above note 10.
21   *Ibid.* at 990 (S.C.R.).

human activity such as politics or the arts. Regulation to ensure "truth in advertising" is familiar, yet it would surely be unthinkable to impose comparable measures in the areas of political or artistic expression.

The pattern revealed by *Ford*, striking down a total ban, and by *Irwin Toy*, reflecting a significant judicial tolerance for more specific laws restricting commercial expression, has been repeated by later decisions of the Court. The Court has upheld as a reasonable limit under section 1 of the *Charter* a *Criminal Code* provision making it illegal to solicit in a public place for the purpose of prostitution.[22] Dickson C.J.C. stated that, when considering the reasonable-limits test, the Court should have in mind the nature of the expression at issue. Solicitation had an overt "economic purpose" and it could "hardly be said that communications regarding an economic transaction of sex for money lie at, or even near, the core of the guarantee of freedom of expression."[23]

However, where the law imposes a total ban on commercial speech rather than targeting the mischief with a more limited and specific measure, the Court has taken a tougher line. In *Rocket v. Royal College of Dental Surgeons*,[24] a dentist challenged regulations imposing a ban on professional advertising. The Supreme Court accepted that a professional body was entitled to regulate advertising by its members to protect the public and that "restrictions on expression of this kind might be easier to justify than other infringements."[25] Yet the Court struck down the regulations on the grounds that they went well beyond what was necessary to protect the public interest and that they prevented dentists from giving straightforward and useful information such as hours of operation and languages spoken. Similarly, in *RJR*,[26] by a majority of five to four, the Supreme Court found that a law imposing a complete ban on advertising of tobacco products could not survive section 1 scrutiny as a minimal infringement of freedom of expression. While the majority accepted that Parliament could limit the right to advertise tobacco with a view to promoting the health of Canadians, the total ban was not shown to be necessary nor had the government shown that more limited alternatives would be ineffective. Parliament enacted a more nuanced piece of legislation in response to the *RJR* decision which prohibited only certain forms of tobacco advertising—lifestyle advertising, advertisements appealing to young per-

---

22   *Reference Re ss. 193 and 195.1(1)(c) of the Criminal Code (Canada)*, [1990] 1 S.C.R. 1123, 56 C.C.C. (3d) 65.
23   *Ibid.* at 1136 (S.C.R.).
24   *Rocket*, above note 12.
25   *Ibid.* at 247 (S.C.R.), McLachlin J.
26   *RJR*, above note 13.

sons and false or misleading advertising—and required manufacturers to include health warning labels of a certain size on their products' packaging. The Supreme Court found these restrictions "represented a genuine attempt by Parliament to craft controls on advertising and promotion that would meet its objectives as well as the concerns expressed by the majority of this Court in *RJR*" and upheld them as a justifiable limitation of the tobacco manufacturers' freedom of expression under section 1.[27]

The right of a consumer to engage in "counter-advertising" was recognized in *R. v. Guignard*.[28] A disgruntled customer used a billboard to make known to the public his dissatisfaction with an insurance company. He was convicted under a municipal bylaw prohibiting billboards in residential areas that mention the name of commercial entities. The Supreme Court struck the bylaw down as an infringement of freedom of expression. "Consumers may express their frustration or disappointment with a product or service. Consumers may share their concerns, worries or even anger with other consumers and try to warn them against the practices of a business."[29] While the Court agreed that municipalities could control and regulate the visual pollution created by public signs, this bylaw did not survive scrutiny as a reasonable limit under section 1. As only signs mentioning commercial entities were prohibited, there was no rational connection to the stated objective of preventing visual pollution. Nor did the bylaw satisfy the minimal-impairment test since it severely curtailed the consumer's right to express his dissatisfaction publicly. In a subsequent case, the Court indicated that a municipal bylaw limiting the size of billboards violated freedom of expression, but was justified under section 1 of the *Charter*.[30] In the same case, the Ontario Court of Appeal unanimously invalidated a bylaw prohibiting all advertising for third parties.[31] These cases fit into the pattern, observed above, of the courts striking down total bans on particular types of advertising while often accepting less drastic restrictions on commercial expression as reasonable.

Expression that appears to be motivated by economic or commercial interests may involve other values protected by the *Charter*. The

---

27   *Canada (Attorney General) v. JTI-Macdonald Corp.*, [2007] 2 S.C.R. 610 at para. 7.
28   [2002] 1 S.C.R. 472, 209 D.L.R. (4th) 549.
29   *Ibid.* at para. 23.
30   *Vann Niagara Ltd. v. Oakville (Town)*, [2003] 3 S.C.R. 158.
31   *Vann Niagara Ltd. v. Oakville (Town)* (2002), 60 O.R. (3d) 1 (C.A.). There was no appeal to the Supreme Court from this aspect of the decision of the Ontario Court of Appeal.

Supreme Court has accorded significant protection to picketing[32] and leafleting[33] in labour disputes as a form of freedom of expression. The Court has stated that the interests of striking workers often go beyond purely economic issues. "Working conditions, like the duration and location of work, parental leave, health benefits, severance and retirement schemes, may impact on the personal lives of workers even outside their working hours."[34] The Court has recognized the importance of picketing as a means of redressing the imbalance of power between powerful commercial interests and vulnerable workers and has modified the common law rules related to secondary picketing.[35]

C. POLITICAL EXPRESSION

As already noted, freedom of expression about political issues lies at the heart of our democratic tradition. But does this mean that Parliament is incapable of intervening in all situations? Expression in the real world of politics is closely tied to economic resources. Those who have money have the means to convey their message to the public; those who lack resources are at a disadvantage and to them the promise of freedom of expression may be ineffectual. Is Parliament entitled to alleviate economic inequalities by regulating election expenses? Such laws are designed to improve debate by ensuring that some voices do not drown out others. Does this laudable goal justify imposing restraints on the political expression of those who have more substantial resources?

In an early *Charter* case, a federal law prohibiting anyone other than a registered party or candidate from spending money during an election campaign to promote a cause or a candidate was struck down.[36] The federal government contended that limiting the right of individuals to participate in campaigns was necessary to ensure the integrity of other provisions controlling expenditures by candidates. An Alberta judge held that the government had failed to prove its case.

---

32   *Retail, Wholesale and Department Store Union, Local 558 v. Pepsi-Cola Canada Beverages (West) Ltd.*, [2002] 1 S.C.R. 156, 208 D.L.R. (4th) 385 [*Retail, Wholesale and Department Store Union*].

33   *United Food and Commercial Workers, Local 1518 (U.F.C.W.) v. KMart Canada Ltd.*, [1999] 2 S.C.R. 1083, 176 D.L.R. (4th) 607; *Allsco Building Products Ltd. v. United Food and Commercial Workers, Local 1288P (U.F.C.W.)*, [1999] 2 S.C.R. 1136, 176 D.L.R. (4th) 647.

34   *Retail, Wholesale and Department Store Union*, above note 32 at 400 (D.L.R.).

35   See chapter 6.

36   *National Citizens' Coalition v. Canada (A.G.)* (1984), 11 D.L.R. (4th) 481 (Alta. Q.B.).

Given the importance of freedom of political expression, he was not satisfied that this significant constraint on the participation of individuals and groups who were not candidates was justifiable.

In 1996 the Alberta Court of Appeal came to a similar conclusion with respect to a federal law prohibiting any advertising between the date an election is called and the twenty-ninth day before voting day, as well as the day before and the day of the election.[37] The law also prohibited third parties from spending more than $1,000 for advertising, promoting, or opposing a particular candidate. These measures followed the recommendations of a royal commission on elections. The "blackout" provision was intended to control escalating campaign costs and to limit the advantage of an incumbent. The third party spending provision was intended to prevent circumvention of spending limits imposed on candidates and to enhance public confidence in the electoral process by avoiding the risk of patronage in return for such spending. The Alberta courts were not persuaded by the evidence adduced by the Attorney General that these measures were justified as limits on freedom of expression under section 1. In the Court of Appeal, Conrad J.A. found that the government's case failed to establish a sufficiently important objective to justify overriding a *Charter* right. In her view, the harm feared from unconstrained advertising and spending was essentially speculative. She also expressed the view that such restrictions, especially those effectively precluding participation by non-candidates, were fundamentally at odds with basic *Charter* values:

> An important justification for the *Charter* guarantees of free expression and association, and an informed vote, is the need in a democracy for citizens to participate in and affect an election. It follows that there can be no pressing and substantial need to suppress that input merely because it might have an impact.[38]

In a case dealing with Quebec's referendum law, the Supreme Court of Canada reached a conclusion similar to that of the Alberta Court of Appeal even while revealing a different perspective.[39] The Court struck down a law imposing spending restrictions but expressly stated that third party spending limits of the kind at issue in the Alberta case could be justifiable. The Quebec referendum law limited expenditures and required that all expenses be paid from the funds of committees specifically authorized to represent one side or the other. The Court

---

37   *Somerville v. Canada (A.G.)* (1996), 136 D.L.R. (4th) 205 (Alta. C.A.).
38   *Ibid.* at 232, Conrad J.A.
39   *Libman v. Quebec (A.G.)*, [1997] 3 S.C.R. 569, 151 D.L.R. (4th) 385.

was entirely sympathetic to the view that limiting election expenses could be justified in order to ensure fairness in a campaign and to prevent the most affluent members of society from exercising a disproportionate influence, but it found that the Quebec law went too far. Individuals or groups not willing or able to affiliate with one of the authorized committees were precluded from even producing leaflets or posters to express their opinion. While limiting the rights of third parties to spend money during a campaign might be necessary to ensure the integrity of spending limits justifiably imposed on candidates or authorized committees, the Quebec law failed the minimal impairment test by prohibiting all third party expenditures and thereby effectively precluding any third party expression of view.

The Supreme Court of Canada considered limits on third party spending under the *Canada Elections Act* in *Harper v. Canada (Attorney General)*. The Act restricted third parties from spending more than $3,000 per riding or $150,000 nationally. Stephen Harper, then leader of the National Citizens Coalition, challenged these restrictions as a limitation on freedom of expression, as well as on freedom of association and the right to vote. In 2000, the Supreme Court set aside an interlocutory injunction restraining the enforcement of the spending limits.[40] In 2004, the Supreme Court decided the case on the merits. It held in a 6 to 3 decision that the spending restrictions violated freedom of expression but were justified under section 1 of the *Charter*.[41]

The majority judgment of Bastarache J. recognized that political expression warrants a high degree of constitutional protection, but also indicated that third party advertising could be less deserving of constitutional protection because of the danger of wealthy third parties manipulating political discourse to their advantage, causing electoral unfairness. He concluded that "on balance, the contextual factors favour a deferential approach to Parliament in determining whether the third party advertising limits are demonstrably justified in a free and democratic society."[42] The restrictions on third party advertising during elections were justified as rationally connected to the objectives of ensuring fair elections by promoting equality in political discourse, protecting the integrity of spending restrictions on political parties and candidates, and ensuring that voters have confidence in the electoral process. The restrictions were proportionate because they only applied to third party advertising that was associated with a political party

---

40   *Harper v. Canada (Attorney General)*, [2000] 2 S.C.R. 764 [*Harper* I]. For further discussion see chapters 11 and 17.
41   *Harper v. Canada (Attorney General)*, [2004] 1 S.C.R. 827 [*Harper* II].
42   *Ibid.* at para. 88.

or candidate, and the beneficial effects of the restrictions in promoting electoral fairness outweighed their harms to free expression. Three judges in dissent accepted that promoting electoral fairness, preventing the wealthy from dominating political discourse, and preserving confidence in the electoral system were pressing and substantial objectives that could limit freedom of expression. Nevertheless, they held that the actual restrictions were disproportionate because they effectively prevented third parties from using effective radio and television ads and resulted in a virtual ban on political expression during elections except through registered political parties and candidates. The entire Court, however, was unanimous that a total ban on third party election advertising on polling day was a reasonable limit on freedom of expression, given the difficulty of responding to any misleading advertising during this time.

Another decision in this area, however, indicates that the Supreme Court will impose a high standard of justification for absolute prohibitions on expression in connection with elections.[43] At issue was a federal law banning the publication of opinion polls in the three days prior to a federal election. The majority found that the law could not be justified under section 1. The contention that it was desirable to provide voters with a period of rest and reflection, free from opinion polls, was rejected as a pressing and substantial objective. Writing for the majority, Bastarache J. stated that "Canadian voters must be presumed to have a certain degree of maturity and intelligence" and that it was an insult to assume that "an individual would be so enthralled by a particular poll result as to allow his or her electoral judgment to be ruled by it."[44] While the Court accepted that measures to ensure an opportunity to assess the accuracy of opinion polls was a valid objective, it found that the law failed to meet the minimal-impairment test. There were other measures that would meet that objective in a manner less intrusive of freedom of expression, such as requiring the publication of the methodology used. Moreover, wrote Bastarache J., by imposing a complete ban on the publication of opinion polls within the three-day period, the law constituted such a serious infringement of freedom of expression that even if it satisfied the minimal-impairment test, its deleterious effects would have outweighed the benefit it sought to achieve.

Issues surrounding restrictions on third party spending during elections are now relatively settled in Canada, with the Supreme Court adopting a deferential approach to restrictions designed to achieve elec-

---

43   *Thomson Newspapers Co. v. Canada (A.G.)* (1998), 159 D.L.R. (4th) 385 (S.C.C.).
44   *Ibid.* at 437.

toral fairness and preventing the wealthy from dominating political discourse. One remaining issue is the regulation of spending during elections by parties and candidates. *MacKay v. Manitoba*,[45] dealt with public subsidies for the campaign expenses of candidates. The plaintiff challenged Manitoba legislation that gave candidates the right to be reimbursed from public funds for a portion of their campaign expenses, provided they secured a specified percentage of the vote. The Court found that there were serious deficiencies in the evidence and that it was being asked to rule in the abstract rather than in response to a specific factual situation. A somewhat similar issue arose almost fifteen years later in *Figueroa v. Canada (Attorney General)*[46] where the leader of the Communist Party of Canada successfully challenged, under section 3 of the *Charter*, the denial of state benefits to parties who ran less than fifty candidates in national elections. An egalitarian as opposed to a libertarian approach to elections may, as in *Harper v. Canada*,[47] defer to state limits on spending during elections but, as in *Figueroa*, may be much less deferential to state benefit schemes that have the effect of excluding small or marginal parties or candidates. In other words, the object in the egalitarian model of elections is on promoting equality and fairness for all.

The Supreme Court's focus on the egalitarian model is further reflected in *R. v. Bryan*.[48] During the 2002 federal election, the accused posted the election results from thirty-two ridings in Eastern Canada onto a website while polls were still open in other parts of the country. He was charged under the *Canada Elections Act* with the offence of disseminating election results from one electoral district to another where the polls were still open. He argued that the prohibition on transmitting election results was a violation of his freedom of expression. A 5 to 4 majority rejected his argument, finding that the prohibition was justified under section 1. The majority held that no evidence was required to show that informational equality between voters in an election was a pressing and substantial objective and, adopting an explicitly deferential approach, found that the restriction met the section 1 proportionality test. The four dissenting judges found the evidence offered to justify the ban to be "speculative, inconclusive and largely unsubstantiated" and that as the "harm or suppressing core political speech" is "profound" any benefits of the legislation were outweighed by its deleterious effects.[49]

---

45   [1989] 2 S.C.R. 357, 61 D.L.R. (4th) 385.
46   [2003] 1 S.C.R. 912 [*Figueroa*], also discussed in chapter 11.
47   *Harper* II, above note 41. See discussion above.
48   [2007] 1 S.C.R. 527.
49   *Ibid.* at para. 107.

Given the close connection between political expression and the exercise of democratic rights, it is not surprising that the Supreme Court has held that the act of voting is protected as freedom of expression under section 2(b).[50] What is perhaps surprising is the Court's conclusion that the entitlement to vote in a referendum or a municipal plebiscite is a matter to be left to the legislature.[51] The Court, however, has left the door open to challenges to discriminatory restrictions on the availability of the right to vote. This is again consistent with an egalitarian model of elections. However, the Court has held that denying a vote in a referendum to those who have recently moved to a province or to those who live in a municipality that has already held its own plebiscite did not result in discrimination in extending the vote.[52] The Court has also ruled that a provincial statutory regime which precluded school employees from being elected as school trustees to any school board in the province, even if they were employed by a different school board, did not violate the employees' freedom of expression.[53] There, the Court found that the employees' freedom of expression was not violated as their claim was grounded in access to a particular statutory regime rather than in the fundamental freedom of expression.[54]

D. HATE SPEECH

The *Criminal Code* prohibits the communication of statements, other than in private conversation, that wilfully promote hatred against an identifiable group.[55] The purpose behind this prohibition is readily understood. In view of Canada's multicultural and multiracial social fabric, Parliament considered it appropriate to take steps to ensure that the values of tolerance, equality, and non-discrimination are respected. But anti-hate speech laws are opposed by many advocates of free speech. While it is impossible to see any redeeming value in the utterances of the hatemonger, it is argued that such laws pose an unjustifiable risk to the competing value of freedom of expression. Race, religion, and cultural difference are important issues of public concern and often give rise to heated public debate. The issues are exceedingly sensitive

---

50   *Haig v. Canada (Chief Electoral Officer)*, [1993] 2 S.C.R. 995.
51   *Ibid.*; *Siemens v. Manitoba (Attorney General)*, [2003] 1 S.C.R. 6.
52   *Ibid.*
53   *Baier v. Alberta*, [2007] 2 S.C.R. 673.
54   See further discussion of this point above in chapter 3.
55   Section 319. See also the related provisions prohibiting the wilful promotion of genocide (s. 318).

and some may take offence at what others regard as fair comment. Is it possible to identify with sufficient clarity and precision that which is truly unworthy and reprehensible without posing a significant risk to honest and vigorous debate?

In *R. v. Keegstra*,[56] a majority of the Supreme Court of Canada answered yes. All members of the Court agreed that, despite its message, hate speech does convey a meaning and therefore constitutes expression within the ambit of the *Charter*. Following the course it had laid out in *Irwin Toy*, the Court refused to exclude hate speech from the protection of the *Charter* on definitional grounds. It held that, if this form of expression was to be limited, the law had to satisfy the reasonable-limits test of section 1. All members of the Court also accepted the argument that the objective of the anti-hate speech law was sufficiently compelling to justify limiting a *Charter* right. Such a law is intended to avoid tangible harm in the form of feelings of humiliation and degradation felt by those targeted. Furthermore, it is designed to enhance a social climate of mutual respect and tolerance. Anti-hate laws, said the Court, were not only consistent with certain international obligations assumed by Canada but also enhanced other important and competing *Charter* values of equality and multiculturalism.

The judges of the Supreme Court divided, however, on the question of minimal impairment. A purposive analysis led the majority to conclude that the minimal impairment test was to be applied less rigorously than in other contexts. While hate speech qualified as expression, in the majority's view, it had to be recognized that hate speech was inimical to the values underlying freedom of expression. It was clearly false, thereby not attracting support from the rationale of the marketplace of ideas. And, while democracy depends upon free and open debate, hate speech denies equal dignity and respect, a precondition for genuine debate. Hate speech also attacks the autonomy rights of those who are its targets. From this perspective, the majority concluded that the anti-hate law could be justified as a minimal impairment of freedom of expression. The law was, in the Court's view, drawn with sufficient precision to avoid posing a threat to honest or worthy expression. It does not prohibit private communications, and the prosecution has to prove as an essential ingredient of the offence that the speech represents the wilful promotion of hatred. The accused is afforded a number of defences, including truth; the good-faith expression of opinion on a religious subject; the reasonable belief in the truth of statements relevant to the public interest, the discussion of which is for

---

56 *Keegstra*, above note 17.

the public benefit; and the conviction that the statement was intended in good faith to remove feelings of hatred. The majority found that the Parliament had carefully tailored the law to its legitimate objective and that it should be upheld on the ground that it minimally impaired freedom of expression.

The dissenting judges saw the effect of the anti-hate law quite differently. While not disputing Parliament's laudable goals, the minority did not agree that the law had a rational connection to those goals. The effect of an anti-hate-law prosecution is to afford the hatemonger an otherwise unattainable platform and level of publicity. Attempts at suppression might only serve to create martyrs. Historical evidence of vigorous anti-hate-law prosecution in pre-Nazi Germany was offered to suggest that such laws were at best ineffective and at worst counterproductive. The dissenting judges also disagreed that the law was sufficiently precise, pointing to instances where prosecutions had been brought or threatened against forms of expression plainly tolerable in a free society. Though such prosecutions might not succeed, the very threat of prosecution could well stifle expression on controversial matters.[57]

In subsequent cases, the Supreme Court upheld the *Canadian Human Rights Act* provisions curtailing hate speech[58] and a decision of a provincial human rights tribunal ordering a school board to remove from the classroom a teacher who had expressed racist views.[59] However, in another case[60] the Supreme Court struck down the "false news" provision of the *Criminal Code*, which had been used in an attempt to silence a well-known purveyor of anti-Semitic and Holocaust-denial literature. The law in question prohibited the publication of statements, known by the speaker to be false, that causes or is likely to cause injury or mischief to a public interest. All members of the Court agreed that, although the law was aimed at deliberate lies, freedom of expression was involved. Even lies convey a meaning, and if that meaning was to be suppressed, the Court held that the law had to satisfy the section 1 reasonable-limits test. However, as in the hate-speech case, the Court was sharply divided on the application of the minimal-impairment test. This time the majority ruled that the law could not be justified. While

---

57   The American courts have tended to strike down restrictions on racist speech: see *Collin v. Smith*, 578 F.2d 1197 (1978); *R.A.V. v. City of St. Paul*, 112 S.Ct. 2538 (1992).

58   *Canada (Human Rights Commission) v. Taylor*, [1990] 3 S.C.R. 892, 75 D.L.R. (4th) 577.

59   *Ross v. New Brunswick School District No. 15*, [1996] 1 S.C.R. 825, 133 D.L.R. (4th) 1.

60   *Zundel*, above note 18.

the "false news" law was being used to combat a modern problem, its objective was shrouded in the mists of time. Its origins could be traced to a thirteenth-century law designed to protect the reputations of the great men of the realm. In the view of the majority, it was impossible to say what objective Parliament had in mind in retaining this ancient provision in the modern *Criminal Code*. The law lacked a clear objective or purpose and the majority held that the objective of a law cannot shift to meet the demands of the reasonable-limits test. Even if the law could be said to relate to the pressing and substantial concern of promoting racial harmony, the majority found that it could not satisfy the minimal-impairment test. Unlike the anti-hate speech law, the "false news" provision was far too broad. Falsity was difficult to determine, and, combined with the virtually unlimited reach of the phrase "injury to a public interest," the provision created an offence that posed a serious threat to freedom of expression. Writing for the majority, McLachlin J. made reference to the significant "chilling effect" this provision could have on protected speech:

> To permit the imprisonment of people, or even the threat of imprisonment, on the ground that they have made a statement which 12 of their co-citizens deem to be false and mischievous to some undefined public interest, is to stifle a whole range of speech, some of which has long been regarded as legitimate and even beneficial to our society. I do not assert that Parliament cannot criminalize the dissemination of racial slurs and hate propaganda. I do assert, however, that such provisions must be drafted with sufficient particularity to offer assurance that they cannot be abused so as to stifle a broad range of legitimate and valuable speech.[61]

McLachlin J. was not persuaded by the argument that the authorities could be trusted to use the law only when appropriate:

> The whole purpose of enshrining rights in the *Charter* is to afford the individual protection against even the well-intentioned majority. To justify an invasion of a constitutional right on the ground that public authorities can be trusted not to violate it unduly is to undermine the very premise upon which the *Charter* is predicated.[62]

---

61   *Ibid.* at 743 (S.C.R.).
62   *Ibid.* at 773 (S.C.R.).

E. PORNOGRAPHY

Pornography poses a problem similar to that of hate speech. Pornography is a form of expression in that it does convey a meaning. However, pornography is degrading, dehumanizing, and inimical to other *Charter* values, especially the equality of women. Defining what constitutes pornography with sufficient precision to avoid threatening legitimate artistic or scientific treatment of eroticism and sexuality is notoriously difficult. Is it possible to criminalize that which is of no redeeming value without posing an unjustifiable risk to the freedom to explore the important human issues of sexuality and eroticism?

The Supreme Court of Canada was confronted with these issues in *R. v. Butler*.[63] The *Criminal Code* makes it an offence to make, publish, or circulate "obscene" materials. An obscene publication has as its "dominant characteristic" "the undue exploitation of sex, or of sex and any one or more of . . . crime, horror, cruelty, and violence."[64] This definition is vague and prosecutions for the offence are susceptible to misuse. The offence was enacted in an era when the use of criminal prosecutions to enforce standards of sexual propriety and decency was readily accepted. Prosecutions against sexually explicit works of literary or artistic merit are certainly not unheard of. On the other hand, the reach of the provision has been to some degree restricted in recent years by judicial decisions that viewed the law as aimed at a different harm, namely, the legitimization or encouragement of sexual violence and victimization of women. These decisions interpreted the law as a means to protect the values of equality, specifically with respect to women, and emphasized the harm of sexual violence, degradation, and dehumanization.

In *Butler*, faced with a challenge to the law on the ground that it infringed freedom of expression, the Supreme Court built upon this interpretive framework for the obscenity offence. The judgment of Sopinka J. first developed a test for determining whether representations of sex in any given case could be described as obscene. That test requires the courts to determine "what the community would tolerate others being exposed to on the basis of the degree of harm that may flow from such exposure."[65] Sopinka J. then went on to describe three categories of pornography: first, explicit sex with violence, which would almost always be punishable; second, explicit sex without violence but that is

---

63   *Butler*, above note 16.
64   Section 163.
65   *Butler*, above note 16 at 485.

degrading and dehumanizing, which would be punishable if the risk of harm is substantial; and, third, explicit sex without violence and that is not dehumanizing or degrading, which would not be punishable unless children are employed in its production.[66] In effect, the Court found that it was possible to interpret an offence originally intended to protect a certain view of sexual morality as having evolved to the point where it now protects against sexual violence and the denial of equality for women. The Court reinterpreted the obscenity offence so that it became an anti-pornography provision.

The Court was unanimous in finding that the offence, interpreted in this way, could withstand *Charter* scrutiny. As with hate speech, the Court had little hesitation in holding that, however reprehensible, pornography is a form of expression since it is intended to convey a meaning. This meant that the law had to be subjected to section 1 analysis. The Court held that the enforcement of decency and sexual propriety is not an objective sufficient to override a *Charter* right because such an objective would be inimical to individual freedom of choice. However, the Court was satisfied, that with the refined definition it accorded to the offence, the law was aimed at values essential to a free and democratic society, namely, the dignity and autonomy of women and the avoidance of degradation and dehumanization. In the Supreme Court's view, this did not conflict with the "false news" case[67] where the Court had refused to accept that the purpose of the law could shift to meet a modern problem.

On the issue of proportionality, pornography, like hate speech, was found to lie outside the core values underlying freedom of expression, and hence a more relaxed form of scrutiny was applied. Indeed, in *Butler*, the Supreme Court adopted an unusually relaxed standard when assessing the strength of the evidence linking pornography to the harm it was alleged to cause. The Court acknowledged that, in this area, the connection was difficult if not impossible to establish, but rather than hold that this gap in evidence was fatal to the section 1 analysis, Sopinka J. stated: "[I]t is reasonable to presume that exposure to images bears a causal relationship to changes in attitude and beliefs."[68] Even with its modern and refined interpretation, the pornography offence is anything but precise. However, the Court frankly admitted that past attempts at a more precise definition had floundered. In this context, the

---

66   Two members of the Court, Gonthier and L'Heureux Dubé JJ., disagreed and said that the depiction of explicit sex could be punished if displayed in certain public settings.

67   *Zundel*, above note 18.

68   *Butler*, above note 16 at 502 (S.C.R.).

Court was prepared to find that the minimal-impairment test could be satisfied by a law that fell well short of perfection.

The Supreme Court took a similar approach in a case involving a challenge to the *Criminal Code* provisions dealing with child pornography.[69] The law prohibited possession of materials showing a person under the age of eighteen engaged in explicit sexual activity. This definition, if applied casually, posed a serious threat to protected expression. However, rather than strike down the vaguely worded prohibition, the Court found it possible to save it through interpretation. By narrowly interpreting the prohibition, liberally interpreting the defences for matters having artistic merit or an educational or scientific purpose, and by reading into the law certain exceptions for purely personal materials that did not involve children in their production, the Court held that its scope was narrowed to a limit on freedom of expression that could be justified under section 1.

In *Little Sisters Book and Art Emporium v. Canada (Minister of Justice)*,[70] the Supreme Court once again adopted a deferential approach to Parliament's efforts to deal with the problem of pornography. The Court found that the *Butler* test applied equally to gay and lesbian materials. By seizing and refusing to allow into Canada gay and lesbian books and magazines that did not violate the *Butler* standard, customs officials had violated the freedom of expression of a Vancouver book store. However, the majority decision, written by Binnie J., refused to strike down the broad powers of customs officials to intercept obscene materials at the border. Binnie J. held that although errors would be made in interpretation, Parliament was entitled to assume that the *Butler* definition would be applied properly by public officials. The dissenting opinion, written by Iacobucci J., would have struck down the provision on the ground that there was a long history of misapplication of the law and an absence of safeguards to ensure that *Charter* rights are respected. Iacobucci's approach appears to have been prescient, as customs officials seized further books and magazines sent to the same book store shortly after the judgment. The book store again launched an action to contest the detention of these materials, and sought to have its costs in the litigation funded in advance by the public. The advance costs issue came before the Supreme Court, and a majority refused the

---

69   *R. v. Sharpe*, [2001] 1 S.C.R. 45, 194 D.L.R. (4th) 1.

70   [2000] 2 S.C.R. 1120. The Court also found that customs officials had violated s. 15 of the *Charter* by discriminating on the basis of sexual orientation in targeting the imports of the Little Sisters, a gay and lesbian book store. See chapter 15 on equality rights for further discussion.

request.[71] Binnie J. in dissent would have granted advance costs, finding the situation to be a "special case."[72]

The *Butler* harm test was further elaborated in *R. v. Labaye*,[73] a case dealing with an adult only "swingers" club charged with the offence of keeping a common bawdy house "for the purpose of indecency". The majority held that the *Butler* harm test should be used to determine whether there was sufficient harm to warrant a criminal conviction. This involves two steps. First, the nature of the harm must be one of three different kinds: the loss of autonomy or liberty of those exposed to the material; harm to society by predisposing others to anti-social conduct; and harm to individuals participating in the production of the material. Second, the harm or risk of harm must be of such a degree that it is incompatible with the proper functioning of society. While *Labaye* did not involve freedom of expression, or any other provision of the *Charter*, it is likely that this more elaborate development of the *Butler* test will serve as the new constitutional standard for prohibiting expression deemed to be obscene.

F. JUDICIAL PROCEEDINGS

The Supreme Court has recognized that, in view of the important role played by the courts in our society, "the courts must be open to public scrutiny and to public criticism of their operation by the public . . . . The press must be free to comment upon court proceedings to ensure that courts are, in fact, seen by all to operate openly in the penetrating light of public scrutiny."[74] This principle led the Supreme Court to strike down legislation prohibiting publication of the details of matrimonial proceedings,[75] and it led the Ontario Court of Appeal to give a narrow definition to the offence of contempt of court for intemperate remarks critical of the judicial system.[76]

Yet another area in which freedom of expression collides with other *Charter* rights is the "free press versus fair trial" debate. The right of everyone charged with an offence to a fair trial on the basis of the evi-

---

71 *Little Sisters Book and Art Emporium v. Canada (Commissioner of Customs and Revenue)*, [2007] 1 S.C.R. 38, discussed in chapter 7.

72 *Ibid.* at para. 137.

73 [2005] 3 S.C.R. 728 [*Labaye*].

74 *Edmonton Journal v. Alberta (A.G.)*, [1989] 2 S.C.R. 1326 at 1337 and 1339, 64 D.L.R. (4th) 577.

75 *Ibid.*

76 *Kopyto*, above note 2.

dence produced in court is reinforced by the *Charter*, section 11(d). The press is plainly entitled to provide the public with information about cases pending before the courts, but in some circumstances pre-trial publicity may be thought to affect the right to a fair trial. Before the *Charter*, there is little doubt but that Canadian courts accorded priority to the right to a fair trial. Where pre-trial disclosure of evidence, the identity of the accused, or details of the offence might possibly prejudice potential jurors against the accused or otherwise impair the right of the accused to a fair trial, the courts did not hesitate to impose gag orders delaying publication of such details until after the trial. Such orders plainly limited freedom of expression and freedom of the press, but since neither right was expressly guaranteed by the constitution, the courts were entitled to give priority to the statutory right to a fair trial.

In *Dagenais v. Canadian Broadcasting Corp.*,[77] the Supreme Court was asked to review this area in light of the *Charter* and the entrenchment of the rights of freedom of expression and freedom of the press. The Court found that the pre-*Charter* rule inappropriately emphasized the right to a fair trial at the expense of freedom of expression. Under the *Charter*, both freedom of expression and the right to a fair trial enjoy constitutional protection, and "*Charter* principles require a balance to be achieved that fully respects the importance of both sets of rights."[78] This led the Court to conclude that a more stringent test should be applied to publication bans so that the balance between these conflicting rights might be achieved. A ban should be ordered only where it was shown to be necessary to prevent a real and substantial risk to fairness of the trial, and where reasonably available alternative measures, such as adjourning the trial, allowing challenges for cause during jury selection, and strong instructions to the jury or change of venue, would not prevent the risk. To this, the Court added the requirement that it be shown that "the salutary effects of the publication ban outweigh the deleterious impact the ban has on free expression."[79]

The decision represents a significant change in the law with respect to gag orders. The case also provides further insight into the manner in which the Supreme Court responds to measures that limit freedom of expression in the name of protecting another *Charter* right or freedom. As in the cases dealing with hate speech and pornography, the Court has rejected the proposition that one right or freedom should be given priority over another. Rather, the Court has said that the appropriate

---

77   [1994] 3 S.C.R. 835, 120 D.L.R. (4th) 12 [*Dagenais*].
78   *Ibid.* at 877 (S.C.R.), Lamer C.J.C.
79   *Ibid.* at 878 (S.C.R.).

approach is to reconcile the competing rights through the proportionality review of section 1, allowing measures intended to protect one
right to limit another but only to the extent necessary and subject to
the minimal-impairment test.

In *R. v. Mentuk*,[80] a publication ban was granted by the trial judge to
protect the identity of undercover police officers and police operational
methods. Here, the competing interests were the protection of freedom
of expression on the one hand and the proper administration of justice on the other. The Supreme Court reformulated the *Dagenais* test in
more general terms to accommodate the various competing interests
that might arise:

> A publication ban should only be ordered when such an order is
> necessary to prevent a serious risk to the proper administration of
> justice, because reasonable alternative measures will not prevent the
> risk, and when the salutary effects of the publication ban outweigh
> the deleterious effects on the rights and interests of the parties and
> the public, including the effects on the right to free expression, the
> right of the accused to a fair and public trial, and the efficacy of the
> administration of justice.[81]

Iacobucci J. stressed that because "the presumption that courts should
be open and reporting of their proceedings should be uncensored is
so strong and so highly valued in our society," a ban should only be
ordered upon "a convincing evidentiary basis."[82]

The Supreme Court found that the public had a right to know about
the use and possible abuse of police powers and that the Crown had
failed to demonstrate that the ban on publishing details of the operational methods of the police was necessary to protect the proper investigation of crime. However, the Court also found that protecting the
identity of undercover police officers for a specifically time-limited period was justified. This ban would protect the personal safety of individ-

---

80 [2001] 3 S.C.R. 442 [*Mentuk*].
81 *Ibid.* at para. 32. See also *Sierra Club v. Canada (Minister of Finance)*, [2002] 2
    S.C.R. 522, applying this test in a case involving a confidentiality order with
    respect to documents concerning financial aid for the construction of nuclear
    reactors in China. In that case, the Court upheld the confidentiality order, hold-
    ing that the protection of commercial interests was sufficiently important to
    restrict the open court principle and that the restriction was justified given the
    narrow scope and the highly technical nature of the information covered by the
    confidentiality order. See also *Toronto Star Newspapers Ltd. v. Ontario*, [2005] 2
    S.C.R. 188, applying the same test to sealing orders for search warrants.
82 *Mentuk, ibid.* at para. 39.

ual police officers engaged in dangerous operations without impairing the right of the public to know how police powers are exercised.

The Supreme Court has reaffirmed the importance of the open court principle, even in the national security context. In *Ruby v. Canada (Solicitor General)*,[83] it held that provisions of the *Privacy Act* requiring a reviewing court to hear all cases involving claims of foreign confidences or national security without either the public or the applicant being present constituted an unjustified violation of freedom of expression. The Court acknowledged that the mandatory closed court provisions were rationally connected to the pressing objectives of protecting foreign confidences and national security, but concluded that the statutory requirement that the entire proceedings be held *in camera* were disproportionate. In the result, the Court read down the offending provision so that the Court had the discretion to close proceedings only when and if the release of information would harm foreign confidences and national security. A similar approach was taken in *Re Vancouver Sun*[84] when the Supreme Court held that a rebuttable presumption of an open court applied to the conduct of investigative hearings under the *Anti-Terrorism Act* to obtain information about terrorist activities. The Court overturned a judge's order that the entire investigative hearing would be held *in camera* without notice to the media or the accused in the ongoing Air India trial. The Court affirmed that the stringent tests for justifying restrictions on the open court principle articulated in *Dagenais* and *Mentuk* should be applied to all discretionary judicial decisions that limit freedom of expression. In other words, any publication ban should be ordered only when necessary to prevent a serious risk to the proper administration of justice because reasonably alternative measures would not prevent the risk, and only if the salutary effects of the publication ban outweighed its deleterious effects. Applying these principles of minimal impairment and proportionality, the Court found that although the application for an investigative hearing and the identity of the person being compelled to reveal information should be kept secret, the existence of the hearing, its subject matter, and the *Charter* challenge to the novel procedure should be open. Two judges dissented on the basis that a presumption of a closed court was justified given the danger of publicity to ongoing terrorism investigations and to those being compelled to reveal information about terrorism. In total, these cases suggest that the open court principle will be the starting point and that any proposed limitation on it will be subject to stringent

---

83 [2002] 4 S.C.R. 3.
84 [2004] 2 S.C.R. 332.

standards of justification, including those of minimal impairment and proportionality.

G. PROTECTION OF REPUTATION

An individual's reputation enjoys the protection of law. Statements that defame and injure reputation may give rise to a civil right of action for libel or slander, permitting the targeted individual to claim damages for the injury to reputation. The law of libel is notoriously complex and difficult but essentially provides that, where the defendant publishes a statement injurious to the plaintiff's reputation, damages are recoverable. While certain defences are available, including the truth of the statement complained of, it is for the defendant to prove a defence, failing which damages are presumed. In recent years, Canadian juries have been willing to award substantial damages, both compensatory and punitive.

Here again, a laudable and important objective is said to require limiting the rights of freedom of expression and freedom of the press. Canadian law makes no distinction between private and public figures. The press must observe the same strict requirements when describing the activities of political and public figures as apply to ordinary citizens. The presumption of falsity means that any time the press makes a statement that might injure reputation, it must be able to prove the truth of what it has said according to the exacting standards of a court of law. Honest belief in the truth of the statement provides no defence, nor does absence of malice or negligence in the writing of the story. The press must, therefore, be more than cautious in what it says; it must be right. Journalists have to avoid publishing stories, even on matters of immediate public interest and concern, unless they are confident that the truth of statements capable of injuring reputation can be proved.

The courts of England,[85] the United States,[86] Australia[87] and New Zealand[88] have seen fit to modify the law of defamation and to accord significantly more weight to freedom of expression.[89] In the United States, this change was premised on the constitutional guarantee of freedom of the press. American law distinguishes between public and

---

85   *Reynolds v. Times Newspapers*, [2001] 2 AC 127.

86   *New York Times Co. v. Sullivan*, 376 U.S. 254 (1964).

87   *Theophanous v. Herald and Weekly Times Ltd.* (1994), 124 A.L.R. 1 (H.C.).

88   *Lange v. Atkinson*, [2000] 3 N.Z.L.R. 385.

89   For a review of these developments from a Canadian perspective, see *Cusson v. Quan* (2007), 87 O.R. (3d) 241 (C.A.) adopting the English "responsible journalism" defence. Leave to appeal to the SCC granted, [2008] 1 S.C.R. xii.

private figures. In the case of a public figure, the presumption of falsity is removed and the plaintiff is required to prove that the defendant acted with malice, that is, that the defendant knew the story was false or was wilfully blind to its falsity.

In *Hill v. Church of Scientology of Toronto*,[90] the Supreme Court of Canada was asked to reconsider the common law of defamation, particularly the presumptions of falsity and damage, in light of the *Charter* protection of freedom of expression. The plaintiff, a crown attorney, sued after a lawyer for the Church of Scientology publicly announced that his client intended to take proceedings alleging the crown attorney had breached an order of the court. These allegations proved to be without foundation, and the jury awarded over one million dollars in damages. As explained in chapter 6, the *Charter* does not apply directly to the common law in such circumstances. While the Supreme Court did not resist the proposition that the common law must evolve and change in light of *Charter* values, the Court was unwilling to make any significant change in the law.[91] Writing for the Court, Cory J. said that defamatory statements are only tenuously connected to the core values protected by freedom of expression, while the right to individual reputation, although not specifically protected by the *Charter*, represents and reflects the innate dignity of the individual, a value that underlies all *Charter* rights. Accordingly, the Court rejected the argument that the law of defamation was in need of significant reformulation and found the balance struck by the existing law in favour of the protection of reputation to be appropriate. The Court adopted a similar approach in *R. v. Lucas*,[92] upholding the *Criminal Code* provisions dealing with defamatory libel. Though finding that the law infringed freedom of expression, the Court reiterated the importance attached to the protection of reputation and held that the law was justifiable under section 1. The Supreme Court has also indicated that defamation actions under Quebec's *Civil Code* strike the correct balance between freedom of expression and the protection of reputation. The Court stressed the need for proof of fault in terms of actions that violate the standards of a reasonable journalist. Binnie J. dissented on the basis that the award of $673,153 in damages for truthful statements made in the public interest but out of their proper context was a violation of freedom of expression.[93]

---

90   [1995] 2 S.C.R. 1130, 126 D.L.R. (4th) 129.

91   The Court did extend the defence of "qualified privilege" to reports of pleadings and other court documents yet to be filed.

92   *Lucas*, above note 18.

93   *Gilles E. Néron Communication Marketing Inc. v. Chambre des notaires du Québec*, [2004] 3 S.C.R. 3.

The Supreme Court's approach to defamation now appears to be changing. The Court gave further consideration to how the *Charter*'s guarantee of freedom of expression should influence the common law of defamation in *WIC Radio Ltd. v. Simpson.*[94] The plaintiff was an outspoken opponent of the introduction to schools of materials dealing with homosexuality. When a radio talk show host criticized the views of the plaintiff on air with comments indicating that the plaintiff condoned violence against gay people, the plaintiff sued for defamation. The host argued that he was protected by the defence of "fair comment" as he had expressed an opinion based on fact on a matter of public interest. Previous cases had held that the defence was only available where the defendant honestly believed the opinion he had expressed and the talk show host did not so swear. The majority held that the *Charter* value of freedom of expression required a change in the common law and that the fair comment defence would be made out if *any person* could honestly express the opinion on the basis of the proved facts. As the Court noted, newspaper editors, who can be liable for comments expressed in their publications, may often not themselves agree with the comments expressed in their publications and if not afforded the more generous defence, public debate on important public issues could be stifled. The *WIC* decision recognizes that "an individual's reputation is not to be treated as regrettable but unavoidable road kill on the highway of public controversy" but also holds that "an overly solicitous regard for personal reputation" should not "be permitted to 'chill' freewheeling debate on matters of public interest."[95] This suggests that the Court may now be willing to reconsider the common law's marked preference for the protection of reputation over freedom of expression.

H. LOCATION OF THE EXPRESSION

Individuals who wish to express themselves often seek to do so in a well-travelled public place. For those who lack the resources to place their message in newspapers or broadcast media, expressing oneself in a public place may be essential if the message is to find an audience. An audience may be found at public places such as roads, squares, parks, and airports. Yet each of these places has a public purpose. How should the individual's right to freedom of expression be reconciled with the rights of others to use these places for their intended purpose? Does the

---

94   *WIC Radio Ltd. v. Simpson,* above note 4.
95   *Ibid.* at para. 2.

state have the right to control access to such places for the purposes of disseminating a message?

In *Committee for the Commonwealth of Canada v. Canada*[96] the Supreme Court of Canada considered this issue in relation to the claim of a group that sought to distribute pamphlets at a major Canadian airport. The Court rejected the contention that the government could preclude the pamphleteers from distributing their materials at the airport. As Lamer C.J.C. noted, government property is held for the benefit of the community at large and ownership does not, by itself, justify refusal of access for expressive purposes. By the same token, however, the right of the individual asserting freedom of expression must be assessed with reference to the public purpose of the place in question. Six of the seven judges sitting on the case found it necessary to write reasons, and hence it is not possible to identify a single rationale for the decision. However, in the end, all the judges agreed that the exercise of the right to freedom of expression did, in the circumstances, include the right to express oneself at the airport.

While the members of the Court found that the pamphleteers' freedom of expression extended to their activities in the airport, they generally accepted that not all types of public property would attract s. 2(b) protection. Two different tests were suggested by the Court to determine whether the freedom of expression was protected in a particular public space. The first was based on an analysis of the primary function of the space, and whether that function was compatible with free expression. The second was based on whether protecting expression in the space would serve the underlying values of the freedom. Given the split in the Court in this case, neither of these tests was definitively adopted.

A subsequent case[97] dealt with posters and came to a similar conclusion. A musician advertised performances of his band by placing posters on hydro poles. Charged under a municipal bylaw prohibiting the placing of posters on public property, he challenged the bylaw as an infringement of freedom of expression. Iacobucci J. was conscious of the importance of posters as a form of expression for those with limited resources: "[P]osters have communicated political, cultural and social information for centuries."[98] All members of the Court agreed that the bylaw's complete ban on posters constituted an undue restriction of freedom of expression. The Court found it unnecessary to determine which of the two tests suggested in *Commonwealth of Canada* was preferable.

---

96   [1991] 1 S.C.R. 139, 77 D.L.R. (4th) 385 [*Commonwealth of Canada*].
97   *Peterborough (City) v. Ramsden*, [1993], 2 S.C.R. 1084, 106 D.L.R. (4th) 233.
98   *Ibid.* at 245 (D.L.R.).

This issue was addressed again in *Montreal (City) v. 2952-1366 Québec Inc.*[99] The respondent operated a strip club in Montreal, and set up a loudspeaker in the entranceway to broadcast music and commentary onto the street, in order to attract customers. The respondent was charged under a municipal bylaw for emitting sound produced by sound equipment which could be heard outside. The respondent challenged the bylaw, claiming that it was an unjustifiable infringement of his freedom of expression. The Court held that on either of the tests proposed in *Commonwealth of Canada*, the public street was a place in which freedom of expression was protected.

While observing that it was unnecessary to do so, the majority went on to articulate a more definitive test for determining whether section 2(b) protection extends to a particular public space. The Court held that the question to be asked is "whether the place is a public place where one would expect constitutional protection for free expression on the basis that expression in that place does not conflict with the purposes which s. 2(*b*) is intended to serve."[100] Two factors were highlighted to be considered in answering this question. First, the historical or actual function of the public place in question, and whether its function or the activities taking place within it are compatible with free expression. Second, whether other aspects of the space indicate that allowing free expression within it would serve to undermine the values underlying the freedom of expression. After determining that the street outside the club was amenable to free expression, the majority went on to find that the bylaw was justified under section 1 as a reasonable measure to prevent noise pollution.

In *Greater Vancouver Transportation Authority v. Canadian Federation of Students—British Columbia Component*,[101] the Supreme Court held that a public transit authority that sold advertising space on the sides of buses could not refuse to accept political advertisements. The transit authority was held to be an arm of government that afforded access to advertising on its buses but imposed a content-based restriction by refusing messages that had political content. The majority judgment, written by Deschamps J., held the claimants were not advancing a claim that the government was required to provide them with a platform for their expression but rather that they were entitled to use "an existing platform . . . without undue state interference with the content of their expression."[102] Applying the *City of Montreal* test, the court

---

99 *Montreal (City) v. 2952-1366 Québec Inc.*, above note 15.
100 *Ibid.* at para. 74.
101 2009 SCC 31.
102 *Ibid.* at para. 35.

found that there was both a history and an actual use of the sides of buses as a space for public expression and that as "the space allows for expression by a broad range of speakers to a large public audience" and that allowing expression "could actually further the values underlying section 2(b)," the side of a bus "was a location where expressive activity is protected by section 2(b) of the *Charter*."[103] Refusing political messages could not be justified as a reasonable limit under section 1. While the Court accepted the sufficiency of the objective of providing a safe, welcoming public transit system, it held that refusing political messages had a rational connection to that objective and, in any event, the blanket refusal to accept political advertisements failed the minimal impairment test and was not proportionate to the claimants' right to express their message.

I. CONCLUSION

The Supreme Court has identified freedom of expression as an important *Charter* guarantee that lies at the heart of a free and democratic society, but it has also refused to accord anything approaching absolute protection to this important freedom. The Court has given expression an exceptionally wide definition, leaving to the section 1 analysis the difficult issues of reconciling this important freedom with other values. The results have been mixed. Despite the importance it has attached to freedom of expression, the Court has demonstrated considerable tolerance for laws that limit freedom of expression in the name of protecting minority interests. Laws prohibiting hate speech, pornography, and third party spending during elections have been upheld under relatively relaxed section 1 scrutiny on the ground that significant countervailing equality values are at stake. Similarly, protection of reputation prevailed over freedom of expression when the Court was asked to reassess the laws of defamation although more recent cases indicate a willingness to adjust the law of defamation to better accommodate freedom of expression. On the other hand, the law relating to reporting judicial proceedings has been significantly modified under the *Charter* in favour of the media. With respect to commercial speech, an area some observers predicted would not be affected by the *Charter*, the Court has insisted upon a relatively high level of proof that legal restraints are required to achieve state objectives.

---

103 *Ibid.* at para. 46.

It is thought by those who place special value on freedom of expression that this pattern of decisions is inconsistent.[104] While the Supreme Court has never denied the importance of freedom of expression, it has certainly been prepared to see this freedom limited in the name of protecting other important interests. Other observers applaud the judicial refusal to place freedom of expression on a special pedestal and welcome the Court's willingness to grant Parliament and the legislatures a degree of latitude in the protection of equality values.[105] These critics contend that, if anything, the Court has been too solicitous of expression in the area of commercial speech. In the end, as this range of opinion suggests, the Court has proceeded very much on a case-by-case basis, avoiding definitive pronouncements on other than the basic structure for analysis of a freedom of expression claim.

FURTHER READINGS

BOROVOY, A.A., *When Freedoms Collide: The Case for Our Civil Liberties* (Toronto: Lester & Orpen Dennys, 1988) c. 2

CAMERON, J., "The Past, Present and Future of Expressive Future under the *Charter*" (1997) 35 Osgoode Hall L.J. 1

DYZENHAUS, D., "Regulating Free Speech" (1991) 23 Ottawa L. Rev. 289

FLOOD, C., "Freedom of Commercial Free Expression: The Most Undervalued *Charter* Right" (2006) 21 N.J.C.L. 271

HUTCHINSON, A.C., "Money Talk: Against Constitutionalising (Commercial) Speech" (1990) 17 Can. Bus. L.J. 2

LEE, I., "Can Economics Justify Freedom of Expression?" (2008) 21 Can. J.L. & Jur. 355

LEPOFSKY, M.D., "The Supreme Court's Approach to Freedom of Expression: *Irwin Toy v. Quebec (Attorney General)* and the Illusion of Section 2(b) Liberalism" (1993) 3 N.J.C.L. 37

---

104 See, for example, A. Borovoy, *When Freedoms Collide: The Case for Our Civil Liberties* (Toronto: Lester & Orpen Dennys, 1988) c. 2.
105 See, for example, K. Mahoney, "The Canadian Constitutional Approach to Freedom of Expression in Hate Propaganda and Pornography" (1992) 55 Law & Contemp. Probs. 77.

MAHONEY, K., "The Canadian Constitutional Approach to Freedom of Expression in Hate Propaganda and Pornography" (1992) 55 Law & Contemp. Probs. 77

MOON, R., "The Supreme Court of Canada on the Structure of Freedom of Expression Adjudication" (1995) 45 U.T.L.J. 419

MOON, R., *The Constitutional Protection of Freedom of Expression* (Toronto: University of Toronto Press, 2000)

REID, C., "Freedom of Expression, Commercial Expression and Tobacco in Canada" (2008) 39 V.U.W.L.R. 343

ROACH, K., & D. SCHNEIDERMAN, "Freedom of Expression in Canada" in G.A. Beaudoin & E. Mendes, eds., *The Canadian Charter of Rights and Freedoms*, 4th ed. (Markham, ON: LexisNexis Butterworths, 2005)

SCHNEIDERMAN, D., ed., *Freedom of Expression and the Charter* (Toronto: Carswell, 1991)

SHARPE, R.J., "Commercial Expression and the *Charter*" (1987) 37 U.T.L.J. 229

WEINRIB, L., "Hate Promotion in a Free and Democratic Society: *R. v. Keegstra*" (1991) 36 McGill L.J. 1416

CHAPTER 10

FREEDOM OF ASSOCIATION

Freedom of association, guaranteed by section 2(d) of the *Charter of Rights and Freedoms*, protects the right of individuals to come together to form a wide array of organizations and relationships, including those with political, religious, and social purposes. The difficult threshold issue for the courts has been whether the guarantee not only recognizes the right of individuals to come together in an organization but also confers constitutional protection on the activities essential to ensure the association's meaningful existence.

Nowhere has the issue of the scope of the guarantee of freedom of association been more hotly debated than with respect to the institutions and practices of collective bargaining. Most of the caselaw on section 2(d) deals with labour relations, especially in the public sector. If section 2(d) protects only the right to come together and form an association, its importance is relatively modest. On the other hand, to the extent that it also protects the essential activities of the group, it has enormous impact, particularly in the realm of labour relations. Another important issue for the collective bargaining regime is whether freedom of association includes the right to refuse to be associated with a group or its views and policies. Does section 2(d) include the right to join the trade union of one's choice, or to refuse to join a union or pay it dues?

A. THE RIGHT TO ENGAGE IN COLLECTIVE BARGAINING

The Supreme Court of Canada first dealt with the claim that section 2(d) protects the right to engage in collective bargaining in a trilogy of cases dealing with legislation limiting the right to strike. In the leading case, *Reference Re Public Service Employee Relations Act*,[1] a majority of the Court held that the guarantee of freedom of association did not encompass the right to bargain collectively or the right to strike. The legislation at issue removed the right to strike from public sector workers and, in the absence of agreement, prescribed mandatory arbitration to determine the contents of the collective agreement. LeDain J. held that the rights to bargain collectively and to strike are not fundamental rights or freedoms. Rather, they are the creatures of legislation that balances a number of competing interests. Clearly, LeDain J. felt that the area of labour relations was one requiring specialized expertise. He was influenced by the fact that this area of law had largely been removed from the courts and assigned to the supervision of labour relations tribunals. LeDain J. limited the protection of section 2(d) to "the freedom to work for the establishment of an association, to belong to an association, to maintain it, and to participate in its lawful activity without penalty or reprisal."[2]

The dissenting judges, Dickson C.J.C. and Wilson J., concluded that the guarantee of freedom of association did include the rights for workers to bargain collectively and to strike. In their view, section 2(d) protected not only the right to join together but also the right of members of the association to pursue together aims that could be lawfully pursued individually. Although there is no individual equivalent to the right to strike, the dissenting judges thought that this activity should be included in section 2(d), given its importance to the protection of the interests of working people. While they would have found the legislation to violate section 2(d), the dissenting judges conceded that certain restraints on the right to strike would be acceptable under section 1. Dickson C.J.C. noted that ensuring essential services during a labour dispute could be a pressing and substantial objective under section 1. However, the legislation at issue was not, in his view, justifiable be-

---

1   *Reference Re Public Service Employee Relations Act (Alberta)*, [1987] 1 S.C.R. 313, 38 D.L.R. (4th) 161 [*Alberta Reference*]. McIntyre J., writing alone and in much greater detail, concluded that s. 2(d) did not include a right to strike, although he did not specify whether it included a right to bargain collectively.

2   *Ibid.* at 391 (S.C.R.).

cause its prohibition on striking was too sweeping and included more than essential workers. Furthermore, Dickson C.J.C. wrote, the arbitration provisions did not adequately safeguard employees' interests, since they provided for government control of access to arbitration and placed restrictions on the items that could be bargained.

In the two companion cases, a majority of the Court held that limitations on the right to strike and bargain did not violate the right guaranteed by section 2(d). In one case, Saskatchewan legislation banning a strike in the dairy industry was upheld,[3] while the other upheld the federal government's price-and-wage control program, which banned strikes and altered the financial compensation scheme.[4] Following these decisions, there was still some doubt whether section 2(d) of the *Charter* might include a right to bargain collectively, even if it did not include a right to strike. However, in the *PIPS* case, the majority of the Supreme Court rejected the argument that the right to bargain collectively was included in section 2(d).[5] The Professional Institute of the Public Service (PIPS) had represented a group of federal government employees transferred to employment with the Northwest Territories government. The public-service legislation of the Northwest Territories provided that a union could not obtain bargaining rights unless it was incorporated under legislation giving it the power to bargain collectively, and PIPS was not incorporated under this legislation. The majority of the Supreme Court held that there was no violation of section 2(d), because the transferred employees remained free to join any union. The incorporation provision was likened to the voluntary recognition provisions in other collective bargaining legislation, which allow employers to recognize a union's right to bargain on behalf of its employees. Here, incorporation was the means by which the Legislative Council of the Territories conferred bargaining rights on a public sector union. As to the argument that this left PIPS with no chance to represent its former members, the Court held that no union could demand collective bargaining rights vis-à-vis an employer, stating that "since the activity of bargaining is not itself constitutionally protected, neither is a legislative choice of the bargainer."[6] Writing for the majority, Sopinka J.

---

3   *R.W.D.S.U., Locals 544, 496, 635, 955 v. Saskatchewan*, [1987] 1 S.C.R. 460, 38 D.L.R. (4th) 277. In this case, Dickson C.J.C. reached the same conclusion as the majority, while Wilson J. was alone in dissent

4   *P.S.A.C. v. Canada (A.G.)*, [1987] 1 S.C.R. 424, 38 D.L.R. (4th) 249. Again Dickson C.J.C. and Wilson J. dissented.

5   *Professional Institute of the Public Service of Canada v. Northwest Territories (Commissioner)*, [1990] 2 S.C.R. 367, 72 D.L.R. (4th) 1 [*PIPS*].

6   *Ibid.* at 406 (S.C.R.).

turned to the reasons of McIntrye J. in the earlier *Alberta Reference* and summarized his view of the meaning of section 2(d):

> ... first, that s. 2(d) protects the freedom to establish, belong to and maintain an association; second, that s. 2(d) does not protect an activity solely on the ground that the activity is a foundational or essential purpose of an association; third, that s. 2(d) protects the exercise in association of the constitutional rights and freedoms of individuals; and fourth, that s. 2(d) protects the exercise in association of the lawful rights of individuals.[7]

Sopinka J. concluded that collective bargaining is not protected by section 2(d): "Restrictions on the *activity* of collective bargaining do not normally affect the ability of individuals to form or join unions."[8]

Cory J., with two others, dissented. In his view, the Legislative Council had to comply with the *Charter* when implementing the decision to permit collective bargaining by its employees. Mandating the incorporation of bargaining agents was seen to be an interference with the employees' right to select, form, or change an association.

This restrictive view of the scope of protection included within freedom of association was applied in the case of a challenge to the statutory exclusion of members of the RCMP from the *Public Service Staff Relations Act*, a federal law governing labour relations in the public service.[9] The majority of the Supreme Court held that section 2(d) did not protect the right of workers to be included in any particular statutory regime as they were free to form a parallel, independent employee association of their own.

However, in *Dunmore v. Ontario (Attorney General)*,[10] the Supreme Court began to move away from the exclusion of collective bargaining rights from the protection of section 2(d) and to breathe significant life into the reach of freedom of association. For years, agricultural workers had been excluded from Ontario's statutory regime governing collective bargaining. The law was amended by a pro-labour government to afford them certain rights, but then quickly repealed by a newly elected government with a different policy on collective bargaining. Agricultural workers challenged the repealing statute, arguing that they could not hope to form an association to protect their interests without the protective umbrella of labour relations legislation because of their highly

---

7   *Ibid.* at 402 (S.C.R.). See also *Canadian Egg Marketing Agency v. Richardson*, [1998] 3 S.C.R. 157, 160 D.L.R. (4th) 1 at 58.

8   *PIPS, ibid.* at 404 (S.C.R.).

9   *Delisle v. Canada (Deputy Attorney General)*, [1999] 2 S.C.R. 989.

10   [2001] 3 S.C.R. 1016, 207 D.L.R. (4th) 193 [*Dunmore*].

vulnerable position. The Supreme Court of Canada agreed and ordered the Ontario government to afford agricultural workers the needed statutory protections.

Writing for the majority, Bastarache J. concluded that "the freedom to collectively embody the interests of individual workers"[11] fell squarely within the protection of section 2(d) and that agricultural workers could not enjoy that freedom without protective legislation. Bastarache J. held that the four-part formulation of the rights protected by section 2(d) adopted in the *Alberta Reference* and *PIPS* should be supplemented:

> [T]here will be occasions where a given activity does not fall within the third and fourth rules but where the state has nevertheless prohibited that activity solely because of its associational nature. These occasions will involve activities which 1) are not protected under any other constitutional freedom, and 2) cannot, for one reason or another, be understood as the lawful activities of individuals.[12]

Particularly noteworthy is Bastarache J.'s recognition of the collective element in freedom of association, a feature of section 2(d) previously rejected by majority opinions. Reverting to Dickson C.J.C.'s dissent in the *Alberta Reference*,[13] Bastarache J. wrote that individuals form associations "not simply because there is strength in numbers, but because communities can embody objectives that individuals cannot."[14]

Also notable in *Dunmore* is the remedy ordered by the Supreme Court. Ordinarily, freedom of association is a "negative freedom," one that precludes state interference rather than requires affirmative state assistance. However, *Dunmore* holds that where a group lacks the means to form an association to protect its interests, and the effect of exclusion from a protective statutory regime, designed to facilitate freedom of association "substantially orchestrates, encourages or sustains the violation of fundamental freedoms,"[15] the state may be required to act.

Dunmore represented a significant shift by the Supreme Court of Canada. The judgment demonstrated a sensitivity to and concern for the rights of workers and for the importance of collective action. To require a legislature to act affirmatively to enhance the enjoyment of section 2(d) rights is novel.

Dunmore recognized that section 2(d) protects the freedom of workers to organize, but stopped short of constitutionalizing the right to

---

11   *Ibid.* at 224 (D.L.R.).
12   *Ibid.* at 213 (D.L.R.).
13   *Alberta Reference*, above note 1.
14   *Dunmore*, above note 10 at 213 (D.L.R.).
15   *Ibid.* at 221 (D.L.R.).

strike or even the right to engage in collective bargaining. However, in *Health Services and Support—Facilities Subsector Bargaining Assn. v. British Columbia*,[16] the Supreme Court of Canada held that section 2(d) protects the "capacity of members of labour unions to engage, in association, in collective bargaining on fundamental workplace issues."[17] British Columbia had passed legislation giving health care employers more flexibility to transfer and reassign employees, to contract out certain services, and to layoff employees. The legislation specified that any provision in an existing collective agreement that was inconsistent with these new employer powers was invalid to the extent of the inconsistency. Unions representing the affected employees challenged the legislation, arguing that it violated their rights under section 2(d) because it invalidated portions of their existing collective agreements and rendered any future collective bargaining on the affected topics largely meaningless. The Court accepted the unions' arguments, and declared certain provisions of the legislation to be unconstitutional.

In the majority judgment, McLachlin C.J. and LeBel J. noted that the protection of inherently collective activities recognized in *Dunmore* required a re-examination of both the *Alberta Reference* and *PIPS*. After reviewing the arguments relied on in those cases, McLachlin C.J. and LeBel J. concluded that "the holdings in the *Alberta Reference* and *PIPS* excluding collective bargaining from the scope of s. 2(d) can no longer stand."[18] The Court was careful to note that the right to bargain collectively does not entail a right to any substantive outcome, but is instead a right to a "general process of collective bargaining, not to a particular model of labour relations, nor to a specific bargaining method."[19]

As the Court characterized the right to bargain collectively as a right to bargain on "fundamental workplace issues," not every interference with collective bargaining will constitute an infringement of section 2(d). It is only when collective bargaining on matters which are "important to the ability of union members to pursue shared goals in concert"[20] are interfered with that section 2(d) will be violated. Moreover, the Court indicated that it may be possible to alter fundamental workplace issues by legislation or conduct without violating section 2(d), provided that the changes were effected following a process of good faith negotiation.[21]

---

16   [2007] 2 S.C.R. 391 [*Health Services*].
17   *Ibid.* at para. 19.
18   *Ibid.* at para. 36.
19   *Ibid.* at para. 91.
20   *Ibid.* at para. 96.
21   *Ibid.* at para. 109.

As *Health Services* dealt with direct government interference with collective bargaining, the case does not necessarily indicate that governments will be obligated to statutorily protect the ability of otherwise vulnerable unions to bargain collectively. However, *Dunmore* has made clear that section 2(d) can impose positive obligations on governments to statutorily protect vulnerable workers. In a recent case before the Court of Appeal for Ontario, agricultural workers challenged the legislation enacted by Ontario following *Dunmore*.[22] That legislation conferred the right to form associations and provided some protection against reprisals and intimidation but did not impose on employers an obligation to bargain in good faith, nor did it provide for the usual dispute resolution mechanisms or for exclusive bargaining rights. The court upheld the agricultural workers' challenge and held that *Health Services* and *Dunmore* required Ontario to enact legislation that provides "sufficient protections to enable agricultural workers to engage in a meaningful process of collective bargaining."[23] The Supreme Court of Canada has granted leave to Ontario to appeal the decision.[24]

While the law regarding section 2(d)'s protection of collective bargaining has significantly changed, there has not yet been any clear indication that the court is willing to rethink its position on the right to strike. In *Health Services*, the court made a point of noting that the case did "not concern the right to strike."[25] However, the court also ruled in that case that the arguments used in the *Alberta Reference* and *PIPS* against recognizing a right to collective bargaining were no longer persuasive, and some of these same arguments were also used to deny the right to strike. The *Dunmore* and *Health Services* decisions demonstrate that the Court is steadily distancing itself from its earlier jurisprudence on section 2(d), but the precise contours of the extent of the protection to be accorded to collective bargaining rights are yet to be determined.

B. THE RIGHT NOT TO ASSOCIATE

To this point, the focus has been on the freedom to associate. But sometimes an individual may not want to associate with another. This claim arose in *Lavigne*, where a community college teacher who was not a

---

22   *Fraser v. Ontario (Attorney General)* (2008), 92 O.R. (3d) 481.
23   *Ibid.* at para. 101.
24   [2009] S.C.C.A. No. 9
25   *Health Services*, above note 16 at para. 19. Similarly, in *Fraser*, above note 22, the court emphasized that the agricultural workers did not seek the right to strike: paras. 57, 82.

union member objected to a collective agreement provision forcing him to pay dues to the union. The compelled payment of dues, known as the "Rand formula" (or the agency shop), differs from compelled membership in the union (or a closed shop provision). Even though Lavigne was not compelled to join the union, he disagreed with a number of purposes for which his union dues were being spent, including opposing cruise missile testing and supporting certain causes, including access to abortion.

The collective agreement was subject to *Charter* scrutiny because the employer, the college's Council of Regents, was closely controlled by government and hence could be considered a Crown agent.[26] Four of seven judges held that the mandatory dues provision did not violate section 2(d), while three members of the court held that s. 2(d) was violated but that the legislation could be saved under s. 1.

Wilson J. and two others concluded that section 2(d) did not include a right not to associate (sometimes called a "negative right"). In her view, however, this did not leave an individual unprotected from the harms that might come from forced association. The section 2(b) guarantee of freedom of expression would be available to an individual who was compelled to be associated with views he or she did not hold.[27] McLachlin J. concluded that some instances of compelled association might violate section 2(d), but not the requirement to pay union dues. In her view, section 2(d) protected only against "coerced ideological conformity." She did not think that Lavigne's payment of dues in fact associated him with the union's causes.[28]

La Forest J., with whom two other judges concurred, found that section 2(d) included a right not to associate, which had been breached in this case. In his view, it is contrary to the *Charter* either to prevent individuals from joining together or to compel them to do so in some circumstances. While certain forced associations are a reality of modern society, La Forest J. found there was a *Charter* violation, since Lavigne was required to contribute to causes beyond the immediate concerns of the bargaining unit. Compelling him to contribute funds to the union for bargaining purposes, including collective agreement administration, served to protect the common good and was consistent with section 2(d), but forced contribution to non-union purposes was not.[29] However, La Forest J. concluded that the compelled payment of

---

26   This point is discussed in greater detail in chapter 6.

27   *Lavigne v. Ontario Public Service Employees Union*, [1991] 2 S.C.R. 211, 81 D.L.R. (4th) 545 at 582–85 [*Lavigne*].

28   *Ibid.* at 645 (D.L.R.).

29   *Ibid.* at 635 (D.L.R.).

dues was justified under section 1. He rejected the idea that individual objectors could be given an opportunity to opt out of paying for matters that were not purely "collective bargaining." Permitting such opting out would seriously undermine the union's financial security and invite paternalistic scrutiny of union activities by government.

The Supreme Court was again badly split on the question of the right not to associate in *Advance Cutting and Coring v. Quebec*.[30] The case involved a challenge to Quebec legislation governing the construction industry that required workers to be members of certain specified unions. This went well beyond the "Rand formula" at issue in *Lavigne* where workers are required to contribute to the union, but free to refuse to become members. Those supporting the law contended that it was necessary to avoid "free riders" who would reap the benefits of union activities, but weaken the union by withholding dues and membership. Four judges held that the law did not infringe freedom of association, four held that it did. The fifth and deciding voice was that of Iacobucci J. who held that the law did infringe freedom of association, but that it could be saved by section 1. L'Heureux-Dubé J. held that freedom of association does not include a negative right. LeBel J. (with whom Gonthier and Arbour JJ. agreed) found that there was a negative element to section 2(d) but that it was not a mirror image of the positive aspect and that it contained certain inner limits necessary to protect the association's "group voice."[31] In the absence of evidence that forced membership in the union would amount to ideological conformity, LeBel J. held that forced union membership did not violate section 2(d). Bastarache J., in dissent (with McLachlin C.J., Major and Binnie JJ.), found that ideological conformity was the inevitable result of forced union membership. The "Rand formula," approved in *Lavigne*, solved the free rider problem while avoiding coerced association.

C. CONCLUSION

The Supreme Court was initially reluctant to intervene in important aspects of the area of labour relations under the *Charter*. Freedom of association was held not to include the right to strike or the right to engage in collective bargaining, and the Court refused to interfere with mandatory dues and union membership. The Court did not grant unions new protection against legislative action curtailing bargaining and strikes,

---

30   [2001] 3 S.C.R. 209, 205 D.L.R. (4th) 385.
31   *Ibid.* at 482 (D.L.R.).

but neither did it give new tools to those opposed to the majoritarian nature of collective bargaining and intent on overturning agency and closed shop provisions. This cautious approach was decried by those who had hoped that the *Charter* would expand the scope of collective bargaining.[32] Others saw it as a middle of the road posture, consistent with the Court's tendency in other areas to refuse to recognize economic activity as worthy of *Charter* protection.[33] In the end, however, the narrow interpretation of section 2(d) was found to be inconsistent with the Court's generally liberal approach to *Charter* interpretation and with the concern shown in other areas for the rights and interests of vulnerable groups. The more generous interpretation of section 2(d) in *Dunmore* and *Health Services* clearly opens a new chapter in which collective bargaining rights are protected although the precise nature and extent of that protection remains a work in progress.

FURTHER READINGS

ADAMS, R., "The Revolutionary Potential of *Dunmore*" (2003) 10 C.L.E.I.J. 117

BAKAN, J., *Just Words: Constitutional Rights and Social Wrongs* (Toronto: University of Toronto Press, 1997) c. 5

BARRETT, S., "*Dunmore v. Ontario (Attorney General)*: Freedom of Association at the Crossroads" (2003) 10 C.L.E.I.J. 83

BEATTY, D.M., *Putting the Charter to Work: Designing a Constitutional Labour Code* (Montreal: McGill-Queen's University Press, 1987)

BEATTY, D.M., "Labouring Outside the *Charter*" (1991) 29 Osgoode Hall L.J. 839

CAMERON, J., "Due Process, Collective Bargaining, and s. 2(d) of the *Charter*: A Comment on *B.C. Health Services*" (2006–7) 13 C.L.E.L.J. 323

FUDGE, J., "Labour is not a Commodity: The Supreme Court and Freedom of Association" (2004) 67 Sask. L. Rev. 425

HUGHES, P., "*Dunmore v. Ontario (Attorney General)*: Waiting for the Other Shoe" (2003) 10 C.L.E.I.J. 27

---

32   See, for example, D.M. Beatty, "Labouring Outside the *Charter*" (1991) 29 Osgoode Hall L.J. 839.
33   See chapters 3, 4, and 13 for further discussion of this point.

NORMAN, K., "Freedom of Association (Section 2(d))" in G.A. Beaudoin & E. Mendes, eds., *The Canadian Charter of Rights and Freedoms*, 4th ed. (Markham, ON: LexisNexis Butterworths, 2005)

POTHIER, D., "Twenty Years of Labour Law and the *Charter*" (2002) 40 Osgoode Hall L.J. 369

SWINTON, K.E., "The *Charter of Rights* and Public Sector Labour Relations" in G. Swimmer & M. Thompson, eds., *Public Sector Collective Bargaining in Canada: Beginning of the End or End of the Beginning?* (Kingston, ON: I.R.C. Press, 1995)

WEILER, P., "The *Charter* at Work: Reflections on the Constitutionalizing of Labour and Employment Law" (1990) 40 U.T.L.J. 117

DEMOCRATIC RIGHTS

A central argument favouring the entrenchment of rights in a constitution is that checks on the political process are needed to protect certain fundamental values. There is often disagreement about the specific rights that should be entrenched or the degree to which legislatures should be restricted by the constitution and subject to judicial review. Yet one area in which there is widespread consensus on the need for some judicial oversight is that of political activity. Participation in fair elections and vigorous public debate are the cornerstones of democracy.

The *Charter of Rights and Freedoms* contains three guarantees designed to ensure the healthy functioning of Canadian parliamentary democracy. Section 3 provides that every citizen has the right to vote in elections for the House of Commons or a provincial legislature and to be qualified for membership in those houses. Section 4 sets a maximum duration of five years for the life of the House of Commons or a provincial legislature, although that period can be extended in time of war or similar national crisis by a two-thirds vote of the members. Finally, section 5 guarantees a sitting of Parliament and the legislatures at least once in every year. The importance—and the primacy—of these sections is shown by the fact that they cannot be overridden by the exercise of the notwithstanding clause in section 33. The Supreme Court of Canada has indicated that such a status for the democratic rights places them "at the heart of our constitutional democracy."[1]

---

1   *Thomson Newspapers Co. v. Canada (Attorney General)*, [1998] 1 S.C.R. 877, 159
    D.L.R. (4th) 385. In that case, the Court chose to decide the constitutionality of

Section 4 of the *Charter* is designed to ensure that Canadians have a regular opportunity to elect federal and provincial representatives, while section 5 is designed to ensure that those elected representatives have a regular opportunity to examine and vote upon the actions of the executive branch of government. Sections 4 and 5 are long-standing parts of the Canadian constitution, which derive from our British tradition of parliamentary democracy. Indeed, section 50 of the *Constitution Act, 1867*, also states that the life of the House of Commons is five years, unless an election is called earlier.

Not surprisingly, since sections 4 and 5 of the *Charter* reflect constitutional conventions that have been widely accepted for a long time, they have not generated any litigation. However, section 3, the right to vote, is a much richer and more controversial provision that has given rise to a number of disputes. These include the legitimacy of residency and other qualifications on the right to vote, the drawing of electoral boundaries, and restrictions on third party spending during election campaigns. Section 3 has also often been raised in conjunction with the guarantees of freedom of expression and association, discussed in the two previous chapters, as well as equality rights, which are discussed in chapter 15 below.

A. VOTER QUALIFICATIONS

Read literally, the right to vote requires that every citizen have the opportunity to cast a ballot in every election. However, election laws have contained a number of qualifications, most commonly restricting the right to vote to those over a certain age, denying the vote to prison inmates and those in psychiatric institutions, to judges, and to citizens not resident in Canada. Historically, the vote was denied to women, Asians, Indians, and others. In addition, many laws require citizens to have been resident within a territory for a specified period, often several months, before they are eligible to vote.

Section 3 of the *Charter* only provides a right for citizens to vote in federal and provincial elections. Lower courts have interpreted section 3 not to apply to the vote at the municipal or school board level.[2] The

---

the restriction on the publication of polls seventy-two hours before an election under s. 2(b) of the *Charter*, which was subject to the override, as opposed to s. 3 of the *Charter*, which was immune from the override. Section 2(b) is often the basis for challenges to direct or indirect restrictions on voting or electoral participation. These cases are discussed in chapter 9.

2   The Ontario courts have held that s. 3 did not give a right to vote in municipal elections or to run for municipal office in *Jones v. Ontario (A.G.)* (1988), 53

Supreme Court has also decided that the right to vote in section 3 of the *Charter* does not apply to referenda. During the 1992 referendum on constitutional amendments known as the Charlottetown Accord, the Court was asked to determine the validity of a residency requirement. Simultaneous referenda were held in all provinces and territories. In Quebec, the referendum was held under provincial legislation, which required six months' residence in the province. In all other parts of Canada, the referenda took place under federal legislation. Graham Haig, having recently moved to Quebec from Ontario, was disqualified under the Quebec legislation because he did not meet the provincial residency requirement. He could not qualify under federal legislation, which required residence in a polling division in the federal referendum area. Haig challenged the failure to include him under the federal election legislation, but his claim was dismissed on the ground that section 3 applied only to federal and provincial elections and did not guarantee the right to vote in a referendum.[3]

Generally, residency requirements have been found to be reasonable limits on voting rights justifiable under section 1 of the *Charter*, in light of the widespread use of territorial representation in the Canadian system of government. As most representatives are elected in a geographically determined riding or constituency, a residency requirement ensures that only individuals with substantial ties to a locality have a right to select its representative. A period of residency also contributes to the voter's knowledge of the issues affecting that community. As well, residency requirements protect the integrity of the election process by preventing individuals from coming into the riding temporarily to disrupt voting patterns.[4]

Some voter qualifications are linked to the concept of competency. For example, the requirement that a voter be eighteen years of age rests on the assumption that a certain age is a standard for measuring matur-

---

D.L.R. (4th) 273 (Ont. H.C.); *Rheaume v. Ontario (A.G.)* (1992), 7 O.R. (3d) 22 (C.A.); and *Nunziata v. Toronto (City)* (2000), 189 D.L.R. (4th) 627 (Ont. C.A.). Courts have also held that s. 3 does not apply to school board elections in *Baker v. Burin School Board District #7* (1999), 178 D.L.R. (4th) 155 (Nfld. S.C.); but that section 3 does apply to elections of the legislative assembly of the territories in *Friends of Democracy v. Northwest Territories (Attorney General)* (1999), 171 D.L.R. (4th) 551 (N.W.T.S.C.).

3   *Haig v. Canada (Chief Electoral Officer)*, [1993] 2 S.C.R. 995, 105 D.L.R. (4th) 577 at 602. Iacobucci J., Lamer C.J.C. concurring, dissented on the ground that the denial of the opportunity to vote violated the guarantee of freedom of expression in s. 2(b) of the *Charter*.

4   *Reference Re Yukon Election Residency Requirement* (1986), 27 D.L.R. (4th) 146 (Y.T.C.A.).

ity and responsibility. Formerly, judges were disqualified from voting in order to preserve the appearance of judicial neutrality and independence from the political process. A successful *Charter* challenge to this disqualification[5] was followed by a 1993 change to the federal *Elections Act* to allow judges to vote.[6] Until the early 1990s, those who were restrained of the liberty of movement or the management of their property by reason of mental disease were deprived of the federal vote. A successful *Charter* challenge to this disqualification[7] was followed by legislative removal of this restriction in 1993. The 1993 amendments also allowed citizens absent from Canada for less than five years to vote in elections, after a successful *Charter* challenge to provincial restrictions on the ability of citizens who were temporally absent from the country to vote.[8]

The most litigated voter qualification provision has been the denial of the franchise to prisoners in penal institutions. The traditional reason for denying inmates the vote was to register society's disapproval of those who had broken its laws and thereby were thought to have disqualified themselves from participating in one of the important elements of citizenship. In effect, the denial of the right to vote was a further penalty for the crime. It has also been argued, in some cases, that inmates must be denied the right to vote to preserve prison security. Finally, it has been suggested that, since prison inmates are detached from the community, they cannot participate meaningfully in the public debate necessary to inform themselves as educated voters.

In two 1992 decisions, appellate courts accepted the argument that a prisoner's section 3 right to vote was infringed and this was not a reasonable limit under section 1.[9] In *Belczowski*,[10] Hugessen J.A. observed that there were some crimes, such as treason, in which the denial of the right to vote was logically linked to the nature of the crime. However, the then existing provision barred an inmate from voting regardless of the nature of the crime committed. Moreover, he held, there was no necessary connection between imprisonment and lack of familiarity with political issues — indeed, many in society would be unfamiliar with important issues, yet they are still allowed to vote. Both decisions were upheld, with very brief reasons, by the Supreme Court of Canada

---

5   *Muldoon v. Canada*, [1988] 3 F.C.R. 628 (T.D.).

6   *Canada Elections Act*, S.C. 1993, c. 19.

7   *Canadian Disability Rights Council v. Canada*, [1988] 3 F.C. 622 (T.D.).

8   *Hoogbruin v. British Columbia* (1985), 24 D.L.R. (4th) 718 (B.C.C.A.).

9   *Sauvé v. Canada (A.G.)* (1992), 89 D.L.R. (4th) 644 (Ont. C.A.); *Belczowski v. Canada* (1992), 90 D.L.R. (4th) 330 (F.C.A.) [*Belczowski*].

10   *Belczowksi, ibid.*

in 1993.[11] The Court held that the blanket prohibition on inmate voting in section 51(e) of the *Canada Elections Act* did not meet the proportionality test under section 1, particularly the minimal-impairment component of the test.

Subsequently, the *Canada Elections Act* was amended in 1993 to limit the prohibition on voting to those sentenced to a term of more than two years. The differentiation between those with less than two-year sentences and those with longer sentences denied the vote only to those who had been convicted of the most serious offences. On the other hand, those who advocate prisoners' right to vote argued that, since no effort was made to tailor the prohibition to the type of offence, the prohibition remained too broad to survive, even in its amended form. The new restriction was challenged under section 3 of the *Charter* in litigation by Richard Sauvé, the same inmate who successfully challenged the earlier voting restriction in the Supreme Court. Sauvé, who was serving a sentence for murder, was still prohibited from voting under the amended Act. The Supreme Court, by a five to four majority, struck down the revised law. The government conceded that the *Canada Elections Act* violated the section 3 rights of prisoners, but argued that it was justified under section 1 because it furthered two collective aims of society: to enhance civic responsibility and respect for the rule of law; and to provide additional punishment or enhance the general purposes of criminal sanction. The Court, however, firmly rejected the government's attempts at justification and was highly critical of the "broad, symbolic" or "rhetorical" objectives advanced by the government. Writing for the majority, Chief Justice McLachlin wrote, "The right to vote is fundamental to our democracy and the rule of law and cannot be lightly set aside. Limits on it require not deference, but careful examination."[12] The government's attempt at justification failed each stage of the section 1 analysis. Gonthier J., writing for the minority, would have accepted that the government had advanced a "reasonable social or political philosophy" justifying the suspension of voting rights for felons to deliver "a message to both the community and the offenders themselves that serious criminal activity will not be tolerated by the community."[13] Felons had broken the "social contract" requiring them to abide by the rule of law; therefore, it was appropriate to tem-

---

11   *Sauvé v. Canada (A.G.)*, [1993] 2 S.C.R. 438. In *Reynolds v. British Columbia (A.G.)* (1984), 11 D.L.R. (4th) 380, a prohibition on voting by those on probation was found to be unconstitutional by the British Columbia Court of Appeal.

12   *Sauvé v. Canada (Chief Electoral Officer)* (1999), 180 D.L.R. (4th) 385 (Fed. C.A.), rev'd [2002] 3 S.C.R. 519 at para. 9, McLachlin C.J.C.

13   *Ibid.* at para. 119 (S.C.R.), Gonthier J.

porarily disenfranchise them, just as it was acceptable to temporarily incarcerate them.

Section 3 of the *Charter* not only gives every citizen the right to vote in federal and provincial elections, but also to be qualified for membership in provincial legislatures and Parliament. The Supreme Court has held that a provincial law that disqualifies a person from sitting as a member of a provincial legislature for five years after a conviction for an elections offence was a reasonable limit on the section 3 right. The limited disqualification applying to specific offences was considered to be a proportionate means to pursue the important objective of protecting the integrity of the electoral system.[14]

B. REGULATING THE ELECTORAL PROCESS

Cases like *Sauvé v. Canada (Chief Electoral Officer)*, discussed in the previous section, involve direct restrictions on the right to vote. The infringement of section 3 in that case was obvious, and the debate between the majority and the minority of the Supreme Court focused on the justification of the infringement under section 1 of the *Charter*. In a democracy, however, the effectiveness of each vote cast depends in large measure on the electoral system created and regulated by the government. The drawing of electoral boundaries, limitations on third party advertising, and restrictions on the availability of funding and other privileges to political parties are all issues that have led to cases that have asked the courts to scrutinize the constitutionality of the electoral process. Because the effect of such regulation on the right to vote or to run for office is indirect, and therefore much harder to gauge than in voter qualification cases, the Supreme Court has been forced to flesh out in greater detail the content of the section 3 right. In three key cases in this area, the Court has defined the section 3 right broadly, finding violations when an individual's right to "effective participation" or the right to play a "meaningful role" in the electoral process has been infringed. At the same time, however, it has endorsed the "egalitarian" model of elections that permits regulation aimed at ensuring that each individual has an equal opportunity to participate in the electoral process. Unlike the so-called "libertarian" model, the egalitarian model allows for measures such as spending limits to prevent the wealthy from monopolizing political debate.

---

14   *Harvey v. New Brunswick (Attorney General)*, [1996] 2 S.C.R. 876, 137 D.L.R. (4th) 142.

1) Electoral Boundaries

The Canadian electoral system is based on territorial representation at both the federal and the provincial level. Individuals vote for a member to represent their constituency in the provincial legislature or the House of Commons. The government is selected on the basis of having the support of a majority of elected members in the House. The Canadian system is also a "first past the post" system, with the individual who receives the greatest number of votes winning the seat, even if he or she did not garner a majority of the votes.

Other countries have quite different electoral systems. Some use proportional representation of parties based on the percentage of votes received, with members of the legislature selected from party lists. Members are not necessarily attached to a particular constituency. Other systems also use proportional representation but still provide for the election of members in a particular constituency.

The rationale for proportional representation is to ensure, to the extent possible, that every vote is reflected by the members elected. On the other hand, the rationale for electing members from a geographic constituency is to facilitate the input of interests within that territory, while also ensuring that an elected member is available to play a problem-solving role for the citizens whom he or she represents.

In the Canadian system and others based on territorial representation, difficult issues arise when drawing electoral boundaries for constituencies. Should the goal be an equal number of voters in each constituency? Should there be departures from that goal in order to serve other interests — for example, to recognize the distinctive interests of communities, or to facilitate travel and contact between voters and their representative? Traditionally, rural voters were thought to have different concerns than urban voters, and electoral boundaries were drawn accordingly. With the increasing ethnic diversity in Canadian society, it might be argued that electoral lines should be drawn so as to maximize the opportunity for an ethnic or religious group to vote for a member of its community, rather than dispersing the votes among other ethnic and religious communities where they would have less voting power should the group choose to vote as a block. One might argue that it is justifiable that rural or northern constituencies have smaller numbers of voters than urban ones because of the difficulties of campaigning and maintaining contact in less-populated areas.

Inevitably, the drawing of electoral-boundary lines raises the spectre of "gerrymandering," a term that connotes the exercise of distasteful self-interest on the part of those in control of the process. Not surprisingly, political incumbents have an interest in drawing boundaries in ways that can help them and undermine support for their opponents. Where the process of constituency line drawing is left to politicians, rather than independent electoral-boundary commissions, there may be good reason for the courts to scrutinize the fairness of the outcome. But no matter the process, one cannot avoid difficult and debatable decisions about the size and design of constituencies. The courts have a delicate role in deciding when the electoral system improperly undermines the right to vote, guaranteed under section 3 of the *Charter*.

The most significant decision to date is that of the Supreme Court of Canada in the *Reference Re Provincial Electoral Boundaries (Saskatchewan)*.[15] Saskatchewan had established an independent electoral-boundaries commission but had also set a strict quota of urban and rural seats and required that the boundaries of urban ridings coincide with the existing boundaries of municipalities. Aside from two sparsely populated northern ridings, the ridings under consideration were within plus or minus 25 percent of the "provincial quotient," the figure determined by dividing the provincial voting population by the number of ridings.

While the Supreme Court of Canada split six to three in upholding the boundaries, all the judges agreed on the general principles underlying the right to vote espoused by the majority judgment of McLachlin J. In reasons supported by four others, she described the meaning of the right to vote as "not equality of voting power *per se*, but the right to 'effective representation.'"[16] The conditions of "effective representation" included not only relative parity of voting power (so that the weight of an individual's vote would not be unduly diluted) but also factors important to "fair" representation of Canada's diversity. In her words,

> Factors like geography, community history, community interests and minority representation may need to be taken into account to ensure that our legislative assemblies effectively represent the diversity of our social mosaic.[17]

McLachlin J. expressly rejected the American model of "one person, one vote," arguing that it is neither consistent with Canadian history nor a practical alternative in the search for effective representation in a country like Canada:

---

15   [1991] 2 S.C.R. 158, 81 D.L.R. (4th) 16 [*Saskatchewan Boundaries*].
16   *Ibid.* at 183 (S.C.R.).
17   *Ibid.* at 184 (S.C.R.).

Respect for individual dignity and social equality mandate that citizens' votes not be unduly debased or diluted. But the need to recognize cultural and group identity and to enhance the participation of individuals in the electoral process and society requires that other concerns also be accommodated.[18]

Applying these principles, McLachlin J. concluded that both the process and the outcome of the Saskatchewan scheme were fair and consistent with section 3 of the *Charter*. In particular, she noted that the division of seats between rural and urban areas approximated the actual population division in the two areas. Moreover, she accepted the argument that rural ridings are more difficult to serve, both because of transportation and communication problems and because rural voters are said to make more demands on their representatives. Finally, discrepancies between ridings were justified on traditional bases such as geography, community interests, and projected population changes.

While accepting these general principles, Cory J., with two other judges, dissented. He found that the underlying process in drawing boundaries in Saskatchewan was contrary to section 3 because the strict rural/urban division interfered with the rights of urban voters and that this was not justifiable under section 1. He was influenced by the fact that Saskatchewan had in the past used electoral boundaries that were closer to equal population standards than the impugned boundaries.[19]

The Saskatchewan case is interesting from several perspectives. We see a distinctive Canadian approach that takes into account concerns about the effectiveness of representation as well as sensitivity to the interests of groups and that can be contrasted with the American courts' insistence on the more individualistic principle of one person, one vote. The result marks the reluctance of the Supreme Court to give

---

18   *Ibid.* at 188 (S.C.R.).

19   Cases in Alberta, Prince Edward Island, and the Northwest Territories have applied the Saskatchewan principles, with the Alberta decision upholding an electoral map that favoured rural over urban ridings (*Reference Re Electoral Boundaries Commission Act (Alberta)* (1991), 120 A.R. 70 (C.A.); and the Prince Edward Island and Northwest Territories decisions finding an unjustified violation of s. 3 of the *Charter*: *MacKinnon v. Prince Edward Island* (1993), 101 D.L.R. (4th) 362 (P.E.I.T.D.); *Friends of Democracy v. Northwest Territories (Attorney General)* (1999), 171 D.L.R. (4th) 551 (N.W.T.S.C.), leave to C.A. refused (1999), 176 D.L.R. (4th) 661 [*Friends of Democracy*]. A subsequent *Charter* challenge to new electoral boundaries in Prince Edward Island was rejected on the basis that variations in voter populations of plus or minus 20 percent and the mixing of some rural and urban districts did not violate the right to effective representation. *Charlottetown (City) v. Prince Edward Island* (1998), 168 D.L.R. (4th) 79 (P.E.I.C.A.), leave refused 179 D.L.R. (4th) vi (S.C.C.).

the judiciary a central role in electoral map drawing. By accepting the legislation's allowance for as much as a 25-percent deviation from the provincial quotient for constituency size, the Court gave a great deal of scope for electoral-boundary commissions or legislatures in drawing boundaries. This also accords with the Court's approach to equality rights in which it often defers to legislative attempts to assist the disadvantaged and does not insist on the same treatment for each person. This reading of equality rights is premised on the idea that departures from equal population standards are meant to assist northern (including Aboriginal) and rural residents as disadvantaged groups. Some, however, argue that robust departures from equal population standards under-represent urban populations and with that, visible minorities.[20] As can be seen, the concept of effective representation can be contested. What is clear, however, is that, consistent with the Court's approach to equality rights as opposed to freedom of expression, the *Saskatchewan Boundaries* case is based on the acceptance of significant definitional limits on the right to vote. One consequence of this approach is that the government does not have to justify all departures from equal population standards under section 1 of the *Charter*.

At the federal level, variation in the size of electoral districts is indirectly mandated by the constitution itself. Section 51A of the *Constitution Act, 1867*, guarantees that no province will have fewer members in the House of Commons than in the Senate. This ensures that Prince Edward Island, a province with a population of about 140,000, will always have four members in the House of Commons. Many of the urban ridings in provinces with rising populations, such as Ontario and British Columbia, are substantially larger than those in P.E.I.[21] Since the House of Commons is unlikely to grow substantially for both political and practical reasons, the result of the "Senate floor" rule is almost certain to create a significant imbalance in constituency size. To the extent that this imbalance is required by other parts of the constitution, it will likely be immune from *Charter* review because of the Court's prior refusal in the context of denominational school rights found in the *Constitution Act, 1982*, to allow *Charter* challenges to other parts of the constitution.[22]

---

20   Michael Pal and Sujit Choudhry, "Is Every Ballot Equal? Visible Minority Vote Dilution in Canada" (2007) 13 Institute for Research on Public Policies Choices.

21   This is discussed further in K.E. Swinton, "Federalism, Representation and Rights" in J. Courtney, P. MacKinnon, & D. Smith, eds., *Drawing Boundaries: Legislatures, Courts, and Electoral Values* (Saskatoon: Fifth House, 1992) at 17 [*Drawing Boundaries*].

22   *Reference Re Bill 30, An Act to Amend the Education Act (Ontario)*, [1987] 1 S.C.R. 1148; *Adler v. Ontario*, [1996] 3 S.C.R. 609 discussed above, chapter 8, section D(2).

It has been asked by some whether there is a requirement of "affirmative gerrymandering" to ensure that electoral boundaries are drawn to ensure maximum voting power to racial and ethnic groups.[23] Some argue that "effective representation" for groups traditionally under-represented in Canadian legislatures requires positive action to promote the election of representatives from these communities. This could be facilitated within the existing system of geographic representation, if all that is required is to draw lines in a manner alert to ethnic or cultural difference. Even then, courts have held that agreements with Aboriginal peoples and Aboriginal rights do not justify large deviations from equal population standards.[24] Even an equality-rights based approach to electoral districting that tolerates or even requires generous departures from equal population standards to assist disadvantaged groups will not work if a group is not concentrated territorially. For example, to ensure greater representation of women, one would have to argue that section 3 of the *Charter* required a different kind of electoral system—either two-person constituencies with male and female members, or a shift to a proportional representation system in which political parties may have a greater incentive to achieve diversity in the lists of people who will be elected depending on the percentage of the popular vote received by the particular party.

Does the Supreme Court's decision in *Saskatchewan Boundaries* indicate that such challenges would be successful? The Court was clearly sympathetic to a system sensitive to the diversity of interests in Canadian politics that allows for deviation from the principle of "one person, one vote" or "treat all the same." Yet the Court did not go so far as to adopt a "mirror" concept of representation that requires individuals to be represented on the basis of sex or ethnicity. Nor did the Court signal any willingness to alter the "procedural representation" that is at the basis of the Canadian system. That system allows individuals, grouped geographically, to decide, from time to time, whether they see their interests aligning with others on the basis of sex, ethnicity, class, religion, or a combination of these and other characteristics. Although minorities might be better represented in other electoral systems that rely on various forms of proportionate representation and party lists, there is little indication that the courts would invalidate the existing first past the post riding system on *Charter* grounds.

---

23   K. Roach, "Chartering the Electoral Map into the Future" in *Drawing Boundaries*, above note 21 at 211–14.

24   *Friends of Democracy*, above note 19.

2) Party Benefits

Political parties play a key role in Canada's electoral system. More than ten years after the Supreme Court wrestled with the issue of re-districting in *Saskatchewan Boundaries*, it examined the relationship between section 3 of the *Charter* and the role of political parties in *Figueroa v. Canada*.[25] The *Canada Elections Act* provides political parties with a number of significant benefits, including the right to issue tax receipts for donations and the right of candidates to have their party affiliation listed on ballots.

In *Figueroa*, the leader of the Communist Party of Canada challenged a restriction that withheld such benefits to parties who failed to nominate fifty candidates for an election. The government's main justification for the fifty-candidate threshold was that it favoured national parties capable of fielding enough candidates to form a majority in Parliament. Under such a system, a voter has a greater chance of having her vote determine which party forms the government. Parties that do not field enough candidates to form a government do not advance the objective of "effective representation" that the Court had found was embodied by section 3.

The Supreme Court rejected the government's argument and declared the government's fifty-candidate threshold unconstitutional. Writing the majority decision, Iacobucci J. expanded on the meaning of "effective representation." He repeated McLachlin J.'s conclusion (in *Saskatchewan Boundaries*) that effective representation gave each citizen the right to an effective representative in Parliament or a provincial legislative assembly. He added, however, that section 3 also guarantees each citizen the right to play a "meaningful role" in the electoral process. The rights under section 3 are therefore participatory in nature, and the right to participate in an election has an "intrinsic value," regardless of the impact on the actual outcome of the elections. Therefore, the right to vote is infringed if a voter's range of options is limited by making it more difficult for small parties to field candidates and to make their candidates' party affiliation known on election day. Finally, Iacobucci J. rejected an approach to section 3, endorsed by the minority, that would have balanced the individual interest in electoral participation against other communal aspects of participation. Iacobucci J. expressly declared that the right of each citizen to play a meaningful role in the electoral process should not be subject to countervailing collective interests.

---

25   *Figueroa v. Canada (Attorney General)*, [2003] 1 S.C.R. 912, rev'g (2000), 50 O.R. (3d) 728 (C.A.), rev'g (1999), 43 O.R. (3d) 728 (Gen. Div.) [*Figueroa*].

Iacobucci J. scrutinized the three goals advanced by the government to justify the fifty-candidate threshold as a reasonable limit under section 1: to improve the electoral process; to protect of the integrity of the electoral financing regime; and to ensure that the process is able to deliver a viable outcome in Parliament. While he accepted the pressing and substantial nature of the first two objectives, he found that they failed the proportionality stage of the section 1 analysis under *R. v. Oakes*.[26] With respect to the third objective, Iacobucci J. said it was "extremely problematic"[27] to advance an objective that favoured a certain kind of outcome in Parliament, namely, a majority government, thereby reducing the chances that candidates from regional or marginal parties would be elected. Iacobucci J. stated that "[l]egislation enacted for the express purpose of decreasing the likelihood that a certain class of candidates will be elected is not only discordant with the principles integral to a free and democratic society, but, rather, is the antithesis of those principles."[28] Iacobucci J. went on to consider the proportionality analysis under the *Oakes* test and found that the fifty-candidate threshold could not reasonably be expected to advance the government's stated objective of encouraging majority governments.

An interesting feature of *Figueroa* is the discussion of the first-past-the-post system of election, a matter of current public debate that could conceivably give rise to a *Charter* challenge on the basis that it gives unduly weight to some votes while minimizing others. The dissenting judges stated that the first past the post system is designed to favour "aggregation and cohesiveness"[29] and that such values must be weighed against the value of individual participation when determining whether section 3 has been violated. Iacobucci J. expressly rejected this suggestion and said "the *Charter* is entirely neutral as to the type of electoral system in which the right to vote or to run for office is to be exercised."[30] While this suggests that the first past the post system is not favoured under the *Charter*, Iacobucci also cautioned "this decision does not stand for the proposition that the differential treatment of political parties will always constitute a violation of s. 3. Nor does it stand for the proposition that an infringement of s. 3 arising from the differential treatment of political parties could never be justified."[31]

---

26   [1986] 1 S.C.R. 103, 26 D.L.R. (4th) 200 [*Oakes*].
27   *Figueroa*, above note 25 at para. 80.
28   *Ibid.*
29   *Ibid.* at para. 153, LeBel J.
30   *Ibid.* at para. 37, Iacobucci J.
31   *Ibid.* at para. 91, Iacobucci J.

3) Third Party Advertising

A year after *Figueroa*, the Supreme Court was faced with another contentious issue in *Harper v. Canada (Attorney General)*,[32] a challenge to election spending limits imposed on third parties by the *Canada Elections Act*. Under the Act, third parties were limited from spending more than $150,000 nationally or $3,000 per riding during election campaigns, among other restrictions. These provisions were challenged by Stephen Harper, then leader of the National Citizens' Coalition, under section 2(b) (freedom of expression),[33] section 2(d) (freedom of association), and section 3 (right to vote).

The majority decision by Bastarache J. held that the restrictions on third party spending during election time engaged the "informational component" of the right to meaningfully participate in the electoral process. This aspect of the right to vote gives each voter the right to be "reasonably informed of all the possible choices" before him. Without spending limits, the affluent might dominate political discourse: "If a few groups are able to flood the electoral discourse with their message, it is possible, indeed likely, that the voices of some will be drowned out." It is the need to prevent the wealthy from monopolizing the public forum that prevents carefully-tailored spending limits from violating an individual's section 3 rights.[34] As the spending limits still allowed third parties to undertake modest national campaigns, there was no violation of section 3.

Bastarache J.'s decision is informed by his acceptance of what has been called the egalitarian model of elections. This model is premised on the idea that political discourse during elections needs to be regulated to ensure that the wealthy do not dominate discourse and that the poor are able to participate. It is contrasted with the libertarian model, under which there would be few, if any, restrictions on election spending. Proponents of the libertarian model view the egalitarian model as paternalistic and they argue that voters are best served by receiving as much information as possible, regardless of the source, and that voters should be credited with sufficient capacity to sort through repeated or unwanted messages and make informed decisions. Bastarache J. holds that the *Canada Elections Act* regime and cases like *Saskatchewan Boundaries* have both embraced the egalitarian model and its goal of creating a "level playing field" so that "no one voice is overwhelmed

---

32 *Harper v. Canada (Attorney General)*, [2004] 1 S.C.R. 827.
33 See chapter 9.
34 *Harper*, above note 32 at paras. 71–73, Bastarache J.

by another."[35] Deference to Parliament's judgment as to how to best achieve the egalitarian model informed Bastarache J.'s analysis of both section 3 and section 1 of the *Charter*:

> Under the egalitarian model of elections, Parliament must balance the rights and privileges of the participants in the electoral process: candidates, political parties, third parties and voters. Advertising expense limits may restrict free expression to ensure that participants are able to meaningfully participate in the electoral process. For candidates, political parties and third parties, meaningful participation means the ability to inform voters of their position. For voters, meaningful participation means the ability to hear and weigh many points of view. The difficulties of striking this balance are evident. Given the right of Parliament to choose Canada's electoral model and the nuances inherent in implementing this model, the Court must approach the justification analysis with deference.[36]

This comment suggests that, even though in *Sauvé* and *Figueroa* the majority of the Supreme Court stressed that potential infringements of section 3 deserve strict scrutiny, the Court will nonetheless be less likely to find a *Charter* violation if the government can argue that a challenged law advances the equality of different voters. This trend continued in *R. v. Bryan*[37] in which a majority of the Court upheld a ban on distributing information on election results while the polls were still open in parts of Canada. The majority accepted that the restriction on expression was a proportionate attempt to ensure informational equality among all Canadian voters. Four judges in dissent, however, found that the goal of informational equality was not important enough to justify limiting political speech.

C. CONCLUSION

The right to vote is one of the most fundamental rights possessed by citizens in a democracy. In the cases that have come before the courts, judges have shown little sympathy for laws that deny the right to vote to particular groups or that discriminate against smaller, more marginal political parties. On the other hand, the courts have respected the historical and representational underpinnings of electoral-bound-

---

35   *Ibid.* at para. 62, Bastarache J.
36   *Ibid.* at para. 87, Bastarache J.
37   [2007] 1 S.C.R. 527.

ary design and hesitated to interfere with legislative judgment that is designed to promote the equality of all voters. The courts have also protected the rights of minority political parties to play a meaningful role in elections.

FURTHER READINGS

BREDT, C., & M. KREMER, "Section 3 of the *Charter*: Democratic Rights at the Supreme Court of Canada" (2005) 17 N.J.C.L. 19

CARTER, M., "Reconsidering the *Charter* and Electoral Boundaries" (1999) 22 Dal. L.J. 53

CHARNEY, R., & Z. GREEN, "It's My Party and I'll Run if I Want To: *Figueroa*, *Harper* and the Animal Alliance Environment Voters Party" (2006–2007) 21 N.J.C.L. 257–70

COURTNEY J., P. MACKINNON, & D. SMITH, eds., *Drawing Boundaries: Legislatures, Courts, and Electoral Values* (Saskatoon: Fifth House, 1992)

COURTNEY, J., *Commissioned Boundaries* (Montreal: McGill-Queen's University Press, 2002)

FEASBY, C., "*Libman v. Quebec (A.G.)* and the Administration of the Process of Democracy under the *Charter*: The Emerging Egalitarian Model" (1999) 44 McGill L.J. 5

FEASBY, C., "Issue Advocacy and Third Parties in the United Kingdom and Canada" (2003) 48 McGill L.J. 11

FRITZ, R., "Challenging Electoral Boundaries Under the *Charter*" (1999) 5 Rev. Const. Stud. 1

GEDDIS, A., "Liberté, Egalité, Argent: Third Party Election Spending and the *Charter*" (2004) 42 Alta. L. Rev. 429

KNIGHT, T., "Unconstitutional Democracy? A *Charter* Challenge to Canada's Electoral System" (1999) 57 U.T. Fac. L. Rev. 1

MANFREDI, C., & M. RUSH, *Judging Democracy* (Peterborough: Broadview Press, 2008)

MANFREDI, C., & M. RUSH, "Electoral Jurisprudence in the Canadian and U.S. Supreme Courts: Evolution and Convergence" (2007) 52 McGill L.J. 1

MORTON, F.L., & R. KNOPFF, "Does the *Charter* Mandate 'One Person One Vote'?" (1992) 30 Alta. L. Rev. 669

PAL, M., & S. CHOUDHRY, "Is Every Ballot Equal? Visible Minority Vote Dilution in Canada" (2007) 13(1) Institute for Research on Public Policies Choices

ROACH, K., "One Person, One Vote? Canadian Constitutional Standards for Electoral Distribution and Districting" in D. Small, ed., *Drawing the Map: Equality and Efficacy of the Vote in Canadian Electoral Boundary Reform* (Toronto: Dundurn Press, 1991) vol. 11

STUDNIBERG, B., "Politics Masquerading as Principles: Representation by Population in Canada" (2009) 34 Queens L.J. 611

CHAPTER 12

MOBILITY RIGHTS

An important element of individual freedom is the right to enter and leave one's country and to move about it freely. In countries with federal systems, such as Canada, it is fundamental to a sense of national citizenship that individuals be able to move to and work in other provinces without prejudice because of their province of origin. The mobility rights protected by section 6 of the *Charter of Rights and Freedoms* are designed to promote and foster these objectives.

Section 6 contains two kinds of mobility rights, one international and the other interprovincial. Section 6(1) guarantees the right of citizens to enter, remain in, and leave Canada, while sections 6(2)(a) and (b) guarantee the right of citizens and permanent residents "to move and take up residence in any province; and to pursue the gaining of a livelihood in any province." The interprovincial guarantee is qualified in two ways. The right is subject to laws of general application in force in a province, provided those laws do not discriminate among individuals primarily on the basis of province of present or previous residence (section 6(3)(a)). Section 6(3)(b) permits reasonable residency requirements for the receipt of publicly provided social services. As well, section 6(4) protects from *Charter* challenge laws and programs aimed at relieving the plight of those who are socially or economically disadvantaged in provinces with rates of unemployment above the national rate. Finally, as with all *Charter* rights, a government may be able to justify laws that violate section 6 under section 1. However, mobility rights are among those rights in the *Charter* that are regarded as so significant that they are not subject to the legislative override in section 33.

A. THE RIGHT TO ENTER AND LEAVE CANADA

Section 6(1) of the *Charter*, the right of citizens to enter and leave Canada, has its origins in the *International Covenant on Civil and Political Rights*. Article 12(2) of that document provides that "[e]veryone shall be free to leave any country, including his own," while Article 12(4) states that "[n]o one shall be arbitrarily deprived of the right to enter his own country." However, the language of section 6(1) of the *Charter* is broader in that it includes a right to "remain in" Canada.

The most obvious uses for this section would be to challenge the denial of a passport, compelled expulsion from the country, or denial of re-entry. Although these scenarios are unlikely in a country with Canada's democratic traditions, national security concerns have given rise to litigation over exclusion of a citizen.[1]

Section 6(1) has been invoked most often when Canadian citizens try to resist extradition to another country for trial. Canada has numerous extradition treaties with other countries, which allow a foreign country to seek the surrender of a Canadian citizen who is alleged to have committed an offence according to that country's law. If the individual is found guilty, he or she would ordinarily be required to serve any sentence in the foreign country, although Canada has arrangements with some countries that allow the convicted person to serve the sentence in a Canadian prison.

In *United States v. Cotroni*,[2] the Supreme Court of Canada concluded that surrender of a citizen pursuant to the *Extradition Act* was a violation of section 6(1) of the *Charter*. Even though the surrender did not amount to an expulsion or banishment, since the individual could return after an acquittal at trial or after serving a sentence, the Court held that the rights in section 6(1) were infringed because the individual was denied the right to remain in Canada.

---

1   Discussed below. The deportation of a permanent resident under the *Immigration Act* after conviction for a serious offence has been upheld. Section 6(1) is not applicable because it applies only to citizens, and s. 7 is not violated (*Chiarelli v. Canada (Minister of Employment and Immigration)*, [1992] 1 S.C.R. 711, 90 D.L.R. (4th) 289).

2   [1989] 1 S.C.R. 1469.

Although section 6(1) was violated, La Forest J., writing for the majority, concluded that the infringement caused by extradition lay far from the core values of section 6(1). In his view, the central thrust of section 6(1) was protection against exile and banishment, "the purpose of which is the exclusion of membership in the national community."[3] This led the majority to take a more flexible approach to the application of section 1 of the *Charter* in the case of extradition. The Court had no difficulty in finding that there was a pressing and substantial objective underlying the extradition law: it aimed at the suppression of crime through international cooperative efforts. On the issue of proportionality of means and ends, the Supreme Court divided (five to two). Cotroni argued that, because he could have been tried in Canada for the same offence he was charged with in the United States, his extradition could not be justified as a reasonable limit. While the two dissenting judges accepted this proposition, the majority disagreed. Cotroni was alleged to have conspired to possess and distribute heroin. His actions occurred in Canada, the heroin was to be distributed in the United States, and most of the witnesses were in that country. Therefore, the Court held, it was reasonable to allow him to be surrendered to the United States for trial and the section 1 test was satisfied.[4] Judicial review on *Charter* grounds of the Minister's decision to surrender the claimant for extradition attracts a standard of reasonableness so that the Minister's decision is given deference and will be upheld so long as it falls within a reasonable range of outcomes.[5]

The right of a Canadian citizen to enter Canada was held to be violated in the case of Abousfian Abdelrazik who had been listed by the United Nations as a person associated with al Qaeda and had been denied travel documents by the Canadian governments that would allow him to return to Canada from Sudan. Although a procedure that allows passports to be denied for reasons of national security has been upheld by the Federal Court of Appeal to be a reasonable limit on the section 6(1) right that was proportionate to the objective of preventing terrorism,[6] this process was not used in this case and the denial of an emergency passport in this case was unreasonable and not justified under section 1 of the *Charter*. In the case of the right to enter and leave Canada, the right entailed positive state obligations with respect to the issuance of a passport.[7] The effective remedy ordered in this case was

---

3   *Ibid.* at 1482.
4   A similar result was reached in *United States of America v. Ross*, [1996] 1 S.C.R. 469.
5   *Lake v. Canada* (Minister of Justice), [2008] 1 S.C.R. 761.
6   *Canada (Attorney General) v. Kamel*, 2009 FCA 21.
7   *Abdelrazick v. Canada (Attorney General)*, 2009 FC 580 at para. 152.

the issuance of an emergency passport and an escort to ensure that Mr. Abdelrazik would be returned to Canada and appear before the judge.[8]

In cases where the accused person would face denial of fundamental rights upon extradition, successful *Charter* challenges have been based on section 7. In *United States of America v. Burns*,[9] two individuals were wanted on three counts of aggravated first-degree murder in Washington state, where a finding of guilt would result in either the death penalty or life in prison without parole. The Minister of Justice ordered the individuals to be extradited without seeking assurances that the death penalty would not be imposed or that, if it were imposed, it would not be carried out. At the Supreme Court of Canada, the individuals argued that extradition without assurances infringed sections 6(1), 12, and 7 of the *Charter*. The Supreme Court held that the real issue was the death penalty and that this issue should be considered under section 7. In the Court's view, "[t]he death penalty is overwhelmingly a justice issue and only marginally a mobility rights issue."[10] As discussed in chapter 13, the Court found that to surrender the two individuals without assurances that they would not face the death penalty would violate their section 7 right not to be deprived of life, liberty, and security of the person except in accordance with the principles of fundamental justice.

B. INTERPROVINCIAL MOBILITY

Section 6 of the *Charter* also protects interprovincial mobility. The section was part of a more ambitious set of proposals by the federal government to strengthen the Canadian economic union. Concerned about barriers to the mobility of labour, capital, goods, and services, the federal government proposed to bolster the common market clause in section 121 of the *Constitution Act, 1867*. That section provides that the articles produced or grown in a province shall be "admitted free" into other provinces. It has been narrowly interpreted by the courts as prohibiting customs duties, but it has been ineffective in protecting against rules discriminating against out-of-province labour, property

---

8   *Ibid.* at para. 160, 166-167
9   [2001] 1 S.C.R. 283, 195 D.L.R. (4th) 1.
10   *Ibid.* at 317 (S.C.R.).

ownership, or access to government contracts.[11] For example, Quebec for many years discriminated against workers from out-of-province in the construction industry, while Prince Edward Island restricted land ownership by non-residents.

Despite federal pressure for more ambitious constitutional language in various efforts at constitutional reform, section 6(2) deals only with mobility for citizens and permanent residents. It has been interpreted by the Supreme Court of Canada as guaranteeing a right of interprovincial mobility that ensures a right to move to another province to take up work there, and the right of a non-resident to work in another province without relocating. It is not, however, a free-standing guarantee of the right to work, and for the right to be invoked, there must be some element of interprovincial mobility at issue.[12] While the British Columbia Court of Appeal in *Wilson* interpreted section 7 as including a right of mobility *within* a province,[13] this must be contrasted with the Supreme Court of Canada's view that section 6(2) is designed to eliminate boundaries between the provinces.[14]

Nor has the section been interpreted as protecting new residents and non-residents from compliance with the general rules applicable to existing provincial residents—for example, occupational qualifications and licence requirements that affect everyone.[15] Section 6(3)(a) makes it clear that residents and non-residents are subject to laws of "general application"—that is, laws that do not discriminate primarily on the basis of province of residence.

The leading cases interpreting section 6(2) and section 6(3)(a) of the *Charter* are *Black v. Law Society of Alberta*[16] and *Canadian Egg Marketing Agency v. Richardson*.[17] In *Black*, the Law Society of Alberta had passed two rules in an effort to control interprovincial law firms—specifically, a partnership between an Alberta firm and an Ontario firm. The first rule prohibited partnerships between lawyers resident in Al-

---

11 See, for example, the discussion of Laskin C.J.C. in *Reference Re Agricultural Products Marketing Act (Canada)*, [1978] 2 S.C.R. 1198 at 1266–68, 84 D.L.R. (3d) 257.

12 *Law Society of Upper Canada v. Skapinker*, [1984] 1 S.C.R. 357, 9 D.L.R. (4th) 161 [*Skapinker*].

13 *Wilson v. British Columbia (Medical Services Commission)* (1988), 53 D.L.R. (4th) 171 (B.C.C.A.).

14 In *Skapinker*, above note 12, Estey J. stated at 181 (D.L.R.): "The two rights (in paras. (a) and (b)) both relate to movement into another province, either for the taking up of residence, or to work without establishing residence."

15 See, for example, *Taylor v. Institute of Chartered Accountants of Saskatchewan* (1989), 59 D.L.R. (4th) 656 (Sask. C.A.).

16 *Black v. Law Society of Alberta*, [1989] 1 S.C.R. 591, 58 D.L.R. (4th) 317 [*Black*].

17 [1998] 3 S.C.R. 157, 166 D.L.R. (4th) 1 [*Canadian Egg*].

berta and non-residents, while the second prohibited partnerships by members in more than one firm. The three-member majority of the Supreme Court of Canada held that both rules infringed section 6(2)(b), because their effect was seriously to impair the ability of non-resident lawyers to carry on a viable business arrangement. These rules did not fall within 6(3)(a), because they were not laws of general application. Their purpose and effect was to discriminate on the basis of residence.

The majority went on to examine the rules in light of section 1 of the *Charter* and concluded that they were not reasonable limits. Even though the Law Society had legitimate concerns about the proper governance of the legal profession, including avoiding conflicts of interest in the practice of law, there were other alternatives that would achieve their ends without impinging upon the rights secured by section 6(2)(b).

McIntyre J., in dissent, argued that the rules about partnership between residents and non-residents or multiple partnerships might violate the right to freedom of association in section 2(d), but there was no violation of the mobility guarantee. In his words, "[n]obody is forbidden entry into Alberta and nobody is prohibited from practising law or forming a partnership in Alberta."[18] In considering section 1, he concluded that the rule forbidding partnerships between residents and non-residents was not a reasonable limit, although he would have upheld the rule against multiple partnerships.

Black dealt with provisions that were directed at non-residents. However, many provincial laws restrict the practice of an occupation and create barriers to mobility, even though their purpose is not to restrict competition from non-residents or new residents. For example, one province may require higher levels of training for nurses than another. Quebec has rules about proficiency in the French language for those practising professions that create obstacles for non-francophones. Most provincial laws of this kind seem safe from a mobility-rights challenge. Even if they have a disproportionate impact on non-residents, they will likely be characterized as laws of general application within section 6(3)(a) that do not discriminate on the basis of province of residence.

The relationship between section 6(2)(b) and section 6(3)(a) of the *Charter* was considered in *Canadian Egg*. That case concerned the constitutionality of an interlocking federal and provincial egg marketing scheme that prevented the interprovincial marketing and export of eggs produced in the Northwest Territories. Egg producers in the Northwest Territories challenged the scheme under section 6. By a five to two majority, the Supreme Court held that there was no violation

---

18   *Ibid.* at 636 (S.C.R.).

of section 6. In the view of the majority, section 6(3)(a) is not a "saving" provision like sections 6(3)(b), 6(4), or 1 of the *Charter*. Rather, section 6(2)(b) and section 6(3)(a) must be read together as defining a single right. Section 6 was engaged because the gaining of a livelihood in another province may be pursued by an attempt to create wealth in that province by production, marketing, or performance. However, the egg marketing scheme did not discriminate primarily on the basis of province of residence. The scheme had a valid and non-discriminatory purpose: to ensure the fair and orderly marketing of eggs in Canada by using historical production patterns to distribute quotas. The exclusion of the Northwest Territories was simply an application of the principle of allocating quota on the basis of historical production patterns. The effect of the scheme on the Northwest Territories egg producers had to be compared against its effect on new egg producers in the destination province who have no quota and wish to market their eggs in the destination province. In the majority's view, the Northwest Territories egg producers had failed to establish that their actual prejudice relative to this comparison group displaced the valid purpose of the scheme.

C. CONCLUSION

If section 6 of the *Charter* was meant to have a major impact on the functioning of the Canadian economic union, its supporters have likely been disappointed, for its reach has been limited so far to cases of direct discrimination on the basis of provincial residence in the pursuit of an individual's livelihood or choice of residence. It does not catch many other barriers to the mobility of goods, services, people, and capital, leaving these to be addressed by other institutions and legal rules.[19]

---

19   See, for example, *Reference Re Prince Edward Island Lands Protection Act* (1987), 40 D.L.R. (4th) 1 (P.E.I.C.A.), where it was found that controls on non-residents' ownership of land did not violate s. 6. For further discussion of such barriers and their legal treatment, see K.E. Swinton, "Courting Our Way to Economic Integration: Judicial Review and the Canadian Economic Union" (1995) 25 Can. Bus. L.J. 280.

FURTHER READINGS

BLACHE, P., "Mobility Rights" in G.A. Beaudoin & E. Mendes, eds., *The Canadian Charter of Rights and Freedoms*, 3d ed. (Toronto: Carswell, 1996)

DE MESTRAL, A., & J. WINTER, "Mobility Rights in the European Union and the *Charter*" (2001) 46 McGill L.J. 979

JACKMAN, M., "Interprovincial Mobility Rights under the *Charter*" (1985) 43 U.T. Fac. L. Rev. 16

LASKIN, J.B., "Mobility Rights under the *Charter*" (1982) 4 Sup. Ct. L. Rev. 89

LEE, T., & M. TREBILCOCK, "Economic Mobility and Constitutional Reform" (1987) 37 U.T.L.J. 268

SWINTON, K.E., "Courting Our Way to Economic Integration: Judicial Review and the Canadian Economic Union" (1995) 25 Can. Bus. L.J. 280

LIFE, LIBERTY, AND SECURITY OF THE PERSON AND THE PRINCIPLES OF FUNDAMENTAL JUSTICE

Section 7 of the *Charter of Rights and Freedoms* provides:

> Everyone has the right to life, liberty and security of the person and the right not to be deprived thereof except in accordance with the principles of fundamental justice.

The section is cast in broad language and the scope of the guarantee is potentially significant and far-reaching. In an early decision, the Supreme Court stated that the process of elaborating the meaning of section 7 would necessarily be a gradual and case-by-case exercise.[1] This is understandable, for the interpretation of section 7 raises difficult questions. As we shall see, many of these questions involve fundamental moral and social issues and call for the courts to consider the scope and limits of judicial review under the *Charter*.

Section 7 has had a significant impact in the criminal law context where it has been held to extend important procedural and substantive guarantees to persons accused of crime. That aspect of section 7 is discussed in chapter 14. This chapter considers the impact of section 7 outside the sphere of guarantees in the criminal process. Here it is significant that section 7 of the *Charter*, unlike the due process protections of the American *Bill of Rights*, does not explicitly protect property rights. Moreover, unlike some other modern rights protec-

---

1   *R. v. Morgentaler*, [1988] 1 S.C.R. 30 at 51, 44 D.L.R. (4th) 385, Dickson C.J.C. [*Morgentaler*].

tion instruments, section 7 of the *Charter* does not explicitly protect socio-economic rights such as the right to welfare or housing or health care.

As will be seen, however, section 7 still has an important and often controversial role to play outside of the criminal justice context. Should section 7 be narrowly interpreted to protect little more than procedural fairness or does the requirement to respect the "principles of fundamental justice" demand review of the substantive content of legislation to ensure that all laws are just and fair? Does section 7 protect the "liberty" to do as one pleases, or should "liberty" be given a narrower interpretation, embracing only physical freedom? All laws constrain "liberty" in its widest sense. It is a basic tenet of our legal system that one is at liberty to do as one pleases unless constrained by some positive law. Yet ours is also a society governed by law and a society that recognizes that laws, and hence constraints on liberty, are required to preserve order and protect the weak and vulnerable. Does "security of the person" entail the right to own property or the right to contract for private health insurance? If so, section 7 could help the "haves" in our society by significantly constraining governmental regulatory and redistributive measures. Does "security of the person" guarantee some minimal level of economic entitlement? If so, section 7 could help the "have-nots" by compelling the creation and extension of government welfare schemes. Opponents of abortion have argued that abortion denies the unborn of the right to "life," while pro-choice advocates contend that laws preventing abortion infringe a woman's rights to "liberty" and "security of the person."

There is also conflict about the sources of the principles of fundamental justice. Are they only found in the basic or traditional tenets of the justice system? Or can they be informed by changing standards of domestic and even international justice? Is there a danger of judges reading their own views of good policy into the principles of fundamental justice? How much of a consensus is required before a principle is recognized as a principle of fundamental justice? How do courts distinguish between legal principles and matters of policy that should be left to elected governments? Finally, what is the appropriate relation between section 7 and section 1 of the *Charter*? Is section 7 of the *Charter* such a special right that violations of section 7 rights will rarely if ever be justified under section 1 of the *Charter*? Has the reluctance of courts to hold that violations of section 7 are justified under section 1 affected the content of the section 7 rights both with respect to the definition of the rights to life, liberty and security of the person and with respect to the definition of the principles of fundamental justice?

In this chapter, we canvass the way the courts have responded to these and other questions. As we shall see, definitive answers have yet to be given in many contentious areas. After almost three decades of litigation, the task of defining the outer limits of "life, liberty and security of the person" as well as the "principles of fundamental justice" is still very much a work-in-progress.

A. THE REQUIREMENTS OF A SECTION 7 VIOLATION

There are a number of steps in establishing a violation of section 7 of the *Charter*. First, the *Charter* applicant must demonstrate that he or she falls within the reference to "everyone" in section 7. This will be easy in the context of natural persons, but not in the case of corporations or other artificial entities. Next, the *Charter* applicant must demonstrate a violation of the right to life, liberty, or security of the person. This will be easy in the context of physical deprivations of liberty, but more contentious in the case of other interests. Demonstrating a violation of the right to life, liberty, or security of the person, however, is insufficient to make out a section 7 claim. For example, a person convicted of a criminal offence and sentenced to jail suffers a loss of liberty. But loss of liberty, standing alone, is not contrary to the *Charter* guarantee. The rights claimant must proceed to the final stage of analysis and show that the denial of a right protected by section 7 is contrary to the principles of fundamental justice. The issue under section 7 is not whether the legislation strikes the right balance between individual and social interests, but whether it results in the deprivation of life, liberty, or security of the person in a manner that does not respect fundamental principles of justice. The claimant under section 7 should not bear the burden of demonstrating that the state's action is disproportionate and not justified.[2]

If all three elements of the section 7 violation have been established, it is still possible that the section 7 violation could be justified by the government under section 1 of the *Charter*. Nevertheless, the courts have indicated that justifications of section 7 violations will be rare. The Supreme Court has observed that "a violation of section 7 will be saved by section 1 only in cases arising out of exceptional conditions,

---

2   *R. v. Malmo-Levine*, [2003] 3 S.C.R. 571 at para. 96 [*Malmo-Levine*]; *Charkaoui v. Canada (Citizenship and Immigration)*, [2007] 1 S.C.R. 350 at para. 21 [*Charkaoui*].

such as natural disasters, the outbreak of war, epidemics and the like."[3] In a more recent case, the Court has observed that:

> The rights protected by section 7—life, liberty, and security of the person—are basic to our conception of a free and democratic society, and hence are not easily overridden by competing social interests. It follows that violations of the principles of fundamental justice, specifically the right to a fair hearing, are difficult to justify under section 1. Nevertheless, the task may not be impossible, particularly in extraordinary circumstances where concerns are grave and the challenges complex.[4]

In that case, the Court held that while the protection of intelligence relating to national security "undoubtedly constitutes a pressing and substantial objective,"[5] the government had failed to justify under section 1 the total denial of adversarial challenge to the intelligence that the government provided to the court to support a non-citizen's detention and possible deportation under a security certificate. In another recent case, the Court has held that the government has failed to justify limiting section 7 rights by requiring young offenders convicted of offences of serious violence to rebut a presumption in favour of an adult sentence and the lifting of a publication ban on their identity.[6] In fact, the majority of the Court has never held that a violation of section 7 of the *Charter* was justified under section 1.

1) Everyone

The reference to "everyone" in section 7 of the *Charter* has been interpreted not to include corporations. This makes sense given that a corporation does not enjoy rights to life, liberty, and security of the person in the same sense as a natural person.[7] However, it does conflict with the interpretation of other sections of the *Charter*, such as freedom

---

3   *Suresh v. Canada*, [2002] 1 S.C.R. 3, 208 D.L.R. (4th) 1 at para. 78 [*Suresh*], citing *Reference Re s. 94(2) of the Motor Vehicle Act (B.C.)*, [1985] 2 S.C.R. 486 at 518, 24 D.L.R. (4th) 536 [*Re B.C. Motor Vehicle Act*]; and *New Brunswick (Minister of Health and Community Services) v. G.(J.)*, [1999] 3 S.C.R. 46, 177 D.L.R. (4th) 124 at para. 9 [*New Brunswick v. G.(J.)*]. See also *R. v. D.B.*, [2008] 2 S.C.R. 3 [*D.B.*].
4   *Charkaoui*, above note 2 at para. 66.
5   *Ibid.* at para. 68.
6   *D.B.*, above note. 3 at paras. 91–92.
7   *Irwin Toy Ltd. v. Quebec*, [1989] 1 S.C.R. 927 at 1004, 58 D.L.R. (4th) 577 [*Irwin Toy*]; *Dywidag Systems International Canada v. Zutphen Brothers Construction Ltd.*, [1990] 1 S.C.R. 705, 68 D.L.R. (4th) 147; *British Columbia (Securities Commission) v. Branch*, [1995] 2 S.C.R. 3, 123 D.L.R. (4th) 462.

of expression and the right against unreasonable search and seizure, under which claims by corporations have been upheld.

The impact of the exclusion of corporations from the ambit of section 7 of the *Charter* is mitigated in a practical sense because the courts have allowed corporations to defend themselves in penal[8] and even civil proceedings[9] by arguing that a law violates the section 7 rights of natural persons and is therefore invalid. A legislature that wanted to insulate a law from section 7 review would thus have to make that law only applicable to corporations, something that is not commonly done.

The word "everyone" is not limited to citizens and includes "every human being who is physically present in Canada and by virtue of such presence amenable to Canadian law."[10] A number of landmark section 7 cases have involved claims made by non-citizens.[11] In one recent case involving the extraterritorial application of the *Charter* to the disclosure of the fruits of interviews that Canadian officials conducted with Omar Khadr at Guantanamo Bay, Cuba, the Supreme Court seemed to base its holding that section 7 of the *Charter* imposes disclosure obligations on the government in part on the fact that Mr. Khadr is a Canadian citizen.[12] The effect of the mention of Khadr's citizenship in this context is not clear and in any event it related to the extraterritorial application of the *Charter*. It is well established that non-citizens in Canada are protected under section 7's reference to "everyone".

There may, however, be other limits on the meaning of "everyone" In holding that a foetus is not protected under Quebec's *Charter of Human Rights and Freedoms*, the Supreme Court has hinted that a foetus is not included in the reference to "everyone" in section 7 of the Canadian *Charter*.[13]

2) Life, Liberty, and Security of the Person

Before it is even possible to determine whether the state has respected the principles of fundamental justice, an applicant under section 7 of the *Charter* must establish that his or her interest "falls within the ambit of section 7: 'if no interest in life, liberty or security of the person

---

8   R. v. Wholesale Travel Group Inc., [1991] 3 S.C.R. 154.
9   *Canadian Egg Marketing Agency v. Richardson*, [1998] 3 S.C.R. 157, 166 D.L.R. (4th) 1.
10 *Singh v. Minister of Employment and Immigration*, [1985] 1 S.C.R. 177 at 202.
11 *Suresh*, above note 3; *Charkaoui*, above note 2.
12 *Canada (Justice) v. Khadr*, [2008] 2 S.C.R. 125 at para. 31 [*Khadr*].
13 *Daigle v. Tremblay*, [1989] 2 S.C.R. 530 [*Daigle*].

is implicated, the section 7 analysis stops there.'"[14] The courts interpret life, liberty, and security of the person as three analytically distinct interests. The courts have largely taken a case-by-case approach and not offered a comprehensive definition of what interests are protected by the rights to life, liberty, and security of the person.

a) The Right to Life

To date, the Supreme Court of Canada has not addressed the scope of the right to life. Even in a case dealing with the extradition of fugitives to face the death penalty, the Court concluded that the rights to liberty and security of the person were violated and that the lives of the fugitives "are potentially at risk."[15] Similarly, the Court found that section 7 was engaged in a case involving deportation of a refugee applicant to face the substantial risk of torture, by noting that "it is conceded that 'everyone' includes refugees and that deportation to torture may deprive a refugee of liberty, security and perhaps life."[16] Given the interest at stake, a risk to life may itself violate the right to life in section 7 of the *Charter*.

b) The Right to Liberty

The Supreme Court has been divided with respect to the scope of the right to liberty. Some judges, notably Wilson and La Forest JJ., were prepared to interpret the right to include matters involving the right to make fundamental personal decisions without state interference, such as where to live,[17] or whether to permit medical treatment for one's children,[18] and how to educate them.[19] Other judges, most notably Lamer C.J.C., took a more restrictive approach that emphasized freedom from physical restraint by the state. In a 1995 case, he was prepared to restrict the scope of section 7 to

> the conduct of the state when the state calls on law enforcement officials to enforce and secure obedience to the law, or invoke the law

---

14 *Blencoe v. British Columbia (Human Rights Commission)*, [2000] 2 S.C.R. 307, 190 D.L.R. (4th) 513 at para. 48 [*Blencoe*].

15 *United States of America v. Burns*, [2001] 1 S.C.R. 283, 195 D.L.R. (4th) 1 at para. 59 [*Burns*].

16 *Suresh v. Canada*, above note 3 at para. 44.

17 *Godbout v. Longueil*, [1997] 3 S.C.R. 844, La Forest J. (L'Heureux-Dubé and Gonthier JJ. concurring).

18 *B.(R.) v. Children's Aid Society*, [1995] 1 S.C.R. 315, 122 D.L.R. (4th) 1, La Forest J. (L'Heureux-Dubé, Gonthier, and McLachlin JJ. concurring) [*B.(R.)*]; *New Brunswick*, above note 3, L'Heureux-Dubé (McLachlin J. concurring).

19 *Jones v. R.*, [1986] 2 S.C.R. 284, 31 D.L.R. (4th) 569, Wilson J.

to deprive a person of liberty through judges, magistrates, ministers, board members etc.[20]

A majority of the Supreme Court opted for a more generous approach in *Blencoe v. British Columbia (Human Rights Commission)*. Bastarache J. (McLachlin C.J.C., L'Heureux-Dubé, Gonthier, and Major JJ. concurring) declared that "the liberty interest protected by section 7 of the *Charter* is no longer restricted to mere freedom from physical restraint."[21] This conclusion was qualified by a number of factors. First, Bastarache J. indicated that "although an individual has the right to make fundamental personal choices free from state interference, such personal autonomy is not synonymous with unconstrained freedom."[22] Second, on the facts of the case, he found that the rights to both liberty and security of the person were not violated by a thirty-month delay in processing a human rights complaint about sexual harassment. He concluded: "freedom from the type of anxiety, stress and stigma suffered by the respondent in this case should not be elevated to the stature of a constitutionally protected section 7 right."[23] The issue is also complicated by the fact that the four remaining judges did not decide the section 7 issue in this case, holding that the *Charter* applicant was entitled to an independent administrative law remedy.

Most cases involving fundamental personal choices have arisen from the *Charter* claimant's interaction with the justice system. The extent to which such a claim may arise outside the administration of justice is still unclear. In *Gosselin*, McLachlin, writing for the majority, agreed with Bastarache J. that

> the dominant strand of jurisprudence on s. 7 sees its purpose as guarding against certain kinds of deprivation of life, liberty and security of the person, namely, those "that occur as a result of an individual's interaction with the justice system and its administration."

While accepting that "an adjudicative context might be sufficient," McLachlin found it unnecessary to decide categorically that it was required to ground a section 7 claim.[24]

What "fundamental personal choices" will attract *Charter* protection under section 7? In *Morgentaler*, Wilson J. described "the decision

---

20   B.(R.), above note 18 at 340 (S.C.R.).

21   *Blencoe*, above note 14 at para. 49.

22   *Ibid.* at para. 54.

23   *Ibid.* at para. 97.

24   *Gosselin v. Quebec (Attorney General)*, [2002] 4 S.C.R. 429 at paras. 77–79 [*Gosselin*].

of a woman to terminate her pregnancy"[25] as a fundamental personal choice that would attract section 7 protection. Privacy has been described as being "at the heart of liberty in a modern state"[26] but the content of the right of privacy outside the criminal justice system remains uncertain. In *R. v. Clay*, the Supreme Court held that "the liberty right within s. 7 is thought to touch the core of what it means to be an autonomous human being blessed with dignity and independence in 'matters that can properly be characterized as fundamentally or inherently personal.'"[27] Applying this test, the Court rejected the proposition that recreational marijuana smoking constitutes an inherently personal activity deserving section 7 protection.

c)   The Right to Security of the Person

The right to security of the person has been interpreted to include serious state-imposed psychological stress. In *New Brunswick v. G.(J.)*,[28] the Supreme Court held that state apprehension of a child from parental custody violated the parent's security of the person. "As an individual's status as a parent is often fundamental to personal identity, the stigma and distress resulting from a loss of parental status is a particularly serious consequence of the state's conduct."[29] The Court hastened to add, however, that "not every state action which interferes with the parent-child relationship will restrict a parent's right to security of the person." For example, a parent's security of the person is not violated when his or her child is sentenced to jail, conscripted into the army, or even negligently shot by the police.

The fact that security of the person is not violated by ordinary stresses and anxiety caused by state action was underlined by the Supreme Court's statement in *Blencoe*[30] that security of the person would only be violated "where the state interferes in profoundly intimate and personal choices" such as "a woman's choice to terminate her pregnancy, an individual's decision to terminate his or her life, the right to raise one's children and the ability of sexual assault victims to seek therapy without fear of their private records being disclosed." As mentioned above, the Court held in that case that a person's security of the person was not violated by a thirty-month delay in processing a human rights complaint of sexual harassment. At the same time, the Court

---

25   *Morgentaler*, above note 1 at 171.

26   *R. v. Dyment*, [1988] 2 S.C.R. 417 at 427.

27   *R. v. Clay*, [2003] 3 S.C.R. 735 at paras. 31–32.

28   *New Brunswick*, above note 3.

29   *Ibid.* at para. 61.

30   *Blencoe*, above note 14 at paras. 83, 86.

has held that state-imposed delays in access to abortions[31] and delays imposed by waiting lists for medical treatments[32] infringe the security of the person by causing psychological and physical suffering.

Any infringement of the rights to life, liberty, and security of the person must be caused by the state. In *Blencoe*, the Court distinguished between the prejudice caused by the complaint of sexual harassment and the prejudice caused by the state's processing of the complaint. In an early *Charter* case challenging the testing of cruise missiles, the Court held that the causal connection between such actions and threats to life, liberty, or security of the person was too "uncertain, speculative and hypothetical to sustain a cause of action" under section 7 of the *Charter*.[33] At the same time, however, the Court has found a sufficient causal connection between Canada's decisions to either extradite or deport people and the infliction of the death penalty or torture in foreign lands to find a violation of the rights to life, liberty, and security of the person.[34]

In *R. v. D.B.*,[35] a majority of the Court held that section 7 of the *Charter* was violated by a provision that required a young offender to justify the maintenance of a publication ban upon conviction of a violent offence. The majority made reference to the young offender's right to privacy, the stigmatizing effects of publication, and the greater psychological and social stress that would be caused by publication of the offender's name.[36] Four judges in dissent argued that the lifting of the publication ban did not affect the young offender's liberty or security. With respect to the latter, they argued that there was no state action because any harm caused to the young offender would be caused by the media and third parties and not the state.[37] The majority's approach in *D.B.* may signal a more flexible approach to the requirement of the state-imposed stress in *Blencoe* that will be more generous to *Charter* claimants and more realistic in recognizing the state's role in initiating a process in which both the state and third parties, such as the media, cause harm to a person's security interests.

---

31 *Morgentaler*, above note 1 at 59 (S.C.R.), Dickson C.J.C.; at 105–6 (S.C.R.), Beetz J.
32 *Chaoulli v. Quebec (Attorney General)*, [2005] 1 S.C.R. 791 at para. 119, McLachlin C.J.C. and Major J.; at para. 205–6, Binnie and LeBel JJ. [*Chaoulli*].
33 *Operation Dismantle v. R.*, [1985] 1 S.C.R. 441 at 447, 18 D.L.R. (4th) 481.
34 *Burns*, above note 15; *Suresh*, above note 3.
35 *D.B.* above note 3.
36 *Ibid.* at paras. 84–87.
37 *Ibid.* at para. 178.

3) Principles of Fundamental Justice

Section 7 of the *Charter* does not allow the courts to "engage in a free-standing inquiry under s. 7 into whether a particular legislative measure 'strikes the right balance' between individual and societal interests in general."[38] To establish a section 7 violation, the applicant must also show that his or her right to life, liberty, or security of the person has been denied contrary to an identifiable principle of fundamental justice. As we shall see from the following discussion, the definition of the principles of fundamental justice has been a fruitful source of debate and inquiry.

a)   Substance, Procedure, and the Basic Tenets of the Justice System

Fair procedure is a matter that falls within the traditional expertise of the judiciary. Judges are experts at the fact-finding processes of the adversarial system and have a keen sense of the procedural values needed to ensure fairness to all who come before the courts. In the common law tradition, judges have also played an important role in monitoring the administrative apparatus of the state to ensure that individuals are dealt with fairly. The common law has evolved "rules of natural justice," which include the right to notice and a hearing if one's rights are affected. There is strong evidence to suggest that, at the time of the *Charter's* adoption, it was widely believed that the phrase "principles of fundamental justice" was restricted to procedural values of this kind.[39] Procedural fairness, the precise meaning of which will depend upon the particular context of the case,[40] is undoubtedly an important element of the principles of fundamental justice.

However, in its first important judgment on section 7, the Supreme Court rejected a narrow interpretation that would have limited the "principles of fundamental justice" to procedural fairness. In *Re B.C. Motor Vehicle Act*,[41] the Court held that section 7 should be given a more generous meaning, namely, that it allowed the courts to review, from the perspective of substantive as well as procedural justice, laws infringing "life, liberty or security of the person." This means that the courts have the right to strike down laws that do not conform to the judicial view of what is fundamentally just. In *Re B.C. Motor Vehicle Act*, the Court struck down a law imposing a mandatory jail sentence upon

---

38   *Malmo-Levine*, above note 2 at para. 96
39   The relevance of the drafters' original intention in *Charter* interpretation is discussed in chapter 3.
40   See *Ruby v. Canada (Solicitor General)*, [2002] 4 S.C.R. 3 at para. 39 [*Ruby*].
41   *Re B.C. Motor Vehicle Act*, above note 3.

conviction for driving while under suspension even when the accused was not aware of the suspension. In the Court's view, this was at odds with the fundamental principle that the severe sanction of imprisonment should be imposed only in cases of moral blameworthiness.[42]

Lamer J., who wrote the majority opinion, recognized that the case raised "fundamental questions of constitutional theory, including the nature and very legitimacy of constitutional adjudication under the *Charter* as well as the appropriateness of various techniques of constitutional interpretation."[43] While finding that section 7 conferred a mandate on the courts to assess the substantive justice of laws, Lamer J. took pains to impose two important qualifications. First, he noted that the very structure of section 7 made it clear that the "principles of fundamental justice" were not a free-standing guarantee but rather could be invoked only where a law violated the right to "life, liberty or security of the person." Second, Lamer J. tied the principles of fundamental justice to what he described as "the basic tenets of our legal system" and to the "domain of the judiciary as guardian of the justice system," distinguishing the latter from what he described as "the realm of general public policy."[44] He made reference, as well, to "the spectre of a judicial 'super-legislature'";[45] to the need to give meaningful content to section 7 while avoiding adjudication of policy matters; and to the necessity for "objective and manageable standards."[46] While this is admittedly imprecise, it does reflect a judicial awareness of the need to limit the power of judicial review to matters for which the courts have some claim to institutional competence and expertise.

In subsequent decisions the Supreme Court has, with one notable exception, affirmed its commitment to the idea that the principles of fundamental justice are found in the basic tenets of the legal system, as opposed to general policy informed by philosophy and social science, which is outside of the inherent domain of the judiciary.[47] In *R. v. Malmo-Levine*; *R. v. Caine*,[48] the Court expanded upon Sopinka J.'s analysis in the *Rodgriquez* case where he held that a principle of fundamental justice is a legal principle generally accepted among reasonable people as "vital or fundamental to our societal notion of justice . . . [and] capable of being identified with some precision and applied

42   This point is discussed in greater detail in chapter 14.
43   *Re B.C. Motor Vehicle Act*, above note 3 at 495 (S.C.R.).
44   *Ibid.* at 503.
45   *Ibid.* at 498.
46   *Ibid.* at 499.
47   *Suresh*, above note 3 at para. 45.
48   *Malmo-Levine*, above note 2.

to situations in a manner which yields an understandable result."[49] In *Malmo-Levine*, the Court refused to strike down the criminalization of simple possession of marijuana, rejecting the argument that it is a principle of fundamental justice "that the *absence* of demonstrated harm to others deprives Parliament of the power to impose criminal liability."[50] The majority ruled that the "harm principle" did not qualify as "a legal principle about which there is significant societal consensus that it is fundamental to the way in which the legal system ought fairly to operate . . . identified with sufficient precision to yield a manageable standard against which to measure deprivations of life, liberty or security of the person." According to the majority, there is no general consensus that the criminal law had to be limited to conduct causing actual harm to others. To the extent that some minimal level of harm was accepted as a necessary underpinning of a criminal prohibition, there was no agreement on the nature of harm required and, hence, the harm principle lacked sufficient precision to serve as a principle of fundamental justice.

The Supreme Court followed a similar line of reasoning in *Canadian Foundation for Children, Youth and the Law v. Canada (Attorney General)*[51] when it rejected "the best interests of the child" as a principle of fundamental justice and refused to strike down a *Criminal Code* provision allowing parents and teachers to use reasonable corrective force to discipline children. McLachlin C.J.C. described the requirements of a principle of fundamental justice:

> First, it must be a legal principle. This serves two purposes. First, it "provides meaningful content for the s. 7 guarantee"; second, it avoids the "adjudication of policy matters" . . . . Second, there must be sufficient consensus that the alleged principle is "vital or fundamental to our societal notion of justice" . . . . The principles of fundamental justice are the shared assumptions upon which our system of justice is grounded. They find their meaning in the cases and traditions that have long detailed the basic norms for how the state deals with its citizens. Society views them as essential to the administration of justice . . . . [T]he alleged principle must be capable of being identified with precision and applied to situations in a manner that yields predictable results.[52]

---

49   *Rodriguez v. R.*, [1993] 3 S.C.R. 519 at 590–91, 107 D.L.R. (4th) 342 [*Rodriguez*].
50   *Malmo-Levine*, above note 2 at para. 103.
51   [2004] 1 S.C.R. 76 [*Canadian Foundation for Children*].
52   *Ibid.* at para. 8 (case references omitted).

The "best interests of the child" is a legal principle, but the majority held that as it is only one factor to be considered among others in cases involving children, it is not a foundational principle vital or fundamental to societal notions of justice, nor is it susceptible to precise and predictable application.

In *R. v. D.B.*,[53] a majority of the Supreme Court applied the test outlined above to hold that the presumption that young people had diminished moral blameworthiness and culpability when they commit offences was a principle of fundamental justice. Abella J. for the majority held that this principle was a long established legal principle recognized in the tradition of separate legislation for young offenders. There was also a domestic and international consensus that age plays a role in the development of judgment and moral sophistication. Finally, the Court stated that the principle could be identified with sufficient precision to provide a manageable standard to determine whether infringements of life, liberty, or security of the person violated the principles of fundamental justice. In the result, the Court held the presumption that young people convicted of serious violent offences would receive adult sentences violated the principle of diminished responsibility as did the onus on the young offender to justify a publication ban on their name. The Court did not rule out the possibility of young offenders receiving adult sentences or having their names published, but held that the Crown must justify such measures in each individual case. Four judges dissented. They argued that the lifting of the publication ban did not engage the young person's liberty or security interests because any stigma or labelling would not be caused by state action. They also stressed that the presumption of an adult sentence was rebuttable and concluded that the onus on the young offender reflected a reasonable balance of the competing interests of the offender and society. Although the principle of the diminished responsibility of youth articulated in *D.B.* could have far-reaching implications, the decision relates to a traditional "basic tenet of the justice system" rather than a broad issue of social or economic policy, namely, the onus Parliament had placed on young offenders to displace presumptions that they would receive adult sentences and have their names published.

The decision in *Chaoulli v. Quebec (Attorney General)*[54] suggests that not all members of the Supreme Court are wedded to defining the principles of fundamental justice in strictly legal terms in order to avoid the "adjudication of policy matters." At issue was a Quebec law prohibiting

---

53   Above note 3.
54   *Chaoulli*, above note 32.

insurance to obtain private health care services available under the public system. The purpose of the law was to discourage the growth of a parallel private health care system and to protect the maintenance of a single-tier public health care system. The design of an appropriate public health care system is one of the most contentious and difficult issues of social and economic policy confronting the Canadian public. It is the very sort of issue the Court had, until 2005, studiously avoided on the principle that courts and judges are ill-equipped to decide complex, multi-faceted issues of social and economic policy. However, three members of the court (McLachlin C.J.C. and Major J. with Bastarache J. concurring) applied the concept of "arbitrariness" to strike down the law: "A law is arbitrary where 'it bears no relation to, or is inconsistent with, the objective that lies behind [it].' To determine whether this is the case, it is necessary to consider the state interest and societal concerns that the provision is meant to reflect."[55] They held that in light of the experience in other countries where private and public health care delivery coexist, the connection between limiting the availability of private health care insurance and maintaining a healthy public health care delivery system was so weak that it could be described as "arbitrary." This represents a striking departure from the Court's consistent deference to legislative judgment on broad policy issues such as the criminalization of marijuana, the proper approach to the correction of children, and whether social welfare benefits were adequate. The fourth member of the majority, Deschamps J., decided the case under Quebec's *Charter of Human Rights and Freedoms* without commenting on section 7 of the Canadian *Charter*. The Quebec *Charter* only requires a deprivation of security of the person and not that the deprivation be in violation of the principles of fundamental justice. Nevertheless, Deschamps J.'s analysis closely resembles that of McLachlin C.J.C. and Major J. in the stress on the arbitrariness of waiting lists. All four judges seemed to conclude that waiting lists were in themselves arbitrary as the case did not involve the particular circumstances of a person on a waiting list or a claim that errors had been made in determining priorities on the waiting list.

Binnie and LeBel JJ. (Fish J. concurring) insisted, in a strongly-worded dissent, that deciding the appropriate mix of public and private health care was a matter far removed from the realm of adjudication. They pointed out that the question had been the subject of several elections and government-sponsored studies and that, as both the trial judge and the Quebec Court of Appeal had found, there was no consen-

---

55   *Ibid.* at para. 130, citing *Rodriguez*, above note 49 at 594–95 (S.C.R.).

sus that allowing private health care based upon insurance would not undermine the public system. There was no "manageable constitutional standard" to determine what level of health care is required and "[t]he resolution of such a complex fact-laden policy debate does not fit easily within the institutional competence or procedures of courts of law."[56] Binnie and LeBel JJ. stated that "the appellants' case does not rest on constitutional law but on their disagreement with the Quebec government on aspects of its social policy. The proper forum to determine the social policy of Quebec in this matter is the National Assembly."[57] Relying on the Court's earlier decisions defining the principles of fundamental justice, Binnie and LeBel JJ. insisted that the challengers failed to demonstrate a violation:

> . . . the formal requirements for a principle of fundamental justice are threefold. First, it must be a *legal* principle. Second, the reasonable person must regard it as vital to our societal notion of justice, which implies a significant *societal consensus*. Third, it must be capable of being *identified with precision* and applied in a manner that yields *predictable results*. These requirements present insurmountable hurdles to the appellants. The aim of "health care to a reasonable standard within reasonable time" is not a *legal* principle. There is no "societal consensus" about what it means or how to achieve it. It cannot be "identified with precision." As the testimony in this case showed, a level of care that is considered perfectly reasonable by some doctors is denounced by others. Finally, we think it will be very difficult for those designing and implementing a health plan to predict when its provisions cross the line from what is "reasonable" into the forbidden territory of what is "unreasonable," and how the one is to be distinguished from the other.[58]

Binnie and LeBel JJ. accepted "arbitrariness" as a principle of fundamental justice, but insisted that in light of the objective of protecting a one-tier public health care system, it was not "arbitrary" for Quebec to discourage the growth of private health insurance: "Prohibition of private health insurance is directly related to Quebec's interest in promoting a need-based system and in ensuring its viability and efficiency. Prohibition of private insurance is not 'inconsistent' with the state interest; still less is it 'unrelated' to it."[59] They rejected the "global challenge to the entire single-tier plan" but "would not foreclose indi-

---

56   *Ibid*. at paras. 163–64.
57   *Ibid*. at para. 167.
58   *Ibid*. at para. 209.
59   *Ibid*. at para. 256.

vidual patients from seeking individual relief tailored to their individual circumstances."[60]

Because the judges who decided the *Charter* issue were evenly divided and as only seven judges sat on the case, it remains to be seen whether *Chaoulli* signals a permanent shift in the general direction of section 7 jurisprudence. In any event, it is clear that there will be increased litigation of health care claims under section 7 of the *Charter*.

In *United States v. Burns*,[61] the Supreme Court held, contrary to its earlier decisions, that extradition without assurances that the foreign state would not apply the death penalty would in all but exceptional cases violate section 7 of the *Charter*. The Court stressed that it was not concerned with the death penalty as a matter of public policy or philosophy but rather with "the narrower aspects of the controversy"[62] that fell "squarely within 'the inherent domain of the judiciary as guardian of the justice system.'"[63] These matters included the growing recognition of wrongful convictions in Canada, the United Kingdom, and the United States; the trauma experienced by those awaiting execution; and international trends with respect to the death penalty. Although this decision affirms the Court's commitment to focusing on only the basic tenets of the justice system when determining the principles of fundamental justice, it also demonstrates that these tenets can evolve to take into account new developments. The Court also made clear that it was not bound by public opinion about the death penalty in determining whether section 7 of the *Charter* would be violated by extradition to face the death penalty.

b)   Vagueness

It is a fundamental value of our legal system that citizens are entitled to fair notice of the conduct that is permitted or prohibited so that they can regulate their activities accordingly. A related concept is that the law should set appropriate limits on officials who exercise discretion in applying and enforcing the law. McLachlin C.J.C. has explained the vagueness principle as follows:

> A law must set an intelligible standard both for the citizens it governs and the officials who must enforce it. The two are interconnected. A vague law prevents the citizen from realizing when he or she is entering an area of risk for criminal sanction. It similarly makes it

---

60   *Ibid.* at para. 264.
61   *Burns*, above note 15.
62   *Ibid.* at para. 71.
63   *Ibid.* at para. 38.

difficult for law enforcement officers and judges to determine whether a crime has been committed. This invokes the further concern of putting too much discretion in the hands of law enforcement officials, and violates the precept that individuals should be governed by the rule of law, not the rule of persons. The doctrine of vagueness is directed generally at the evil of leaving "basic policy matters to policemen, judges, and juries for resolution on an *ad hoc* and subjective basis, with the attendant dangers of arbitrary and discriminatory application": *Grayned v. City of Rockford*, 408 U.S. 104 (1972), at p. 109.[64]

In chapter 4, we considered these points from the aspect of section 1, the *Charter*'s limitation clause, which requires a certain minimal level of precision in laws that impinge upon protected rights. Where government seeks to uphold a law that infringes a protected right on the ground that the law is justifiable as a reasonable limit, it must show that the limit is "prescribed by law."

The Supreme Court has accepted the argument that the "principles of fundamental justice" include the requirement that laws not be so vague as to fail to respect these values of fair notice and control of discretionary power.[65] On the other hand, the Court has made it clear that there is an inherent element of uncertainty in any legal standard of general application and that it is unrealistic to expect precision and predictability in all cases. While the Court has insisted that the standard supplied must be intelligible and capable of providing a basis for legal debate and rational decision making, it has consistently resisted the argument that a legal norm or standard must provide crystal clear and immediate answers.

In *Irwin Toy*,[66] the 1989 decision challenging a restraint on advertising as an infringement of freedom of expression that we considered in detail in chapter 9, the majority wrote:

> Absolute precision in the law exists rarely, if at all. The question is whether the legislature has provided an intelligible standard according to which the judiciary must do its work. The task of interpreting how that standard applies in particular instances might always be characterized as having a discretionary element, because the standard can never specify all the instances in which it applies. On the other hand, where there is no intelligible standard and where the

---

64 *Canadian Foundation for Children*, above note 51 at para. 16.
65 The following discussion is taken from R.J. Sharpe, "The Application and Impact of Discretion in Commercial Litigation" (1998) 17 Adv. Soc. J. (No. 1) 4.
66 *Irwin Toy*, above note 7 at 617 (D.L.R.).

legislature has given a plenary discretion to do whatever seems best in a wide set of circumstances, there is no "limit prescribed by law."

The notion of "an intelligible standard" was echoed in the judgment of Lamer J. in the *Prostitution Reference* where he speaks of "an ascertainable standard of conduct, a standard that has been given sensible meaning by courts."[67] The theme was taken up again by Gonthier J. in *R. v. Nova Scotia Pharmaceutical Society*.[68] There, the Court had to contend with the offence of conspiracy to lessen undue competition under the *Competition Act*, a measure that was challenged as failing to respect the principles of fundamental justice:

> Legal rules only provide a framework, a guide as to how one may behave, but certainty is only reached in instant cases, where law is actualized by a competent authority . . . .
>
> By setting out the boundaries of permissible and non-permissible conduct, these norms give rise to legal debate. They bear substance, and they allow for discussion as to their actualization. They therefore limit enforcement discretion by introducing boundaries, and they also sufficiently delineate an area of risk to allow for substantive notice to citizens.
>
> Indeed, no higher requirement as to certainty can be imposed on law in our modern state. Semantic arguments, based on a perception of language as an unequivocal medium, are unrealistic. Language is not the exact tool some may think it is. It cannot be argued that an enactment can and must provide enough guidance to predict the legal consequences of any given course of conduct in advance. All it can do is enunciate some boundaries, which create an area of risk. But it is inherent in our legal system that some conduct will fall along the boundaries of the area of risk; no definite prediction can then be made. Guidance, not direction, of conduct is a more realistic objective . . . .
>
> A vague provision does not provide an adequate basis for legal debate, that is for reaching a conclusion as to its meaning by reasoned analysis applying legal criteria . . . . [I]t fails to give sufficient indications that could fuel legal debate.[69]

These statements indicate a judicial recognition that the problem of uncertainty of result in any given case is pervasive and inherent in any

---

67   *Reference Re ss. 193 and 195.1(1)(c) of the Criminal Code (Canada)*, [1990] 1 S.C.R. 1123, 56 C.C.C. (3d) 65 at 91 [*Prostitution Reference*].

68   [1992] 2 S.C.R. 606, 93 D.L.R. (3d) 36.

69   *Ibid.* at 638–40 (S.C.R.).

standard phrased broadly enough to provide us with guidance in more than one situation.[70] The objective of law is not and cannot be complete predictability of results—that must be left to judgment in each case. At the same time, however, the idea of law does require a minimum "intelligible standard," "an ascertainable standard of conduct," a norm that "give[s] rise to legal debate" or "provide[s] an adequate basis for legal debate" and "give[s] sufficient indication that could fuel legal debate."

Claims that legislation is so vague as to violate the principles of fundamental justice have almost invariably been rejected. Broadly worded statutes have been narrowly interpreted to avoid constitutional infirmity.[71] A statute providing for the release of those found not criminally responsible because of mental disorder if they did not present a "significant threat to the safety of the public" was held not to be excessively vague.[72] The Supreme Court also found that undefined references to "terrorism" and "threats to the security of Canada" in immigration legislation were not unconstitutionally vague. Although such terms require judicial interpretation, the Court held that the meaning of the word "terrorism," for example, was not "so unsettled that it cannot set the proper boundaries of legal adjudication."[73]

c) Overbreadth

Legislation drafted more broadly than is necessary to attain its objective and thereby impinging unduly upon a protected right or freedom may be struck down under section 7 of the *Charter* on grounds of overbreadth. Overbreadth is related to, but distinct from, vagueness. Overbreadth does not depend upon vagueness. The intended effect of a statute may be perfectly clear and not suffer from vagueness, but may be overly broad in its application. On the other hand, vagueness often entails overbreadth. Uncertainty flowing from the vague wording of a statute may have the effect of overly broad application.[74] Overbreadth is also closely related to section 1 proportionality analysis, discussed in Chapter 4.

In *R. v. Heywood*,[75] the Supreme Court of Canada struck down a *Criminal Code* provision making it a crime for persons convicted of

---

70 For another case reiterating the point, see *R. v. Lucas*, [1998] 1 S.C.R. 439, 157 D.L.R. (4th) 423, dealing with the offence of defamatory libel.

71 *Canadian Foundation for Children*, above note 51.

72 *Winko v. British Columbia*, [1999] 2 S.C.R. 625, 175 D.L.R. (4th) 193.

73 *Suresh*, above note 3 at para. 96.

74 *R. v. Heywood*, [1994] 3 S.C.R. 761 at 791–92, applying *R. v. Zundel* (1987), 58 O.R. (2d) 129 (C.A.) at 157–58.

75 *Ibid.*

specified offences to be "found loitering in or near a school ground, playground, public park or bathing area" on the ground that it was overly broad and therefore infringed the liberty interest protected by section 7 of the *Charter*. The provision was aimed at the protection of children; however, it applied to all parks, not just those frequented by children; it was unlimited in time and offered no process of review; it applied to those convicted of offences not involving children; and it could be enforced without notice to the accused. Cory J. explained the overbreadth principle in the following way:

> Overbreadth analysis looks at the means chosen by the state in relation to its purpose. In considering whether a legislative provision is overbroad, a court must ask the question: are those means necessary to achieve the State objective? If the State, in pursuing a legitimate objective, uses means which are broader than is necessary to accomplish that objective, the principles of fundamental justice will be violated because the individual's rights will have been limited for no reason. The effect of overbreadth is that in some applications the law is arbitrary or disproportionate.[76]

The overbreadth principle was applied again in *R. v. Demers*, invalidating a *Criminal Code* provision that denied those permanently unfit to stand trial the possibility of an absolute discharge. The Supreme Court held that "the continued subjection of an unfit accused to the criminal process, where there is clear evidence that capacity will never be recovered and there is no evidence of a significant threat to public safety, makes the law overbroad because the means chosen are not the least restrictive of the unfit person's liberty and are not necessary to achieve the state's objective."[77]

B. INTERESTS PROTECTED BY SECTION 7

Although section 7 of the *Charter* can be broken up into its component parts of "everyone," "rights to life, liberty or security of the person," and the right not to be deprived of these rights "except in accordance with the principles of fundamental justice," it is also helpful to take a more holistic approach to whether a section 7 violation has been established. In the remainder of this chapter, we take such an approach and

---

76   *Ibid.* at 792–93.
77   *R. v. Demers*, [2004] 2 S.C.R. 489 at para. 43.

examine some important contexts in which laws and state actions have been challenged under section 7.

1) Control of the Body: Abortion, Assisted Suicide, and Access to Health Care

The Supreme Court of Canada has had two opportunities to examine the extent to which section 7 protects the individual in making significant decisions about the body. The first was *R. v. Morgentaler*,[78] in which the Court held that the abortion provisions of the *Criminal Code* violated section 7 of the *Charter*; the second, *Rodriguez v. R.*,[79] narrowly upheld the prohibition on assisted suicide in the *Criminal Code*.

a) Abortion

R. v. Morgentaler dramatically demonstrated the *Charter*'s impact on highly contested matters of public policy. The *Criminal Code* provision at issue prohibited abortions but also provided an exemption if a woman seeking an abortion obtained a certificate from a therapeutic-abortion committee consisting of three physicians. Such a certificate could be issued if the committee concluded that the woman's life or health would be endangered by the continuation of the pregnancy. These committees could operate only in accredited hospitals, and the doctor performing the abortion could not be included on the committee. Evidence was led to show that access to abortion varied significantly across the country. Many hospitals did not provide abortions at all, while others imposed rules more stringent than those set out in the *Criminal Code*, for example, denying abortions to married women.

The Supreme Court struck down the *Criminal Code* prohibition of abortion, but the Court was sharply divided in its reasoning. Beetz J., writing for himself and Estey J., found it possible to strike down the law on relatively narrow grounds. He focused on the fact that the law had a direct impact on a woman's health. In his view, the law infringed the woman's right to security of the person by requiring committee approval of medical treatment necessary to protect her life or health. He also found that the therapeutic-abortion committee procedure was not in accordance with the principles of fundamental justice, since it was applied in an arbitrary and uneven fashion, often based on factors not reasonably linked to the protection of the life or health of the woman or her foetus.

---

78 *Morgentaler*, above note 1.
79 *Rodriguez*, above note 49.

Wilson J. adopted a much more expansive interpretation. In her view, there was a violation of both the right to liberty and the right to security of the person. The right to liberty, Wilson J. wrote, "guarantees to every individual a degree of personal autonomy over important decisions intimately affecting their private lives."[80] A woman's decision whether to continue a pregnancy is hers and hers alone, and state interference with her personal autonomy in making that decision violates her right to liberty. In addition, Wilson J. found, the state violated the woman's right to security of the person by forcing her to continue a pregnancy. The woman's autonomy right was infringed for she was being treated as "a means to an end which she does not desire," in that she was "the passive recipient of a decision made by others as to whether her body is to be used to nurture a new life."[81]

The third set of majority reasons was written by Dickson C.J.C., with Lamer J. concurring. Some of his language echoed that of Wilson J.:

> Forcing a woman, by threat of criminal sanction, to carry a foetus to term unless she meets certain criteria unrelated to her own priorities and aspirations, is a profound interference with a woman's body and thus a violation of security of the person.[82]

However, other passages suggest an approach closer to that of Beetz J., because of the emphasis on the threat to a woman's physical and psychological health created by procedures that prevented, or at least delayed, access to important medical treatment under the threat of criminal sanction.

McIntyre J. in dissent, with La Forest J. concurring, rejected the view that section 7 included a right to an abortion in any circumstances. In his view, neither the language of the *Charter* nor "the history, traditions and underlying philosophies of our society would support the proposition that a right to abortion could be implied in the *Charter*."[83]

While all the majority judges rejected arguments made under section 1 to save the legislation, they also made it clear that some restrictions on a woman's access to abortion could be justified under section 1 in order to protect the foetus. Beetz J., however, rejected the proposition that Parliament could prevent access to an abortion necessary to protect maternal life or health. Wilson J. suggested that Parliament's case for intervention to protect the foetus would become stronger as the pregnancy progressed. This suggested an approach similar to that

---

80   *Morgentaler*, above note 1 at 171 (S.C.R.).
81   *Ibid.* at 173 (S.C.R.).
82   *Ibid.* at 56–57 (S.C.R.).
83   *Ibid.* at 143, 144 (S.C.R.).

of the United States Supreme Court, which, in *Roe v. Wade*,[84] had concluded that increasing restrictions on access to abortion were justified in the later stages of pregnancy.

Morgentaler generated much debate about whether Parliament could enact new legislation limiting abortions that would survive judicial scrutiny. The federal government attempted to do so shortly following the decision with the introduction of Bill C-43, which would have required a doctor to certify that a woman's health was endangered by the continuation of the pregnancy. The bill passed in the House of Commons but was defeated as a result of a tie vote in the Senate. The result is that there is currently no prohibition of abortion in Canada's criminal law. Some provinces have attempted to control access to abortion, particularly by restrictions on free-standing abortion clinics, but some of those initiatives have been found to be unconstitutional under the distribution of powers in the federal system. For example, in *Morgentaler 1993*, the Supreme Court of Canada struck down Nova Scotia's regulation as an attempt to legislate in the area of criminal law, which is within exclusive federal jurisdiction.[85]

There have also been attempts to litigate the abortion issue from the perspective of foetal rights. Joseph Borowksi, a pro-life activist, brought an action seeking a declaration that the abortion provisions in the *Criminal Code* violated the foetus's right to life under section 7. He was unsuccessful in the lower courts of Manitoba. By the time the case reached the Supreme Court of Canada, the Court had struck down the abortion provisions of the *Criminal Code* in *Morgentaler*, and the Court declined to consider his case on the merits on the basis that the issue was moot — that is, there was no legal issue, given the invalidity of the legislation.[86]

In *Daigle v. Tremblay*,[87] a man sought an injunction to prevent his former partner from obtaining an abortion. The case involved the interpretation of Quebec's *Charter of Human Rights and Freedoms*, specifically, the scope of the foetus's and prospective father's rights. The Supreme Court of Canada determined that a foetus is not a person with rights under the Quebec *Charter*, but it did not address the issue of whether "everyone" in section 7 of the Canadian *Charter* includes a foetus, since no law was being challenged and the Canadian *Charter* did not apply to a proceeding involving private parties.

---

84   410 U.S. 113 (1973).

85   *R. v. Morgentaler*, [1993] 3 S.C.R. 463, 107 D.L.R. (4th) 537 [*Morgentaler 1993*].

86   *Borowski v. Canada (A.G.)*, [1989] 1 S.C.R. 342, 57 D.L.R. (4th) 231. See chapter 7 for a discussion of mootness.

87   *Daigle*, above note 13.

b)   Assisted Suicide

Rodriguez v. R.[88] raised the issue of the scope of section 7 in relation to another important personal decision, namely, the right to determine the timing of one's death through assisted suicide. Sue Rodriguez was terminally ill, suffering from Lou Gehrig's disease, which had attacked her neurological system. She wanted to be able to end her own life when she felt that the quality of her life made it no longer worth living. Given the nature of her disease, at that point, she might be unable physically to accomplish the necessary acts, and hence she might need some assistance. Attempting suicide is not a crime, but section 241(b) of the *Criminal Code* makes it an offence for anyone to assist another person to commit suicide. Rodriguez argued that the section violated section 7 of the *Charter* by denying her the right to terminate her life when she wished.

The Supreme Court of Canada divided five to four on the issue of the constitutionality of the provision. Sopinka J., writing for the majority, held that the legislation did violate the right to security of the person. His reasons drew upon those of Wilson J. in *Morgentaler*. He concluded:

> . . . personal autonomy, at least with respect to the right to make choices concerning one's own body, control over one's physical and psychological integrity, and basic human dignity are encompassed within security of the person, at least to the extent of freedom from criminal prohibitions which interfere with these.[89]

On the facts of the case, Sopinka J. held that denying Ms. Rodriguez assistance to commit suicide would deprive her of personal autonomy and cause physical pain and psychological distress. However, when Sopinka J. went to the next level of analysis, he found that the restriction on assisted suicide did not violate principles of fundamental justice. The purpose of the legislation, he found, was to protect those in a vulnerable situation from exploitation. The prohibition of assisted suicide was grounded in the state interest in the sanctity of human life, a fundamental value of Canadian society. Sopinka J. conceded that there are exceptions to the principle of the sanctity of life in our law. For example, the law allows for the termination of life through the refusal or consented withdrawal of medical treatment. On the other hand, Sopinka J. noted, the law has drawn a distinction between passive and active euthanasia. In Sopinka J.'s opinion, there was no general societal

---

88   *Rodriguez*, above note 49.
89   *Ibid.* at 588 (S.C.R.).

consensus that active euthanasia is acceptable. Absent that consensus and given the value placed on human life, the majority of the Court held that it should not find the assisted-suicide prohibition in violation of the principles of fundamental justice.

McLachlin J., who wrote one of the three dissenting opinions, held that the law did not accord with the principles of fundamental justice, because it was arbitrary in its application to individuals such as Ms. Rodriguez. In her view, Parliament has not taken a consistent attitude with respect to decisions to terminate life—for example, it does not prohibit passive euthanasia or suicide. Therefore, she found it arbitrary to deny access to suicide to an individual like Ms. Rodriguez who was able to make a free and informed decision about the continuation of her life.[90]

Rodriguez illustrates the difficulty facing judges in determining the scope of the principles of fundamental justice. While the early section 7 cases stated that the principles of fundamental justice are found in the basic tenets of the legal system,[91] the Supreme Court has found it difficult to identify a similar grounding for the meaning of fundamental justice in cases like *Rodriguez* that raise complex moral issues.

c)   Access to Health Care

In *Chaoulli v. Quebec (Attorney General)*,[92] the Supreme Court held that although there is no free-standing right to health care, where the public health care system fails to provide timely access, laws restricting access to private health care services may be subject to *Charter* scrutiny. The court held that delays in the public health care system were serious, widespread, and potentially life threatening. Three judges held that a Quebec law, prohibiting insurance to provide access to private health care services, should be struck down as an arbitrary interference with the section 7 right to timely access to necessary health care services. The three judges (McLachlin C.J.C. and Major J., Bastarache J. concurring) relied on the judgment of Beetz J. in *Morgentaler* for the broad proposition "that rules that endanger health arbitrarily do not comply with the principles of fundamental justice."[93] A fourth judge came to a similar conclusion, but on the basis of Quebec's *Charter of Human Rights and Freedoms* which only requires the deprivation of life and security of the person and not that the deprivation be in viola-

---

90   Lamer C.J.C. dissented, but relied on the equality right in s. 15 of the *Charter*, rather than s. 7.

91   *Re B.C. Motor Vehicle Act*, above note 3.

92   *Chaoulli*, above note 32.

93   *Ibid.* at para. 133.

tion of principles of fundamental justice. The three dissenting judges (Binnie and LeBel JJ., Fish J. concurring) agreed that access to health care fell within the right to life and security of the person protected by section 7 of the Canadian *Charter*, but strongly disagreed that there was a violation of the principles of fundamental justice. They held that the *Morgentaler* case was distinguishable on the basis that abortions were restricted by the criminal sanction and they were also arbitrarily prohibited because they could not be legally performed in certain parts of the country where there were no accredited abortion committees or hospitals that performed abortions.[94] The majority decision, discussed above in relation to the principles of fundamental justice, represents a potentially dramatic expansion of the reach of section 7.

2) Privacy, the Family, and Fundamental Personal Choices

In *B.(R.) v. Children's Aid Society of Metropolitan Toronto*,[95] four members of the Supreme Court held that the right to liberty guaranteed by section 7 of the *Charter* must allow an individual "to make decisions that are of fundamental personal importance."[96] In *B.(R.)*, the parents were Jehovah's Witnesses who, based upon their religious beliefs, refused medical treatment for their child that would likely have involved a blood transfusion. In the words of La Forest J., "the right to nurture a child, to care for its development, and to make decisions for it in fundamental matters such as medical care, are part of the liberty interest of a parent."[97] In this view, any state intervention to protect a child's interests must be justified as conforming with the principles of fundamental justice.

Lamer C.J.C. took issue with this broad reading of section 7 and reiterated the view he had expressed in other cases limiting the protection of the section:

> The liberty in question must therefore be one that may be limited through the operation of some mechanism that involves and actively engages the principles of fundamental justice. Principles of fundamental justice pertain to the justice system. They are designed to govern both the means by which one may be brought before the ju-

---

94   *Ibid.* at paras. 259–63.
95   *B.(R.)*, above note 18.
96   *Ibid.* at 368 (S.C.R.).
97   *Ibid.* at 370 (S.C.R.).

dicial system and the conduct of judges and other actors once the individual is brought within it.[98]

Lamer C.J.C. would restrict the scope of section 7 to

> the conduct of the state when the state calls on law enforcement officials to enforce and secure obedience to the law, or invokes the law to deprive a person of liberty through judges, magistrates, ministers, board members, etc.[99]

Sopinka J. found it unnecessary to deal with the point, while the remaining three judges held that the liberty interest in section 7 did not allow a parent to deny necessary medical treatment to a child. In their view, the child's right to life, also guaranteed by section 7, placed limits on the parent's right to liberty.

All members of the Court agreed in the result, however, namely, that the wardship order depriving the parents of the right to decide for their child should be upheld. For the majority, La Forest J. found that the parents' case could not survive the second stage of the section 7 analysis relating to the principles of fundamental justice. He found that the wardship provisions of the provincial child-welfare legislation conformed to the principles of fundamental justice. The parents had received notice of the wardship application, there had been a hearing before a judge, and they had been afforded an opportunity to present their views.

The Court examined a related issue in *A.C. v. Manitoba (Director of Child and Family Services)*.[100] In that case a medically required blood transfusion was ordered for a fourteen-year-old Jehovah's Witness. The Court upheld the constitutionality of provincial legislation that allowed medical treatment to be ordered for children under sixteen years of age when it was in their best interests while recognizing that those sixteen years or older could refuse treatment. The Court agreed that the ordering of treatment without the fourteen year old's consent violated her rights to liberty and security of the person. Nevertheless, the Court held that the legislation did not violate the principles of fundamental justice given that the best interest standard was sufficiently flexible to accommodate the autonomy interests of mature children. In other words, the legislation reflected "a proportionate response to the goal of protecting vulnerable young people from harm, while respecting the individuality and autonomy of those who are sufficiently

---

98 *Ibid.* at 340 (S.C.R.).
99 *Ibid.*
100 2009 SCC 30.

mature to make a particular treatment decision."[101] The legislation also contemplated that children would be given notice and an opportunity to participate in the decision-making process, though that was not possible in this case of emergency treatment. Binnie J. dissented in large part because he interpreted the statute as creating an irrebutable presumption of incapacity. He thus found it violated the principles of fundamental justice because it was an arbitrary measure that could not advance the legitimate purpose of protecting children who were not capable of making decisions about medical treatment and because in his view (but not the majority's) it denied those under sixteen years of age an ability to rebut a presumption of incapacity.[102]

In *New Brunswick (Minister of Health and Community Services) v. G.(J.).*,[103] a mother was denied legal aid when the state sought an order extending its custody of her three children for an additional six months. The Supreme Court found the denial of legal aid to be a violation of section 7 of the *Charter*. Lamer C.J.C. found that the decision affected that mother's security of the person by constituting a serious state interference with her psychological integrity. In a concurring judgment, Justice L'Heureux-Dubé (Gonthier and McLachlin JJ. concurring) added that the section 7 interests should be assessed with attention to concerns about gender equality and the disproportionate effects of child protection proceedings on single mothers. Consistent with a broader approach to the right to liberty, these judges also saw the case as implicating liberty interests.

Lamer C.J.C. held that "the principles of fundamental justice in child protection proceedings are both substantive and procedural. The state may only relieve a parent of custody when it is necessary to protect the best interests of the child, provided that there is a fair procedure for making this determination."[104] For the hearing to be fair, the parent must be able to participate effectively. Given the seriousness of the interests at stake, the complexity of the proceedings, and the mother's capacities, Lamer C.J.C. concluded that her right to a fair hearing required that she be represented by counsel. This decision was made on the facts of the particular case and the Court warned as follows:

> . . . a parent need not always be represented by counsel in order to ensure a fair custody hearing. The seriousness and complexity of a hearing and the capacities of the parent will vary from case to case.

---

101 *Ibid.* at para. 115.
102 *Ibid.* at paras. 223–24.
103 *New Brunswick*, above note 3.
104 *Ibid.* at para. 70.

Whether it is necessary for the parent to be represented by counsel is directly proportional to the seriousness and complexity of the proceedings, and inversely proportional to the capacities of the parent.[105]

The Court emphasized the connection between a fair process and the substantive goal of the hearing by concluding that "without the benefit of counsel, the appellant would not have been able to participate effectively at the hearing, creating an unacceptable risk of error in determining the children's best interests and thereby threatening to violate both the appellant's and her children's section 7 right to security of the person."[106] The Court's recognition in this case of the intimate connection between procedural and substantive justice was consistent with the Court's rejection in the 1985 *Motor Vehicle Act* case of a strict and artificial dichotomy between the two concepts.

In *Winnipeg Child and Family Services v. K.L.W.*,[107] the Supreme Court agreed that even the temporary apprehension of a mother's newborn child who is deemed in need of protection violated the mother's security of the person. However, the Court went on to hold that section 7 of the *Charter* was not violated because, in the context of protecting vulnerable children, prior judicial authorization of the state's apprehension of the child was not necessary. Two judges dissented on the basis that prior judicial authorization was necessary because, unlike in *B.(R.)*, apprehension of the child was not an emergency.[108] L'Heureux-Dubé J. for the majority, however, stressed the difficulty of distinguishing between emergencies and non-emergencies in the child protection context. The Court did indicate that "the seriousness of the interests at stake demands that the resulting disruption of the parent-child relationship be minimized as much as possible by a fair and prompt post-apprehension hearing." As contemplated in *G.(J.)*, "in order to be fair, the hearing must involve reasonable notice with particulars to the parents, as well as an opportunity for them to participate meaningfully in the proceedings."[109]

Future cases are likely to raise difficult questions about the scope of the personal autonomy and privacy interests protected by section 7. They may arise, for example, with respect to government regulation of medical procedures, such as access to new reproductive technologies or with respect to parental control of children.

---

105 *Ibid.* at para. 86.
106 *Ibid.* at para. 81.
107 [2000] 2 S.C.R. 519.
108 *Ibid.* at para. 3, Arbour J. (McLachlin C.J.C. concurring).
109 *Ibid.* at paras. 122, 123.

3) Extradition and Deportation to Face Death or Torture and National Security Matters

In *United States v. Burns*,[110] the Supreme Court decided that the extradition of any fugitive without assurances from the foreign state that the death penalty would not be applied would, except in "exceptional cases," violate section 7 of the *Charter*. The decision marked a departure from two decisions by the Court a decade earlier in which it held that extradition of fugitives to the United States to face the death penalty was consistent with the *Charter*.[111] Although the principles of fundamental justice were still located in the basic tenets of the legal system, these tenets were informed by developments such as a growing recognition of wrongful convictions and an international trend against the imposition of the death penalty. The Court also decided the case on broad principles that would apply to all fugitives. The decision did not, for example, depend on the fact that the fugitives in the particular case were Canadian citizens or young persons.

The Court emphasized that the ultimate issue under section 7 must be to ensure compliance with the principles of fundamental justice when depriving individuals of their rights to life, liberty, or security of the person. The idea that punishment or treatment that "shocks the conscience" would violate section 7 of the *Charter* should not be associated with public opinion polls. The words were not intended to signal an abdication by judges of their constitutional responsibilities in matters involving fundamental principles of justice. The Supreme Court quoted with approval the following passage written by President Arthur Chaskalson of the Constitutional Court of South Africa in declaring unconstitutional the death penalty in that country:

> Public opinion may have some relevance to the enquiry, but, in itself, it is no substitute for the duty vested in the Courts to interpret the Constitution and to uphold its provisions without fear or favour. If public opinion were to be decisive, there would be no need for constitutional adjudication. The protection of rights could then be left to Parliament, which has a mandate from the public, and is answerable to the public for the way its mandate is exercised . . . . The very reason for establishing the new legal order, and for vesting the

---

110 *Burns*, above note 15.

111 *Reference Re Ng Extradition (Can.)*, [1991] 2 S.C.R. 858, 84 D.L.R. (4th) 498; *Kindler v. Canada (Minister of Justice)*, [1991] 2 S.C.R. 779, 84 D.L.R. (4th) 438. For criticisms of the Court for not overruling these decisions, see R. Haigh, "A Kinder, Gentler Supreme Court" (2001) 14 Sup. Ct. L. Rev. 139 (2d).

power of judicial review of all legislation in the courts, was to protect the rights of minorities and others who cannot protect their rights adequately through the democratic process. Those who are entitled to claim this protection include the social outcasts and marginalised people of our society. It is only if there is a willingness to protect the worst and the weakest amongst us that all of us can be secure that our own rights will be protected.[112]

Although the Supreme Court of Canada played an anti-majoritarian role in enforcing the constitution, it also emphasized that the interpretation of section 7 of the *Charter* required a balance of conflicting interests. It considered the state interests that would be advanced by extradition without assurances that the death penalty would not be applied but concluded that, except in undefined exceptional cases, these interests could be served by extradition with assurances that the death penalty would not be applied. For example, Canada could still honour its international obligations to assist in the return of fugitives to justice and could avoid becoming a "safe haven" for criminals if fugitives were extradited to foreign countries to face long prison sentences as opposed to the death penalty. The Court concluded:

> The arguments in favour of extradition without assurances would be as well served by extradition with assurances. There was no convincing argument that exposure of the respondents to death in prison by execution advances Canada's public interest in a way that the alternative, eventual death in prison by natural causes, would not. The arguments against extradition without assurances have grown stronger since this Court decided *Kindler* and *Ng* in 1991. Canada is now abolitionist for all crimes, even those in the military field. The international trend against the death penalty has become clearer. The death penalty controversies in the requesting State—the United States—are based on pragmatic, hard-headed concerns about wrongful convictions. None of these factors is conclusive, but taken together they tilt the section 7 balance against extradition without assurances.[113]

In *Suresh v. Canada*,[114] the Supreme Court decided that the deportation of terrorists to face torture in a foreign country would, except in exceptional cases, violate section 7 of the *Charter*. The Court looked

---

112 *Burns*, above note 15 at para. 67, citing *S. v. Makwanyane*, 1995 (3) SA 391 at para. 88.

113 *Ibid.* at paras. 130–31.

114 *Suresh*, above note 3.

to both Canadian and international law to determine that torture offended the principles of fundamental justice. The Court held that section 7 would be violated even though the ultimate harm of torture, like the ultimate harm of death in *Burns*, would not be imposed by the Canadian government. There was a "sufficient causal connection between our government's participation and the deprivation ultimately effected."[115]

As in *Burns*, the Court emphasized that the interpretation of section 7 required a balance of conflicting interests. In *Suresh* the Court reasoned:

> On the one hand stands the state's genuine interest in combatting terrorism, preventing Canada from becoming a safe haven for terrorists, and protecting public security. On the other hand stands Canada's constitutional commitment to liberty and fair process. This said, Canadian jurisprudence suggests that this balance will usually come down against expelling a person to face torture elsewhere.[116]

The Court, however, refused to articulate an absolute rule against deportation to face torture. It stated:

> We do not exclude the possibility that in exceptional circumstances, deportation to face torture might be justified, either as a consequence of the balancing process mandated by s. 7 of the *Charter* or under s. 1. We may predict that it will rarely be struck in favour of expulsion where there is a serious risk of torture. However, as the matter is one of balance, precise prediction is elusive. The ambit of an exceptional discretion to deport to torture, if any, must await future cases.[117]

In cases in which there is a substantial risk of torture, section 7 of the *Charter* requires heightened procedural protection for a person who might be deported or extradited.[118] These procedural rights are informed by common law standards of procedural fairness that, the Court recognized, are basic tenets of the justice system. A full oral or judicial hearing is not required, but the applicant should be able to make written submissions, examine the materials considered by the Minister, and receive written reasons for the decision whether to deport. In *Ahani v. Canada*, a companion case to *Suresh*, the Court held

---

115 *Ibid.* at para. 54.

116 *Ibid.* at para. 58.

117 *Ibid.* at para. 78. For an argument that extradition to face torture would violate Canada's international law obligations, see K. Roach, "International, Domestic and Remedial Dialogues: The Canadian Experience" (2005) 40 Texas Int. L.J. 537.

118 *Application under s. 83.28 of the Criminal Code (Re)*, [2004] 2 S.C.R. 248.

that the person subject to deportation to Iran had not demonstrated a substantial risk of torture and section 7 of the *Charter* had not been violated.[119] Subsequently, Ahani unsuccessfully argued that he had a right under section 7 of the *Charter* to remain in Canada until his appeal to the United Nations Human Rights Commission was heard.[120]

A related question is whether section 7 is violated by procedures that allow the government to make submissions to a court without the affected party being present or having access to the information because of concerns about protecting national security and confidences received from foreign governments. In *Chiarelli v. Canada*,[121] the Supreme Court held that security certificate procedures in immigration law did not violate section 7 of the *Charter*. The Court, however, stressed that the affected party whom the government sought to remove from Canada would have access to a summary of information presented to the judge. In *Ruby v. Canada*,[122] the Supreme Court held that provisions in the *Privacy Act* that allow the government to make submissions about matters affecting national security and foreign confidences without the affected party being present did not violate section 7 of the *Charter*. The Court stressed, however, that fairness could be achieved through other procedural safeguards such as subsequent disclosure, judicial review, and rights of appeal.

In *Charkaoui v. Canada*[123], the Court significantly qualified its prior holding in *Chiarelli v. Canada*[124] and held that the security certificate process used under immigration law to detain those believed to be threats to national security violated section 7 of the *Charter* because it prevented any adversarial challenge to secret intelligence submitted by the government to the reviewing judge. Chief Justice McLachlin ruled for an unanimous Court that the detainees's rights to liberty and security of the person were violated even if, as non-citizens, they did not have a right not to be deported from Canada.[125] In a subsequent case involving the same detainee, the Court recognized the reality that "the consequences of security certificates are often more severe than those of many criminal charges."[126] This underlines that section 7 applies

---

119 *Ahani v. Canada*, 2002 SCC 2, 208 D.L.R. (4th) 57.

120 *Ahani v. Canada* (2002), 58 O.R. (3d) 107 (C.A.).

121 [1992] 1 S.C.R. 711.

122 *Ruby*, above note 40.

123 *Charkaoui*, above note 2.

124 [1992] 1 S.C.R. 711.

125 *Charkaoui*, above note 2 at paras. 12-18.

126 *Charkaoui v. Canada*, 2008 SCC 38 at para. 54. In that case, the Court held that section 7 of the *Charter* supported its interpretation of s. 12 of the *Can-*

beyond the criminal context. The Court in *Charkaoui* recognized that the national security context would affect the content of the principles of fundamental justice but that "they cannot be permitted to erode the essence of section 7. The principles of fundamental justice cannot be reduced to the point where they cease to provide the protection of due process that lies at the heart of section 7 of the *Charter*."[127] In the end, the Court determined that the detainees had been denied their rights to a fair hearing and the right to know and answer the case against them because there was no adversarial challenge to the secret intelligence that the government provided to the judge to support the security certificate. The Court held that the government had not justified this violation of section 7 of the *Charter* under section 1 because there was a variety of more proportionate alternatives that would allow adversarial challenge to the secret intelligence while protecting the state's interests in preventing harms to national security and persons that would be caused by the disclosure of the information. The Court suspended its declaration of invalidity for 12 months and during that time Parliament enacted new provisions that allow security cleared special advocates, but not the detainee or the detainee's own lawyers, to see and challenge the secret intelligence that the government provides to the reviewing judge to justify the security certificate.[128]

In *Khadr v. Canada*,[129] the Supreme Court of Canada held that Canadian officials had violated the *Charter* and international law when they interrogated Omar Khadr in 2002 and 2003 while he was detained at the American military base at Guantanamo Bay, Cuba. The Court's decision that this case required the extraterritorial application of the *Charter* has been discussed above in chapter 6. Having found that the

---

adian Security Intelligence Service Act, R.S.C. 1985, c. C-23 as requiring that all intelligence collected about the detainee be retained and made available to the Ministers and judges who reviewed the security certificate.

127 *Charkaoui*, above note 2 at para. 27.

128 The detainees brought other *Charter* challenges to the security certificate regime with mixed success. The Court held that a prolonged lack of review of the detention of foreign nationals as opposed to permanent residents violated the rights against arbitrary detention under s. 9 of the *Charter* and the right to *habeas corpus* under s. 10(c) of the *Charter*. At the same time, the Court held that prolonged detention did not amount to cruel and unusual punishment under s. 12 because the detainees would have regular opportunities to review their detention. The Court also held that the lack of appeal rights and automatic detention did not violate unwritten rule of law principles and that the security certificate scheme which only applies to non-citizens did not violate their equality rights.

129 *Khadr*, above note 12.

Charter applied in this case, the Court found a violation of section 7. What is significant, however, is that the content of the section 7 violation was not based on general principles of disclosure in domestic criminal cases under *R. v. Stinchcombe*.[130] Rather the content of the disclosure duty was "defined by the nature of Canada's participation in the process that violated Canada's international human rights obligations."[131] In the context of this case, this meant that Omar Khadr only received disclosure of the records of the interviews that Canadian officials conducted with him at Guantanamo and the information that Canada gave to the United States as a direct consequence of the interviews at Guantanamo, interviews which, the Court held, violated Canada's international human rights obligations and required extraterritorial application of the *Charter*. Omar Khadr thus received far less disclosure than he would have under *Stinchcombe*.[132] Nevertheless, the case raises the interesting question of whether violations of Canada's international human rights obligations will necessarily also constitute violations of the principles of fundamental justice under section 7. If they do, then Canada's international human rights obligations may effectively have been constitutionalized as principles of fundamental justice under section 7, at least in the limited context of attempts to apply the *Charter* to the activities of Canadian officials acting outside Canada. If so, this could be a major step towards moving Canada away from a dualist tradition in which its international commitments have to be specifically incorporated into domestic law, to one with less of a distinction between Canada's international and its domestic constitutional obligations.

4) Economic Rights

The extent to which the *Charter* should protect economic rights has been the subject of debate from its inception. The language of section 7 would seem to offer a basis to argue against restrictions on economic activity, since its guarantee of the right to liberty could arguably include a right to economic liberty. The right to security of the person, similarly, could encompass a right to economic security in the form of basic rights to social assistance or public housing. To be weighed against these claims, however, is the legislative history of the *Charter*,

---

130 [1991] 3 S.C.R. 326 as discussed in chapter 14.
131 *Khadr*, above note 12 at para. 3.
132 The government was given an opportunity to make national security confidentiality claims before the material was actually disclosed. See *Khadr v. Canada (Attorney General)*, 2008 FC 807.

for property rights were expressly excluded from section 7 and subsequent efforts to add property rights have failed.

To date, the courts have, for the most part, been unsympathetic to those seeking to vindicate pure economic rights through the *Charter*. "The ability to generate business revenue by one's chosen means is not a right that is protected under s. 7 of the *Charter*."[133] There have, however, been some successes in the lower courts. In *Wilson*, the British Columbia Court of Appeal upheld a challenge by doctors to provincial regulation of the number of doctors practising in the province and the location of their practices.[134] The weight of authority, however, is to the effect that section 7 does not protect a right to engage in a particular type of professional activity.[135]

More generally, as Dickson C.J.C. stated, the right to liberty protected by section 7 "is not synonymous with unconstrained freedom" in the economic sphere and does not extend "to an unconstrained right to transact business whenever one wishes."[136] In a similar vein, Dickson C.J.C. wrote that care must be taken lest the *Charter* "become an instrument of better situated individuals to roll back legislation which has as its object the improvement of the condition of less advantaged persons."[137] The Supreme Court has flatly rejected the possibility "that economic rights as generally encompassed by the term 'property' are not within the perimeters of the s. 7 guarantee," and it has held as well that corporations cannot claim the protection of economic rights under section 7.[138]

The question whether section 7 protects a basic minimum of social assistance still has not yet been conclusively resolved.[139] Social-welfare advocates have pressed for constitutional amendments to add a "social charter" with court-enforced economic and social rights. There was a vigorous debate about the merits of such a change in the last major round of constitutional reform, but ultimately it was not included in

---

133 *Siemens v. Manitoba (Attorney General)*, [2003] 1 S.C.R. 6 at para. 46.

134 *Wilson v. British Columbia (Medical Services Commission)* (1988), 30 B.C.L.R. (2d) 1 (C.A.), leave to appeal to S.C.C. denied. See also *Mia v. British Columbia (Medical Services Commission)* (1985), 17 D.L.R. (4th) 385 (B.C.S.C.).

135 *Biscotti v. Ontario Securities Commission* (1990), 74 O.R. (2d) 119 (H.C.J.).

136 *Edwards Books & Art Ltd. v. R.*, [1986] 2 S.C.R. 713 at 785–86, 35 D.L.R. (4th) 1.

137 *Ibid.* at 779 (S.C.R.).

138 *Irwin Toy*, above note 7 at 1003 (S.C.R.). It should be noted, however, that s. 1(a) of the *Canadian Bill of Rights* does protect the right of property. As discussed in chapter 1, the *Bill of Rights* applies only to federal laws.

139 For discussion see: M. Jackman, "The Protection of Welfare Rights under the *Charter*" (1988) 20 Ottawa L. Rev. 257; I. Johnstone, "Section 7 of the *Charter* and Constitutionally Protected Welfare" (1988) 46 U.T. Fac. L. Rev. 1.

the 1992 Charlottetown Accord.[140] In an early decision, Wilson J. noted that the broad language of section 7 might extend to the provision of basic necessities, referring to the *Universal Declaration of Human Rights*, which includes a guarantee of "the right to a standard of living adequate for . . . health and well-being . . . including food, clothing, housing and medical care and necessary social services."[141] Interestingly, when rejecting the argument that section 7 includes property rights, the Supreme Court gave the following caveat, suggesting that consideration of this question is not altogether foreclosed:

> This is not to declare, however, that no right with an economic component can fall within "security of the person." Lower courts have found that the rubric of "economic rights" embraces a broad spectrum of interests, ranging from such rights, included in various international covenants, as rights to social security, equal pay for equal work, adequate food, clothing and shelter, to traditional property—contract rights. To exclude all of these at this early moment in the history of *Charter* interpretation seems to us precipitous. We do not, at this moment, choose to pronounce upon whether these economic rights fundamental to human life and survival are to be treated as though they are of the same ilk as corporate-commercial economic rights.[142]

The majority decision in *Gosselin v. Quebec (Attorney General)*[143] disappointed those who hoped to gain *Charter* protection for basic welfare rights. For the time being, the Supreme Court refused to take that momentous step, but the decision explicitly leaves open the possibility that an affirmative right to basic subsistence might one day be protected by section 7. This cautious approach coincides with the Court's general reluctance to interpret *Charter* guarantees as including economic rights as well as the Court's tendency to defer to legislatures where complex economic and social policy choices are at issue[144] and reflects a judicial unwillingness to become embroiled in social-welfare policy. Writing for the majority in *Gosselin*, McLachlin C.J.C. disagreed with Bastarache

---

140 P. Macklem & C. Scott, "Constitutional Ropes of Sand or Justiciable Guarantees? Social Rights in a New South African Constitution" (1992) 141 U. of Penn. L. Rev. 1; J. Bakan & D. Schneiderman, eds., *Social Justice and the Constitution: Perspectives on a Social Union for Canada* (Ottawa: Carleton University Press, 1992).

141 *Singh v. Canada (Minister of Employment & Immigration)*, [1985] 1 S.C.R. 177 at 206–7.

142 *Irwin Toy*, above note 7 at 1003–4 (S.C.R.).

143 *Gosselin*, above note 24.

144 See especially chapter 4.

J. that section 7 is necessarily limited to situations directly involving the administration of justice. However, McLachlin C.J.C. ruled that the evidence of hardship in the case was insufficient to require the Court to interpret section 7 as having an affirmative element requiring the state to provide the elements necessary to the enjoyment of life, liberty, or security of the person. On the other hand, invoking the living tree metaphor, she explicitly left open the possibility that section 7 might one day evolve to embrace social welfare rights. Arbour J., with whom L'Heureux-Dubé J. agreed, wrote a strong dissent urging her colleagues to adopt an expansive definition of section 7 as including a positive component including the right to basic needs.

C. CONCLUSION

Section 7 gives rise to some of the most difficult issues arising under the *Charter*. The right to life, liberty, and security of the person invites the courts to engage a wide array of difficult moral and ethical issues. The Supreme Court's insistence that the principles of fundamental justice have substantive and not merely procedural content signalled an activist role for the Court. Until recently, the Court proceeded cautiously in determining the ambit of section 7. However, the Court's recent extension of section 7 to the guarantee of timely access to health care services potentially opens the door to a host of contentious health care and other issues formerly regarded as falling outside the limits of constitutional adjudication. It is a virtual certainty that, in the years to come, the courts will continue to be asked to resolve the conflict between the individual's right to control his or her own body and the broader social interest in the protection of the sanctity of life. These issues have arisen in the past in relation to abortion and assisted suicide and are likely to arise in the future in connection with life-choice and health issues generated by the remarkable scientific advances in genetics. It is also likely that both the "haves" and the "have-nots" will continue to press for recognition of economic or social-welfare rights. So far, the Court has shied away from interpreting the *Charter* to include economic rights, but equally it has refused unequivocally to preclude the protection of a right to basic rights of social assistance and housing.

FURTHER READINGS

BAKAN, J., & D. SCHNEIDERMAN, eds., *Social Justice and the Constitution: Perspectives on a Social Union for Canada* (Ottawa: Carleton University Press, 1992)

BALA, N., "*D.B.* and the Principles of Youth Justice" (2009) Sup. Ct. L. Rev. (2d) (forthcoming)

BRODIE, J., *et al.*, *The Politics of Abortion* (Don Mills, ON: Oxford University Press, 1992)

CAMERON, J., "Positive Obligations under the *Charter*" (2003) 20 Sup. Ct. L. Rev. (2d) 65

CANADIAN BAR ASSOCIATION, *The Right to Publicly-Funded Legal Representation in Canada* (Ottawa: Canadian Bar Association, 2002)

COLVIN, E., "Section 7 of the *Charter of Rights and Freedoms*" (1989) 68 Can. Bar Rev. 560

DOWNIE, J., *Dying Justice: A Case for Decriminalizing Euthanasia and Assisted Suicide in Canada* (Toronto: University of Toronto Press, 2004) c. 12

GARANT, P., "Vie, Liberté, securitie at justice fundamentale" in G. Beaudoin and E. Mendes, eds. *Canadian Charter of Rights and Freedoms*, 4th ed (Toronto: LexisNexis, 2005)

JACKMAN, M., "The Protection of Welfare Rights under the *Charter*" (1988) 20 Ottawa L. Rev. 257

JACKMAN, M., "Poor Rights: Using the *Charter* to Support Social Welfare Claims" (1993) 19 Queen's L.J. 65

JOHNSTONE, I., "Section 7 of the *Charter* and Constitutionally Protected Welfare" (1988) 46 U.T. Fac. L. Rev. 1

MORTON, F.L., & R. KNOPFF, *Charter Politics* (Scarborough, ON: Nelson, 1992) c. 10

ROACH, K., "*Charkaoui* and Bill C-3: Some Implications for Anti-Terrorism Policy and Dialogue Between Courts and Legislatures" (2008) 42 Sup. Ct. L. Rev. (2d) 281

ROACH, K., "The *Charter* and National Security" in J. Kelly & C. Manfredi, eds. *Contested Constututionalisms* (Vancouver: University of British Columbia Press, 2009)

SINGLETON, T., "The Principles of Fundamental Justice, Societal Interests and Section 1 of the *Charter*" (1995) 74 Can. Bar Rev. 407

WISEMAN, D., "The *Charter* and Poverty: Beyond Injusticability" (2001) 51 U.T.L.J. 425

CHAPTER 14

CHARTER RIGHTS IN THE CRIMINAL PROCESS

The *Charter of Rights and Freedoms* has had a profound impact in the area of criminal law. *Charter* claims are routinely asserted in criminal proceedings. There have been thousands of cases decided by the courts involving detailed consideration of investigative techniques, pre-trial procedures, and the trial process itself. We offer here a sampling of some of the most significant issues that are raised by the *Charter*.

One way to examine the impact of the *Charter* is to use the abstract models of the criminal process first put forward by the American scholar Herbert Packer to assess the influence of the American Bill of Rights on the criminal justice system.[1] The first is the "crime control model" in which the focus of the criminal justice system is to find and punish the guilty through efficient police and prosecutorial work, usually leading to a guilty plea. The second is the "due process" model in which the focus is on controlling the exercise of police powers through an elaborate series of procedural guarantees, violation of which results in the release of the accused regardless of guilt or innocence. The Canadian criminal justice system, in common with the systems of other liberal democracies, has always exhibited features of both models.

Crime control is bound to be a central feature of any system of criminal justice. The fundamental reason for the existence of the crim-

---

1   H. Packer, *The Limits of the Criminal Sanction* (Stanford: Stanford University Press, 1968). See also K. Roach, *Due Process and Victims' Rights: The New Law and Politics of Criminal Justice* (Toronto: University of Toronto Press, 1999).

inal law is to protect society from those individuals whose behaviour causes serious harm. The severe sanction of deprivation of liberty and imprisonment is justified by the criminal's significant departure from the norms of civil society and by the need to punish such conduct in order to protect society from further transgressions.

Our system of criminal justice has always recognized, however, that crime control is achieved through the assertion of coercive state power, which inevitably involves risks of abuse and oppression. To guard against these risks, the criminal process has evolved a range of procedural protections, designed to ensure that individuals suspected of crime are dealt with fairly and humanely. These guarantees, products of both the common law tradition and statutes enacted by Parliament, include such basic rights as the presumption of innocence, the right to silence, *habeas corpus*, and the right to be tried by a jury of one's peers. These procedural norms, identified as elements of the "due process" model, restrain the exercise of coercive power in a significant way. They are designed to protect the innocent and to avoid the risk of wrongful conviction. But they also benefit the guilty, since they ensure that everyone caught up in the criminal process should be treated fairly. A part of our tradition is the principle that it is better that ten guilty persons should go free than one innocent person be convicted. It is not possible to have a scheme of rights that protects only those who are innocent of wrongdoing. Procedural rights often cause consternation when they assist the guilty. Yet, that is a price to be paid in a free society where rights are enjoyed by all individuals.

The criminal justice system is continually striving to strike an appropriate balance between crime control and the protection of society on the one hand, and fairness to accused persons and the prevention of abuse of police powers on the other. The courts have always played an important role in this exercise. However, by entrenching a number of procedural rights in the constitution, the *Charter of Rights and Freedoms* has increased the courts' responsibility to delineate the line between crime control and due process. In addition, other values are relevant such as the right of privacy and other rights of victims of crime, and the equality rights of groups such as women, children, and minorities who may be disproportionately subject to some crimes. While the fundamental purpose of the Canadian criminal justice system remains the protection of society, there can be little question that the result of the courts' efforts has been to move Canada closer towards the due-process end of the spectrum. At the same time, many of the *Charter* decisions examined in this chapter demonstrate the reality of dialogue between courts and legislatures under the *Charter*. Parliament has frequently responded to the Supreme Court's due-process decisions with new legislation that while accommodating due-process rights also advances society's interests in controlling crime.

A. SECTION 7 AND THE PRINCIPLES OF FUNDAMENTAL JUSTICE

1) The Fault Element

As noted in chapter 13, a crucial question that was faced in the early years of the *Charter* was whether the very general language of section 7 permitted the courts to review the substance of laws or whether judicial review was restricted to procedural matters. In *Reference Re s. 94(2) of the Motor Vehicle Act (B.C.)*,[2] the Supreme Court held that "the principles of fundamental justice" are not restricted to procedural values but have substantive content as well. The case involved a fundamental issue in the criminal law, namely, the extent to which moral blameworthiness should be a requirement for conviction. Criminal offences typically require proof of two elements, harm and fault. Ordinarily, the fact that harm has resulted from someone's conduct is not enough to support a conviction. To label someone a criminal, we must also be satisfied that the individual charged is morally blameworthy. The behaviour of the individual accused of a crime must be shown to have fallen short of an expected standard by intending, or at least foreseeing, the forbidden harm. However, the fault requirement is often difficult to prove, and the legislature may judge it to be in the public interest to impose a sanction without proof of fault of the accused. *Re Motor Vehicle Act* involved such a law. It imposed a mandatory penalty of imprisonment for driving an automobile while one's licence was under suspension. There were a number of situations that could lead to a licence suspension without the knowledge of the licence-holder. An individual might not have even been aware of a licence suspension, and so the result was that a person who had no criminal intent could face a mandatory jail sentence. In the Supreme Court of Canada's view, such a situation violated the principles of fundamental justice:

> A law that has the potential to convict a person who has not really done anything wrong offends the principles of fundamental justice and, if imprisonment is available as a penalty, such a law then violates a person's right to liberty under s. 7 of the *Canadian Charter of*

---

2   [1985] 2 S.C.R. 486, 24 D.L.R. (4th) 536 [*Re Motor Vehicle Act*].

> *Rights and Freedoms* . . . . In other words, absolute liability and im-
> prisonment cannot be combined.[3]

The Supreme Court has subsequently indicated that convicting a
person of an offence without the proof of any fault would be acceptable under the *Charter*, provided that the person was not sentenced to
imprisonment.[4] Even though conviction of the blameless would violate
the principles of fundamental justice, it would only violate section 7
of the *Charter* if the conviction resulted in a deprivation of the right to
life, liberty, or security of the person.

The Supreme Court has given further consideration to the principles limiting the imposition of no-fault liability in criminal law in
a number of situations. It struck down a "statutory rape" offence that
made sex with a girl under fourteen years of age a crime punishable by
life imprisonment, even if the accused honestly believed that the girl
was older and had consented. The Court's concern was that "a person
who is mentally innocent of the offence—who has no *mens rea* [or
fault] with respect to an essential element of the offence—may be convicted and sent to prison."[5] Parliament responded with new offences to
protect children from sexual interference that required the accused to
take all reasonable steps to ascertain the age of the child.

The *Criminal Code* "constructive murder" provisions, obviating the
need to prove an intent to kill if death is caused in the commission
of certain offences and in specified circumstances, were challenged as
violating the principles of fundamental justice. While there is no question that an individual who causes death in the commission of an offence is guilty of manslaughter, itself a serious crime, the issue was
whether an accused who did not intend to kill and did not even foresee
the possibility that death might result should be convicted of murder.
The Supreme Court ruled that, absent proof of moral blameworthiness
connected to the death, such an individual could not be found guilty of
murder, the most serious offence known to the law. At a minimum, said
the majority, there must be proof beyond a reasonable doubt of at least
subjective foreseeability that the conduct could result in death:[6]

> The punishment for murder is the most severe in our society and the
> stigma that attaches to a conviction for murder is similarly extreme.
> . . . [T]here must be some special mental element with respect to the

---

3   *Ibid.* at 492 (S.C.R.), Lamer J.
4   *R. v. Pontes*, [1995] 3 S.C.R. 44, 100 C.C.C. (3d) 353.
5   *R. v. Hess*, [1990] 2 S.C.R. 906, 59 C.C.C. (3d) 161 at 168.
6   *R. v. Vaillancourt*, [1987] 2 S.C.R. 636, 47 D.L.R. (4th) 399 [*Vaillancourt*]; see also
    R. v. Martineau, [1990] 2 S.C.R. 633, 58 C.C.C. (3d) 353.

death before a culpable homicide can be treated as a murder. That special mental element gives rise to the moral blameworthiness which justifies the stigma and sentence attached to a murder conviction.[7]

The Court's list of the most serious "stigma" based offences that require subjective fault in relation to all aspects of the offence has remained short. It includes murder, attempted murder,[8] and war crimes,[9] but does not include other serious criminal offences such as manslaughter.

Regulatory offences are at the other end of the seriousness spectrum. They are enacted to enforce non-criminal behaviour with regard to matters that are not inherently unlawful but that require standards to protect an important public interest. These offences do not carry the same moral connotation and have long been regarded as different from traditional criminal law offences. In a 1991 decision, the Supreme Court held that the *Charter* does not require the same degree of moral culpability as a prerequisite for conviction of a regulatory offence. Where such offences carry the possibility of imprisonment, section 7 does require a minimal degree of fault, but that is satisfied by a standard of negligence. Requiring the accused to establish on a balance of probabilities that he or she was not negligent was also accepted as a reasonable limit on the presumption of innocence protected under section 11(d) of the *Charter*.[10]

Between these two extremes are criminal offences less serious than murder but more grave than regulatory offences. In this grey area, the Supreme Court has insisted upon a minimal level of culpability as a prerequisite for conviction. The constitutional standard is satisfied by conduct judged blameworthy on an objective standard and fault need not relate to all aspects of the harm being punished. Thus, offences such as unlawfully causing bodily harm,[11] dangerous driving,[12] and manslaughter[13] have been upheld despite the fact that they require proof of fault on an objective rather than a subjective standard. Negligence is measured on the basis of a reasonable person standard. The Court has, however, recently stressed that section 7 of the *Charter* requires more than negligence that would produce civil liability but proof of a marked departure from the standards of a reasonable person. The Court was concerned that

---

7   *Vaillancourt, ibid.* at 653–54 (S.C.R.), Lamer J.

8   *R. v. Logan*, [1990] 2 S.C.R. 731, 58 C.C.C. (3d) 391.

9   *R. v. Finta*, [1994] 1 S.C.R. 701, 88 C.C.C. (3d) 417.

10   *R. v. Wholesale Travel Group Inc.*, [1991] 3 S.C.R. 154, 84 D.L.R. (4th) 161.

11   *R. v. DeSousa*, [1992] 2 S.C.R. 944, 95 D.L.R. (4th) 595.

12   *R. v. Hundal*, [1993] 1 S.C.R. 867, 79 C.C.C. (3d) 97.

13   *R. v. Creighton*, [1993] 3 S.C.R. 3, 105 D.L.R. (4th) 632.

if every departure from the civil norm is to be criminalized, regard-less of the degree, we risk casting the net too widely and branding as criminals persons who are in reality not morally blameworthy. Such an approach risks violating the principle of fundamental justice that the morally innocent not be deprived of liberty.[14]

The marked departure standard has now emerged as a constitutional minimum whenever negligence is used as a form of criminal liability.

2) Defences

Section 7 of the *Charter* has been interpreted not only to influence fault elements, but also to influence the substance of a number of defences to crimes. In the controversial *Daviault* case, a majority of the Supreme Court held that the denial of a defence of extreme intoxication to a charge of sexual assault violated section 7 of the *Charter* because it could allow a person who was not at fault at the time of the offence to be convicted of the offence.[15] Parliament quickly responded with new legislation deeming that the act of being so extremely intoxicated so that a person would not be aware that he or she was committing an assault or a sexual assault was a sufficient form of fault to convict that person of assault or sexual assault. Lower courts have been divided about the constitutionality of this provision and the Supreme Court will eventually have to decide the issue.

Section 7 of the *Charter* has also been interpreted to prevent the conviction of a person who acted in a morally involuntary manner because, for example, he or she was acting under duress and was responding reasonably to threats. The Supreme Court held that *Criminal Code* requirements that the threats must be of immediate death or bodily harm from a person who is present at the time that the crime was committed were too strict and violated the *Charter*.[16] Like the fault cases discussed above, this case affirms that section 7 is not limited to the procedural requirement of a fair hearing, but also involves the substantive fairness of laws. There are limits to the degree to which the *Charter* will affect the substantive law of defences in criminal law. The Supreme Court has refused to invalidate section 43 of the *Criminal Code*, which authorizes the use of reasonable corrective force against children on the basis that the defence is inconsistent with the best interests of children. As discussed in chapter 13, the Court concluded that there was not enough

---

14   *R. v. Beatty*, [2008] 1 S.C.R. 49 at para. 34.
15   *R. v. Daviault*, [1994] 3 S.C.R. 63, 93 C.C.C. (3d) 21.
16   *R. v. Ruzic*, [2001] 1 S.C.R. 687, 153 C.C.C. (3d) 1.

consensus to justify enforcing the best interests of the child principle as a principle of fundamental justice under section 7 of the *Charter*.[17] At the same time, the Court placed new limits on this defence as a matter of statutory interpretation.

3) Procedural Rights

The general language of section 7 has been found by the Supreme Court of Canada to incorporate and require respect for certain procedural rights that are not specifically guaranteed by sections 8 to 14 of the *Charter*. In a variety of situations, the Court has held that the "principles of fundamental justice" are broader than the specific rights enjoyed at common law or under particular provisions of the *Charter*. This has had significant implications for all stages of the criminal process.

a)   Right to Silence

R. v. Hebert[18] dealt with the issue of a statement made by an accused person, detained in custody, to an undercover police officer posing as a fellow prisoner. The accused had received legal advice and indicated that he did not wish to make a statement. The undercover officer engaged the accused in conversation and an incriminating statement was made. The specific right to counsel (section 10(b)) and right against self-incrimination (section 11(c)) conferred by the *Charter* did not apply in these circumstances. The Supreme Court held, however, that the principles of fundamental justice implicitly include a broader right to silence. An accused person has the right to choose whether or not to speak to the authorities. The police are permitted to question an accused person, but they are not entitled to use their superior power to override the accused's decision to assert his legal rights. The Court viewed the use of an undercover agent as a trick, designed to deprive the accused of the choice he had made upon legal advice to remain silent in the face of questioning. It found that the accused's right not to be deprived of life, liberty, or security of the person except in accordance with the principles of fundamental justice had been denied. A later decision[19] applied this principle where a statement was elicited by a prisoner acting as a police informer since, in the circumstances, the informer was an agent of the state and, but for his intervention, the statement would not have been given by the accused. A subsequent case, however, held the right

---

17   *Canadian Foundation for Children, Youth and the Law v. Canada (Attorney General)*, [2004] 1 S.C.R. 76.

18   [1990] 2 S.C.R. 151, 57 C.C.C. (3d) 1.

19   *R. v. Broyles*, [1991] 3 S.C.R. 595, 68 C.C.C. (3d) 308.

to silence was not violated simply by the accused's conversation with an undercover police officer posing as a fellow prisoner.[20]

The Court has held that the right to silence under s.7 of the *Charter* was not violated in a case where the accused was arrested for murder, consulted with counsel, and was repeatedly questioned despite telling the police on numerous occasions that he did not wish to talk to them. The majority of the Court held that in the case of police interrogations, the right to silence will not be violated so long as the accused's subsequent statement to the police was voluntary. It rejected a requirement that the police hold off questioning those who assert a right to silence on the basis that such a requirement would not strike the appropriate balance between the state's interest in the investigation of crime and the protection of the accused from the superior resources of the state. Four judges in dissent argued that the persistence of the police in this case violated the accused's rights to silence and counsel. They stressed that police simply ignored the detainee's choice to remain silent. They argued that there was no evidence that respecting the accused's choice whether to speak to the police would have a devastating impact on criminal investigations. In addition, they argued that under a purposive approach, an accused's right to silence could be violated even though the accused's statement would satisfy common law requirements that statements given to the police be proven to be voluntary.[21]

b) Right against Self-Incrimination

Although there are more specific protections against self-incrimination in sections 11(c) and 13 of the *Charter*, which will be examined below, there is also an important residual right against self-incrimination under section 7 of the *Charter*. The Supreme Court has not interpreted this right to allow a person "to take the Fifth" (as in the United States) by refusing to answer questions. Rather, it has held that the right will be protected if a person is protected from the use and derivative use of compelled statements in subsequent proceedings. For example, business people can be compelled to produce records and be examined on them under a *Securities Act*, but the fruits of such compelled incrimination or evidence derived from such information cannot be used against them in subsequent proceedings. If the predominant purpose of the state was to obtain evidence to be used against that person, section 7 of the *Charter* would exempt the person from having to testify.[22] Use and

---

20 *R. v. Liew*, [1999] 3 S.C.R. 227, 137 C.C.C. (3d) 353.
21 *R. v. Singh*, [2007] 3 S.C.R. 405.
22 *British Columbia (Securities Commission) v. Branch*, [1995] 2 S.C.R. 3, 97 C.C.C. (3d) 505 [*Branch*].

derivative use immunity has been applied to motorists who are compelled under a *Motor Vehicle Act* to provide an accident report,[23] but the right against self-incrimination does not apply to fishing logs that must be kept to prevent over-fishing.[24] The Court has thus taken a contextual approach to the right against self-incrimination.

In 2004, the Supreme Court upheld the constitutionality of investigative hearings introduced after the September 11, 2001 terrorist attacks as a means to compel people to disclose information about terrorism. The majority of the Court held that the new procedure was consistent with the right against self-incrimination under section 7 of the *Charter* because no evidence compelled from a person at an investigative hearing or evidence derived from such evidence could be used in subsequent proceedings, with the exception of a perjury prosecution. The Court, however, extended the statutory use and derivative use immunity provisions to apply in subsequent extradition and immigration proceedings, as well as in criminal proceedings.[25] The Court also indicated that an investigative hearing conducted for the predominant purpose of obtaining evidence to be used in a subsequent criminal trial of a suspect would violate the right against self-incrimination in section 7 of the *Charter*. Three judges dissented on the basis that it was an abuse of process to attempt to use an investigative hearing with respect to a reluctant witness in the middle of the ongoing Air India terrorism trial. Two judges dissented on the more general basis that the procedure violated judicial independence by requiring judges to preside over what were essentially police investigations.[26] The majority, however, stressed the important role that the presiding judge and counsel representing the reluctant witness would play at an investigative hearing, as well as the rebuttable presumption that the investigative hearing be held in open court.[27]

c)   Right to Disclosure of the Prosecution's Case

In *R. v. Stinchcombe*,[28] the Supreme Court interpreted section 7 to impose upon the Crown a duty of disclosure. The Court was clearly influenced by a number of recent Canadian *causes célèbres* where miscarriages of

---

23   *R. v. White*, [1999] 2 S.C.R. 417.

24   *R. v. Fitzpatrick*, [1995] 4 S.C.R. 154.

25   The right against self-incrimination in s. 7 of the *Charter* also requires that use and derivative use immunity apply to any breaches of solicitor-client privilege that may be necessary because someone's innocence is at stake: *R. v. Brown*, [2002] 2 S.C.R. 185.

26   *Application under s. 83.28 of the Criminal Code*, [2004] 2 S.C.R. 248.

27   *Re Vancouver Sun*, [2004] 2 S.C.R. 332.

28   [1991] 3 S.C.R. 326, 68 C.C.C. (3d) 1.

justice had occurred because the Crown had failed to disclose information important to the defence. It held that, while the defence has no obligation to assist the prosecution, the Crown is obliged to use the information it has in the interests of justice. The Crown, said the Court, must disclose prior to trial any evidence it intends to use and also any evidence that might assist the accused, even if the Crown does not intend to adduce such evidence at trial. The position of Crown counsel, representing the public interest in seeing that justice be done, is not that of an ordinary adversary. Crown counsel are expected to act in the interest of justice, and the fruits of a police investigation must be used in a manner that respects the right of the accused to make full answer and defence, "one of the pillars of criminal justice on which we heavily depend to ensure that the innocent are not convicted."[29] This decision has had a profound effect on the behaviour of both police and Crown counsel. Disclosure to the accused has now become a routine step in pre-trial proceedings. The Supreme Court has stressed the breadth of the Crown's duty to disclose evidence whenever there is a reasonable possibility that it will be useful to the accused in making full answer and defence. The Crown's disclosure obligations include evidence that the Crown does not propose to use in its case.[30] The Court has recently affirmed this broad right to disclosure noting that the police, like the Crown, have a duty to disclose all relevant evidence including information about police misconduct that could reasonably impact on the case.[31] .

d) Right to Make Full Answer and Defence

Section 7 of the *Charter* protects the fair trial rights of accused persons and has had a significant impact upon the trial process. The accused's right to full answer and defence is related to the accused's right to disclosure of the prosecution's case, but the right to full answer and defence will only be violated if there is a reasonable possibility that the failure to disclose affected the outcome of the trial or its overall fairness. The minimum remedy for a violation of this important right will be the order of a new trial.[32]

The right to make full answer and defence has played an important and controversial role in the prosecution of sexual assault cases. In *Seaboyer*, a *Criminal Code* provision limiting the right of an accused charged with sexual assault to cross-examine a complainant as to prior sexual conduct was struck down as being inconsistent with the principles of

---

29   *Ibid.* at 336 (S.C.R.), Sopinka J.
30   *R. v. Taillefer; R. v. Duguay*, [2003] 3 S.C.R. 307 [*Taillefer*].
31   *R. v McNeil*, [2009] 1 S.C.R. 66 [*McNeil*].
32   *Ibid.*

fundamental justice.[33] While the majority recognized the importance of protecting complainants in sexual assault cases from unjustified and unwarranted inquiry into their personal histories, it concluded that a complete ban on any questions regarding past sexual conduct went too far and might preclude the trial court from hearing a legitimate defence. As McLachlin J. explained, eliminating the possibility that the judge and jury might draw unwarranted and inappropriate conclusions based on sexist or stereotypical attitudes carried the risk of convicting the innocent:

> [I]t exacts as a price the real risk that an innocent person may be convicted. The price is too great in relation to the benefit secured, and cannot be tolerated in a society that does not countenance in any form the conviction of the innocent.[34]

The *Seaboyer* decision was decried by feminist groups that had lobbied for the law and saw it as vital in encouraging women to come forward to the police with complaints. The sting of the judgment was, however, softened by the Court. While the law was struck down, the Court did impose strict guidelines defining the specific circumstances in which such questions would be permitted. The issue was subsequently addressed by legislation, which prohibits the introduction of evidence that the complainant has engaged in sexual activity other than the subject matter of the charge unless a judge determines at a special hearing that the evidence is relevant and that its evidentiary value is not substantially outweighed by the danger of prejudice to the proper administration of justice. The judge is instructed to take into account not only the accused's right to make full answer and defence but also society's interests in encouraging the reporting of sexual assaults, non-discriminatory fact-finding, potential prejudice to the complainant's dignity and privacy, and the right of the complainant to personal security and the full protection and benefit of the law.[35] This legislative reply to *Seaboyer* has subsequently been upheld as being consistent with the *Charter* on the basis that the procedural aspect of the rule does not require the accused to testify and its substantive part only excludes evidence that is not relevant to the charge against the accused.[36]

A similar issue arose over whether the accused in sexual assault cases should have access to private records of the complainant as part of the right to full answer and defence. This is a difficult issue because

---

33   *R. v. Seaboyer*, [1991] 2 S.C.R. 577, 83 D.L.R. (4th) 193 [*Seaboyer*].
34   *Ibid.* at 274 (D.L.R.).
35   *Criminal Code*, s. 276.
36   *R. v. Darrach*, [2000] 2 S.C.R. 443, 191 D.L.R. (4th) 539.

it pits at least two *Charter* rights against one another—the accused's right to full answer and defence and the complainant's right to privacy. In 1995, a majority of the Supreme Court in *R. v. O'Connor* held that the appropriate procedure was to have a judge balance or reconcile the accused's right to full answer and defence with the complainant's right to privacy before ordering that the complainant's private records be disclosed to the accused. Four judges dissented and would have imposed more restrictions on both the judge's and the accused's access to the complainant's private documents by requiring consideration of society's interests in encouraging the reporting of sexual assaults and the equality rights of women and children before the judge even examined the private documents.[37] Parliament responded to the ruling with new legislation following the minority judgment. The new legislation required the accused's rights to full answer and defence to be balanced with the complainant's rights to privacy and equality before private records were produced for the trial judge's inspection. This legislation only applies to confidential records in sexual assault cases and the Court has recently affirmed that the accused's right to full answer and defence in other cases will generally require that the accused receive information held by third parties that is truly relevant to the accused's case because it relates to an issue in the trial.[38]

In *R. v. Mills*,[39] the Supreme Court upheld the new legislation noting that it was a legitimate response to the Court's earlier decision, that the accused had no right to evidence that would distort the fact-finding process, and that balancing the respective rights was appropriate, both at the stage of production to the trial judge as well in deciding upon disclosure to the accused. The Court added:

> Courts do not hold a monopoly on the protection and promotion of rights and freedoms; Parliament also plays a role in this regard and is often able to act as a significant ally for vulnerable groups. This is especially important to recognize in the context of sexual violence. The history of the treatment of sexual assault complainants by our society and our legal system is an unfortunate one. Important change has occurred through legislation aimed at both recognizing the rights and interests of complainants in criminal proceedings, and debunking the stereotypes that have been so damaging to women and children, but the treatment of sexual assault complainants remains an ongoing problem. If constitutional democracy is meant to ensure that due re-

---

37   *R. v. O'Connor*, [1995] 4 S.C.R. 1411, 103 C.C.C. (3d) 1.
38   *McNeil*, above note 31.
39   [1999] 3 S.C.R. 668, 180 D.L.R. (4th) 1 [*Mills*].

gard is given to the voices of those vulnerable to being overlooked by the majority, then this court has an obligation to consider respectfully Parliament's attempt to respond to such voices.[40]

The *Mills* decision demonstrates that a robust dialogue can occur between Parliament and the Court regarding the appropriate balance of values in the criminal law without resort to section 33 of the *Charter*.

In a 5 to 4 decision, the Supreme Court decided that the accused's right to full answer and defence is not infringed by section 651(3) of the *Criminal Code*, which requires counsel for the accused to make his or her closing address to the jury first if witnesses are called and examined by the defence. The majority recognized that in certain cases, however, it might be necessary to give the accused a right of reply to the prosecutor's closing address.[41]

e) Detention of Those Found Not Guilty by Reason of Mental Disorder

Post-trial proceedings have not escaped the reach of section 7 of the *Charter*. In *R. v. Swain*,[42] the Supreme Court held that the *Criminal Code* provision for the automatic detention of an accused person found not guilty by reason of insanity at "the pleasure of the Lieutenant Governor" violated the principles of fundamental justice. The *Criminal Code* made no provision for a hearing or for any other procedural protection, and to hold someone indefinitely without according such rights was found to be inconsistent with the *Charter*. The Court recognized, however, that striking down the section immediately could result in a number of dangerous people being released and, accordingly, it declared the law to be valid for a stated period to afford Parliament the opportunity to enact legislation conferring the appropriate procedural protections. Parliament's new legislation, which provided for the release of a person found not guilty by reason of insanity unless that person was a significant threat to the safety of the public, was subsequently upheld by the Supreme Court under both sections 7 and 15 of the *Charter*. The Court found that the law did not impose a presumption or a stereotype of dangerousness on those found not criminally responsible by reason of a mental disorder and that the new legislation represented an appropriate balance of individual and social interests.[43] In subsequent cases, the

---

40 *Ibid.* at para. 58.

41 *R. v. Rose*, [1998] 3 S.C.R. 262, 129 C.C.C. (3d) 449.

42 [1991] 1 S.C.R. 933, 63 C.C.C. (3d) 481.

43 *Winko v. British Columbia (Forensic Institution)*, [1999] 2 S.C.R. 625, 175 D.L.R. (4th) 193.

Court has continued to uphold the new legislation while also stressing the need for the least onerous and restrictive disposition that is consistent with public safety.[44] The Court has also held that the indefinite deprival of the liberty of a person found unfit to stand trial because of a mental disorder violates section 7 of the *Charter* in those cases in which a permanently unfit accused does not pose a significant threat to society.[45]

B. UNREASONABLE SEARCH AND SEIZURE

Section 8 of the *Charter* states:

> Everyone has the right to be secure against unreasonable search or seizure.

The right conferred by section 8 is of ancient origin. The common law tradition has long recognized the need to protect the property and privacy of citizens against unwarranted incursions by state agents.

This section of the *Charter* has produced a significant volume of caselaw. Many, if not most, criminal trials involve the introduction of evidence seized by the police, and the propriety of the investigative methods employed by the police in obtaining evidence now comes under close scrutiny. Before the *Charter*, illegally obtained evidence was admissible. Now, under section 24 (discussed in greater detail below), evidence obtained in a manner that violates a *Charter* right "shall be excluded if it is established that, having regard to all the circumstances, the admission of it in the proceedings would bring the administration of justice into disrepute." This provides accused persons with a powerful incentive to raise *Charter* challenges to the manner in which the incriminating evidence was obtained.[46]

While the protection of an individual's right to privacy can be readily understood, that right has to be reconciled with the competing state interest to conduct searches and seize evidence as part of the law-enforcement process. The right conferred by section 8 is, by its very terms,

---

44   *Penetanguishene Mental Health Centre v. Ontario (Attorney General)*, [2004] 1 S.C.R. 498; *Pinet v. St. Thomas Psychiatric Hospital*, [2004] 1 S.C.R. 528.

45   *R. v. Demers*, [2004] 2 S.C.R. 489.

46   The Court has, however, held that an accused does not have his own privacy in a girlfriend's apartment or standing to argue in his trial that the search violated the rights of his girlfriend: *R. v. Edwards*, [1996] 1 S.C.R. 128. Passengers have been held not to have a reasonable expectation of privacy in a search of a car: *R. v. Belnavis*, [1997] 3 S.C.R. 341.

a relative one since the individual is protected only against *unreason-able* searches and seizures. To determine when a search or seizure is unreasonable, it is necessary to consider and balance, on the one hand, the right of the individual to be left alone, and on the other, the legitimate public interest in effective law enforcement.

In one of the Supreme Court's first *Charter* decisions, *Hunter v. Southam Inc.*,[47] the Court set out the basic framework for analysis of these issues. It started by interpreting section 8 generously. The section was found to confer a broad and general right to be secure from unreasonable search and seizure. This right extended beyond the protection of property and encompassed the protection of an individual's reasonable expectation of privacy. From that basic purpose of the right, the Court reasoned that certain procedural elements had to be imposed to reconcile the competing values of privacy and law enforcement. The first was the need for prior judicial authorization. The justification for a search should be assessed before it has been conducted. It would be inconsistent with the notion of an individual right to hold that, if the police find something, the search was reasonable, for that is to invite searches on a whim. Protecting individuals against unjustified state intrusion requires preventative measures prior to the search, and hence the Court held that there is a presumption of unreasonableness where a search has been undertaken without a warrant obtained from an officer charged with the duty of acting judicially. The Court added that, to obtain a warrant, the authorities should be required to justify the need for the search by sworn evidence that satisfies an objective standard. The general standard was "probable cause" or reasonable grounds to believe that a crime was committed and that the search would reveal evidence of the crime. The Court recognized that there could be "exigent" circumstances where the police had to act quickly and where circumstances did not allow time to obtain a warrant, but those cases, said the Court, were very much the exception to the general rule that a warrant is required.

A number of subsequent search-and-seizure cases have turned upon what constitutes a "reasonable" expectation of privacy in particular circumstances. In *R. v. Dersch*,[48] for example, the acquisition of blood samples by police, initially taken by physicians for medical purposes while the accused was unconscious in hospital, was found to constitute an unreasonable search and seizure under section 8. The accused was found to have a reasonable expectation that such informa-

---

47   [1984] 2 S.C.R. 145, 11 D.L.R. (4th) 641.
48   [1993] 3 S.C.R. 768, 85 C.C.C. (3d) 1.

tion would be kept confidential. In a number of cases,[49] the Supreme Court has dealt with non-consensual taking of bodily substances. It has taken a tough line on this issue, holding that the individual's right to bodily integrity must take priority and that the police have no right to require suspects to give such samples. Legislation has been enacted authorizing the police to obtain a warrant to take bodily substances for DNA testing without the consent of the suspect and this legislation has been upheld under the *Charter*.[50] Although the police can generally frisk search a person being arrested, the Court has held that because of section 8 of the *Charter* this power does not extend to delayed inventory searches of cars,[51] to routine strip searches,[52] or to the seizure of DNA samples without a judicial warrant.[53]

In *R. v. Mann*,[54] the Court held that the police can briefly detain people for investigative purposes if there are reasonable grounds to suspect that they are connected with crime. During such periods of detention, the police can, if reasonably necessary to protect their safety, conduct a protective pat-down search of the detainee. The Court, however, held that a more intrusive search of the accused's pocket after a soft and presumably non-dangerous object was detected was unreasonable and a violation of section 8 of the *Charter*. The object turned out to be illegal drugs that were excluded under section 24(2) of the *Charter*. In a subsequent case, the Court held that section 8 was not violated when the police searched two people who they detained when responding to a 911 call that guns were seen in the area. The Court stressed that the searches, which discovered two illegal hand guns, were justified because the officers had reasonable grounds to believe that their safety or the safety of others was at risk when responding to a gun call.[55]

In two complicated cases involving the use of sniffer dogs that detected drugs in a bag of a passenger in a bus station and in a backpack at a high school,[56] the Supreme Court held that the use of the dog

---

49   R. v. *Dyment*, [1988] 2 S.C.R. 417, 45 C.C.C. (3d) 244; R. v. *Pohoretsky*, [1987] 1 S.C.R. 945, 33 C.C.C. (3d) 398; R. v. *Stillman*, [1997] 1 S.C.R. 607, 144 D.L.R. (4th) 193 [*Stillman*].

50   R. v. *S.A.B.*, [2003] 2 S.C.R. 678.

51   R. v. *Caslake*, [1998] 1 S.C.R. 51, 121 C.C.C. (3d) 97.

52   R. v. *Golden*, [2001] 3 S.C.R. 679, 207 D.L.R. (4th) 18. To conduct a strip search there must be reasonable and probable grounds to believe that such a strip is necessary to protect the police or prevent the destruction of evidence, and the strip search must be conducted in a reasonable manner.

53   *Stillman*, above note 49.

54   [2004] 3 S.C.R. 59 [*Mann*].

55   R. v. *Clayton*, [2007] 2 S.C.R.725 [*Clayton*].

56   R. v. *A.M.*, [2008] 1 S.C.R. 259; R. v. *Kang-Brown*, [2008] 1 S.C.R. 456.

constituted a search; that the search was unreasonable in the circumstances, and that the drugs should be excluded under section 24(2) of the *Charter*. The Court agreed that the dog sniff was a search and distinguished the use of the dog from the use of technology that can detect excess heats emanating from houses, which the Court had found not to constitute a search.[57] The Court was, however, divided on the appropriate standard that should be applied in subsequent dog sniff cases. Four judges would only allow the use of sniffer dogs when there were reasonable and probable grounds to believe that such searches would discover evidence of crime while four other judges would allow such searches on the less restrictive grounds of reasonable suspicion. The fifth judge held that a reasonable suspicion standard was reasonable but that suspicion need not even relate to a particular person. It thus appears that there is majority support for a reasonable suspicion standard, albeit with almost all judges requiring that the grounds relate to a specific individual as opposed to suspicious areas.

The validity of the *Criminal Code* provisions authorizing judicial warrants for electronic surveillance has been upheld,[58] as have provisions that also allow a warrant to be obtained without notice to convicted offenders to obtain DNA samples.[59] However, the Supreme Court has not hesitated to limit some other police investigative techniques that are not authorized by a warrant. In *R. v. Duarte*,[60] the Court found that surreptitiously recording a communication the originator expects will not be intercepted by anyone other than the intended recipient violates section 8 of the *Charter* unless authorized by warrant. The police had used the familiar technique of equipping an informer with a body-pack recorder to tape a conversation with a suspect. No warrant had been obtained since it was thought that the procedure was legal where one party, here the informer, consented. The Court decided that a reasonable expectation of privacy demanded that the police obtain a warrant authorizing such procedures. Parliament subsequently applied a new warrant procedure for consent intercepts and also authorized such intercepts without judicial authorization to prevent bodily harm and in urgent or exigent circumstances.[61] Similarly in *R. v. Wong*,[62] the Court held that surreptitious video surveillance constitutes a search

---

57   *R. v. Tessling*, [2004] 3 S.C.R. 432 [*Tessling*].
58   *R. v. Finlay* (1985), 23 D.L.R. (4th) 532 (Ont. C.A.), leave to appeal to S.C.C. refused, [1986] 1 S.C.R. ix; *R. v. Garofoli*, [1990] 2 S.C.R. 1421, 60 C.C.C. (3d) 161.
59   *R. v. Rodgers*, [2006] 1 S.C.R. 554.
60   [1990] 1 S.C.R. 30, 65 D.L.R. (4th) 240.
61   *Criminal Code*, ss. 184.1–184.6.
62   [1990] 3 S.C.R. 36, 60 C.C.C. (3d) 460.

and seizure requiring prior judicial authorization when conducted in circumstances in which the suspect had a reasonable expectation of privacy. In that case, individuals engaged in illegal gambling in a hotel room were found to have a reasonable expectation of privacy. Parliament again responded with a new general warrant provision that would allow a judge to authorize any investigative technique (other than an invasion of bodily integrity) that might otherwise violate a person's privacy and constitute an unreasonable search and seizure.[63]

In *R. v. Kokesch*,[64] the Supreme Court found that a warrantless "perimeter search," during which the police trespassed on the accused's property and peered into his windows to confirm a suspicion that he was cultivating marijuana, constituted a violation of section 8. The Court has also upheld the individual's privacy interest in a dwelling-house by finding that the police violated section 8 by forcible entry to make a warrantless arrest absent circumstances of "hot pursuit" of a fleeing suspect.[65] Parliament again responded with a new warrant procedure and also statutory authorization for warrantless entry into homes to make arrests in exigent circumstances, in which it was impracticable to obtain a warrant and there were reasonable grounds to suspect that entry was necessary to prevent imminent death or bodily harm or reasonable grounds to believe that it was necessary to prevent imminent loss or destruction of evidence.[66]

A distinction has been drawn between personal information, which is protected against unreasonable search and seizure, and routine commercial records, which are not. In *R. v. Plant*,[67] the police used information regarding electricity consumption, obtained in the course of a drug investigation from the utility commission, to incriminate the accused who was charged with cultivating marijuana. No warrant had been issued to obtain the records, but the seizure was not found to trigger a section 8 violation. Since these commercial records were not of a personal and confidential nature and did not reveal intimate details of the accused's lifestyle or personal choices, there was not a reasonable expectation that they would be protected from state surveillance. The Supreme Court subsequently applied this precedent in *R. v. Tessling*[68] to hold that the warrantless use of heat detection technology from an airplane did not violate section 8 of the *Charter*. The Court concluded

---

63   *Criminal Code*, s. 487.01.
64   [1990] 3 S.C.R. 3, 61 C.C.C. (3d) 207.
65   *R. v. Feeney*, [1997] 2 S.C.R. 13, 146 D.L.R. (4th) 609.
66   *Criminal Code*, ss. 529–529.5.
67   [1993] 3 S.C.R. 281, 84 C.C.C. (3d) 203.
68   *Tessling*, above note 57.

that the technology only detected information exposed to the public and did not expose any intimate details or core biographical data of the occupants. The case might have been differently decided if the technology could reveal what activities in the house were producing the excess heat. In *R. v. Patrick*, the Court held that there was no reasonable expectation of privacy in garbage bags placed in a back lane for pick-up but distinguished this from garbage in a person's garage or near his porch.[69]

The Supreme Court has also drawn a distinction between the requirements of a reasonable search in the regulatory context and in the criminal context. Generally, the Court has indicated that the *Hunter v. Southam* standard of prior judicial authorization on the basis of probable cause that a crime has been committed "will not usually be the appropriate standard for a determination made in an administrative or regulatory context. The greater the departure from the realm of criminal law, the more flexible will be the approach to the standard of reasonableness."[70] In a complex case investigating alleged anti-competitive behaviour,[71] the Court was deeply split, but in the result the majority found that compelled production of documents pursuant to anti-combines legislation did not constitute a seizure within the meaning of section 8. This result was confirmed in a subsequent case holding that demands for information and documents pursuant to the *Income Tax Act* do not constitute seizures under section 8.[72] In *R. v. Jarvis*,[73] however, the Court indicated that even in the income tax context, all *Charter* protections used in the criminal context apply when the state is acting with the predominant purpose of determining penal liability. The result is that the requirements of section 8 will vary with the context. For example, school officials must conduct searches reasonably, but they do not require a judicial warrant or reasonable and probable grounds to believe that a crime has been committed.[74] At the other end of the scale, the Court has indicated that searches of a lawyer's office require special safeguards such as notification of the privilege holder because of the need to protect solicitor-client confidences and privilege.[75]

---

69 *R. v. Patrick*, 2009 SCC 17.

70 *Branch*, above note 22 at para. 52 (S.C.R.).

71 *Thomson Newspapers Ltd. v. Canada (Director of Investigation & Research)*, [1990] 1 S.C.R. 425, 54 C.C.C. (3d) 417.

72 *R. v. McKinlay Transport Ltd.*, [1990] 1 S.C.R. 627, 55 C.C.C. (3d) 530.

73 [2002] 2 S.C.R. 757.

74 *R. v. M.(M.R.)*, [1998] 3 S.C.R. 393, 129 C.C.C. (3d) 361.

75 *Lavallee, Rackel and Heintz v. Canada*, [2002] 3 S.C.R. 209; *Maranda v. Richer*, [2003] 3 S.C.R. 193.

C. ARBITRARY DETENTION AND IMPRISONMENT

Section 9 of the *Charter* guarantees:

> Everyone has the right not to be arbitrarily detained or imprisoned.

The meaning of "detention," a term crucial to both sections 9 and 10, was first considered in the context of section 10. In *R. v. Therens*,[76] an impaired-driving case, the issue of the accused's right to retain and instruct counsel depended upon whether he was "detained" within the meaning of section 10 when asked to go to the police station to give a breath sample. Rejecting the notion of detention as limited to instances of physical constraint, the Supreme Court instead defined the term as including any occasion when a police officer, by some form of compulsion or coercion, "assumes control over the movement of a person by a demand or direction which may have significant legal consequence."[77] The Court found that, even where the individual was not subjected to physical force or to a legally enforceable demand, "psychological compulsion, in the form of a reasonable perception of suspension of freedom of choice"[78] could result in detention within the meaning of the *Charter*. The Supreme Court has subsequently indicated that "the constitutional rights recognized by sections 9 and 10 of the *Charter* are not engaged by delays that involve no significant or psychological restraint."[79] The Court has thus avoided the extremes of detention being limited to physical constraint or expanded to include fleeting delays or interferences, and has held that there is detention under sections 9 and 10 whenever there is significant physical or psychological restraint.[80]

By its very terms, the right that section 9 secures is a relative one. There are clearly situations where the authorities must have the power to detain or imprison individuals, and the *Charter* right is engaged only where denial of freedom is arbitrary. Yet the Supreme Court has interpreted "arbitrarily" in a manner that favours individual liberty. The Court has recognized the danger posed by giving the police unfettered discretion to detain. There must be some objective standard, defined by the law, governing the power. *R. v. Hufsky*,[81] and *R. v. Ladouceur*[82]

---

76   [1985] 1 S.C.R. 613, 18 D.L.R. (4th) 655.
77   *Ibid.* at 642 (S.C.R.).
78   *Ibid.* at 644 (S.C.R.).
79   *Mann*, above note 54 at para. 19.
80   *R. v. Grant*, 2009 SCC 32 at paras. 24 and 28.
81   [1988] 1 S.C.R. 621, 40 C.C.C. (3d) 398.
82   [1990] 1 S.C.R. 1257, 56 C.C.C. (3d) 22.

dealt with provincial legislation authorizing random "spot checks" for impaired drivers. The Court found that stopping a motorist amounted to a detention under section 9 and that such a detention was arbitrary. The selection of which cars would be stopped was at the absolute discretion of the individual officer, and when establishing the program, the authorities had failed to provide any criteria for the exercise of this discretion, leaving it subject to the whim of each officer. The Court went on to consider whether a random stop of a driver could be justified under section 1. In view of the importance of highway safety and the deterrent function served by these stops, legislation authorizing random spot checks was found to be a reasonable limit on the right conferred by section 9. In a later decision,[83] the Court limited the powers of the police conducting random spot checks under this legislation. In the absence of reasonable and probable grounds for a more intrusive investigation, questioning by the police, when acting under this legislation, is constitutionally restricted to checking the driver's licence and insurance, the driver's sobriety, and the mechanical fitness of the vehicle.

In *R. v. Mann*, the Supreme Court recognized a common law power of investigative and warrantless detention that is consistent with both sections 8 and 9 of the *Charter*. The Court indicated that "police officers may detain an individual for investigative purposes if there are reasonable grounds to suspect in all the circumstances that the individual is connected to a particular crime and that such a detention is necessary."[84] If the officer has reasonable grounds to believe that his or her safety is at risk, a protective pat-down search is allowed if conducted in a reasonable manner. The Court added "that the investigative detention should be brief in duration and does not impose an obligation on the detained person to answer questions for the police."[85] In addition, the person detained should be informed of the reasons for the detention as required by section 10(a) of the *Charter*. In a subsequent case, a majority of the Court held that section 9 of the *Charter* was not violated when the police stopped a car and detained its occupants, eventually searching the occupants and discovering illegal handguns. The Court stressed that the car and its occupants matched the description of "black guys" in four vehicles openly displaying hand guns in the parking lot of the Million Dollar Saloon. The Court stressed the need to balance the seriousness of the risk to public safety against the liberty of the individuals.[86] Three judges reached the same result, but through

---

83 *R. v. Mellenthin*, [1992] 3 S.C.R. 615, 76 C.C.C. (3d) 481 [*Mellenthin*].

84 *Mann*, above note 54 at para. 45.

85 *Ibid.*

86 *Clayton*, above note 55 at para. 31, Abella J.

a different process. They held that the stop was an arbitrary detention contrary to section 9 of the *Charter* but was justified under section 1 as a reasonable limit on the right that was proportionate to the objective of protecting the public from handguns.[87] The exact parameters of the power of investigative detention and its relation to the right against unreasonable search and seizure in section 8 of the *Charter* and of the right to retain and instruct counsel without delay and to be informed of that right under section 10(b) of the *Charter* will undoubtedly continue to be fleshed out in subsequent cases. The Court affirmed in *R. v. Grant*[88] that psychological detention could exist under sections 9 and 10 when a person either has a legal obligation to comply, or when a reasonable person would conclude that he or she had no choice but to comply with a police demand. There was psychological detention in this case because the police went beyond general questioning of a youth on the street and interrogated him in an adversarial fashion while telling him to keep his hands in front of him. The detention was arbitrary because it was unlawful and exceeded a brief investigative stop on the basis of reasonable suspicion. As will be discussed below, however, the Court admitted as evidence a gun that was discovered as a result of the arbitrary detention, and this was despite a failure by the police to provide the right to counsel upon detention, in part because the legal obligations of the police in this situation were not clear and this mitigated the seriousness of the Charter violation.

Detention following a conviction will not be arbitrary, but in *R. v. Lyons*[89] it was argued that the dangerous-offender provision, which allows a judge to impose a sentence of indefinite imprisonment where certain stated criteria were met and where the convicted person posed a serious threat to public safety, was arbitrary. The Court rejected this argument, finding that Parliament had adequately defined the class of offenders subject to this sentence. Similarly, the Court has upheld the *Criminal Code* provisions providing for minimum periods of imprisonment for first-degree murder without eligibility for parole.[90] At the same time, automatic indeterminate detention following a verdict of not guilty by reason of insanity has been held to be arbitrary because of the absence of standards.[91] As mentioned above, new legislation enacted in response to this decision has been upheld under the *Charter*.

---

87   *Ibid.* at para 105*ff*, Binnie J.
88   Above note 80 at para. 44.
89   [1987] 2 S.C.R. 309, 37 C.C.C. (3d) 1 [*Lyons*].
90   *R. v. Luxton*, [1990] 2 S.C.R. 711, 58 C.C.C. (3d) 449 [*Luxton*].
91   *R. v. Swain*, [1991] 1 S.C.R. 933, 63 C.C.C. (3d) 481.

D. RIGHTS ON DETENTION AND ARREST

Section 10 of the *Charter* confers certain specific rights that apply upon arrest or detention. As noted above, "detention" has been given a broad interpretation so that the rights conferred under this section may be invoked in circumstances well short of incarceration. Section 10 provides as follows:

> Everyone has the right on arrest or detention
> (a) to be informed promptly of the reasons therefor;
> (b) to retain and instruct counsel without delay and to be informed of that right; and
> (c) to have the validity of the detention determined by way of *habeas corpus* and to be released if the detention is not lawful.

1) Right to Be Informed of the Reasons for Arrest or Detention

Under our system of criminal justice, police powers are limited by law, and before the police interfere with the liberty of an individual, they must be able to justify their actions. Arrest and detention represent a serious interference with personal liberty, and it is a basic right of the individual arrested or detained to know the reason. Requiring the authorities to state promptly the reasons for an arrest or detention permits the person arrested or detained to assess the situation and to decide upon an appropriate response, including submitting to the arrest, seeking counsel, and responding to police questions.

The right to be advised of the reasons arises upon arrest, but it may arise again if the reason for the arrest changes. For example, in *R. v. Borden*,[92] the accused was told that he had been arrested for one sexual assault that did not involve intercourse; on this occasion, he agreed to provide a blood sample. He was not told that the police wanted the sample in relation to another sexual assault of which he was also suspected. The Supreme Court held that the accused's section 10(a) right to be informed of the reason for his detention had been violated. Similarly, in *R. v. Black*,[93] the accused was arrested for attempted murder. The victim died while she was in custody. The accused was told that she was now charged with murder, but she was not told again of her right to

---

92   [1994] 3 S.C.R. 145, 119 D.L.R. (4th) 74. A sample can, however, be used in connection with a subsequent crime if neither the police nor the accused place limits on its use when the sample was obtained. See *R. v. Arp*, [1998] 3 S.C.R. 339.

93   [1989] 2 S.C.R. 138, 50 C.C.C. (3d) 1.

counsel under section 10(b). The Court held that sections 10(a) and (b) required that the police fully advise her of rights again when the reason for the arrest changed. On the other hand, in *R. v. Evans*,[94] the Court held that, although the police did not specifically inform an individual arrested on a drug charge that he was also suspected of two murders, it was clear to the accused from the nature of the questions being asked that he was being held for the murders as well. In *R. v. Mann*,[95] the Supreme Court indicated that a person subject to investigative detention should be "advised, in clear and simple language, of the reasons for the detention." At the same time, however, the Court expressed concerns that reading a person subject to brief investigative detention his or her rights to retain and instruct counsel under section 10(b) "cannot be transformed into an excuse for prolonging, unduly and artificially" investigative detentions that should be brief.[96]

2) Right to Retain and Instruct Counsel and to Be Informed of That Right

The courts have been vigilant in upholding the right to counsel. The rationale for this right is the need to ensure that everyone who is detained has the opportunity to learn immediately of his or her rights and obligations under the law. An individual in police custody is in a vulnerable situation and is entitled to the assistance of someone knowledgeable in the law and independent of the state:

> [W]hen an individual is detained by state authorities, he or she is put in a position of disadvantage relative to the state. Not only has this person suffered a deprivation of liberty, but also this person may be at risk of incriminating him- or herself.[97]

The right to counsel is triggered upon arrest or detention. The reference in section 10(b) to the right to retain and instruct counsel without delay requires immediate provision of the right to counsel upon either arrest or detention.[98] At the same time, a person, even one who is being investigated by the police, will not be detained by a brief encounter with the police that does not result in significant physical or psychological restraint in the sense that a reasonable person would conclude that he or she must comply with the police. The Court has held that

---

94   [1991] 1 S.C.R. 869, 63 C.C.C. (3d) 289.
95   *Mann*, above note 54 at para. 21.
96   *Ibid.* at paras. 19, 22.
97   *R. v. Bartle*, [1994] 3 S.C.R. 173 at 191, 92 C.C.C. (3d) 289, Lamer C.J.C.
98   *R. v. Suberu*, 2009 SCC 33 at para 42.

the plaintiff was not detained, and the right to counsel not triggered, when he was told by a police officer "wait a minute. I need to talk to you before you go anywhere"[99] as he tried to leave a parking lot after his friend was detained because of the possible fraudulent use of a credit card. The majority of the Court held that the accused was only momentarily delayed and subject to general questioning, as opposed to focused interrogation which could result in detention for *Charter* purposes. The Court warned: "[t]o simply assume that a detention occurs every time a person is delayed from going on his or her way because of the police accosting him or her during the course of an investigation, without considering whether or not the interaction involved a significant deprivation of liberty would overshoot the purpose of the *Charter*."[100]

Section 10(b) of the *Charter* affords not only the right to counsel but also the right to be informed of that right. In *R. v. Manninen*,[101] it was made clear that this is more than a formal or hollow right. There, the Supreme Court held that the police must provide the accused with a reasonable opportunity to exercise the right to consult counsel, and they must desist from questioning the accused or attempting to elicit information until he or she has had an opportunity to confer with counsel. Another case, *R. v. Brydges*,[102] dealt with the situation of an accused who could not afford counsel. The Court held that, where it appeared to the police that the accused wished to consult a lawyer but thought that his inability to afford legal counsel would prevent him from exercising the right, it was incumbent upon the police to advise the accused of the availability of legal aid and duty counsel provided under the legal aid scheme.

While *Brydges* required police to inform a detainee of the availability of free legal advice where it is provided, the Court did not go so far as mandating the legislative enactment of such a system. In *R. v. Matheson*[103] and *R. v. Prosper*,[104] the Court rejected the suggestion that section 10(b) imposes a positive obligation on governments to provide free preliminary legal advice through a duty-counsel system. The police instead have a twofold duty to inform detainees of legal services available in the jurisdiction and then to "hold off" questioning until a detainee has had a reasonable opportunity to consult counsel. It has also been held that a detained person must be reasonably diligent in

---

99   *Ibid.* at para. 10.
100 *Ibid.* at para. 24.
101 [1987] 1 S.C.R. 1233, 34 C.C.C. (3d) 385.
102 [1990] 1 S.C.R. 190, 53 C.C.C. (3d) 330 [*Brydges*].
103 [1994] 3 S.C.R. 328, 118 D.L.R. (4th) 323.
104 [1994] 3 S.C.R. 236, 118 D.L.R. (4th) 154.

attempting to seek the advice of counsel, failing which the police are entitled to proceed with questioning the suspect.[105]

The right to counsel guaranteed under section 10(b) continues to check police conduct after the initial charges have been laid. In *R. v. Burlingham*,[106] police impropriety in the plea-bargaining process was found to violate the accused's right to counsel. The police belittled the defence counsel with the express purpose of undermining the relationship between the accused and his lawyer, and they then pressured the accused, in the absence of counsel, to accept a plea bargain. Both aspects of their conduct were found to violate the section 10(b) right to counsel.

Limitations on section 10(b) rights can be justified as reasonable limits under section 1 of the *Charter*. The Court has held that the denial of the right to counsel is both authorized, prescribed by law, and justified in the case of roadside breathalyzer tests[107] and roadside sobriety tests.[108] In both cases, the Court recognized that the objective of detecting intoxicated drivers was important enough to justify limiting the right to counsel and that the limit on the right to counsel was proportionate and required to allow prompt checks of the sobriety of drivers.

3) Right to *Habeas Corpus*

Habeas corpus is a common law remedy against unlawful detention. It is of ancient origin and permits anyone who is detained to require the person having custody to bring the detainee immediately before a court and to provide legal justification for the detention. If the jailer is unable to satisfy the judge that the detention is lawful, the subject has the right to immediate release. The rights secured by this common law remedy are guaranteed by other *Charter* provisions: the right to be secure from arbitrary arrest and detention, the right to a speedy trial, and the right not to be denied reasonable bail. The effect of section 10(c) is to reinforce the common law remedy and to require that any legislative curtailment of the remedy satisfy the exacting standards of section 1.

The Supreme Court has affirmed that

> *habeas corpus* is a crucial remedy in the pursuit of two fundamental rights protected by the *Canadian Charter of Rights and Freedoms*: (1) the right to liberty of the person and the right not to be deprived thereof except in accordance with the principles of fundamental jus-

---

105 *R. v. Tremblay*, [1987] 2 S.C.R. 435, 37 C.C.C. (3d) 565.
106 [1995] 2 S.C.R. 206, 124 D.L.R. (4th) 7.
107 *R. v. Thomsen*, [1988] 1 S.C.R. 640.
108 *R. v. Orbanski; R. v. Elias*, [2005] 2 S.C.R. 3.

tice (s. 7 of the *Charter*); and (2) the right not to be arbitrarily detained or imprisoned (s. 9 of the *Charter*).[109]

The Court held that prisoners in federal institutions can seek *habeas corpus* in the superior courts as an alternative to judicial review in the Federal Court. The Court has also emphasized that superior courts should only decline to exercise its *habeas corpus* jurisdiction "in limited circumstances," such as when a court of appeal has statutory jurisdiction to correct errors of a lower court and release the applicant or if there is "a complete, comprehensive and expert procedure for review of an administrative decision."[110]

E. RIGHTS OF PERSONS CHARGED WITH AN OFFENCE

Section 11 of the *Charter* deals with the rights of persons charged with an offence. This section applies only to criminal or quasi-criminal proceedings and proceedings that give rise to penal consequences. Accordingly, it does apply to prosecutions for criminal offences proper, as well as to prosecutions under provincial legislation. Professional and other similar disciplinary proceedings will be caught only where the consequences are truly penal in nature, reflecting an attempt to redress a wrong done to society as a whole.[111] Section 11 reads:

Any person charged with an offence has the right
(a) to be informed without unreasonable delay of the specific offence;
(b) to be tried within a reasonable time;
(c) not to be compelled to be a witness in proceedings against that person in respect of the offence;
(d) to be presumed innocent until proven guilty according to law in a fair and public hearing by an independent and impartial tribunal;
(e) not to be denied reasonable bail without just cause;
(f) except in the case of an offence under military law tried before a military tribunal, to the benefit of trial by jury where the maximum punishment for the offence is imprisonment for five years or a more severe punishment;

---

109 *May v. Ferndale Institute*, [2005] 3 S.C.R. 809 at para. 21.
110 *Ibid.* at para. 44.
111 *R. v. Wigglesworth*, [1987] 2 S.C.R. 541, 45 D.L.R. (4th) 235 [*Wigglesworth*]. A person subject to forfeiture procedures under the *Customs Act* is not a person charged with an offence for the purpose of s. 11 of the *Charter*. *Martineau v. Minister of National Revenue*, [2004] 3 S.C.R. 737.

(g) not to be found guilty on account of any act or omission unless, at the time of the act or omission, it constituted an offence under Canadian or international law or was criminal according to the general principles of law recognized by the community of nations;

(h) if finally acquitted of the offence, not to be tried for it again and, if finally found guilty and punished for the offence, not to be tried or punished for it again; and

(i) if found guilty of the offence and if the punishment for the offence has been varied between the time of commission and the time of sentencing, to the benefit of the lesser punishment.

1) Right to Be Informed without Unreasonable Delay of the Specific Offence

An accused person needs to know the precise nature of the charges he or she faces for a number of reasons. Identification of the specific offence will enable the accused to challenge the proceedings if they are unlawful or to prepare a defence if they are not. The right to be informed of the offence without unreasonable delay also defines and narrows the proceedings, thereby limiting the scope of the prosecution and the powers of the police.

2) Right to Be Tried without Unreasonable Delay

It has often been said that "justice delayed is justice denied." Delay in prosecution may result in unfairness to the accused since it may well become more difficult to defend oneself after the passage of time. Quite apart from the unfairness, all parties—victims, accused persons, and society at large—have an obvious interest in speedy justice.

Delay in bringing criminal charges to trial has been the subject of a number of controversial decisions of the courts. The most significant was *R. v. Askov*,[112] where the Supreme Court considered a case that had taken twenty-four months to come to trial and where the cause of the delay was no more than the product of an overburdened system. The Court ruled that systemic delay could trigger a section 11(b) claim. While the Court indicated that it was mindful that the allocation of resources was a matter for political decision, the right to a speedy trial was vital to both the accused and the community at large, and solutions to systemic delay had to be found. The Court found that in the circumstances of the case, which arose in one of the busiest and

---

112 [1990] 2 S.C.R. 1199, 59 C.C.C. (3d) 449 [*Askov*].

most congested judicial districts in Canada, a two-year delay between committal and trial was unacceptable and in violation of the *Charter's* guarantee. The impact of the decision was enormous. Thousands of criminal charges were either dropped or stayed and the entire issue of court delay and the allocation of judicial resources has come under intense scrutiny. Though the Court softened its approach somewhat in a subsequent case,[113] the effects of *Askov* continue to be felt, and the risk of having a prosecution stayed for want of a speedy trial acts as a powerful incentive for the authorities to bring prosecutions forward to trial on a timely basis.

A distinction has been drawn, however, between pre- and post-charge delay. In Canada, there is no statute of limitations for serious criminal offences. In recent years, significant numbers of sexual assault charges have been laid years after the occurrence of the alleged offence. The Supreme Court has stated that delay in bringing charges will only rarely be relevant to the right to be tried without unreasonable delay.[114] In certain circumstances, unexplained or unjustified delay in initiating proceedings may give rise to a section 7 claim.[115]

3) Right against Self-Incrimination

The right against self-incrimination is protected in a variety of ways under the *Charter*. This right has already been mentioned under section 7. It is also embodied in section 13 of the *Charter*, discussed below, which protects witnesses from having incriminating evidence used against them in subsequent proceedings. The right conferred by section 11(c) relates specifically to the trial of the accused and protects the accused from having to testify.

Silence of an accused cannot, by statute, be the subject of comment by counsel or by the judge. Yet, while an accused person does not have to testify, to what extent does section 11(c) protect the accused who elects to remain silent from having the judge or jury draw an adverse inference from his or her silence? In a 1994 decision,[116] the Supreme Court suggested that it would be a violation of the right against self-incrimination to draw an adverse inference where the prosecution has failed to make out any case against the accused. But where there is "a

---

113 *R. v. Morin*, [1992] 1 S.C.R. 771, 71 C.C.C. (3d) 1. But see *R. v. Godin*, 2009 SCC 26 (thirty-month delay before trial unreasonable).

114 *R. v. Mills*, [1986] 1 S.C.R. 863, 29 D.L.R. (4th) 161; *R. v. Carter*, [1986] 1 S.C.R. 981, 26 C.C.C. (3d) 572.

115 *R. v. Kalanj*, [1989] 1 S.C.R. 1594, 48 C.C.C. (3d) 459.

116 *R. v. P.(M.B.)*, [1994] 1 S.C.R. 555, 89 C.C.C. (3d) 289.

case to meet," the accused who fails to answer must risk the possibility that his failure to testify may lead the judge or jury to convict.

The Supreme Court has held that a corporation is not entitled to claim the protection of section 11(c), and that an officer of an accused corporation can be compelled to testify,[117] a decision that corresponds to the Court's general tendency to avoid applying the *Charter* to protect purely commercial or corporate interests.

4) Presumption of Innocence and Right to a Fair Hearing by an Independent and Impartial Tribunal

a) Presumption of Innocence

The presumption of innocence has long been an important common law principle in Canada. The accused does not have to prove anything. It is for the prosecution to prove the guilt of the accused beyond a reasonable doubt, failing which the accused is entitled to an acquittal. However, before the *Charter*, this principle was subject to legislation overriding the presumption and Parliament frequently enacted reverse-onus provisions. A "reverse-onus" provision alters the usual rule and requires the accused to prove innocence. A significant body of caselaw challenging legislation of this kind has now developed under the *Charter*.

The case of *R. v. Oakes*,[118] better known for its articulation of the proportionality test under section 1, provides an example. Narcotics legislation provided that where, on a charge of possession for the purposes of trafficking, it was shown that an accused person was in possession of a prohibited drug, the burden shifted to the accused to prove that he or she was not in possession of the drug for the purposes of trafficking. Describing the presumption of innocence as "essential in a society committed to fairness and social justice," the Supreme Court held that the presumption of innocence was violated and that the violation could not be sustained under section 1. The reverse-onus provision applied even where an accused was in possession of very small quantities of narcotic, and in light of the lack of a rational connection between the proved fact, possession, and the presumed fact, trafficking, the provision was found to create an unjustifiable risk of conviction without proof of guilt and an unwarranted limitation on the presumption of innocence.

However, many reverse-onus provisions have survived as reasonable limits under section 1. For example, the Supreme Court upheld as

---

117 *R. v. Amway Corp.*, [1989] 1 S.C.R. 21, 56 D.L.R. (4th) 309.
118 *R. v. Oakes*, [1986] 1 S.C.R. 103, 26 D.L.R. (4th) 200, also discussed at length in chapter 4.

a reasonable limit the presumption applicable to drinking and driving cases that, where the accused is found behind the wheel of a car, care and control of the vehicle, an essential element of the offence, shall be presumed absent proof to the contrary.[119] Similarly, the Court upheld as a reasonable limit the presumption that an accused lives off the avails of prostitution if the fact is proved that he lives with or is habitually in the company of prostitutes.[120]

In some situations, a reverse-onus provision may be part of a package that benefits the accused and that would not be made available without the reverse-onus provision. Parliament may be willing to establish a defence but requires the accused to prove it. An example is the anti-hate law, which makes truth a defence but which requires the accused to make out the defence of truth. The Supreme Court found this to be justifiable under section 1.[121] In the Court's opinion, Parliament was not required to afford the defence of truth. It had done so as a concession to the value of freedom of expression. As Dickson C.J.C. explained,

> Parliament has used the reverse onus provision to strike a balance between two legitimate concerns. Requiring the accused to prove on the civil standard that his or her statements are true is an integral part of this balance, and any less onerous burden would severely skew the equilibrium.[122]

The effect of striking down such a reverse-onus clause might well be to make matters worse for the accused since Parliament would be entitled to remove the defence altogether.

One of the most significant cases upholding a reverse-onus provision dealt with the insanity defence.[123] Information regarding the state of the mental health of the accused is a matter particularly within the control of the accused. Without the cooperation of the accused, the prosecution would have great difficulty in proving sanity. The Supreme Court found that it would be virtually impossible for the Crown to secure convictions if it had to bear the onus of proving sanity. While the Court accepted that there were a variety of measures that might have been enacted to alleviate the problem, in the end, it found that the adoption of the traditional common law presumption of sanity was justifiable. The Court has been similarly tolerant of judge-made common law rules that arguably violate the presumption of innocence. Rules

---

119 *R. v. Whyte*, [1988] 2 S.C.R. 3, 51 D.L.R. (4th) 481.
120 *R. v. Downey*, [1992] 2 S.C.R. 10, 90 D.L.R. (4th) 449.
121 *R. v. Keegstra*, [1990] 3 S.C.R. 697, 61 C.C.C. (3d) 1.
122 *Ibid.* at 70–71 (C.C.C.).
123 *R. v. Chaulk*, [1990] 3 S.C.R. 1303, 62 C.C.C. (3d) 193.

requiring the accused to establish the defences of extreme intoxication and non-mental disorder automatism on a balance of probabilities have been crafted[124] despite authority suggesting that common law limitations on *Charter* rights should receive no deference and be held to the highest form of section 1 justification.[125]

Another important limitation on the presumption of innocence accepted by the Supreme Court under section 1 is that an accused charged with a regulatory offence must generally establish on a balance of probabilities a defence of due diligence or lack of negligence. A majority of the Court has stressed that it is reasonable for those who enter a regulated field to be required to demonstrate that they took reasonable care to avoid harms such as misleading advertising and health and safety violations.[126]

b) Right to a Fair Hearing by an Independent and Impartial Tribunal

Though the right to trial by "an independent and impartial tribunal" is conferred upon an accused person, it indirectly guarantees the independence of the judges who preside in criminal cases. In a 1985 decision,[127] the Supreme Court of Canada identified the three essential attributes of judicial independence. First, independence requires tenure of office and that judges be removable only for a cause related to their capacity to perform a judicial function.[128] Second, independence requires financial security so that judges need not fear diminution in their salary or benefits because of judgments that are unpopular or unfavourable to the government.[129] Third, the Court held that institutional independence in relation to the administration of the courts is a necessary element, in particular, the assignment of judges to particular cases and the establishment of court lists.

---

124 *R. v. Daviault*, [1994] 3 S.C.R. 63, 93 C.C.C. (3d) 21; *R. v. Stone*, [1999] 2 S.C.R. 290, 134 C.C.C. (3d) 353.

125 *R. v. Swain*, [1991] 1 S.C.R. 933, 63 C.C.C. (3d) 481.

126 *R. v. Wholesale Travel Group Inc.*, [1991] 3 S.C.R. 154, 67 C.C.C. (3d) 193.

127 *Valente v. R.*, [1985] 2 S.C.R. 673, 24 D.L.R. (4th) 161.

128 The Court has found that the removal of justices of the peace from office did not violate judicial independence when this was done as a rational means to improve their qualifications for office. *Ell v. Alberta*, [2003] 1 S.C.R. 857.

129 The Court has found that this facet of judicial independence requires independent commissions to make recommendations about judicial salaries and requires justification by the legislature for departures from such recommendations. *Reference Re Public Sector Pay Reduction Act (P.E.I.), s. 10* (1997), 150 D.L.R. (4th) 577 (S.C.C.).

5) Right to Reasonable Bail

The judicial interim-release provisions of the *Criminal Code* strongly favour affording accused persons bail pending their trial, but one element of the *Code*'s package was found wanting in *R. v. Morales*.[130] In addition to detaining a person to ensure attendance at trial and to protect the public from a substantial likelihood that, if released, the accused will commit a criminal offence, the *Code* provided as a tertiary ground for denying bail that the detention of the accused "is necessary in the public interest." This was held to be unacceptably vague and imprecise. It imposed a "standardless sweep" that was found to infringe section 11(e) of the *Charter* and could not be saved under the section 1 proportionality test. Parliament responded some time later with a new tertiary ground based on "any other just cause" including where detention is necessary to maintain confidence in the administration of justice having regard to factors such as the strength of the prosecution's case, the circumstances of the alleged offence, the gravity of the offence, and the potential of a lengthy term of imprisonment.[131] The Supreme Court subsequently held that the reference to "any other just cause" was excessively vague but that the reference to the need to maintain confidence in the administration of justice was constitutional because it constituted a just cause for the denial of bail. Four judges dissented from the later decision on the basis that public fears about the release of a person charged but not convicted of a crime did not justify pre-trial detention and that the new tertiary ground was in its entirety excessively vague.[132]

6) Right to Jury Trial

Section 11(f) of the *Charter* provides that everyone charged with an offence who faces five or more years imprisonment has the right to a trial by jury. The right to trial by jury has been held to be infringed by a judge's action in instructing a jury that an accused, charged with growing marijuana for his own use, had no defence in law and that

---

130 [1992] 3 S.C.R. 711, 77 C.C.C. (3d) 91. The Crown generally has to establish grounds for detaining the accused, but the Court has upheld a reversal of this onus in the case of those already on bail and those charged with trafficking in narcotics.

131 *Criminal Code*, s. 515(10)(c).

132 *R. v. Hall*, [2002] 3 S.C.R. 309.

they must convict. In a jury trial, the jury, not the judge, must decide whether the accused is guilty.[133]

The *Criminal Code* confers the right to a jury trial in virtually all serious offences even though section 11(f) itself limits the *Charter* right to a jury trial to cases where the accused faces five years imprisonment or more. *R. v. Lee*[134] dealt with an exception. The accused had initially failed to appear for trial, and the *Criminal Code* provided that, as a consequence, he lost his right to be tried by a jury. The Supreme Court found that the provision violated section 11(f) of the *Charter* but could be upheld as a reasonable limit under section 1. Parliament was entitled to protect the integrity of the criminal process from delay, inconvenience, and expense. Denying the right to a jury trial in such circumstances was held to be proportional to this legitimate governmental objective.

An individual is not required to take advantage of his or her constitutional rights and ordinarily those rights may be waived. In *R. v. Turpin*,[135] the accused was charged with murder, an offence at the time required by the *Criminal Code* to be tried by jury. The accused argued that the right to a jury trial implicitly carried with it the right to waive trial by jury and be tried by a judge alone. The Supreme Court did not agree and held that there was no inconsistency between the right to be tried by jury and the statutory requirement that certain offences must be tried by jury. The Court has also held that common law and statutory rules protecting the secrecy of the jury's deliberations are consistent with the *Charter*.[136]

7) *Ex Post Facto* Laws

While the section 11(g) requirement that an act or omission constitute an offence at the time it was committed is an important right, it has not been the subject of substantial litigation since attempts to prosecute individuals for offences created after the fact are extremely rare. The issue was raised, however, in the complex case of *R. v. Finta*,[137] which dealt with war crimes relating to the Nazi occupation of Hungary. The accused, a captain in the Royal Hungarian Gendarmerie during the Second World War, was charged with war crimes and crimes against humanity for allegedly participating in the unlawful confinement, kidnapping,

---

133 *R. v. Krieger*, [2006] 2 S.C.R. 501.
134 [1989] 2 S.C.R. 1384, 52 C.C.C. (3d) 289.
135 [1989] 1 S.C.R. 1296, 48 C.C.C. (3d) 8.
136 *R. v. Pan*, 2001 SCC 42, 200 D.L.R. (4th) 577.
137 [1994] 1 S.C.R. 701, 112 D.L.R. (4th) 513.

robbery, and in some cases manslaughter of over 8,000 people. The Supreme Court rejected the accused's claim under section 11(g). It stated that justice required the retroactive punishment of those who committed acts that were internationally illegal and known to be morally objectionable, regardless of the fact that the acts were not formally criminal under positive law at the time. The accused was acquitted at trial on other grounds, however, and the Crown's appeals were rejected.

8) Double Jeopardy

Though much of the law on double jeopardy is governed by pre-*Charter* jurisprudence, there have been some significant cases under section 11(h). In *R. v. Wigglesworth*,[138] an RCMP officer, having been convicted under the *Royal Canadian Mounted Police Act* for assaulting a prisoner, was then charged with criminal assault for the same incident. The Supreme Court allowed the second set of proceedings to continue, noting a "double aspect" to the wrongful conduct. That is to say, while the accused had already answered to his profession through the private sanctions of internal discipline, he must still be made to account to society at large for his actions. The word "offence" in section 11(h) was thus defined narrowly so as to include only truly criminal or penal offences. This approach was applied and affirmed in *R. v. Shubley*,[139] a case involving a charge of criminal assault where the accused had already been subject to prison discipline in relation to the same incident. Applying the two-stage test from *Wigglesworth*, the Court found that, since the prison discipline was neither by its nature criminal nor did it impose true penal consequences, no violation of section 11(h) had occurred.

9) Benefit of Lesser Punishment

This guarantee confirms a pre-*Charter* common law principle similar to the preclusion of conviction for matters that were not an offence at the time the act was committed (section 11(g)). The guarantee rests on a fundamental principle of legality, namely, that an individual's conduct is to be assessed on the basis of the law in force at the time and that it would be unfair to impose penalties not then provided for by law. It has been applied to require a judge to consider the lesser punishment of a determinate long-term offender designation as opposed to an indeterminate dangerous offender designation even though the offender's

---

138 *Wigglesworth*, above note 111.
139 [1990] 1 S.C.R. 3, 65 D.L.R. (4th) 193.

predicate offences were committed before the introduction of long-term offender designation in 1997.[140]

F. CRUEL AND UNUSUAL PUNISHMENT

Section 12 of the *Charter* provides:

> Everyone has the right not to be subject to any cruel and unusual treatment or punishment.

Laws requiring minimum sentences for specified offences have been the exception rather than the rule in Canadian criminal law, though their use has increased in recent years. In *Smith v. R.*,[141] the Supreme Court struck down a minimum punishment of seven years' imprisonment for importing narcotics. Too wide a range of activities was caught by the prohibition against importing drugs, from large-scale trafficking of dangerous drugs by organized crime to the importation of a small quantity of marijuana for personal consumption. While the Court did not settle on a precise definition of "cruel and unusual," a majority found that imposing a minimum sentence of such length would, in many instances, be so grossly disproportionate to the gravity of the offence committed by the accused as to outrage standards of decency and thus offend the guarantee under section 12. The Court was not willing to trust the matter to prosecutorial discretion to charge minor offenders with simple possession, since that would amount to an unacceptable delegation of decision-making authority in a situation where a fundamental right was at issue.

Other challenges to mandatory minimum sentences have, however, failed. The Supreme Court has upheld mandatory life imprisonment without eligibility for parole for twenty-five years for first degree murder[142] and without eligibility for parole for ten years for second degree murder.[143] In both cases, the Court has stressed that the penalty was not grossly disproportionate given the seriousness of the offence.

The Court has also upheld a mandatory minimum penalty of seven days' imprisonment for knowingly driving with a suspended licence[144] and a mandatory ten-year firearm prohibition upon a drug conviction. In the latter case, the Court stressed both that the prohibition was re-

---

140 *R. v. Johnson*, [2003] 2 S.C.R. 357 at para. 45.
141 [1987] 1 S.C.R. 1045, 34 C.C.C. (3d) 97.
142 *R. v. Luxton*, [1990] 2 S.C.R. 711, 58 C.C.C. (3d) 449.
143 *R. v. Latimer*, [2001] 1 S.C.R. 3, 193 D.L.R. (4th) 577.
144 *R. v. Goltz*, [1991] 3 S.C.R. 485, 67 C.C.C. (3d) 481.

lated to the legitimate sentencing goal of protecting the public and that the *Criminal Code* allowed the judge to make exceptions when firearms were required for employment or sustenance reasons.[145]

The Court has also upheld mandatory minimum penitentiary terms when firearms are used to commit serious offences. In *R. v. Morrisey*, it upheld a minimum sentence of four years' imprisonment for criminal negligence causing death with a firearm[146] and in *R. v. Ferguson* it upheld a mandatory minimum sentence of four years' imprisonment for manslaughter with a firearm.[147] The Court in *Morrisey* stressed that in determining whether a particular punishment is grossly disproportionate the court can consider both the circumstances of the particular offender, and of reasonable hypothetical offenders that may be convicted under the offence and subject to the mandatory penalty. The Court in *R. v. Ferguson* held that the appropriate remedial response to a finding of gross disproportionality is to strike the mandatory sentence down under section 52(1) of the *Constitution Act, 1982* for all offenders as opposed to crafting a constitutional exemption for particular offenders.[148] Such a remedial approach, in the Court's view, respects Parliament's intent in creating mandatory sentences and the remedial structure of the *Charter*. It means that any exemption from mandatory penalties will have to be fashioned by Parliament and not by the courts on a case-by-case basis.

In *Steele v. Mountain Institution (Warden)*,[149] the Court found that the continued detention after thirty-five years' incarceration of a sexual psychopath could no longer be justified in light of the evidence of experts as to his present state. The Parole Board was charged with responsibility for assessing such cases, but there had been serious procedural and substantive flaws in the Parole Board's proceedings. The Court held that detention of the prisoner had become so grossly disproportionate to the circumstances of his case as to constitute cruel and unusual punishment, and it ordered that he be released on a *habeas corpus* application.

G. RIGHT AGAINST SELF-INCRIMINATION

The right against self-incrimination is dealt with under a variety of *Charter* provisions. As already noted, aspects of the right against self-

---

145 *R. v. Wiles*, [2005] 3 S.C.R. 895.
146 *R. v. Morrisey*, [2000] 2 S.C.R. 90, 191 D.L.R. (4th) 86.
147 *R. v. Ferguson*, [2008] 1 S.C.R. 96.
148 *Ibid.*
149 [1990] 2 S.C.R. 1385, 60 C.C.C. (3d) 1.

incrimination may be invoked under section 7. Under section 11(c), an accused person cannot be required to testify at his or her own trial. Section 13 of the *Charter* provides as follows:

> A witness who testifies in any proceeding has the right not to have any incriminating evidence so given used to incriminate that witness in any other proceedings, except in a prosecution for perjury or for the giving of contradictory evidence.

The right against self-incrimination is narrower in Canadian law than it is under the common law or under the Fifth Amendment of the American constitution. In Canada, there is no right to refuse to give evidence in a proceeding in which the witness is not the accused.[150] The right conferred by section 13 of the *Charter* is restricted to not having that evidence used against the witness in a subsequent proceeding.

In *R. v. Dubois*,[151] this protection was extended to an accused who had testified at his trial, was convicted, appealed, and was given a new trial. The Supreme Court of Canada held that the testimony given at the first trial could not be used at the new trial. The guarantee was further extended in *R. v. Mannion*[152] where, in similar circumstances, the Court held that the previous testimony could not even be used to cross-examine the accused at his retrial. However, in *R. v. Kuldip*,[153] the Court held that evidence given at a previous trial could be used to cross-examine as to the credibility of the accused as distinct from the use of such evidence to prove guilt.[154]

In *R. v. Henry*,[155] the Court attempted to reconcile the confusing jurisprudence in this area and return to first principles. It overruled the extension of the protections against self-incrimination in *Mannion* on the basis that the purpose of the right against self-incrimination was not engaged when an accused chooses to testify at his retrial. In such circumstances, the accused is not being compelled to engage in self-incrimination. The Court also partially overruled *Kuldip* by holding that the accused's prior voluntary testimony on the same indictment could be used in the new trial either to impeach the credibility of the accused or as evidence supporting the accused's guilt. Although *Henry*

---

150 *Canada Evidence Act*, R.S.C. 1985, c. C-5, s. 5(2).
151 [1985] 2 S.C.R. 350, 22 C.C.C. (3d) 513.
152 [1986] 2 S.C.R. 272, 28 C.C.C. (3d) 544.
153 *R. v. Kuldip*, [1990] 3 S.C.R. 618, 61 C.C.C. (3d) 385.
154 See also *R. v. Noel*, [2002] 3 S.C.R. 433, holding that the Crown had violated the right against self-incrimination by trying to have the accused adopt incriminating parts of his prior testimony.
155 [2005] 3 S.C.R. 609.

withdraws section 13 protections in cases involving the accused's voluntary testimony in his or her own trial and retrial, it extends protection against self-incrimination by holding that prior testimony that was compelled from the accused as a witness cannot be used in a subsequent trial of that person either as evidence of guilt or to impeach the accused's credibility. The underlying rationale is the difficulty of segregating the use of prior testimony as evidence of guilt or for the purpose of impeaching the accused's credibility. *Henry* is also noteworthy in demonstrating the Court's willingness to overrule and reinterpret prior *Charter* precedents in an attempt to rationalize the law.

H. RIGHT TO AN INTERPRETER

Section 14 of the *Charter* guarantees parties and witnesses the right to an interpreter:

> A party or witness in any proceeding who does not understand or speak the language in which the proceedings are conducted or who is deaf has the right to the assistance of an interpreter.

The *Charter* also contains English- and French-language guarantees that apply to criminal proceedings in certain provinces, as discussed in chapter 16.

The leading case on the section 14 right to an interpreter is *R. v. Tran.*[156] Convicted of sexual assault, the accused's interpreter at trial failed to translate much of the key testimony in full and instead merely summarized the evidence. Embracing a "liberal interpretation and principled application" of the right to an interpreter, the Supreme Court allowed the accused's appeal and ordered a new trial. Grounded in the basic requirement that a person charged with a criminal offence has the right to hear the case against him or her and to be given a full opportunity to answer it, the Court stated section 14 guarantees that those who need an interpreter must be given assistance that is continuous, precise, impartial, competent, and contemporaneous. Not every deviation from perfection will constitute a violation of section 14, however. The claimant must establish that the lapse in interpretation involved procedure, evidence, or law and not merely some collateral or extrinsic matter.

---

156 [1994] 2 S.C.R. 951, 117 D.L.R. (4th) 7.

I. REMEDIES IN THE CRIMINAL PROCESS

One of the most difficult issues the courts face is determining the appropriate remedy for a *Charter* breach. Typically, *Charter* rights are asserted by accused persons because the police have obtained incriminating evidence as a result of the conduct that forms the basis for the *Charter* claim. A judicial decision that a *Charter* right has been infringed will have a declaratory effect. The authorities may be expected to abide by court rulings and alter their practices and procedures to comply with the dictates of the *Charter* in subsequent cases. But what of the individual who is before the court and whose rights have been infringed? A decision that merely declares that his or her rights have been infringed will ring hollow if no further action is taken. Can a system of justice premised on respect for certain fundamental rights countenance continuation of the proceedings or reliance on evidence obtained in violation of those rights? On the other hand, if the evidence obtained as a result of the *Charter* breach is not admitted by the court, relevant facts are excluded and the search for the truth is inhibited. As a result, a guilty person may go free. Is exclusion of evidence acceptable in these circumstances? Is this an appropriate way to control police behaviour?

Chapter 17 considers remedial issues in general, while the specific issues of stay of proceedings and exclusion of evidence in criminal proceedings is dealt with here. Section 24 of the *Charter* provides as follows:

> (1) Anyone whose rights or freedoms, as guaranteed by this *Charter*, have been infringed or denied may apply to a court of competent jurisdiction to obtain such remedy as the court considers appropriate and just in the circumstances.
>
> (2) Where, in proceedings under subsection (1), a court concludes that evidence was obtained in a manner that infringed or denied any rights or freedoms guaranteed by this *Charter*, the evidence shall be excluded if it is established that, having regard to all the circumstances, the admission of it in the proceedings would bring the administration of justice into disrepute.

1) Stay of Proceedings

In certain cases, a prosecution may be so tainted by the *Charter* breach that a stay of proceedings is appropriate. A stay of proceedings is an order that forbids the prosecutor from taking any further steps against the accused on the charges before the court. It is obviously a drastic remedy. Before the *Charter*, stays were available in cases where the court found that a prosecution amounted to an abuse of the court's process. Since the *Charter*'s enactment, the common law stay has been assimilated and adapted as a *Charter* remedy. The Supreme Court had made it clear that, given its severity, the remedy of a stay should be granted only

> "in the clearest of cases," where the prejudice to the accused's right to make full answer and defence cannot be remedied or where irreparable prejudice would be caused to the integrity of the judicial system if the prosecution were continued.[157]

A stay of proceedings will only be ordered if the prejudice caused by the abuse will be aggravated by the trial and no other remedy is reasonably capable of removing that prejudice. In cases of uncertainty, the judge will balance the interests in favour of a stay against society's interest in having a final decision on the merits.[158] The minimum remedy for a violation of the accused's right to full answer and defence will be the order of a new trial, and a stay of proceedings will only be appropriate and just in the exceptional circumstances of an irreparable violation of the right.[159] In contrast, the Supreme Court decided in the early years of the *Charter* that a stay of proceedings was the minimum remedy for a violation of the right to a trial in a reasonable time under section 11(b) of the *Charter*, on the basis that a trial after that time would not be fair and would aggravate the prejudice caused by the pre-trial delay.[160]

2) Exclusion of Evidence

The most commonly ordered remedy for a breach of *Charter* rights in the criminal process is exclusion of evidence. Prior to the enactment of the *Charter*, illegally obtained evidence was admissible, even where it was obtained in a manner that violated a right guaranteed by the *Canadian Bill of Rights*.[161] Section 24(2) of the *Charter* alters that rule but stops short of a presumptive exclusionary rule.

The first question is whether the "evidence was obtained in a manner that infringed or denied any rights or freedoms guaranteed by this *Charter*." The issue here is the extent to which it must be shown that there was a causal link between the *Charter* breach and obtaining the evidence. Evidence found following an unreasonable search may well

---

157 *R. v. O'Connor* (1995), 103 C.C.C. (3d) 1 at 43, L'Heureux-Dubé J.
158 *R. v. Regan*, [2002] 1 S.C.R. 297, 209 D.L.R. (4th) 41.
159 *Taillefer*, above note 30.
160 *R. v. Rahey*, [1987] 1 S.C.R. 588.
161 *Hogan v. R.*, [1975] 2 S.C.R. 574, 48 D.L.R. (3d) 427.

have been uncovered in any event. Was it obtained "in a manner which violated" a *Charter* right? The Supreme Court has interpreted these words of section 24(2) not to require a strict causal connection. In *R. v. Strachan*,[162] Dickson C.J.C. stated that the inquiry should focus on the "entire chain of events" and that, ordinarily, a temporal link between the *Charter* breach and discovery of the evidence will be sufficient. The case involved a search and arrest at the home of the accused. The police refused to allow the accused to telephone his lawyer and proceeded to find drugs. Despite the tenuous causal connection between the *Charter* breach of denial of counsel and the discovery of the drugs, the Court found that section 24(2) was engaged. In the end, the majority held that the drugs could be admitted into evidence, but the case stands for the proposition that a strict causal relationship between the *Charter* breach and the discovery of the evidence is not required.

If this initial hurdle is satisfied, the Court must turn to a second issue and the central component of section 24(2), namely, whether admission of the evidence "would bring the administration of justice into disrepute." A significant body of caselaw has developed on the admissibility of evidence where a *Charter* right has been infringed. The basic framework for analysis was set out in the Supreme Court of Canada's 1987 decision in *R. v. Collins*[163] and confirmed in the 1997 *Stillman* decision.[164] As will be seen, it has recently been altered.

In *Collins*, the Supreme Court stated that the purpose of section 24(2) was not to control the conduct of the police but rather to protect the integrity of the judicial system. Lamer J. identified as relevant the "disrepute that will result from the admission of the evidence that would deprive the accused of a fair hearing, or from judicial condonation of unacceptable conduct by the investigatory and prosecutorial agencies."[165] The Court rejected the suggestion that disrepute should be assessed on the basis of public opinion or shock to the community. That, said Lamer J., would be contrary to the very purpose of the *Charter*, to protect the individual from the majority. The question of bringing the administration of justice into disrepute is, accordingly, to be assessed on a judicial and dispassionate basis. The relevant question is "[W]ould the admission of the evidence bring the administration of justice into disrepute in the eyes of a reasonable man, dispassionate and fully apprised of the circumstances of the case?"[166] Very often,

---

162 [1988] 2 S.C.R. 980, 46 C.C.C. (3d) 479.
163 [1987] 1 S.C.R. 265, 33 C.C.C. (3d) 1 [*Collins*].
164 *Stillman*, above note 49.
165 *Collins*, above note 163 at 16–17 (C.C.C.).
166 *Ibid.* at 18 (C.C.C.).

those who assert *Charter* claims and seek to exclude evidence as a result are undeserving of public sympathy, but *Charter* protections apply to all. As Iacobucci J. explained,

> [W]e should never lose sight of the fact that even a person accused of the most heinous crimes, and no matter the likelihood that he actually committed those crimes, is entitled to the full protection of the *Charter*. Short-cutting or short-circuiting those rights affects not only the accused, but also the entire reputation of the criminal justice system. It must be emphasized that the goals of preserving the integrity of the criminal justice system, as well as promoting the decency of investigatory techniques, are of fundamental importance in applying s. 24(2).[167]

Collins, and subsequently *Stillman*, set out a three-step test for the determination of whether the admission of the evidence would bring the administration of justice into disrepute. The first set of factors to be considered is the way the evidence affects the fairness of the trial. If the court concludes that admission of the evidence would adversely affect the fairness of the trial, the evidence will almost always be excluded. *Stillman* draws a distinction between "conscriptive" and "non-conscriptive" evidence.[168] Conscriptive evidence is obtained when, in violation of *Charter* rights, an accused "is compelled to incriminate himself at the behest of the state by means of a statement, the use of the body, or the production of bodily samples."[169] "Non-conscriptive" evidence is that which is obtained by the state without the accused's participation or which existed independently of any *Charter* breach. Conscriptive evidence will ordinarily be excluded without considering any other factors, unless the prosecutor can show that it would have been discovered by non-conscripted means. The admission of conscriptive evidence would strike at a fundamental tenet of a fair trial, the right against self-incrimination. Statements obtained following denial of the right to counsel

---

167 *R. v. Burlingham*, [1995] 2 S.C.R. 206, 124 D.L.R. (4th) 7 at 31. See also *R. v. Feeney*, [1997] 2 S.C.R. 13 at para.83, Sopinka J.:

> If the exclusion of this evidence is likely to result in an acquittal of the accused as suggested by L'Heureux-Dubé J. in her reasons, then the Crown is deprived of a conviction based on illegally obtained evidence. Any price to society occasioned by the loss of such a conviction is fully justified in a free and democratic society which is governed by the rule of law.

168 *Stillman*, above note 49.

169 *Ibid.* at 655 (S.C.R.), Cory J.

have frequently been excluded.[170] The notion of evidence emanating from the accused has been extended to exclude evidence obtained as a result of a police line-up following the denial of the right to counsel since such evidence could be obtained only through the participation of the accused.[171] Similarly, body samples obtained as a result of a *Charter* breach have been considered conscriptive evidence.[172]

On the other hand, non-conscriptive evidence—most often, tangible evidence that exists independently of the accused (such as a weapon or drugs)—will ordinarily not render the trial unfair. To determine whether such evidence should be admitted, it is necessary to proceed to consider the next two steps.

The second set of factors is the seriousness of the *Charter* breach and the reasons for it. Technical or minor violations do not attract the same censure as serious ones. A distinction has been drawn between situations where the police have acted in good faith, relying on what is believed to be the existing state of the law, and cases where the police intentionally or carelessly abuse the rights of the accused.[173] In the latter category of cases, evidence has often been excluded, while, in the former, the good faith of the police will be a factor favouring admissibility.

The third set of considerations involves weighing the effect of excluding the evidence against the effect of admitting it. Disrepute to the administration of justice could result if evidence were excluded because of a trivial breach. The seriousness of the charge is also a factor to be considered.

In *R. v. Grant*,[174] the Supreme Court recognized that while the *Collins/Stillman* tests outlined above had "brought a measure of certainty to the section 24(2) inquiry," the tests had resulted in decisions about the admissibility of evidence that were inconsistent with the language and objectives of section 4(2) in facilitating a balancing of the competing interests in all the circumstances of each case. In particular, the Court was concerned about the nearly automatic exclusion of conscriptive evidence, such as unconstitutionally obtained statements, bodily samples, and evidence derived from such evidence that would not have been inevitably discovered without a *Charter* violation. The Court articulated a new three-part test under section 24(2) in which trial judges

---

170 See, for example, *Clarkson v. R.*, [1986] 1 S.C.R. 383, 26 D.L.R. (4th) 493; *R. v. Brydges*, [1990] 1 S.C.R. 190, 53 C.C.C. (3d) 330.
171 *R. v. Leclair*, [1989] 1 S.C.R. 3, 46 C.C.C. (3d) 129.
172 *Stillman*, above note 49.
173 *Collins*, above note 157.
174 2009 SCC 32.

must assess and balance the effect of admitting the evidence on society's confidence in the justice system having regard to: (1) the seriousness of the *Charter*-infringing state conduct (admission may send the message the justice system condones serious state misconduct), (2) the impact of the breach on the *Charter*-protected interests of the accused (admission may send the message that individual rights count for little), and (3) society's interest in the adjudication of the case on its merits.[175]

This new and more flexible test for applying section 24(2) has much in common with the previous tests. The focus remains on upholding the long-term repute of the justice system as opposed to deterring the police or compensating the accused. The test for measuring the seriousness of the violation has also not changed. As before, deliberate, wilful, flagrant, or reckless violations of the *Charter* may require the court to exclude the unconstitutionally obtained evidence to avoid condoning serious violations. On the other hand, inadvertent, minor, or good faith violations of the *Charter* are less serious and less likely to require exclusion.

The most significant change in the new test is the abandonment of the singular focus on the effects of admitting evidence unconstitutionally conscripted from the accused on the fairness of the trial, in favour of a more general concern about the impact of the *Charter* breach on "the interests protected by the right infringed."[176] Following a purposive approach to rights, these interests will differ with the particular right. For example, the focus will be on the effects of a section 8 search and seizure violation on privacy, bodily integrity and dignity, and on effects of the principle against self-incrimination and the right to silence when statements are unconstitutionally obtained from the accused. The abandonment of the focus on fair trials also means that, in cases of unconstitutionally obtained statements and bodily samples, courts should consider whether the seriousness of the *Charter* violation and society's interests in adjudication of the case on the merits also require exclusion. In particular, the Court has opened the door to admission of statements obtained through minor or technical *Charter* violations of the right to counsel or in circumstances where the statement would have been made notwithstanding the *Charter* breach. Nevertheless, the Court has maintained the presumption that most statements obtained in violation of the *Charter* should be excluded.[177] The Court has also opened the door to admission of unconstitutionally obtained bodily

---

175 *Ibid.* at para. 71.
176 *Ibid.* at para. 76.
177 *Ibid.* at paras. 92 and 96.

samples, particularly breath samples, in cases where the *Charter* violation is not serious and where the impact of the violation on privacy, bodily integrity, and dignity is not great. The Court has also recognized that the reliability of bodily samples as opposed to statements "may well tip the balance in favour of admission."[178]

Society's interest in adjudicating a case on its merits may require consideration of the reliability of the evidence, its importance to the prosecution's case, and the seriousness of the offence charged. At the same time, the Court indicated that the seriousness of the offence charged can "cut both ways" because "while the public has a heightened interest in seeing a determination on the merits where the offence charged is serious, it also has a vital interest in having a justice system that is above reproach, particularly where the penal stakes for the accused are high."[179]

In *Grant*, the Court held that a handgun unconstitutionally discovered as a result of an arbitrary detention and a violation of the right to counsel in the course of an investigative stop should be admitted under section 24(2). Although the impact of the *Charter* violations on the accused's *Charter* interests was significant because the police would not have discovered the gun had they not unconstitutionally detained and questioned the accused, the *Charter* violations were not deliberate or in bad faith in part because the applicable law was uncertain at the time. In addition, the admission of the gun as evidence was "essential to a determination on the merits"[180] for various firearm offences. In a companion case,[181] the Court reversed a trial judge's decision to admit evidence of 35 kilograms of cocaine that was obtained after an arbitrary detention and an unconstitutional search of a car. The Court stressed that the blatant and flagrant nature of these *Charter* violations was a significant, albeit not egregious, intrusion on *Charter*-protected interests. The Court held that the trial judge had erred by placing too much emphasis on the third factor, namely the effect of exclusion on society's interests in a determination of the criminal case on the merits. The trial judge had erred by stressing that the police misconduct was less serious than the crimes charged. "The fact that a *Charter* breach is less heinous than the offence charged does not advance the inquiry mandated by section 24(2). We expect police to adhere to higher standards than alleged criminals."[182]

---

178 *Ibid.* at para. 110.
179 *Ibid.* at para. 84.
180 *Ibid.* at para. 140.
181 *R. v. Harrison*, 2009 SCC 34.
182 *Ibid.* at para. 41.

J. CONCLUSION

It will be evident from this survey that Canadian criminal law has been significantly affected by the *Charter of Rights and Freedoms* and that judges have assumed an important law-making role. Not surprisingly, *Charter* decisions have provoked debate concerning both the substantive content of fundamental rights and freedoms and the appropriateness of judicial review as a way of protecting rights.

There are two core principles to be considered here. First is the issue of the legitimacy of judicial review, a matter considered more broadly in chapter 2. Judicial review qualifies majority rule, and it is evident from the cases considered in this chapter that Canadian judges have not hesitated to exercise the power to strike down laws that they consider violate *Charter* guarantees. One point to be noted, however, particularly in the realm of the criminal law, is that more often than not, what is at issue is not the solemn pronouncement of Parliament but rather the action of a police officer or prosecutor. The number of cases challenging the constitutionality of police conduct or that of other unelected state officials far exceeds the number of cases challenging the constitutionality of laws enacted by the representatives of the people. Judicial review of the propriety of the conduct of law-enforcement officials is considerably less controversial and very much more in keeping with the common law tradition. Control of the exercise of power by state officials through judicial review is a cornerstone of the rule of law, and subjecting the actions of police and other state officials to judicial scrutiny is one of the hallmarks of a civilized society. The *Charter* bolsters judicial powers in this area and, in so doing, does not conflict with democratic principles. In addition, it is also significant that many of the *Charter* challenges to both legislation and police conduct examined in this chapter have been the subject of a legislative reply by Parliament in the exercise of its jurisdiction over criminal law and procedure. The constitutionality of this reply legislation has not been considered in all cases, but the Supreme Court has generally determined that the reply legislation was a reasonable balance of the competing interests.

The second tension concerns the competing conceptions of the appropriate focus of the criminal law, identified at the beginning of this chapter, crime control and due process. Crime control is a matter of paramount concern in most modern societies and Canada is no exception. Condemning anti-social behaviour, convicting the guilty, and punishing wrongdoers for their transgressions represent central and important purposes of the criminal law. In recent years, concerns about the effects of some crimes on disadvantaged groups such as women and children have also strengthened the state's interest in crime control. At the same time, however, the criminal law involves the assertion of state power over citizens, and the tradition of liberal democracy requires that coercive powers be limited by law and that those who assert power comply with specified standards. Due-process standards are designed to ensure that the state respects the human dignity of all citizens, even those accused of serious wrongdoing. The *Charter of Rights and Freedoms*, as interpreted and applied by our courts, pushes Canada decidedly in the due-process direction. It has to be recognized, however, that the imposition of limits on the authority of state officials and the extension of procedural protections to persons accused of crime not only benefit the innocent but also make it more difficult to convict the guilty.

FURTHER READINGS

CAMERON, J., ed., *The Charter's Impact on the Criminal Justice System* (Toronto: Carswell, 1996)

CAMERON, J., & J. STRIBOPOULOS, eds., *The Charter and Criminal Justice Twenty Five Years Later* (Toronto: LexisNexis, 2008)

COHEN, S., *Privacy, Crime and Terror : Legal Rights and Security in a Time of Peril* (Toronto: LexisNexis, 2005)

COUGHLAN, S., *Criminal Procedure* (Toronto: Irwin Law, 2008)

PACIOCCO, D.M., *Charter Principles and Proof in Criminal Cases* (Toronto: Carswell, 1987)

PACIOCCO, D.M., *Getting Away with Murder: The Canadian Criminal Justice System* (Toronto: Irwin Law, 1999)

PACIOCCO, D.M., "Competing Constitutional Rights in an Age of Deference: A Bad Time to Be Accused" (2001) 14 Sup. Ct. L. Rev. (2d) 111

QUIGLEY, T., *Procedure in Canadian Criminal Law*, 2d ed. (Toronto: Carswell, 1997)

ROACH, K., *Due Process and Victims' Rights: The New Law and Politics of Criminal Justice* (Toronto: University of Toronto Press, 1999)

ROACH, K., *Criminal Law*, 4th ed. (Toronto: Irwin Law, 2009)

STUART, D., *Charter Justice in Canadian Criminal Law*, 4th ed. (Toronto: Carswell, 2005)

CHAPTER 15

EQUALITY

The guarantee of equality contained in section 15 of the *Charter of Rights and Freedoms* states:

(1) Every individual is equal before and under the law and has the right to the equal protection and equal benefit of the law without discrimination and, in particular, without discrimination based on race, national or ethnic origin, colour, religion, sex, age or mental or physical disability.

(2) Subsection (1) does not preclude any law, program or activity that has as its object the amelioration of conditions of disadvantaged individuals or groups including those that are disadvantaged because of race, national or ethnic origin, colour, religion, sex, age or mental or physical disability.

The equality rights jurisprudence under the *Charter* is complex and it defies any attempt at a quick and accurate summary. This is hardly surprising. Equality is a fundamental value in a democratic society and yet its precise meaning is elusive in political and legal discourse. As a legal concept, it includes the notion that every individual is entitled to dignity and respect and that the law should apply to all in an even-handed manner. Equality thus involves comparisons between individuals or groups but there is considerable debate about proper comparisons—who should be equal to whom, and what constitutes equal treatment? Should there be absolute equality, with everyone treated identically? How should differences be taken into account? Should advantaged groups be able to enjoy the benefit of equality rights? Are affirmative action measures that favour disadvantaged individuals and groups acceptable? Some theories of equality emphasize equal opportunity; others emphasize equality of outcomes.[1] These are value-laden issues that cannot be simply resolved by the mechanical application of any test.

Equality rights claims are challenging because they frequently present controversial moral, social, or political issues that many argue should not even be before the courts. For example, can equality rights be invoked to protect the rights of children not to be spanked?[2] Does section 15 give same-sex couples the right to marry?[3] Equality rights cases are also contentious when used as a vehicle to extend legislative benefits such as pensions, social assistance, or health care coverage. Such cases inevitably have significant policy or budgetary implications, making them the kinds of cases with which courts are the least comfortable.

These are complex and difficult issues, and the search for appropriate responses continues. This chapter begins by tracing the pre-*Charter* origins of equal rights protection in Canada. It next discusses the Supreme Court's attempts to come to grips with a general framework of the analysis of equality rights under the *Charter*. Finally, it discusses how the courts have dealt with particular kinds of discrimination under section 15.

A. EQUALITY UNDER THE *CANADIAN BILL OF RIGHTS*

In order to understand the scope of the *Charter*'s equality guarantee, it is useful to consider briefly the Supreme Court of Canada's treatment of equality under section 1(b) of the *Canadian Bill of Rights*, which guaranteed "the right to equality before the law and the protection of the law." As noted in chapter 1, the Court's performance under the *Bill of Rights* was generally regarded as a disappointment. The most expansive inter-

---

1   For further discussion of the debate about equality, see M. Schwarzschild, "Constitutional Law and Equality" in D. Patterson, ed., *A Companion to Philosophy of Law and Legal Theory* (Cambridge: Blackwell, 1996) at 156; W. Black & L. Smith, "The Equality Rights" in G.A. Beaudoin & E. Mendes, eds., *The Canadian Charter of Rights and Freedoms*, 4th ed. (Markham, ON: LexisNexis Butterworths, 2005) at 14-17 to 14-29.

2   *Canadian Foundation for Children, Youth and the Law v. Canada (Attorney General)*, [2004] 1 S.C.R. 76 [*Canadian Foundation for Children*].

3   *Reference Re Same-Sex Marriage*, [2004] 3 S.C.R. 698 [*Same-Sex Marriage Reference*].

pretation of the equality guarantee was reached in *R. v. Drybones*,[4] the 1969 decision where the Court found inoperative a section of the *Indian Act* that made it an offence for an Indian to be intoxicated off a reserve. The *Indian Act* provision was held by the Court to deny racial equality because it imposed more onerous constraints on Aboriginals than did the general liquor ordinance of the Northwest Territories, which merely prohibited drunkenness in a public place.

While *Drybones* was widely applauded as an important affirmation of the equality principle, the Supreme Court quickly retreated. In *Lavell*,[5] the Court upheld a provision of the *Indian Act* depriving of status an Indian woman who married a non-Indian while not imposing a similar disability on Indian men who married non-Indian women. Despite the blatantly discriminatory nature of this law, a majority refused to find that it violated the equality guarantee of the *Bill of Rights*. Similarly, in *Canard*,[6] the Court upheld a provision preventing an Indian from acting as the administrator of the estate of a deceased Indian, leaving that role to a federal official. In the Court's view, this was not a form of racial discrimination. In *Bliss*,[7] the Court upheld limitations on the rights of pregnant women to unemployment-insurance benefits, finding that discrimination on the basis of pregnancy was not sex discrimination and holding that since the legislation conferred a benefit, it could not be challenged. In these and other cases, the Court used a variety of rationales to uphold legislation—describing the law as designed to meet a valid federal objective, characterizing it as beneficial rather than burdensome, and focusing narrowly on the question of whether the law was equally applied in the courts without regard to its substantive effect.[8]

B. DRAFTING THE *CHARTER'S* EQUALITY GUARANTEE

In the debates about the appropriate wording of the equality provision of the *Canadian Charter of Rights and Freedoms*, there was a significant lobbying effort to strengthen the guarantee so as to prevent a repetition

---

4   [1970] S.C.R. 282, 9 D.L.R. (3d) 473 [*Drybones*].

5   *Canada (A.G.) v. Lavell*, [1974] S.C.R. 1349, 38 D.L.R. (3d) 481 [*Lavell*].

6   *Canard v. Canada (A.G.)*, [1976] 1 S.C.R. 170, 52 D.L.R. (3d) 548 [*Canard*].

7   *Bliss v. Canada (A.G.)*, [1979] 1 S.C.R. 183, 92 D.L.R. (3d) 417 [*Bliss*]. The benefit lay in the fact that pregnant women, unlike other unemployment-insurance claimants, did not have to prove they were available for work.

8   A good overview is found in W.S. Tarnopolsky, *The Canadian Bill of Rights*, 2d rev. ed. (Toronto: McClelland and Stewart, 1975) c. 8.

of the experience under the *Canadian Bill of Rights*. It is therefore significant that section 15 of the *Charter* provides that "every individual is equal before and under the law and has the right to the equal protection and equal benefit of the law." The insistence in the careful wording of section 15 that the guarantee includes equality *before* and *under* the law, as well as *equal protection* and *equal benefit* of the law, was meant to signal to the courts that section 15 was intended to be a much more powerful instrument of protection than its predecessor. In particular, the reference to "equal protection" echoed the Fourteenth Amendment to the United States' constitution, which had proved to be a powerful tool in the fight against racial discrimination. The reference to "equal benefit" was a signal that the reasoning in *Bliss*, distinguishing benefits and burdens, was no longer acceptable. Similarly, the explicit protection in section 15(2) of programs designed to ameliorate the conditions of disadvantaged individuals and groups is intended to ensure that legislatures will not be discouraged from taking affirmative measures to enhance equality.

C. THE SCOPE OF THE EQUALITY GUARANTEE

While section 15 of the *Charter* was clearly a departure from section 1(b) of the *Bill of Rights*, its precise meaning was far from clear. The early cases had to confront questions about the scope of the guarantee, particularly the issue of who could claim its protection. As well, there was debate (which continues to the present) about the appropriate method of interpreting section 15 and its interrelation with section 1.[9]

Section 15 contains a list of characteristics that should not be the basis for discriminatory treatment. This list incorporates the most common grounds for discrimination found in human rights codes: race, national or ethnic origin, sex, age, religion, and physical or mental disability.[10] These are commonly referred to as the "enumerated grounds" of discrimination. Although the original draft of section 15 treated the list of enumerated grounds as more limited in its coverage, the final wording that was adopted makes it clear (because it includes the words

---

9   Section 15 came into effect three years after the rest of the *Charter* (on 17 April 1985), in order to allow governments time to bring their statutes into line with the section.

10   The first draft of the *Charter* was more limited in its coverage, listing only race, national or ethnic origin, colour, religion, age, and sex.

"in particular") that the list of prohibited grounds of discrimination is not exhaustive and that further grounds may be added by the courts. As a result, the Supreme Court has accepted that other "analogous grounds" can also form the basis of equality claims.

Many early cases dealt with laws challenged on grounds not included in the "enumerated" grounds in section 15. These cases involved challenges to laws setting shorter limitation periods for suing municipalities, regulatory provisions of various kinds including the ban on actions in tort for work-related accidents covered by workers' compensation legislation, and regulations prohibiting the use of aluminum cans in order to protect the steel industry from competition. The courts were required to consider the purpose underlying section 15 to decide whether to allow these claims. Since all laws make distinctions between individuals and groups, it is almost always possible to say that a law discriminates in that it imposes burdens or confers benefits on some but not others. Was section 15 meant to give the courts a mandate to oversee the general rationality of the legislative process? Did it forbid different treatment of individuals unless there could be shown in a court of law to be a reasonable basis for doing so? Or did the words "without discrimination" signal a narrower purpose, namely, that the section was meant only to address the adverse treatment of certain groups on the basis of characteristics like those listed, which have led to prejudice, stereotype, and unjust disadvantage in many societies, including our own?[11]

Initially, some lower courts adopted a broader approach and were prepared to consider reviewing a wide range of laws under section 15. This raised concerns, similar to those raised in relation to section 7, that the courts would exceed their institutional role by requiring the government to justify under section 1 the mass of legislative distinctions drawn in the modern statute book. This was a cause for concern among advocacy groups, in particular those representing women and the disabled. They feared that, if section 15 were to be applied to such a wide range of laws, it might well lead the judiciary to adopt a relaxed interpretation of section 1 in order to avoid frequent second-guessing of legislatures' decisions. There were also concerns that more advantaged groups and individuals would benefit the most from the equality rights that many believed were enacted to protect and provide remedies for disadvantaged groups and individuals. These concerns have largely dissipated because the Supreme Court has said that section 15 may

---

11   Section 15 guarantees equality to "individuals," which has been interpreted to mean that people, not corporations, can invoke its protection.

only be invoked to challenge legislative distinctions based on enumerated or analogous grounds.

The concern has also been laid to rest by the Supreme Court's embrace of the ideal of "substantive" equality. This is a term that requires some explanation. One of the tensions arising under section 15 is between so-called "formal equality" and "substantive equality." The term "formal equality" is used to refer to a conception of equality commonly associated with the use of the "similarly situated" test, reminiscent of certain undesirable aspects of American equal protection jurisprudence. This test has venerable roots in the teachings of Aristotle, who stated that "things that are alike should be treated alike." The test is deceptively simple and superficially attractive.[12] For example, in applications for admission to university, one might argue that anyone receiving a certain grade on a standardized test should be admitted and that no other distinctions should be made. But problems quickly emerge from a mechanical application of this concept of equality. What if there was no oral or braille examination available so that a blind individual could not apply? Is it really consistent with a commitment to equality to ignore visual disability and treat that individual in precisely the same way as sighted individuals? May it not be necessary to look beyond the formal legal rule to ask whether there is equality in substance?

The determination of similarity and difference can be made only in relation to some criterion, which is often the purpose behind the rule or the law. As Ryder, Faria, and Lawrence have stated, "The focus of formal equality is on the individual's situation, and on the relevance of the personal characteristic at issue to the objectives of the challenged law or policy."[13] The similarly situated test essentially asks whether the legislative distinction that is being attacked is relevant to the legislation's objectives. Critics of the similarly situated test argue that this makes the test inherently unreliable because determining the purpose is uncertain and subject to manipulation. It also, in and of itself, provides no guidance for determining whether a certain legislative objective is discriminatory. The *Bliss* decision, finding that pregnant women could be treated differently from other unemployment-insurance claimants since they were not generally available for work, is often cited as an example of the perils of the similarly situated approach. As under

---

12   This approach is sometimes called equality of process. See, for example, K. Crenshaw, "Race, Reform and Retrenchment: Transformation and Legitimation in Anti-Discrimination Law" (1988) 101 Harv. L. Rev. 1331.

13   B. Ryder, C.C. Faria, & E. Lawrence, "What's *Law* Good For? An Empirical Overview of *Charter* Equality Rights Decisions" (2004) 24 Sup. Ct. L. Rev. (2d) 103 at 106.

section 1, there was a danger that if the purpose of the law was defined too narrowly and uncritically, then the law would almost always be upheld.

It was argued that, if the promise of equality is to be meaningful, the formal similarly situated test had to be rejected and the emphasis placed on a substantive equality approach that emphasizes consideration of the impact of laws on members of groups subject to stereotyping and historic disadvantage.[14] This approach was reflected by the jurisprudence developed in the interpretation of Canadian human rights codes, which seemed concerned about the actual impact of rules on groups. For example, the Supreme Court found rules requiring everyone to work Saturday in a retail store to be discriminatory. While seemingly grounded in a valid business purpose and not obviously treating anyone differently on the basis of religion, such rules do have an adverse impact on those for whom Saturday is a day of worship. Saturday observers are required to sacrifice their religious beliefs or their job.[15] Similarly, the failure to move furniture in an office to give space for a wheelchair to pass, while seemingly inoffensive, might have the effect of denying access to employment to a person with physical disabilities. The human rights jurisprudence had determined that "adverse-effects" discrimination of this sort gave rise to a duty to accommodate the group adversely affected unless such accommodation would produce undue hardship.[16]

D. THE SUPREME COURT SPEAKS: *ANDREWS V. LAW SOCIETY OF BRITISH COLUMBIA*

Andrews,[17] the first equality case to reach the Supreme Court of Canada, was of fundamental importance in charting the future direction of section 15 interpretation. A number of intervenors made submissions, including the Women's Legal Education and Action Fund (LEAF) and the

---

14   An early example of this type of writing is G. Brodksy & S. Day, *Canadian Charter Equality Rights for Women: One Step Forward or Two Steps Back?* (Ottawa: Canadian Advisory Council on Status of Women, 1989).

15   *Simpsons Sears v. Ontario (Human Rights Commission)*, [1985] 2 S.C.R. 536, 23 D.L.R. (4th) 321; *Central Alberta Dairy Pool v. Alberta (Human Rights Commission)*, [1990] 2 S.C.R. 489, 72 D.L.R. (4th) 417.

16   This jurisprudence is discussed in greater detail in K.E. Swinton, "Accommodating Equality in the Unionized Workplace" (1995) 33 Osgoode Hall L.J. 703.

17   *Andrews v. Law Society (British Columbia)*, [1989] 1 S.C.R. 143, 56 D.L.R. (4th) 1 [*Andrews*].

Coalition of Provincial Organizations of the Handicapped (COPOH). The case involved a challenge to the citizenship requirement for admission to the Law Society of British Columbia. The Court held, in a four to two decision, that this violated section 15, and was not justified under section 1 of the *Charter.*

The most significant aspect of the case was the Court's conceptualization of section 15. It soundly rejected exclusive reliance on formal equality and the similarly situated test, which the Court said "cannot be accepted as a fixed rule or formula for the resolution of equality questions arising under the *Charter.*"[18] The Court emphasized that the purpose behind section 15 was to protect vulnerable groups from discrimination. In the Court's view, this meant that section 15 could not be used to challenge every differential treatment created by a law. To succeed in a section 15 claim, a litigant would have to show (1) that there had been a denial of one of the four equality provisions in section 15—equality before or under the law or equal benefit or protection of the law—and (2) that this differential treatment was discriminatory on the basis of a personal characteristic constituting an enumerated or analogous ground within section 15.

The Court also made it clear that there was a threshold requirement for invoking section 15: there must be discrimination on an enumerated or analogous ground. The enumerated grounds were described as "the most common and probably the most socially destructive and historically practised bases of discrimination."[19] No attempt was made to define "analogous grounds" precisely at this point. McIntyre J. noted that "[t]he enumerated grounds in s. 15(1) are not exclusive and the limits, if any on grounds for discrimination which may be established in future cases await definition."[20] The insistence on enumerated or analogous grounds significantly restricted the reach of section 15 and closed the door on attempts to use the equality guarantee to review all legislative distinctions.[21] The Court insisted, however, that the restriction of section 15 to discrimination on enumerated and analogous grounds was needed to ensure that when it did apply, the guarantee could be given a vigorous interpretation and afford effective protection to members of disadvantaged groups.

---

18   *Ibid.* at 168 (S.C.R.).
19   *Ibid.* at 175 (S.C.R.).
20   *Ibid.*
21   See, for example, *Reference Re Workers' Compensation Act, 1983 (Newfoundland)*, [1989] 1 S.C.R. 922, 56 D.L.R. (4th) 765, holding that being denied a right to sue for work-related accidents is not an analogous ground of discrimination.

The other two important developments in *Andrews* were McIntyre J.'s definition of what constitutes discrimination and his discussion of the respective roles of section 15 and section 1 in the analysis of equality rights claims.

Discrimination was described by McIntyre J. in the following manner:

> . . . a distinction, whether intentional or not but based on grounds relating to personal characteristics of the individual or group, which has the effect of imposing burdens, obligations, or disadvantages on such individual or group not imposed upon others, or which withholds or limits access to opportunities, benefits, and advantages available to other members of society. Distinctions based on personal characteristics attributed to an individual solely on the basis of association with a group will rarely escape the charge of discrimination, while those based on an individual's merits and capacities will rarely be so classed.[22]

Thus, in deciding whether discrimination has occurred, the Court indicated that it would look at the legislature's purpose — for example, whether it acted out of prejudice against a group or on the basis of unjustified stereotypes about its members' capacity. But it would go further and consider as well the impact of laws on a group claiming section 15 protection. This willingness to look at both purpose and effects signalled that the Court would take the same approach under section 15 as it had taken in the interpretation of other *Charter* rights and human rights codes.

Finally, the Court remained true to past *Charter* cases in drawing a sharp line between the consideration of whether a right was violated and whether that infringement was justified under section 1. Some of the lower court cases, including the British Columbia Court of Appeal's decision in *Andrews*, had dealt with the justification for differential treatment within section 15 itself. This seemed to put the onus on the rights claimant to show that the differential treatment was not justified — an approach that the Supreme Court rejected in *Andrews*. McIntyre J. emphasized that the justification for discriminatory treatment under section 1 should be on the government.

In applying this structure to the facts in *Andrews*, all members of the Court agreed that section 15 had been violated. The law drew a distinction between citizens and non-citizens, and citizenship was held to be an analogous ground within section 15. Discrimination resulted

---

22   *Andrews*, above note 17 at 175 (S.C.R.).

from the burden placed on the non-citizen's ability to practise law until citizenship was acquired. A majority of the Court held that the law was not justified under section 1, because there were other ways to address the Law Society's justifiable concerns about a lawyer's competence and familiarity with Canadian institutions than through a citizenship requirement—for example, by testing or the requirement of a Canadian law degree. Justice Wilson stressed for the majority of the Court that "given that s. 15 is designed to protect those groups who suffer social, political and legal disadvantage in our society, the burden resting on government to justify the type of discrimination against such groups is appropriately an onerous one."[23]

E. A DIVIDED COURT: THE 1995 TRILOGY

Despite the unanimity of the Supreme Court in *Andrews* with respect to section 15 claims, three equality decisions, issued at the same time in the spring of 1995, revealed a Court divided on the proper approach to section 15. *Egan*[24] dealt with a challenge to the spousal allowance under the *Old Age Security Act*, which provided a benefit for the spouse of a pensioner who was between sixty and sixty-five when the couple's combined income fell below a certain level. "Spouse" was defined as a person of the opposite sex to whom the pensioner was married or with whom he or she lived in a common-law relationship as husband and wife. Egan was a gay man, whose partner, Norris, applied for the spousal benefit and was turned down because he was not a spouse as defined by the Act. He argued that this amounted to discrimination on the basis of sexual orientation. *Miron*[25] involved a challenge to a provision of the *Ontario Insurance Act*, which gave married spouses involved in accidents against uninsured motorists accident benefits for loss of income or damages but did not give the same benefit to common-law spouses. Miron, injured in a car accident by an uninsured motorist, sought benefits under his common-law spouse's insurance policy, arguing that the law was discriminatory on the basis of marital status and not justified under section 1 of the *Charter*. Finally, *Thibaudeau*[26] in-

23   *Ibid.* at 153 (S.C.R.). McIntyre J. was in dissent in holding that the s. 15 violation was justified under s. 1 of the *Charter* and in indicating that "the standard of 'pressing and substantial' may be too stringent" given "the necessity for the Legislature to make many distinctions between individuals and groups," *ibid.* at 184.
24   *Egan v. Canada*, [1995] 2 S.C.R. 513, 124 D.L.R. (4th) 609 [*Egan*].
25   *Miron v. Trudel*, [1995] 2 S.C.R. 418, 124 D.L.R. (4th) 693 [*Miron*].
26   *Thibaudeau v. Canada*, [1995] 2 S.C.R. 627, 124 D.L.R. (4th) 449 [*Thibaudeau*].

volved a challenge to a provision of the *Income Tax Act*, which provided that child-support payments are taxable to the recipient and deductible to the payor. It was argued that this scheme disproportionately burdened women, who were much more likely to be the custodial parent while the payors were more likely to be male.

The decisions in these cases reveal three distinct approaches to section 15 of the *Charter*. More particularly, the difference focused on when a legislative distinction would be viewed as discriminatory; that is, the second part of the test from *Andrews*. Four judges (La Forest, Gonthier, Major JJ., and Lamer C.J.C.) used what can be called an "internal-relevance" approach that builds on earlier cases such as *Conway*[27] and *Hess*.[28] Four others (McLachlin, Cory, Iacobucci, and Sopinka JJ.) continued to use the *Andrews* approach, while L'Heureux-Dubé J. adopted her own distinctive approach.

The judges adopting the internal-relevance approach stated that there is no discrimination within section 15 if the distinction drawn between two groups by legislation is relevant "to the functional values underlying the legislation,"[29] even though the distinction is made on the basis of an enumerated or analogous ground. Therefore, according to Gonthier J. in *Miron*, one must decide whether a distinction is relevant to "some objective physical or biological reality, or fundamental value."[30] Another requirement was that the "functional values" of the legislation themselves could not be discriminatory.[31]

In both *Miron* and *Egan*, the judges adopting the internal-relevance approach held that the legislative scheme was designed to support the institution of marriage, an institution of fundamental and long-standing importance in Canadian society. In *Miron*, Gonthier J. concluded that the legislature had no obligation to confer all the benefits of marriage on common-law couples. Indeed, to do so "would interfere directly with the individual's freedom to voluntarily choose whether to enter the institution of marriage by imposing consequences on cohabitation without any regard to the will of the parties."[32] Similarly, in *Egan*, marriage was described by La Forest J. as "by nature heterosexual" and,

---

27 *Conway v. R.*, [1993] 2 S.C.R. 872, 105 D.L.R. (4th) 210 [*Conway*]. For a discussion of *Conway*, see section H(4) below.

28 *R. v. Hess*, [1990] 2 S.C.R. 906, 59 C.C.C. (3d) 161 [*Hess*]. For a discussion of *Hess*, see section H(4) below.

29 *Miron*, above note 25 at 436 (S.C.R.), Gonthier J.

30 *Ibid.* at 446 (S.C.R.).

31 *Ibid.* at 436 (S.C.R.).

32 *Ibid.* at 463 (S.C.R.).

given its societal importance, Parliament should be able to give it special support:

> Neither in its purpose or effect does the legislation constitute an infringement of the fundamental values sought to be protected by the *Charter*. None of the couples excluded from benefits under the Act are capable of meeting the fundamental social objectives thereby sought to be promoted by Parliament. These couples undoubtedly provide mutual support for one another, and that, no doubt, is of some benefit to society. They may, it is true, occasionally adopt or bring up children, but this is exceptional and in no way affects the general picture. I fail to see how homosexuals differ from other excluded couples in terms of the fundamental social reasons for which Parliament has sought to favour heterosexuals who live as married couples . . . .[33]

In contrast, another group of four judges, represented by McLachlin J. in *Miron* and Cory J. in *Egan*, rejected the internal-relevance approach as unjustifiably narrow. As McLachlin J. stated in *Miron*:

> If the basis of the distinction on an enumerated or analogous ground is clearly irrelevant to the functional values of the legislation, then the distinction will be discriminatory. However, it does not follow from a finding that a group characteristic is relevant to the legislative aim, that the legislator has employed that characteristic in a manner which does not perpetuate limitations, burdens and disadvantages in violation of s. 15(1). This can be ascertained only by examining the effect of the distinction in the social and economic context of the legislation and the lives of the individuals it touches.[34]

The purpose of section 15, McLachlin J. wrote, is "the avoidance of stereotypical reasoning and the creation of legal distinctions which violate the dignity and freedom of the individual, on the basis of some preconceived perception about the attributed characteristics of a group rather than the true capacity, worth or circumstances of the individual."[35] While past cases indicated that some distinctions on an enumerated or analogous ground might not constitute discrimination within section 15, that situation would be rare—arising where "the distinction may be found not to engage the purpose of the *Charter* guarantee" or where the effect of the law is not to impose a real disadvantage, given the larger social and political context.

---

33   *Egan*, above note 24 at 538 (S.C.R.).
34   *Miron*, above note 25 at 742 (D.L.R.).
35   *Ibid.* at 748 (D.L.R.).

Applying this approach in *Miron*, McLachlin J. found the distinction between married and common-law couples was discriminatory on the basis of marital status, a ground analogous to those enumerated in section 15. This denial of equality was not justified under section 1. Common-law couples, like married couples, could suffer economic dislocation if one member was injured in an accident, and there was no reason to bar them from benefits.

In *Egan*, Cory J. similarly concluded that the distinction drawn between homosexual couples and heterosexual couples living in a common-law relationship was discriminatory. Noting that discrimination is to be determined from the perspective of the individual claiming a *Charter* violation, he said:

> The definition of "spouse" as someone of the opposite sex reinforces the stereotype that homosexuals cannot and do not form lasting, caring, mutually supportive relationships with economic interdependence in the same manner as heterosexual couples. The appellants' relationship vividly demonstrates the error of that approach. The discriminatory impact can hardly be deemed trivial when the legislation reinforces prejudicial attitudes based on such faulty stereotypes. The effect of the impugned provision is clearly contrary to s. 15's aim of protecting human dignity . . .[36]

L'Heureux-Dubé J. took a distinctive position, critical of what she described as the "categorical" approach of her colleagues, arguing that the inquiry in section 15 cases should turn on the nature of the group adversely affected by a distinction and the nature of the interest adversely affected.

For a time, the Supreme Court dealt with this basic disagreement about section 15, by referring to the two approaches and then justifying the result under both. For example, La Forest J. stated in *Eldridge*:

> While this Court has not adopted a uniform approach to s. 15(1), there is broad agreement on the general analytic framework; see *Eaton v. Brant County Board of Education*, [1997] 1 S.C.R. 241, at para. 62, *Miron, supra* and *Egan, supra*. A person claiming a violation of s. 15(1) must first establish that, because of a distinction drawn between the claimant and others, the claimant has been denied "equal protection" or "equal benefit" of the law. Secondly, the claimant must show that the denial constitutes discrimination on the basis of one of the enumerated grounds listed in s. 15(1) or one analogous thereto. Before concluding that a distinction is discriminatory, some members of this

---

36   *Egan*, above note 24 at 604 (S.C.R.).

Court have held that it must be shown to be based on an irrelevant personal characteristic; see *Miron, supra* (*per* Gonthier J.), and *Egan, supra* (*per* La Forest J.). Under this view, s. 15(1) will not be infringed unless the distinguished personal characteristic is irrelevant to the functional values underlying the law, provided that those values are not themselves discriminatory. Others have suggested that relevance is only one factor to be considered in determining whether a distinction based on an enumerated or analogous ground is discriminatory; see *Miron, supra* (*per* McLachlin J.), and *Thibaudeau v. Canada*, [1995] 2 S.C.R. 627 (*per* Cory and Iacobucci JJ.).[37]

Again in *Benner*, the Supreme Court openly acknowledged the three approaches to its interpretation of equality rights.[38] In *Eaton*, Sopinka J. declared that there was agreement among members of the Court on certain principles, noting that the majority in *Miron* (the McLachlin view) had agreed with the internal-relevance approach to the extent that it was acknowledged that, in rare cases, distinctions on an enumerated or analogous ground might not constitute discrimination.[39]

F. A UNITED COURT: *LAW v. CANADA*

The Supreme Court of Canada resolved its differences in the 1999 decision in *Law v. Canada*[40] by holding that a section 15 violation of the *Charter* would require proof of discrimination on an enumerated or analogous ground and substantive discrimination that violated human dignity. The case involved a claim of age discrimination by a thirty-year-old widow who would not qualify for *Canada Pension Plan* survivor benefits until she was sixty-five. She would have received the benefits if she had dependent children or was either disabled or forty-five years of age or older. The Court held that, even though the law imposed a formal and unequal distinction on the basis of the enumerated ground of age, it did not violate section 15 of the *Charter* because it did not violate the human dignity of those under forty-five and, accordingly, did not

---

37   *Eldridge v. British Columbia*, [1997] 3 S.C.R. 624, 151 D.L.R. (4th) 577 at 614 [*Eldridge*].

38   In *Benner v. Canada (Secretary of State)*, [1997] 1 S.C.R. 358, 143 D.L.R. (4th) 577 [*Benner*], the Court struck down a provision in the *Citizenship Act* that imposed more onerous requirements for the acquisition of Canadian citizenship for the children of women who married non-Canadians at a given period than of men who married non-citizens.

39   *Eaton v. Brant County*, [1997] 1 S.C.R. 241 at 271, 142 D.L.R. (4th) 385 [*Eaton*].

40   *Law v. Canada*, [1999] 1 S.C.R. 497 [*Law*].

amount to substantive discrimination. Although the law treats younger people differently, the differential treatment

> does not reflect or promote the notion that they are less capable or less deserving of concern, respect, and consideration . . . . Nor does the differential treatment perpetuate the view that people in this class are less capable or less worthy of recognition or value as human beings or as members of Canadian society . . . . [T]he legislation does not stereotype, exclude or devalue adults under 45. The law functions not by the device of stereotype, but by distinctions corresponding to the actual situation of individuals it affects.[41]

The Court noted that "adults under the age of 45 have not been consistently and routinely subjected to the sorts of discrimination faced by some of Canada's discrete and insular minorities."[42] Moreover, the legislature was entitled to rely on "informed statistical generalizations"[43] rather than stereotypes that younger people could more easily replace their deceased partner's income and that they should not receive the survivor's pension until reaching the age of sixty-five years.

The framework for section 15 claims set out in *Law* draws on *Andrews* by stressing the need for a purposive and contextual approach to equality rights, requiring proof of both differential treatment and substantive discrimination on enumerated or analogous grounds. As in *Andrews*, the Court stressed that equality is a comparative concept and that a comparator group must be selected in order to ground the section 15 analysis. The Court added that "the claimant generally chooses the person, group, or groups with whom he or she wishes to be compared for the purpose of the discrimination inquiry."[44] However, as explained below, where necessary, a court may refine the comparison group with attention to the subject matter of the impugned legislation, its effects, and the context.

The Supreme Court also made several new statements in *Law*. None of these has proved as important as the Court's use of the concept of "essential human dignity" in its analysis. The Court said in unequivocal terms that the purpose of section 15 was to prevent the violation of "essential human dignity" and "to promote a society in which all persons enjoy equal recognition at law as human beings or as members of Canadian society, equally capable and equally deserving of concern, respect and

---

41 *Ibid.* at para. 102.
42 *Ibid.* at para. 95.
43 *Ibid.* at para. 106.
44 *Ibid.* at para. 6.

consideration."[45] Moreover, the determination of whether or not substantive discrimination had been established turns on whether the legislative distinction violated the "essential human dignity" of the *Charter* claimant. In turn, whether the claimant's dignity was violated depended on the analysis of four "contextual factors," to be analyzed from the claimant's perspective. This use of "dignity" as an analytical tool has been difficult to come to grips with and may play less of a role in the future.

Law is generally seen as having established a three-part test for the determination of equality claims:

1) Does the impugned law (a) draw a formal distinction between the claimant and others on the basis of one or more personal characteristics, or (b) fail to take into account the claimant's already disadvantaged position within Canadian society resulting in substantively differential treatment between the claimant and others on the basis of one or more personal characteristics?

2) Is the claimant subject to differential treatment based on one or more enumerated and analogous grounds? and

3) Does the differential treatment discriminate by imposing a burden upon, or withholding a benefit from, the claimant in a manner that reflects the stereotypical application of presumed group or personal characteristics, or that otherwise has the effect of perpetuating or promoting the view that the individual is less capable or worthy of recognition or value as a human being or as a member of Canadian society, equally deserving of concern, respect, and consideration?

Law added factors to the section 15 analysis not found in *Andrews*. The most important is the requirement that a section 15 applicant demonstrate not only differential treatment on enumerated or analogous grounds of discrimination, but also that the differential treatment results in a loss of human dignity:

> What is human dignity? . . . Human dignity means that an individual or group feels self-respect and self-worth. It is concerned with physical and psychological integrity and empowerment. Human dignity is harmed by unfair treatment premised upon personal traits or circumstances which do not relate to individual needs, capacities, or merits. It is enhanced by laws which are sensitive to the needs, capacities, and merits of different individuals, taking into account the context underlying their differences. Human dignity is harmed when individuals and groups are marginalized, ignored, or devalued, and is enhanced when laws recognize the full place of all individuals and groups within

---

45   *Ibid.* at para. 88.

Canadian society. Human dignity within the meaning of the equality guarantee does not relate to the status or position of an individual in society *per se*, but rather concerns the manner in which a person legitimately feels when confronted with a particular law. Does the law treat him or her unfairly, taking into account all of the circumstances regarding the individuals affected and excluded by the law? [46]

Harm to human dignity is to be determined by examining four contextual factors:

1) pre-existing disadvantage;
2) correspondence between the grounds and the claimants' actual needs, capacities, and circumstances;
3) ameliorative purposes or effects; and
4) the nature and scope of the interest affected by the impugned law.

Although the Court stated at the time that this list of factors was "open," no new contextual factors have been added to the list since *Law*. The importance of the contextual factors cannot be overstated. In the decade following *Andrews*, most unsuccessful section 15 claims failed because they were not brought under an enumerated or analogous ground. Under *Law*, most section 15 cases fail because an analysis of the contextual factors persuades a court that the claimant's essential human dignity has not been violated by the impugned legislative distinction.[47]

The additional requirement of an affront to human dignity was determinative in Ms. Law's case. She established differential treatment on the enumerated grounds of age, but her claim was rejected because the Court was "at a loss to locate any violation of human dignity. The impugned distinctions do not stigmatize young persons, nor can they be said to perpetuate the view that surviving spouses under age 45 are less deserving of concern, respect or consideration than any others. Nor do they withhold a government benefit on the basis of stereotypical assumptions."[48]

The *Law* test was criticized for its complexity and for placing additional burdens on section 15 applicants to prove a violation of human dignity and contextual factors that should have been reserved for section 1 analysis. There were also concerns that it follows the functional relevance test by placing too much emphasis on the government's purpose in enacting the law. On the other hand, *Law* was been praised for its insistence on a substantive and contextual approach consistent with the purposes of section 15 and the need for attention to context.

---

46 *Ibid.* at para. 53.
47 See Ryder *et al.*, above note 13 at 116.
48 *Law*, above note 40 at para. 108.

G. *R. v. KAPP: LAW* QUALIFIED AND SIMPLIFIED?

In the 2008 case of *R. v. Kapp*,[49] the Court, in a joint judgment by Chief Justice McLachlin and Justice Abella, qualified the *Law* test for equality and signaled its preference for the simpler 1989 *Andrews* test. As discussed above, the *Andrews* test for equality focused on the two-part test of whether a law created a distinction based on an enumerated or analogous ground and whether the distinction creates or perpetuates disadvantage or stereotyping.

The Court in *Kapp* noted that *Law* had succeeded in unifying what had, since *Andrews,* become a divided approach to equality rights, and that *Law* "was an important contribution to our understanding of the conceptual underpinnings of substantive equality."[50] Nevertheless, the Court recognized that the focus on human dignity had created an additional burden on equality claimants. Even with the guidance of the four contextual factors outlined in *Law*, the human dignity concept had become "confusing and difficult to apply."[51] The Court warned that the four contextual factors should not be read as rigid requirements but rather "as a way of focusing on the central concern of section 15 identified in *Andrews*—combating discrimination, defined in terms of perpetuating disadvantage and stereotyping."[52] The *Law* contextual factors should be used as a tool to focus on stereotyping in the form of attributed characteristics that affect the degree of correspondence between the differential treatment and the reality of the claimant's group or the perpetuation of pre-existing disadvantage. The ameliorative purpose or effect of the law was most relevant to whether it qualified as an affirmative action program under section 15(2), but the Court stated, without deciding, that it could also be relevant to determining whether the law would perpetuate disadvantage.[53]

The impact of *Kapp* remains to be seen. The bulk of the judgment was devoted to the conclusion that a fishing program that provided preferential treatment for three Aboriginal bands was an ameliorative program under section 15(2) and, for that reason, it was not necessary to evaluate whether the law infringed the section 15 rights of non-Aboriginal fishers. That said, it is likely that *Kapp* will have a sig-

---

49   [2008] 2 S.C.R. 483 [*Kapp*].
50   *Ibid.* at para. 20.
51   *Ibid.* at para. 22.
52   *Ibid.* at para. 24.
53   *Ibid.* at para. 23.

nificant impact on the evolution of equality rights jurisprudence. In *Ermineskin Indian Band and Nation v. Canada*,[54] the Court applied the two-part test articulated in *Kapp* to reject a section 15 challenge to provisions of the *Indian Act* that prohibited investment of a band's oil and gas royalties. The Court held that while the Act drew distinctions on prohibited grounds, the distinctions were not discriminatory because they allowed bands some control over the funds and did not draw a distinction that perpetuates disadvantage through prejudice or stereotyping. The unanimous Court made no mention of the *Law* test including its reference to human dignity and the four contextual factors used to make judgments about the effect of a law on human dignity.

The Court continued to ignore the *Law* test in *A.C. v. Manitoba (Director of Child and Family Services)*[55] where it upheld a provincial law that allowed medically necessary treatment to be ordered when in the best interests of children under sixteen years of age. Citing *Kapp*, Abella J. concluded that because the law allowed children under sixteen "to lead evidence of sufficient maturity to determine their medical choices, their ability to make treatment decisions is ultimately calibrated in accordance with maturity, not age, and no disadvantaging prejudice or stereotype based on age can be said to be engaged. There is therefore no violation of s. 15."[56] Chief Justice McLachlin also cited *Kapp* to conclude that the legislative decision was "ameliorative, not invidious."[57] The two-part test in *Andrews* and *Kapp* may be simpler and better at vindicating the purpose of protecting substantive equality. While the *Law* focus on human dignity appears to have been abandoned, the four contextual factors outlined in *Law* are arguably still relevant in determining whether there has been discrimination.

H. IMPORTANT ASPECTS OF THE TEST FOR EQUALITY

1) Analogous Grounds

It has been accepted, at least since *Andrews*, that equality rights claims can be based not only on one of the nine particular grounds of discrimination listed in section 15(1), of the *Charter* but also on grounds

---

54   [2009] 1 S.C.R. 222 at paras. 201–2.
55   2009 SCC 30 [*A.C. v. Manitoba*]
56   *Ibid.* at para. 111.
57   *Ibid.* at para. 152.

of discrimination analogous to those listed. To date, the Supreme Court has accepted that marital status,[58] sexual orientation,[59] citizenship (or non-citizenship),[60] and off-reserve residence for Aboriginals[61] constitute analogous grounds of discrimination that fall within section 15(1)'s ambit. On the other hand, marijuana users,[62] workers denied the right to sue their employers by workers compensation schemes,[63] as well as RCMP officers and health care workers who are treated differently from other employees for the purpose of labour relations, have been held not to constitute groups discriminated against on analogous grounds.[64]

---

58   *Miron*, above note 25; *Nova Scotia (Attorney General) v. Walsh*, [2002] 4 S.C.R. 325.

59   *Egan*, above note 24; *Vriend v. Alberta*, [1998] 1 S.C.R. 493, 156 D.L.R. (4th) 385 [*Vriend*]; *M. v. H.*, [1999] 2 S.C.R. 3.

60   *Andrews*, above note 17; *Lavoie v. Canada*, [2002] 1 S.C.R. 769.

61   *Corbière v. Canada (Minister of Indian and Northern Affairs)*, [1999] 2 S.C.R. 203, 173 D.L.R. (4th) 1 [*Corbière*]. The Court has repeatedly rejected the argument that residence can be an analogous ground for non-Aboriginals: *R. v. Turpin*, [1989] 1 S.C.R. 1296; *Haig v. Canada (Chief Electoral Officer)*, [1993] 2 S.C.R. 995; *Siemens v. Manitoba (Attorney General)*, [2003] 1 S.C.R. 6.

62   *R. v. Malmo-Levine; R. v. Caine*, [2003] 3 S.C.R. 571 at paras. 184–85, in which Gonthier and Binnie JJ. for the majority state that:

> [a] taste for marihuana is not a "personal characteristic" in the sense required to trigger s. 15 protection . . . . As *Malmo-Levine* argues elsewhere, it is a lifestyle choice. It bears no analogy with the personal characteristics listed in s. 15, namely race, national or ethnic origin, colour, religion, sex, age, or mental or physical disability. It would trivialize this list to say that "pot" smoking is analogous to gender or religion as a "deeply personal characteristic that is either unchangeable or changeable only at unacceptable personal costs."

63   See *Reference Re Workers' Compensation Act, 1983 (Newfoundland)*, above note 21 at 924 (S.C.R.), where La Forest J. rejected the claim of victims of work-related accidents: "The situation of the workers and dependants here is in no way analogous to those listed in s. 15(1), as a majority in *Andrews* stated was required to permit recourse to s. 15(1)."

64   *Delisle v. RCMP*, [1999] 2 S.C.R. 989, where the status of being an RCMP officer was not an analogous ground of discrimination.; *Health Services and Support-Facilities Subsector Bargaining Assn. v. British Columbia*, [2007] 2 S.C.R. 391 at para. 165, where restrictions on bargaining by health care workers were found not to amount to discrimination because "the differential and adverse effects of the legislation on some groups of workers relate essentially to the type of work they do, and not to the persons they are. Nor does the evidence disclose that the Act reflects stereotypical application of group or personal characteristics." See also *Rudolf Wolff & Co. v. Canada*, [1990] 1 S.C.R. 695 at 702, in which the Court rejected the claim of those seeking relief against the federal Crown and challenging the statutory requirement that they sue in the Federal Court of Canada:

How is a court to determine whether or not a ground is similar enough to be included as analogous? The Supreme Court has usually identified unacceptable forms of discrimination as focusing on "personal characteristics," that is, characteristics that are somehow inherently part of an individual's identity. Moreover, the Court seems to require such characteristics be either "immutable" — in the way that, say, race or ethnic origin cannot be changed — or "constructively immutable." By constructive immutability, the Court is referring to a characteristic that "the government has no legitimate interest in expecting us to change to receive equal treatment under the law."[65]

The Supreme Court engaged in its most comprehensive examination of analogous grounds in *Corbière v. Canada*.[66] The case involved a section 15 claim by Indian band members who were denied the right to vote in their band's elections if they did not reside on their band's reserve. The Court found that "Aboriginality residence" or the off-reserve status of band members was an analogous grounds of discrimination. The Court took a contextual approach and stressed that "the ordinary 'residence' decisions faced by the average Canadian should not be confused with the profound decisions Aboriginal band members make to live on or off their reserves, assuming choice is possible. The reality of their situation is unique and complex. Thus no new water is charted, in the sense of finding residence, in the generalized abstract, to be an analogous ground."[67] Discriminating on the basis of residence is an analogous ground of discrimination for Aboriginal people but not for non-Aboriginal people.

The majority's discussion of how to identify analogous grounds was as follows:

> What then are the criteria by which we identify a ground of distinction as analogous? The obvious answer is that we look for grounds of distinction that are analogous or like the grounds enumerated in s. 15 — race, national or ethnic origin, colour, religion, sex, age, or mental or physical disability. It seems to us that what these grounds have in common is the fact that they often serve as the basis for stereo-

---

[I]t cannot be said that individuals claiming relief against the Federal Crown are . . . a "discrete and insular minority" or a "disadvantaged group in Canadian society within the contemplation of s. 15." Rather, they are a disparate group with the sole common interest of seeking to bring a claim against the Crown before a court.

65 *Corbière*, above note 61 at para. 13 (S.C.R.).
66 *Corbière*, above note 61.
67 *Ibid.* at para. 15.

typical decisions made not on the basis of merit but on the basis of a personal characteristic that is immutable or changeable only at unacceptable cost to personal identity. This suggests that the thrust of identification of analogous grounds at the second stage of the *Law* analysis is to reveal grounds based on characteristics that we cannot change or that the government has no legitimate interest in expecting us to change to receive equal treatment under the law. To put it another way, s. 15 targets the denial of equal treatment on grounds that are actually immutable, like race, or constructively immutable, like religion. Other factors identified in the cases as associated with the enumerated and analogous grounds, like the fact that the decision adversely impacts on a discrete and insular minority or a group that has been historically discriminated against, may be seen to flow from the central concept of immutable or constructively immutable personal characteristics, which too often have served as illegitimate and demeaning proxies for merit-based decision making.[68]

The majority in *Corbière* also stressed that analogous grounds, once identified and accepted by the courts, will always "serve as jurisprudential markers for suspect distinctions associated with stereotypical, discriminatory decision making"[69] This differs from the approach of L'Heureux-Dubé J., who would have limited the finding of analogous grounds to the case at hand. The entire Court in *Corbière* agreed that there was substantive discrimination because the denial of the vote to off-reserve band members was based on a stereotype that they were not interested in or affected by the decisions of their band.

2) Comparator Groups

The Supreme Court has stressed repeatedly that equality is a comparative concept. For each step of the *Law* test, a comparison must be made between a group with which the claimant identifies and some other group. A great deal turns on the "comparator group" selection. As stated by Binnie J. in *Hodge v. Canada*, "a misidentification of the proper comparator group at the outset can doom the outcome of the whole s. 15(1) analysis."[70]

Hodge is the most important discussion of comparator groups to emerge from the Court. In that case, Binnie J. stated that while it was up to the claimant to make the initial choice of the comparator group,

---

68   *Ibid.* at para. 13.
69   *Ibid.* at paras. 11, 7.
70   [2004] 3 S.C.R. 357 at para. 18 [*Hodge*].

the correctness of that choice was a matter of the law for the court to decide on the following principle:

> The appropriate comparator group is the one which mirrors the characteristics of the claimant (or claimant group) relevant to the benefit or advantage sought except that the statutory definition includes a personal characteristic that is offensive to the *Charter* or omits a personal characteristic in a way that is offensive to the *Charter*.[71]

This creates a kind of "but for" test. The comparator group is the group entitled to the legal benefit that the claimant is deprived of and resembles the claimant's group in all relevant respects, except that its members do not share the personal characteristic that is the basis for exclusion. The claimants belong to the group that would be entitled to the legal benefit being sought but for possessing the disqualifying personal characteristic; the comparator group gets the legal benefit because it does not share that disqualifying characteristic.

In *Hodge*, the claimant had been in a common-law relationship with the deceased for twenty-two years, but left him because of alleged verbal and physical abuse. When he died five months later, she sought but was denied a survivor's pension under the *Canada Pension Plan* because at the time of his death she was no longer considered to be his "spouse." Had they been married but separated she would have received the pension. Ms. Hodge argued that she belonged to the category of "separated common-law spouses," whose treatment under the *CPP* was discriminatory compared to the treatment of "separated married spouses." Binnie J. disagreed and found that the appropriate comparison was to formerly married spouses who had divorced their husband or wife. Both divorcées and common-law spouses who no longer lived with their partners were former spouses, and neither was eligible for a *CPP* survivor's pension. Therefore, while the claimant had identified the right group (separated spouses) she could not meaningfully compare her treatment under the *CPP* to that group, because she was in fact a *former* (that is, not a separated) spouse. *Hodge* establishes that a court does not have to defer to the claimant's choice of comparator group. As Binnie J. put it, "the correctness of the choice is a matter of law for the court to determine."[72]

Auton (Guardian ad litem of) v. British Columbia (Attorney General)[73] demonstrates the importance of this approach to comparator groups.

---

71   *Ibid.* at para. 23.
72   *Ibid.* at para. 21.
73   [2004] 3 S.C.R. 657 [*Auton*].

The claimants were infants suffering from the developmental disorder autism. They claimed the provincial government discriminated against them by not funding a particular kind of behavioural therapy. They contended that they should be compared either to non-disabled Canadian children or adults with mental illness who received funding for medically necessary treatment, and this argument succeeded both in the British Columbia Supreme Court and the British Columbia Court of Appeal. McLachlin C.J.C., writing for the majority, rejected these comparators. The behavioural therapy that the petitioners sought was only now emerging, but the groups that they wanted to be compared to typically received funding only for therapies that were well-established.[74] McLachlin C.J.C. concluded:

> the appropriate comparator for the petitioners is a non-disabled person or a person suffering a disability other than a mental disability (here autism) seeking or receiving funding for a non-core therapy important for his or her present and future health, which is emergent and only recently becoming recognized as medically required.[75]

McLachlin C.J.C. found that the evidence did not show that the provincial government had responded to requests for new therapies or treatments by non-disabled or otherwise disabled people any differently than it had for autistic children. Even if the government could have acted more quickly to fund the autism treatment, there was no evidence it had been laggard when compared to other new therapies for non-disabled persons or persons with another kind of disability, and the claim was therefore dismissed.

3) The Perspective of the Claimant

As we have noted, human dignity has taken on a central role in the analysis of section 15 claims. Discrimination will be held to be established if a legislative distinction has the purpose or effect of demeaning an individual's human dignity. From whose perspective is the claimant's human dignity to be measured? On this score, the Supreme Court stated in *Law* that the effect of the legislative distinction must be assessed from the perspective of the reasonable claimant:

> The appropriate perspective is subjective-objective. Equality analysis under the *Charter* is concerned with the perspective of a person in circumstances similar to those of the claimant, who is informed

---

74   *Ibid.* at para. 55.
75   *Ibid.*

of and rationally takes into account the various contextual factors which determine whether an impugned law infringes human dignity, as that concept is understood for the purpose of s. 15(1).[76]

This assessment of whether the human dignity of the reasonable claimant is infringed has, at times, been a source of disagreement. In cases like *Gosselin v. Quebec (Attorney General)*,[77] dealing with social welfare rights, and *Canadian Foundation for Children, Youth and the Law*, the child spanking case, the Supreme Court divided on the factors that would be considered by a reasonable claimant. In *Gosselin*, the majority held that age-based distinctions were commonly used and that conferring different benefits to young welfare recipients with a view to getting them back into the work force affirmed rather than infringed their human dignity. The minority regarded the age-based distinction as the product of stereotypical thinking that demeaned and disadvantaged a vulnerable group. In the child spanking case, the majority held that a reasonable person, knowing of the limitations the law imposes on abusive conduct directed towards children and aware of the harms of criminalization, would not conclude that a child's dignity would be violated by use of corrective force. The dissenting judges disagreed and would have held that the denial of the law's protection against physical force was disrespectful of children and treated them as second-class citizens.

4)   The Contextual Factors

As noted above, the contextual factors were the crucial element of the *Law* test, though the Court has now warned in *Kapp*[78] that they "should not be read literally as if they were legislative dispositions, but as a way of focusing on the central concern of section 15 identified in *Andrews*—combating discrimination, defined in terms of perpetuating disadvantage and stereotyping." The four factors are:

1)   *Pre-existing disadvantage*: This factor requires a court to examine whether or not the claimant belongs to a group that has historically been vulnerable or the subject of stereotyping and prejudice. If a law has the effect of further disadvantaging an already disadvantaged group, then it is more likely to be found to be discriminatory.

2)   *Correspondence*: This factor looks at whether the legislative distinction that is being attacked corresponds to the actual needs, capaci-

---

76   *Law*, above note 40 at paras. 59–61.
77   [2002] 4 S.C.R. 429 [*Gosselin*].
78   *Kapp*, above note 49 at para 24.

ties, or circumstances of the claimant. If the legislative distinction is the result of a deliberate design, which is not in itself discriminatory and which has sought to take into account the claimant's traits or circumstances, it will be more difficult to establish discrimination. On the other hand, the distinction will be more difficult to justify if it is based on stereotyping in the form of attributed as opposed to actual characteristics.

3) *Ameliorative purpose*: This factor looks at whether or not the impugned law is actually aimed at improving the situation of a group more disadvantaged than the claimant's group. Thus, if a law is aimed at a greater need than the claimant's, it is less likely to be discriminatory. The Court in *Kapp*[79] cast some doubt on this factor under section 15(1) noting that it was most relevant to section 15(2) and that it "would suggest, without deciding here, that the third *Law* factor might also be relevant to the question under section 15(1) as to whether the effect of the law or program is to perpetuate disadvantage."[80]

4) *The nature and scope of the interest affected*: The more severe and localized the consequences of the legislation on the affected group, the greater the chance that it discriminates. Thus, for example, if a fundamental interest of the claimant is at stake—for instance, his liberty interest or his physical integrity—then the court is more likely to find discrimination.

In *Law*, the Supreme Court suggested that pre-existing disadvantage was "probably the most compelling factor favouring a conclusion that differential treatment imposed by legislation is truly discriminatory."[81] However, in subsequent cases, the second factor—correspondence—has generally proven to be decisive. One study suggests that in fifteen cases released by the Supreme Court since *Law*—up to *Canadian Foundation for Children* in 2004—the outcome of the Court's analysis of the correspondence factor matched the outcome of the overall inquiry into the existence of discrimination. In contrast, the first, third, and fourth factors have matched the outcome of the discrimination inquiry seven, six, and eight times out of fifteen, respectively.[82] On a purely

---

79   *Ibid.* at para 24. One objection to the relevance of ameliorative purpose under section 15(1) would be that it would allow the government to argue that the law did not violate section 15(1) because it was ameliorative after having lost the argument that the law as an ameliorative program was justified under section 15(2).

80   *Ibid.* at para. 23.

81   *Law*, above note 40 at para. 63.

82   Ryder *et al.*, above note 13 at 122.

quantitative level, then, the correspondence factor has dominated in the application of the *Law* test.

This is readily apparent when one reads the cases. Examples of cases where the correspondence factor is discussed at length include *Canadian Foundation for Children*[83] and *Nova Scotia (Workers' Compensation Board) v. Martin; Nova Scotia (Workers' Compensation Board) v. Laseur.*[84] In his partial dissent in *Canadian Foundation for Children*, Binnie J. warns that the correspondence factor may amount to a reversion to the "relevance" requirement rejected in Law and also import considerations best left to section 1 into the section 15 analysis.[85] The Court in *Kapp*[86] might have had the correspondence factor in mind when it recognized that "criticism has also accrued for the way *Law* has allowed the formalism of some of the Court's post-*Andrews* jurisprudence to resurface in the form of an artificial comparator analysis focussed on treating likes alike." A focus on stereotyping and attributed rather than real characteristics can perhaps save the correspondence factor from descending into an artificial and formalistic exercise that depends on the choice of comparator groups.

5) Section 15(2)

The Supreme Court first considered the relationship between sections 15(1) and 15(2) of the *Charter* in *Lovelace v. Ontario.*[87] It held that section 15(2) should not be considered as a defence or an exemption from section 15(1) but rather as an "interpretative aid" that is "confirmatory and supplementary" to section 15(1) of the *Charter*. Reading sections 15(1) and 15(2) together "ensures the internal coherence of the *Charter* as a working statute."[88] The Court thus held that a casino project targeting Aboriginal bands did not violate the section 15(1) rights of Aboriginal people not organized in bands. The casino was a partnered and ameliorative program and it responded to the actual circumstances and abilities of the bands. The Court conducted a full section 15 analysis under the *Law* test and much depended on its conclusion that there was a correspondence between the program and providing benefits to bands and not other Aboriginal people. This conclusion about correspondence, however, could be debated. It avoided the claimant's

---

83 *Canadian Foundation for Children*, above note 2.
84 [2003] 2 S.C.R. 504 [*Martin*].
85 *Canadian Foundation for Children*, above note 2 at paras. 97–98.
86 *Kapp*, above note 49 at para. 22.
87 [2000] 1 S.C.R. 950, 188 D.L.R. (4th) 193.
88 *Ibid.* at paras. 105–6.

arguments that, as Aboriginal people who were not in government recognized bands, they were equally, if not more disadvantaged, as the bands that were the beneficiary of the casino project. *Lovelace* meant that governments would not know whether a law or program would be accepted as a legitimate affirmative action measure to ameliorate the conditions of a disadvantaged group until a full section 15 analysis was conducted in each case.

In the 2008 decision in *R. v. Kapp*[89] the Court changed course from the idea that section 15(2) was only an interpretative aid to section 15. The Court in *Kapp* held that if the government could demonstrate that a law or program satisfies the criteria of section 15(2), it would be unnecessary to determine whether it violated section 15(1). In other words, a law would not violate section 15(1) if the government demonstrates under section 15(2) that one of its purposes in enacting the law was to ameliorate the conditions of a disadvantaged group(s). The government will have an ameliorative purpose if it was rational for the state to conclude that the means chosen would contribute to amelioration.[90] The focus is on the government's purposes, not the effects of the programs. It is not necessary that the government's sole purpose be the amelioration of the conditions of disadvantaged groups, and in this case one of the purposes of the program was to manage the fishery. It is also not necessary that every member of the targeted disadvantaged group be disadvantaged. [91] In the result, the Court held that fishing preferences granted to three Aboriginal bands fell under section 15(2) because they rationally addressed long standing disadvantages suffered by Aboriginal people that continue to this day. The fact that some individual members of the bands did not suffer disadvantage "does not negate the group disadvantage suffered by band members."[92]

The new test under section 15(2), articulated in *Kapp*, should prove simpler than the previous test in *Lovelace* that required a full section 15 analysis in all cases. Governments will now know that their section 15(2) analysis will be based largely on the purposes that underlie the impugned law or program and not on the effects that the program may have on others. *Kapp* was, however, a simpler case than *Lovelace* because the applicants did not claim to be a similar disadvantaged group claiming that the affirmative action program was under-inclusive. The abandonment of full section 15 analysis for section 15(2) programs may make it even more difficult for affirmative action programs to be

---

89 *Kapp*, above note 49.
90 *Ibid.* at paras 49–51.
91 *Ibid.* at para 55.
92 *Ibid.* at para 59.

successfully challenged on the basis that they are unconstitutionally under-inclusive.

I. GROUNDS OF DISCRIMINATION

So far, we have discussed section 15 of the *Charter* in terms of its analytical parts. In what follows, we take a more contextual and holistic approach by examining the reasoning, outcomes, and remedies in section 15 cases in some of the most important contexts of potential discrimination.

1) Discrimination against Gays and Lesbians

In *Egan v. Canada*,[93] the Supreme Court unanimously accepted sexual orientation as an analogous ground of discrimination. La Forest J. stated

> that whether or not sexual orientation is based on biological or physiological factors, which may be a matter of some controversy, it is a deeply personal characteristic that is either unchangeable or changeable only at unacceptable personal costs, and so falls within the ambit of section 15 protection as being analogous to the enumerated grounds.

Cory J. stressed the historical disadvantage and prejudice suffered by gays and lesbians and the decisions to include sexual orientation as a prohibited ground of discrimination in most human rights codes. La Forest J., with the concurrence of three other judges, however, held that the exclusion of same-sex couples from old-age security benefits did not violate section 15 of the *Charter* because the exclusion of such couples was relevant to the purposes of the legislation. Cory J. with the concurrence of three other judges held that the exclusion of same-sex couples constituted unjustified discrimination. Sopinka J. was the decisive fifth vote. He held that the exclusion violated section 15 of the *Charter* but was justified under section 1 because the government was entitled to deference in deciding whether to extend benefits to same-sex couples. He noted that this was the Court's first case to recognize sexual orientation as an analogous ground of discrimination and concluded that "given the fact that equating same sex couples with heterosexual spouses, either married or unmarried, is still generally regarded

---

93   *Egan*, above note 24.

as a novel concept, I am not prepared to say that by its inaction to date the government has disentitled itself to rely on s. 1 of the *Charter*."[94]

In *Vriend v. Alberta*,[95] the Supreme Court held that the omission of protection against discrimination on the basis of sexual orientation from Alberta's human rights code constituted unjustified discrimination against gays and lesbians. Although the human rights code regulated private conduct and the discrimination was in the form of a legislative omission, the Court held that the *Charter* still applied to the decision of the Alberta legislature to exclude sexual orientation. The omission of sexual orientation imposed burdens on gays and lesbians by making them vulnerable to private discrimination on the basis of sexual orientation in a manner that heterosexuals were not exposed to discrimination. The Court strongly stated: "the exclusion sends a message to all Albertans that it is permissible, and perhaps even acceptable, to discriminate against individuals on the basis of their sexual orientation."[96] With one judge dissenting, the Court decided that the appropriate remedy was to read sexual orientation into Alberta's human rights code as opposed to striking the entire code down subject to a suspended declaration of invalidity.

A year later in *M. v. H.*,[97] the Supreme Court applied the *Law* analysis to hold that the limitation of support provisions in Ontario's family law legislation to opposite-sex partners was an unjustified violation of section 15 of the *Charter*. The Court held that the law imposed a differential burden on same-sex partners who could not avail themselves of court-ordered support payments. Following *Egan* and *Vriend*, this differential treatment was on the analogous ground of sexual orientation. Finally, the differential treatment resulted in substantive discrimination because it was based on stereotypes that same-sex partnerships could not be as lasting or as meaningful as heterosexual partnerships. The majority of the Court rejected the idea that an ameliorative purpose of ensuring the fair treatment of women after the break up of a common-law partnership justified the exclusion of same-sex partners. The Court declared the Ontario law to be invalid subject to a six-month period of suspension during which the Ontario legislature responded by adding the category of "same-sex partners" to much of its legislation conferring spousal benefits and obligations. In *Little Sisters Book and Art Emporium v. Canada (Minister of Justice)*,[98] which came a year after

94 *Ibid.* at 576 (S.C.R.).
95 *Vriend*, above note 59.
96 *Ibid.* at para. 101 (S.C.R.).
97 *M. v. H.*, above note 59.
98 [2000] 2 S.C.R. 1120, 193 D.L.R. (4th) 193 at para. 120.

M. v. H., the Court found that customs authorities had violated section 15 and discriminated on the basis of sexual orientation by targeting the imports of a gay and lesbian book store when they did not target the imports of "so-called XXX sex shops that specialize in hard core heterosexual material even though, unlike in the case of Little Sisters, little if any of their stock is found routinely on display in the Vancouver Public Library."[99] The Court found that this discrimination on the basis of sexual orientation was the result of the actions of customs officials and it was not authorized in customs legislation allowing officials to detain obscene material. The majority of the Court determined that the appropriate remedy was a declaration that section 15 rights had been violated. A minority of the Court felt this was not a strong enough remedy given the systemic problems with the administration of the legislation. The minority would have struck down the customs legislation subject to an eighteen-month period of suspension.

The most important development in this area has been debate concerning same-sex marriage. The best-known decisions were those of the Courts of Appeal of British Columbia[100] and Ontario[101] and a trial level decision in Quebec,[102] all of which struck down the traditional common law opposite-sex definition of marriage. The reasoning of the Court of Appeal for Ontario is illustrative. The court identified an 1866 English decision as the source of opposite-sex definition of marriage at common law. In that early case, Lord Penzance wrote: "I conceive that marriage, as understood in Christendom, may for this purpose be defined as the voluntary union for life of one man and one woman, to the exclusion of all others."[103] The Court of Appeal rejected the argument that the word "marriage," as used in the *Constitution Act, 1867*, constitutionally entrenched the legal definition of marriage that existed at the time of Confederation as contrary to the notion of the constitution as a "living tree" capable of growth and change over time. The court also declined to find that the issue engaged freedom of religion under section 2(a) of the *Charter*, holding that "[t]his case is solely about the legal institute of marriage. It is not about the religious validity or invalidity

---

99   *Ibid.*

100 *EGALE Canada Inc. v. Canada (Attorney General)* (2003), 225 D.L.R. (4th) 472 (B.C.C.A.), rev'g [2001] 11 W.W.R. 685 (B.C.S.C.).

101 *Halpern v. Canada (Attorney General)* (2003), 65 O.R. (3d) 161 (C.A.), varying (2002), 60 O.R. (3d) 321 (Div. Ct.) [*Halpern*].

102 *Hendricks v. Quebec (Procureur général)*, [2002] R.J.Q. 2506 (Sup. Ct.).

103 *Hyde v. Hyde and Woodmansee* (1866), L.R. 1 P.&D. 130 at 133, a case dealing with the validity of a potentially polygamous marriage.

of various forms of marriage."[104] Turning to section 15(1), the Court of Appeal applied the *Law* test in a straightforward manner. It found that the opposite-sex definition of marriage created a formal distinction between opposite-sex couples and same-sex couples on the basis of their sexual orientation. Finally, it found that an analysis of the contextual factors pointed to the conclusion that the opposite-sex definition of marriage resulted in substantive discrimination. Unlike the Quebec and British Columbia courts, which had delayed their declarations of invalidity, the Ontario Court of Appeal refused to grant a temporary suspension of invalidity and struck down the opposite-sex definition of marriage immediately.

What happened next is interesting from the point of view of legal process. The Liberal government voiced its support for gay marriage and its intention to pass legislation enshrining a neutral definition. Rather than appeal any of the lower court decisions, it directed a reference to the Supreme Court asking about the constitutionality of proposed legislation stating (1) that marriage for civil purposes is the lawful union of two persons to the exclusion of all others and (2) that nothing about that definition would affect the freedom of religious officials to refuse to perform marriages that conflict with their religious beliefs. The Supreme Court held that the first part of this legislation was within the jurisdiction of Parliament under section 91(26) of the *Constitution Act, 1867*, but not the second, since only the provinces are able to legislate exemptions to existing requirements regarding the solemnization of marriage. The Court then held that the proposed definition of marriage was consistent with the *Charter*. Importantly, the Court also found that it did not trench upon the equality rights or the freedom of religion of groups who oppose gay marriage. With respect to equality rights, the Court found that the new definition did not draw any distinctions nor did it withhold any benefits or impose burdens on a differential basis. For that reason, the section 15 challenge to the new definition failed on the first step of *Law*. With respect to freedom of religion, the Court held that no conflict had been shown to exist between the new definition and the section 2(a) rights of those who opposed same-sex marriages. The Court also found that freedom of religion would protect religious officials from being compelled by the government to perform same-sex marriages contrary to their religious beliefs.

The Supreme Court, however, declined to answer arguably the most important of the reference questions: whether the opposite-sex requirement for marriage was consistent with the *Charter*. The Court held that

---

104 *Halpern*, above note 101 at para. 53.

it would be "unwise and inappropriate to answer the question"[105] because the government had said it intended to proceed to amend the marriage definition regardless of the answer. It also refused to answer because the parties to the lower court decisions had relied on the findings that the opposite-sex definition of marriage was unconstitutional. Many same-sex couples had since wed. The Court stated that it would be unfair to jeopardize the rights acquired through litigation by answering the reference question in the affirmative, which was one possible outcome. Finally, the Court held that answering the question in the negative would potentially undermine the government's stated goal of achieving uniformity in respect of civil marriage across Canada. This was in part because it was unclear what the effect of an advisory opinion would have on the lower court opinions that had held the opposite-sex definition unconstitutional. As the Court said, "[t]he result would be confusion, not uniformity."[106] As a result, the Supreme Court itself has not addressed the constitutionality of the opposite-sex definition of marriage, but in 2005 Parliament passed the *Civil Marriage Act*, making same-sex marriage the law across Canada.[107]

In *Hislop v. Canada*,[108] the Court dealt with a set of complex legislative amendments designed to provide but also limit retroactive benefits that same-sex partners could receive under the self-funded *Canada Pension Plan*. The Court held that two legislative provisions that limited the benefits of same-sex partners violated section 15 of the *Charter*. Both provisions discriminated against same-sex couples as compared to heterosexual couples. The Court rejected the government's arguments that the comparator group should be further defined to include express distinctions in the impugned legislation, or that section 15 should be interpreted in a manner that recognized the evolution in the legal and social recognition of same-sex couples.[109] In both cases, the Court held that the government had failed to demonstrate a pressing objective for the different treatment of same-sex couples under section 1 of the *Charter*.[110] These holdings of the Court are consistent with its strong recognition of the equality rights of gays and lesbians in the cases discussed above.

---

105 *Same-Sex Marriage Reference*, above note 3 at para. 64.
106 *Ibid.* at para. 70.
107 Bill C-38, *An Act Respecting Certain Aspects of Legal Capacity for Marriage for Civil Purposes*, 1st Sess., 38th Parl., 2005 (as passed by the House of Commons, 28 June 2005).
108 [2007] 1 S.C.R. 429.
109 *Ibid.* at paras. 38, 41.
110 *Ibid.* at paras. 55, 65.

The Court, however, refused to recognize claims that would have given same-sex couples pension benefits retroactive to the coming into force of equality rights on 17 April 1985. The Court refused to invalidate a facially neutral provision which limited all survivors arrear benefits to 12 months before the applications were received. The plaintiffs argued that this provision had adverse effects on same-sex partners who were unable, until remedial legislation was adopted in 2000, to claim survivor benefits. They also argued that they should be entitled to fully retroactive benefits from when the equality rights in section 15 of the *Charter* took effect. The Court held that it need not decide the validity of this adverse effect discrimination claim because even if the claim was valid, it would not be appropriate to award the retroactive remedy that the applicants had requested. The Court's decision on remedy will be more fully examined in chapter 17, but the Court found that the government had placed reasonable reliance on the law as it existed before *M. v. H.* The Court also justified its decision not to provide retroactive relief on the basis that the plaintiffs would receive some relief.

2) Age Discrimination

McKinney,[111] the first significant case after *Andrews*, dealt with a constitutional challenge to the mandatory retirement at age sixty-five years of university professors employed at a number of Ontario institutions. Two companion cases, *Harrison* and *Stoffman*, dealt with mandatory retirement in British Columbia universities and hospitals.[112] In each of these cases, there was a preliminary issue of whether the *Charter* applied directly to universities and hospitals so as to allow a *Charter* challenge to their employment policies, as discussed above in chapter 6. The majority of the Supreme Court of Canada held that the *Charter* did not apply, but nevertheless proceeded to deal with the constitutionality of the mandatory-retirement policies. In *McKinney* and *Harrison*, the provincial human rights codes were also challenged, since both protected against discrimination in employment on the basis of age, but then defined age with an upper limit of sixty-five years, thereby precluding complaints by workers faced with mandatory retirement at age sixty-five. If that cap on the definition was impermissible under the *Charter*, mandatory retirement could be challenged through a hu-

---

111 *McKinney v. University of Guelph*, [1990] 3 S.C.R. 229, 76 D.L.R. (4th) 545 [*McKinney*].

112 *Harrison v. University of British Columbia*, [1990] 3 S.C.R. 451, [1991] 77 D.L.R. (4th) 55 [*Harrison*]; *Stoffman v. Vancouver General Hospital*, [1990] 3 S.C.R. 483, 76 D.L.R. (4th) 700 [*Stoffman*].

man rights complaint, and past cases involving mandatory retirement at ages caught by the human rights codes would have succeeded.[113]

Speaking for the majority in *McKinney*, La Forest J. noted that age, as a ground of discrimination, differed from other enumerated grounds in section 15, in that "[t]here is a general relationship between advancing age and declining ability." While courts should protect against age-based discrimination resulting from unfounded assumptions or stereotypes about the capacity of older individuals, courts should also be conscious of the justification for granting or withholding certain social benefits on the basis of age. La Forest J. found that both mandatory retirement and the cap on age in the human rights codes violated section 15 because of the burden imposed on older workers, but he then went on to apply a relaxed test under section 1 of the *Charter*. In so doing, he stressed the complexity of mandatory-retirement schemes, which also protected older workers through deferred-compensation arrangements and by allowing departure from the workplace in dignity without unpleasant merit reviews. As well, mandatory retirement served the need for renewal through hiring younger workers with different skills and qualities. Moreover, with respect to the human rights codes' protection for existing mandatory-retirement schemes, La Forest J. noted that their widespread use in the private sector was generally beneficial in nature. This justified the legislative action, which provided a reasonable balance of competing social values. Finally, with respect to the human rights codes, La Forest J. noted that a legislature should be permitted to proceed incrementally in enacting legislation addressing the problems of discrimination, provided that there was a reasonable basis for its cut-off point, as there was here.

Both Wilson and L'Heureux-Dubé JJ. dissented. In their view, the legislation and the mandatory-retirement policies could not be justified under section 1 since there were other ways to meet the concerns for productivity and employment turnover that would allow a more individualized treatment of older workers.

In a later case, the Supreme Court unanimously concluded that there was age discrimination in the *Unemployment Insurance Act* provision preventing those over sixty-five from receiving insurance benefits and restricting them to a lump-sum payment equivalent to three weeks' benefits. This restriction could not be justified, said the Court, because it denied access to benefits to those over sixty-five who needed to con-

---

113 For example, *Ontario (Human Rights Commission) v. Etobicoke (Borough)*, [1982] 1 S.C.R. 202, 132 D.L.R. (3d) 14.

tinue to work because of inadequate pension entitlements.[114] The Court struck down the exclusion of senior citizens, effectively extending the benefits to this group.

Three of the most important and controversial equality rights cases have involved claims of age discrimination, including *Law*,[115] the leading case. As discussed above, *Law* involved restrictions on survivors benefits that affected widows and widowers under the age of forty-five. Although this clearly denied a benefit on the basis of age, the Supreme Court found no substantive discrimination. The age distinction was not based upon stereotypes about the respective needs of younger and older persons. Persons under forty-five years of age were not a disadvantaged group and they would eventually receive the survivor's pension upon reaching sixty-five years of age.

Gosselin v. Quebec (Attorney General)[116] involved a challenge to Quebec's social welfare scheme lowering the amount of social assistance payable to those under thirty unless they participated in education or work experience programs. The scheme was challenged under section 15 on the ground of age discrimination, as well as under section 7 of the *Charter*, and section 45 of the Quebec *Charter of Human Rights and Freedoms*, on the ground that it failed to provide an adequate standard of living. The discussion here will focus on section 15. The debate on section 7 is dealt with in chapter 13.

By a majority, the Supreme Court rejected the section 15 challenge. The legislation distinguished welfare recipients under thirty from those thirty years and older, and thereby created a distinction based on an enumerated ground. However, the majority concluded that the claim should be rejected on the basis of the first two contextual factors from *Law*, historical disadvantage and correspondence. McLachlin C.J.C. found that, "[b]oth as a general matter, and based on the evidence and our understanding of society, young adults as a class simply do not seem especially vulnerable and undervalued"[117] and that, "[i]f anything, people under 30 appear to be advantaged over older people in finding employment."[118] With respect to the second factor, she found that the purpose and design of the legislative scheme "far from being stereotypical or arbitrary, corresponded to the actual needs and circumstances of

---

114 *Canada (Employment and Immigration Commission) v. Tétreault-Gadoury*, [1991] 2 S.C.R. 22, 81 D.L.R. (4th) 358.

115 *Law*, above note 40.

116 *Gosselin*, above note 77.

117 *Ibid.* at para. 33.

118 *Ibid.* at para. 34.

individuals under 30"[119] because the scheme was designed to encourage young adults to further their education and training so that they could become more employable. Moreover, she relied on the finding of the trial judge that Ms. Gosselin had failed to show any adverse effects to welfare recipients under the age of thirty. Ultimately, McLachlin C.J.C. found as follows:

> A reasonable welfare recipient under 30 might have concluded that the program was harsh, perhaps even misguided. (As noted, it eventually was repealed.) But she would not reasonably have concluded that it treated younger people as less worthy or less deserving of respect in a way that had the purpose or effect of marginalizing or denigrating younger people in our society. If anything, she would have concluded that the program treated young people as more able than older people to benefit from training and education, more able to get and retain a job, and more able to adapt to their situations and become fully participating and contributing members of society.[120]

The dissenting judges all took exception to McLachlin C.J.C.'s analysis to varying degrees. L'Heureux-Dubé J. wrote that McLachlin C.J.C.'s decision threatened to "presumptively exclude youth from s. 15 protection."[121] Bastarache J. argued that McLachlin C.J.C. did not give sufficient weight to the fact that age was enumerated in section 15, and so distinctions based on age are inherently suspect. Moreover, Bastarache J. was prepared to recognize that welfare recipients as a class constituted a vulnerable group, something that McLachlin C.J.C. said was irrelevant when considering an age-based distinction between two different groups of welfare recipients.

At issue in *Canadian Foundation for Children*[122] was section 43 of the *Criminal Code*, which allows parents or teachers to use corrective force towards children. As with *Gosselin*, the case also involved a section 7 claim, discussed in chapter 13.

McLachlin C.J.C. wrote the majority judgment. She interpreted the reach of the section 43 defence narrowly, holding that despite its broad language, it does not apply when force is used against children under two or over twelve, does not allow for the use of objects or blows or slaps to the head, and that teachers can only apply force to remove a child from the classroom. The section 15 claim had to be measured accordingly. McLachlin C.J.C. ruled that the claim could not be assessed

119 *Ibid.* at para. 38.
120 *Ibid.* at para. 69.
121 *Ibid.* at para. 110.
122 *Canadian Foundation for Children*, above note 2.

from the perspective of a reasonable preschooler. Rather, McLachlin C.J.C. chose to assess the claim from the perspective of "a reasonable person acting on behalf of a child."[123] She held that the first two parts of the *Law* test were met because section 43 makes a distinction on the basis of age. Furthermore, she held that three of the four elements of the *Law* test favoured a finding of discrimination in this case: children are a highly vulnerable group, whose physical integrity was at stake as a result of a statutory provision that was not aimed at ameliorating the situation of an even more disadvantaged group. The key element of McLachlin C.J.C.'s section 15 analysis, however, was the correspondence factor from *Law*. Section 43, she held, struck a balance between the need to protect children from abuse and the need to provide them with guidance and discipline.[124]

Both Binnie and Deschamps JJ., in dissent, found violations of section 15, although Binnie J. found that section 43 could be justified under section 1 with respect to parents. (Arbour J. wrote the third dissenting opinion, finding an unjustified infringement of section 7.) Binnie J. was particularly critical of the Chief Justice's reliance on the correspondence factor, through which he said she had made the scope of section 15 protection too narrow. The Chief Justice, he argued, had imported into the correspondence factor matters best left to section 1 and, moreover, her analysis threatened to revive the idea of relevancy with respect to a statute's functional values that was adopted by some members of the Court during the mid-1990s. Like Binnie J., Deschamps J. found a violation of section 15. Her criticism of the majority, however, focused on its narrow interpretation of section 43. Because the provision, properly interpreted, in fact allowed a broader range of "corrective force" than the majority suggested, she found that the provision did not correspond to the actual needs and capacities of children: "It cannot be seriously argued that children need corporal punishment to grow and learn."[125]

In *A.C. v. Manitoba (Director of Child and Family Services)*,[126] the Supreme Court held that a provincial law that allowed medically necessary treatment to be ordered when in the best interests of children under 16 years of age did not violate the equality rights. Abella J. stressed that the law did not engage any "disadvantaging prejudice or stereotype based on age" because it allowed those under 16 years of age to argue that they were mature enough to make the decision.[127] Chief

---

123 *Ibid.* at para. 53.
124 *Ibid.* at paras. 58–59.
125 *Ibid.* at para. 230.
126 *A.C. v. Manitoba*, above note 55.
127 *Ibid.* at para. 111.

Justice McLachlin also concluded that there was no section 15 violation because the age-based distinction "is ameliorative, not invidious. First, it aims at protecting the interests of minors as a vulnerable group. Second, it protects the members of the targeted group—children under 16—in a way that gives the individual child a degree of input into the ultimate decision on treatment. In my view, this is sufficient to demonstrate that the distinction drawn by the Act, while based on an enumerated ground, is not discriminatory within the meaning of s. 15."[128]

3) Disability

In *Swain*,[129] the Supreme Court upheld a common law rule allowing the Crown to raise the issue of the accused's insanity in a criminal trial, either after conviction or if the accused led evidence that put his capacity for criminal intent in question. Even though this rule drew a distinction on the basis of mental disability, there was no discrimination within section 15 of the *Charter*, said Lamer C.J.C., because the rule did not impose a burden or disadvantage on those with mental disabilities. In his words, "it is a principle of fundamental justice that the criminal justice system not convict a person who was insane at the time of the offence."[130] This case raised the question whether the determination of burdens and disadvantages should be made from the perspective of the rights claimant or from a more objective standpoint. From Swain's perspective, it might well seem burdensome to allow the Crown to raise the issue of his insanity, if the outcome was an acquittal by reason of insanity that would lead to indeterminate detention because of his mental state. In contrast, and more beneficial from his perspective, a conviction might have resulted in a fixed sentence, perhaps without incarceration.

In the subsequent case of *Winko v. British Columbia*,[131] the Supreme Court held that provisions providing for the possibly indeterminate detention of those found not criminally responsible because of a mental disorder did not violate section 15 of the *Charter*. Although a distinction between accused persons was drawn on the basis of mental disorder, there was no substantive discrimination. The legislation did not presume or stereotype those with mental disorders as dangerous but rather required an individualized demonstration of a significant threat

---

128 *Ibid.* at para. 152.
129 *R. v. Swain*, [1991] 1 S.C.R. 933, 63 C.C.C. (3d) 481 [*Swain*].
130 *Ibid.* at 509 (C.C.C.).
131 [1999] 2 S.C.R. 625, 175 D.L.R. (4th) 193.

to the public. The appropriate perspective was a reasonable person with the same characteristics as the *Charter* applicant.

The question of perspective was also raised in *Eaton*,[132] a case involving a challenge to the special-education provisions in Ontario under which a child with cerebral palsy had been assigned to a special-education class after three years in an integrated classroom. Her counsel argued that the decision contravened section 15 of the *Charter*, because it discriminated on the basis of physical disability. The Supreme Court of Canada disagreed, concluding that while integrated classes might benefit some with disabilities, it might be a burden to others. A special-education tribunal, after considering extensive evidence about the child's abilities and needs, had concluded that a special classroom was in her best interests. Therefore, said the Court, there was no discrimination in that there was no burden or disadvantage placed on the child, nor was she denied a benefit. Genuine and subjective perceptions by a *Charter* applicant of discrimination are not sufficient. There must also be an objective basis for the finding of discrimination so that a reasonable person with the same characteristics and circumstances of the *Charter* applicant would perceive there to be discrimination and denial of human dignity.

While *Eaton* was a disappointment to many advocates of the rights of those with disabilities, the Supreme Court's subsequent decision in *Eldridge*[133] was greeted with delight. In that case, individuals with hearing disabilities successfully argued that the failure to provide them with sign-language interpreters when they receive medical services violated section 15 of the *Charter* and was not justified under section 1. This was a case of adverse-effects discrimination, said the Court, which essentially adopted the same approach here as has been used in the interpretation of human rights codes. In the words of La Forest J., sign-language interpretation "is the means by which deaf persons may receive the same quality of medical care as the hearing population."[134] He then went on to say that the *Charter* includes a duty to make reasonable accommodation, up to the point of undue hardship, for those adversely affected by a rule—a principle that he concluded should be addressed under section 1.[135] Clearly, cost would be a relevant consideration, since governments have to make difficult decisions about the appropriate allocation of limited public resources. The Court issued a declaration

---

132 *Eaton*, above note 39.
133 *Eldridge*, above note 37.
134 *Ibid.* at 620 (D.L.R.).
135 *Ibid.* at 624 (D.L.R.).

with a six-month delay to allow governments to take steps to comply with this judgment.

Although the section 15 claim advanced in *Granovsky v. Canada*[136] — the first case following *Law* dealing with disability rights — was dismissed, the Supreme Court did embrace a broad definition of disability for section 15 purposes. The claimant failed to qualify for a *Canada Pension Plan* benefit because a temporary disability had prevented him from working and making pension contributions for the required period. Had the interruption in making contributions resulted from a permanent disability, the claimant would have qualified for the benefit. Binnie J., writing for the Court, found there was no violation of the human dignity requirement. Although there was differential treatment on the basis of the enumerated grounds of disability, the Court held that Parliament was entitled to ameliorate the conditions of the permanently disabled without extending the same benefit to those temporarily disabled and to do so did not stigmatize or deny the dignity of the temporarily disabled.

While the claim was rejected, the Court did embrace a broad definition of disability for the purposes of *Charter* analysis. The government had been dismissive of Mr. Granovsky's disability, "suggesting disbelief that a severe backache could rise to the level of a constitutional challenge."[137] Binnie J., however, stated that in disability claims the focus should not be on the nature of the claimant's impairment, but rather on the government response to that impairment. He divided the idea of "disability" into three parts: the actual physical or mental impairment; the functional limitation that arises as a result of that impairment; and the socially constructed handicap, as a result of which the disabled individual may be marginalized:

> Section 15(1) ensures that governments may not, intentionally or through a failure of appropriate accommodation, stigmatize the underlying physical or mental impairment, or attribute functional limitations to the individual that the underlying physical or mental impairment does not entail, or fail to recognize the added burdens which persons with disabilities may encounter in achieving self-fulfilment in a world relentlessly oriented to the able-bodied.[138]

The Court's nuanced appreciation of the nature of disability discrimination was further demonstrated in *Nova Scotia (Workers' Com-*

136 [2000] 1 S.C.R. 703 [*Granovsky*].
137 *Ibid.* at para. 32.
138 *Ibid.* at para. 33.

pensation Board) v. Martin; Nova Scotia (Workers' Compensation Board) v. Laseur.[139] The claimants suffered from chronic pain and were entitled to participate in a four-week "functional restoration program" but were excluded from the broad range of benefits granted to workers suffering from other disabilities by Nova Scotia's workers' compensation scheme. Gonthier J., writing for the Court, held that this exclusion violated section 15(1) of the *Charter* on the basis of disability and could not be justified under section 1. In doing so, he elaborated on the complex nature of disability-based equality claims, in two respects. First, he held a disabled claimant could properly invoke as a comparator another group suffering from a disability of a different type or severity. Thus, in this case, the claimants suffering from chronic back pain could compare themselves to workers with other injuries. Second, when addressing the third step of the *Law* analysis, Gonthier J. suggested that, in disability claims, correspondence would usually be the determinative contextual factor. The reason is that disabilities vary widely from person to person, and programs aimed at accommodating them should be tailored to their individual needs insofar as is reasonable:

> it is vital to keep in mind the rationale underlying the prohibition of discrimination based on disability. As I stated above, this rationale is to allow for the recognition of the special needs and actual capacities of persons affected by a broad variety of different disabilities in many different social contexts. In accordance with this rationale, s. 15(1) requires a considerable degree of reasonable accommodation and adaptation of state action to the circumstances of particular individuals with disabilities. Of course, classification and standardization are in many cases necessary evils, but they should always be implemented in such a way as to preserve the essential human dignity of individuals.[140]

Gonthier J. therefore held: "I am unable to agree that the challenged provisions are sufficiently responsive to the needs and circumstances of chronic pain sufferers to satisfy the second contextual factor."[141] Thus, in both *Granovsky* and *Martin*, the Supreme Court has recognized the unique nature of disability claims and stated that the government has an obligation, within reasonable bounds, to accommodate the particular needs associated with particular forms of disabilities. Otherwise,

---

139 *Martin*, above note 84.
140 *Ibid.* at para. 93.
141 *Ibid.* at para. 97.

it may be compounding the actual physical or mental impairment of a disabled person and aggravating a socially constructed handicap.

In *Auton (Guardian ad litem of) v. British Columbia (Attorney General)*,[142] already discussed above, the Supreme Court rejected the claim of children suffering from autism for a specific form of therapy not provided under the province's medicare scheme. No doubt concerned about becoming embroiled in a complex debate about difficult choices regarding medicare funding, the Court held that the benefit claimed was not one provided by law as the legislation "does not promise that any Canadian will receive funding for all medically required treatment" but leaves funding for non-core medical services (a category found by the Court to include the services sought by the claimants) to the discretion of the province.[143]

4) Sex Discrimination

In several cases coming before the Supreme Court, section 15 *Charter* claims have alleged discrimination on the basis of sex, but few have succeeded. In *Hess*,[144] the accused challenged the statutory-rape provisions of the *Criminal Code*, which made it an offence for a male over fourteen years to have sexual intercourse with a female under that age. The accused argued that this was sex discrimination, because only men could be charged with the crime and only females could be the victims. Wilson J. held that there was no violation of section 15 here, since biological reality determined that only men could commit the offence: "[W]e are therefore dealing with an offence that involves an act that as a matter of biological fact only men over a certain age are capable of committing."[145] Because men and women are different in their ability to commit the offence, she held there to be no discrimination.

But what of the fact that a woman might have intercourse with a young male under fourteen and escape punishment? Does this not demonstrate that the law is non-inclusive on grounds of gender in its coverage of sexual offences against the young? It is up to the legislature to decide whether questions of morality and social disapprobation warrant criminalizing such conduct, and there is no discrimination involved in the legislature proceeding part-way, prohibiting only some sexual misconduct. In contrast, McLachlin J., with Gonthier J. concur-

---

142 *Auton*, above note 73.
143 *Ibid*. at para. 38.
144 *Hess*, above note 28.
145 *Ibid*. at 930 (S.C.R.).

ring, would have found a section 15 violation here, both because of the
burden that the offence placed on men but not women and because of
the protection provided for young females but not for young males.
However, she upheld the legislation as justifiable under section 1, since
it protected a particularly vulnerable group, young women. In any
event, after the "statutory rape" offence was struck down under section
7 of the *Charter*, Parliament enacted new gender neutral offences that
protected both girls and boys from sexual interference and could apply
to both male and female accused.

Wilson J.'s approach in *Hess* was troubling to some, because she
rejected the claim within section 15 itself. Her holding that the differential treatment was, in effect, justified and non-discriminatory because of the nature of the offence and the biological difference between
men and women seemed to import into section 15 itself the issues of
justification, which were usually left to the state to bring forward under
section 1.

Despite these concerns, a majority of the Court followed the same
approach in *Conway*.[146] This case rejected a challenge to the practice in
the prison system whereby male prisoners could be "frisk-searched"
and have their cell areas patrolled by female guards, while the practice in the women's penitentiary was to have women guards perform
these duties, except in emergency situations. In an unusually short
judgment, La Forest J. stated that it was "doubtful" that section 15 was
violated, "given the historical, biological and sociological differences
between men and women." More precisely, because of the history of
violence of men against women, cross-gender searching is "different
and more threatening for women than for men."[147] Note was also taken
of the ameliorative objective of employment equity for women in non-
traditional jobs such as prison guards. Thus, the issue of justification
seemed to enter into the finding of discrimination. In contrast, earlier
cases had suggested that, if the rights claimant felt burdened or disadvantaged by the rule because of sex, the justification would be discussed under section 1 with the government bearing the onus.

It is likely that the finding of no gender discrimination in both
Hess and *Conway* would be affirmed under the *Law* test. The *Charter*
applicant must demonstrate not only a disadvantage on the basis of the
enumerated ground of sex, but also substantive discrimination, and
an affront to human dignity. At this stage of section 15 analysis the
court will examine contextual factors such as whether there is a history

---

146   *Conway*, above note 27.
147   *Ibid.* at 214 (D.L.R.).

of disadvantage, whether, as indicated in *Conway*, there was an ameliorative purpose behind the legal disadvantage, and whether there is correspondence with actual abilities. It will be recalled, however, that some criticize the *Law* test for incorporating justificatory factors that should be left for the government to establish under section 1.

In *Symes v. Canada*,[148] the Supreme Court was asked to determine whether the provisions in the *Income Tax Act* limiting the amount that a taxpayer can deduct for childcare expenses violated section 15 of the *Charter*. This was a difficult case because it required the application of an adverse-effects approach to section 15. On its face, there was no indication of sex discrimination in section 63 of the *Income Tax Act*, which allowed a childcare deduction of a fixed amount to taxpayers while requiring that in families with two supporting parents, the deduction be taken by the lower-income earner. However, the claimant, a self-employed female lawyer, argued that the effect of the legislation was discriminatory against women. It limited her deduction to an amount less than the actual cost that she paid for childcare and prevented her from taking childcare as a business deduction elsewhere in the Act. She argued that this was sex discrimination, because women disproportionately bear the cost of childcare. The denial of a full deduction for childcare, while allowing full deductions for other items that disproportionately benefited businessmen, was said to violate section 15 of the *Charter*.

The majority in the Supreme Court, in reasons written by Iacobucci J., concluded that sex discrimination was not established. Even if the evidence showed that women disproportionately bear the burden of childcare in Canadian society, there was no evidence that they disproportionately bear the *cost* of childcare. In fact, the law requires both parents to provide support and care for their children. While Symes and her husband had made an agreement that she would pay for childcare, this did not change the situation: the cost of childcare is borne by families, not just women. Iacobucci J. went on to discuss the difficulties of proving adverse-effects discrimination. In particular, he noted that there are potential problems when a law has adverse effects on both men and women, implying that it will be difficult to conclude that there is sex discrimination where both men and women are burdened and benefited by legislation.

The Supreme Court allowed a section 15 *Charter* claim based on sex discrimination in *Trociuk v. British Columbia (Attorney General)*.[149] Mr.

---

148 [1993] 4 S.C.R. 695, 110 D.L.R. (4th) 470.
149 [2003] 1 S.C.R. 835 [*Trociuk*].

Trociuk was the estranged father of triplets whose former partner had "unacknowledged" him at the time of their children's birth, as she was permitted to do for any reason under provincial legislation. As a result of this unacknowledgment, she chose the children's last name as her own and his particulars were not recorded on their birth registrations. Moreover, the legislation provided him with no means of having the birth registrations altered. Writing for the Court, Deschamps J. held that the legislation clearly distinguished between mothers and fathers, and therefore resulted in differential treatment on the enumerated ground of sex. Deschamps J. went on to find that the differential treatment resulted in an impairment of dignity. She noted that "[p]arents have a significant interest in meaningfully participating in the lives of their children," with which the legislation interfered. The fact that fathers were not historically disadvantaged was not determinative. The unequal treatment sent the message that fathers' relationship with their children was less important than that of mothers. In addition, the legislation lumped fathers like Mr. Trociuk—who was unacknowledged arbitrarily—with other fathers who were unacknowledged because they had fathered a child through rape or incest: "Such a state of affairs is definitional of discrimination."[150] Finally, Deschamps J. found the section 15(1) violation could not be justified under section 1. The legislation sought to ensure that mothers would not hesitate to register their children because of shame or because of the fear of having a confrontation with the father. However, the Court held it would be a simple matter for the legislature to design a non-intrusive application process, under which a father could seek to have his particulars registered or to have a child's surname changed. Deschamps J. struck down the legislation but delayed the declaration of invalidity for twelve months. She also denied Mr. Trociuk's request to have the Court order his children's names changed immediately, but held that he would have to apply for the change under new legislation.

The most recent case on sex discrimination, *Newfoundland (Treasury Board) v. N.A.P.E.*,[151] is one of the most striking equality rights decisions reached by the Supreme Court under the *Charter*, although the result turns not on section 15 itself, but on the Court's determination that a violation of section 15(1) could be justified under section 1 because of the government's need to cut costs in the face of a severe fiscal crisis. For this reason, the case is discussed in greater detail in chapter 4. The case involved the *Public Sector Restraint Act*, under which the provincial government delayed by three years an agreement it had made to make

---

150 *Ibid.* at para. 24.
151 [2004] 3 S.C.R. 381 [*N.A.P.E.*].

pay equity increases to female employees in the health care sector and also extinguished any arrears owing for those three years, leading to a savings of $24 million. The government argued that it had to take this measure, among others, in response to a severe fiscal crisis. Binnie J., writing for the Court, had little trouble concluding that the *Public Sector Restraint Act* violated section 15(1). Not only did it affect women unequally, but its effect "was to affirm a policy of gender discrimination which the provincial government had itself denounced three years previously."[152] Nonetheless, Binnie J. found the Act could be justified because of the severity of Newfoundland's budgetary problems at the time. Only a year before, the Court had ruled in *Martin*, that "[b]udgetary considerations in and of themselves cannot normally be invoked as a free-standing pressing and substantial objective for the purposes of s. 1 of the *Charter*."[153] The *N.A.P.E.* decision surprised equality advocates who feared that serious violations of section 15 rights might now be more readily justified because of cost.

J. CONCLUSION

The Supreme Court has consistently given section 15 of the *Charter* a restricted meaning, requiring a claimant to show discrimination on a prohibited or analogous ground and substantive discrimination. These decisions seem to preclude wholesale judicial review of all laws that create burdens or confer benefits on some but not others. As in section 7, some may question whether the Court has achieved the appropriate balance between imposing definitional limits on the right and requiring the government to demonstrate under section 1 that limits on the right are reasonable and demonstrably justified. The Court's approach has disappointed those who saw section 15 as a charter of social rights capable of remedying injustice on a more general scale. However, it coincides with the Supreme Court's general inclination under the *Charter* to defer to legislative judgment on questions of distributive justice. It may be seen as consistent with the Court's cautious approach to the interpretation of "life, liberty and security of the person" in section 7 and its refusal to recognize property rights as protected under the *Charter*.

On the other hand, where substantive discrimination has been shown on a prohibited or analogous ground, the Court has adopted a rigorous approach designed to ensure that the promise of equality will

---

152 *Ibid.* at para. 34.
153 *Martin*, above note 84 at para. 109.

be respected. The Court has insisted that the equality guarantee mandates substantive review, avoiding a formalistic approach that would fail to take into account social reality. The Court has rejected the idea that a discriminatory intention must be shown, and it has proved willing to find a denial of equality from the failure to accommodate circumstances of actual disadvantage. It has also interpreted section 15(1) in a manner that, following section 15(2), defers to government's attempts to ameliorate the conditions of the disadvantaged even when this requires distinctions on enumerated or analogous grounds of discrimination. More recently in R. v. Kapp, the Court has confirmed its commitment to substantive equality and the prevention of disadvantage through prejudice and stereotyping in section 15(1) and held that a government can shelter a law from section 15(1) scrutiny by demonstrating that it has, as one of its purposes, the amelioration of the conditions of a disadvantaged group.

Section 15 has yielded significant gains for gays and lesbians, where the decisions of the Supreme Court can be applauded for leading public opinion. The Hislop case disappointed many in not awarding retroactive benefits to same-sex couples, but the Court's decision in that case revolved around an unwillingness to award retroactive remedies given that there had been substantial change in the law in this area and it did not decide whether a facially neutral law limiting retroactive pension benefits would constitute adverse-effects discrimination to same-sex couples who had historically been excluded from the plan. Until recently, the lot of the disabled had not been significantly improved by virtue of section 15, but the Supreme Court has now signalled a willingness to impose significant burdens on governments to ensure access to health services. While women's groups were among the most active in lobbying for a powerful equality guarantee, the gains to women from equality litigation have been modest. On the other hand, there can be little doubt that general public acceptance of and respect for gender equality has been enhanced by the Charter.

FURTHER READINGS

BINNIE, I., "Equality Rights in Canada: Judicial Usurpation or Missed Opportunity?" in G. Huscroft & P. Rishworth, *Litigating Rights* (Oxford: Hart Publishing, 2002)

BLACK, W., & L.A. SMITH, "The Equality Rights" in G.A. Beaudoin & E. Mendes, eds., *The Canadian Charter of Rights and Freedoms*, 4th ed. (Markham, ON: LexisNexis Butterworths, 2005)

BREDT, C., & A. DODEK, "Breaking the Law's Grip on Equality: A New Paradigm for Section 15" (2003) 20 Sup. Ct. L. Rev. (2d) 33

FARADAY, F., M. DENIKE, & K. STEPHENSON, eds., *Making Equality Rights Real; Securing Substantive Equality under the Charter* (Toronto: Irwin Law, 2006)

GIBSON, D., *The Law of the Charter: Equality Rights* (Toronto: Carswell, 1990)

GRESCHNER, D., "Does *Law* Advance the Cause of Equality?" (2001) 27 Queen's L.J. 299

HUGHES, P., "Resiling from Reconciling? Musings on *R. v. Kapp*" (2009) Sup. Ct. L. Rev. (2d) 23 (forthcoming)

JACKMAN, M., "Constitutional Contact with the Disparities in the World: Poverty as a Prohibited Ground of Discrimination under the Canadian *Charter* and Human Rights Law" (1994) 2 Rev. Const. Stud. 76

JACKMAN, M., Health Care and Equality: Is there a cure? (2007) 15 Health L.J. 87–141

LEPOFSKY, M.D., "A Report Card on the *Charter's* Guarantee of Equality to Persons with Disabilities after 10 Years—What Progress? What Prospects?" (1997) 7 N.J.C.L. 263

MARTIN, S., "Balancing Individual Rights to Equality and Social Goals" (2001) 80 Can. Bar Rev. 299

MCINTYRE, S., & S. RODGERS, eds., *Diminishing Returns: Inequality and the Canadian Charter of Rights and Freedoms* (Toronto: LexisNexis 2006)

MCLACHLIN, B., "Equality: The Most Difficult Right" (2001) 14 Sup. Ct. L. Rev. (2d) 17

MOREAU, S., "Equality Rights and the Relevance of Comparator Groups" (2006) 5 J. Law and Equality 81

MORRIS, M., & J. CHENG, "*Lovelace* and *Law* Revisited: The Substantive Equality promise of *Kapp*" (2009) Sup. Ct. L. Rev. (2d) (forthcoming)

REAUME, D., "The Relevance of Relevance to Equality Rights" (2006) 31 Queens L.J. 696

RYDER, B., C. FARIA, & E. LAWRENCE, "What's *Law* Good For? An Empirical Overview of *Charter* Equality Rights Decisions" (2004) 24 Sup. Ct. L. Rev. (2d) 103

SHEPPARD, C., "Grounds of Discrimination: Towards an Inclusive and Contextual Approach" (2002) 81 Can. Bar Rev. 893

CHAPTER 16

LANGUAGE RIGHTS

The appropriate status of the French and English languages has been an ongoing source of debate throughout Canadian history, both in the political and in the legal sphere. The Supreme Court has recognized that minority language rights involve both the rights of individuals and the rights of communities and that language rights must be interpreted in the context of Canada's history. The Court has commented:

> First, the members of the minority communities and their families, in every province and territory, must be given the opportunity to achieve their personal aspirations. Second, on the collective level, these language issues are related to the development and existence of the English-speaking minority in Quebec and the French-speaking minorities elsewhere in Canada. They also inevitably have an impact on how Quebec's French-speaking community perceives its future in Canada, since that community, which is in the majority in Quebec, is in the minority in Canada, and even more so in North America as a whole. To this picture must be added the serious difficulties resulting from the rate of assimilation of French-speaking minority groups outside Quebec, whose current language rights were acquired only recently, at considerable expense and with great difficulty. Thus, in interpreting these rights, the courts have a responsibility to reconcile sometimes divergent interests and priorities, and to be sensitive to the future of each language community. Our country's social context, demographics and history will therefore necessarily comprise the

backdrop for the analysis of language rights. Language rights cannot be analysed in the abstract, without regard for the historical context of the recognition thereof or for the concerns that the manner in which they are currently applied is meant to address.[1]

In other words, language rights are both rights for individuals and for collectivities and they are a crucial element of Canada's complex social contract. Minority language rights have been a part of Canada from the start and they were reaffirmed and expanded in the *Charter of Rights and Freedoms* for specific remedial purposes.

A. THE NATURE OF LANGUAGE RIGHTS

There is a range of options to protect ethnic communities, including those who share a common language. One possibility is to provide a degree of self-government for an ethnic or language community, giving it the powers to preserve and promote a distinct identity. In a federation, a language group may form the majority in a province while representing a minority in the country as a whole. Another option is to provide specific rights that permit groups to use their language or express their culture. Examples are separate-school rights, access to broadcasting outlets, or guarantees that government services will be provided in a certain language. Yet another device is protection against discrimination on the basis of language or culture, preventing the majority from disadvantaging the minority because of language or cultural practice. As will be seen, all of these options have been resorted to in the Canadian constitution.

The territorial principle, adopted in countries such as Belgium and Switzerland, leaves the determination of language rights to each province or territorial unit. The result is linguistic uniformity in most territorial units. While Canada's federal structure, with a francophone majority in Quebec and anglophone majorities in the other provinces, contains elements of the territorial principle, important features of the Canadian constitution see language as an aspect of the individual's personality, which is to be respected wherever one lives in Canada. Even though francophones are a small minority in most provinces, and anglophones are a minority in Quebec, both groups are given constitutional rights that limit the ability of provinces to impose linguistic uniformity.

---

1   *Solski (Tutor of) v. Quebec (Attorney General)*, 2005 SCC 14 at para. 5 [*Solski*].

Language rights in Canada are distinctive because they are "positive" in nature. They entitle an individual to certain action on the part of government, such as funding for schools, printing of bilingual statutes, and service from government offices in one's chosen official language. They are different from most other rights in the *Charter*, which constrain government from acting but do not require positive action. For example, the guarantee of freedom of expression does not, as a general rule, require the government to ensure equality of access to funds to ensure that one's voice is heard.[2] The positive nature of language rights requires governments to spend funds to respect language rights and to provide facilities for minority language education instruction where numbers warrant. In some cases, judges may play an active role in ensuring adequate remedies for such positive rights.[3]

B. THE *CONSTITUTION ACT, 1867*

The original Confederation bargain in 1867 was shaped very much by Canadian dualism—that is, by the desires and needs of French- and English-speaking communities to express and protect their identities. For the French-speaking population of Quebec, federalism was the primary method to protect its interests. Federalism ensured that the French-speaking majority in that province would have the powers necessary for cultural preservation—notably, education and civil law.

"Language" was not expressly mentioned as a subject of either federal or provincial legislative jurisdiction in sections 91 and 92 of the *Constitution Act, 1867*, the sections that distribute legislative powers between federal and provincial governments. Accordingly, it is treated as an "ancillary" matter—that is, either government can legislate with respect to language when acting within other assigned legislative fields. For example, Parliament has enacted the *Official Languages Act*, which regulates bilingualism in the federal public service.[4] Similarly, Quebec has the authority to require that French be used as the language of business in the province and to regulate the use of English in signs (although these laws are now subject to the *Charter* rights described below).[5]

---

2   *Native Women's Association of Canada v. Canada*, [1994] 3 S.C.R. 627, 119 D.L.R. (4th) 224.

3   *Doucet-Boudreau v. Nova Scotia*, [2003] 3 S.C.R. 3 [*Doucet-Boudreau*], discussed in chapter 17.

4   R.S.C. 1985, c. O-3. The constitutionality of this Act was determined in *Jones v. New Brunswick (A.G.)*, [1975] 2 S.C.R. 182, 45 D.L.R. (3d) 583 [*Jones*].

5   *Devine v. Quebec (A.G.)*, [1988] 2 S.C.R. 790, 55 D.L.R. (4th) 641.

In addition, the *Constitution Act, 1867*, contained limited positive rights protecting the use of the French and English languages in certain federal and Quebec institutions. Section 133 provides as follows:

> Either the English or French Language may be used by any Person in the Debates of the Houses of Parliament of Canada and of the House of the Legislature of Quebec; and both those Languages shall be used in the respective Records and Journals of those Houses; and either of those Languages may be used by any Person in any Pleading or Process issuing from any Court of Canada established under this Act, and in or from all or any of the Courts of Quebec.

This provision was duplicated in section 23 of the *Manitoba Act* upon Manitoba entering Confederation in 1870,[6] while the provinces of Saskatchewan and Alberta were required to comply with similar obligations by section 110 of the *North-West Territories Act*.[7] Those obligations continued after they became provinces in 1905 because of sections 16(1) of their constituent Acts.[8] However, these language rights were not entrenched and could be changed by legislation, and both provinces have since done so.[9]

The Supreme Court has held that these provisions provide a floor of guaranteed rights but that this does not prevent Parliament or the provincial legislatures from expanding on them.[10] Equally, however, prior to the *Charter*, section 133 of the *Constitution Act, 1867* did not prevent provinces from restricting the use of minority languages in areas other than those mentioned in the constitution. For example, the courts upheld the right of Ontario to abolish French-language instruction in Roman Catholic separate schools in 1912,[11] holding that language of instruction was not protected as an aspect of the denominational school rights conferred by section 93 of the *Constitution Act, 1867*.

---

6   *Manitoba Act, 1870*, S.C. 1870, c. 3, s. 23.

7   R.S.C. 1886, c. 50, s. 110, as amended S.C. 1891, c. 22, s. 18.

8   *Saskatchewan Act*, S.C. 1905, c. 42.

9   The state of language rights in these provinces was discussed by the Supreme Court of Canada in *R. v. Mercure*, [1988] 1 S.C.R. 234, 48 D.L.R. (4th) 1.

10 See *Jones*, above note 4.

11 This was upheld in *Ottawa Roman Catholic Separate School Board v. Mackell*, [1917] A.C. 62, 32 D.L.R. 1 (P.C.) and *Ottawa Roman Catholic Separate School Board v. Ottawa (City)*, [1917] A.C. 76, 32 D.L.R. 10 (P.C.).

C. LANGUAGE RIGHTS AND THE *CHARTER*

With the *Charter of Rights and Freedoms* came new protection for language rights. The language provisions in sections 16 to 23 of the *Charter* were a key component of the 1982 constitutional amendments. The government of Prime Minister Pierre Trudeau saw the *Charter* as a whole, and the language rights in particular, as a way to strengthen Canadians' attachment to their country.[12] The language rights expanded on section 133 of the 1867 constitution, affirming in section 16 that French and English are the two official languages of Canada. To emphasize their importance, sections 16 through 23 were not made subject to the legislative override in section 33 of the *Charter*. The clear message was that French and English minority language communities were to be supported and fostered throughout the country.

After declaring that English and French are the official languages of Canada and New Brunswick, section 16(1) goes on to say that these languages have "equality of status and equal rights and privileges as to their use in all institutions of the Parliament and government of Canada," while section 16(2) makes a similar statement with respect to the institutions of the legislature and government of New Brunswick.[13]

Sections 17 to 20 of the *Charter* affirm and expand on the former section 133 of the 1867 constitution. Section 17 guarantees the right to use English or French in debates and other proceedings of Parliament and the New Brunswick legislature, while section 18 guarantees that the statutes, records, and journals of the federal Parliament and the New Brunswick legislature must be in both languages and that both versions are of equal legal authority. Section 19 guarantees the right to use either French or English in pleadings or processes of federally established courts and those of New Brunswick. Finally, section 20 gives a right for the public to communicate in either language with the head or central office of an institution of the Parliament or government of Canada or any office of an institution of New Brunswick's government or legislature. An individual has a right to communicate with other Canadian government offices if there is "significant demand for communications with and services from that office" in French or English, or "due to the nature of the office, it is reasonable that communications with and services from that office" be available in both languages.

---

12   P.H. Russell, "The Political Purposes of the *Canadian Charter of Rights and Freedoms*" (1983) 61 Can. Bar Rev. 30.

13   The term "Canada" here refers to the federal level of government.

In addition to these "institutional bilingualism" provisions, there is a right to publicly funded minority language education in section 23 of the *Charter*. This section gives a right to education in the minority language of a province to two groups of children: those of Canadian citizens whose first language learned is that of the French or English minority in the province in which they reside,[14] and children of citizens educated in primary school in Canada in the language of the minority of the province in which they reside. Where some children of a family are receiving education in the minority language because of this section, all children in the family have the same entitlement. This right is qualified by the requirement that the numbers of children warrant receiving public funding for minority language instruction (section 23(3)(a)). Where the number warrants, the right extends to instruction in minority language educational facilities (section 23(3)(a)).

D. FREEDOM OF EXPRESSION AND LANGUAGE

In *Ford*, the Supreme Court of Canada held that the guarantee of freedom of expression in section 2(b) of the *Charter* includes the right to speak in the language of one's choice.[15] Accordingly, section 2(b) provides a check on government action designed to restrict the use of certain languages or to compel expression in a particular language. In effect, this interpretation of section 2(b) protects linguistic minorities against state discrimination and demands tolerance with respect to the use of their languages. Unlike the specific language rights of sections 16 to 23, section 2(b) protects all languages.

Ford, as we have seen, arose out of a challenge to Quebec's language legislation prohibiting the use of any language other than French on commercial signs or firm names. The Court rejected the argument that the constitution's specific language rights were a complete code that belied constitutional protection for any other languages. Instead, the Court quoted from an earlier decision involving the Manitoba language guarantees, where it had stated:

---

14   This clause is not in force in Quebec because of s. 59 of the *Constitution Act, 1982*. Section 59 responds to Quebec concerns about immigrants' refusal to assimilate into the francophone community.

15   *Ford v. Quebec (A.G.)*, [1988] 2 S.C.R. 712, 54 D.L.R. (4th) 577 [*Ford*], discussed in greater detail in chapter 9.

The importance of language rights is grounded in the essential role that language plays in human existence, development and dignity. It is through language that we are able to form concepts; to structure and order the world around us. Language bridges the gap between isolation and community, allowing humans to delineate the rights and duties they hold in respect of one another, and thus to live in society.[16]

The Court went on to say:

Language is so intimately related to the form and content of expression that there cannot be true freedom of expression by means of language if one is prohibited from using the language of one's choice. Language is not merely a means or medium of expression; it colours the content and meaning of expression.[17]

Language is a central way in which a group expresses its cultural identity and individuals express their personal identity. It follows that laws restricting the use of one's language will infringe section 2(b) and have to be justified under section 1.

It was acknowledged that Quebec had a pressing and substantial objective in enacting the legislation, given the vulnerable position of French in Quebec because of declining birth rates among francophones, a tendency for new immigrants to gravitate to the anglophone community in Quebec, and a predominance of English in the more important economic sectors. The Court accepted that the attempt to assure Quebeckers that the *visage linguistique* of Quebec reflected the predominance of French was a serious and legitimate objective. However, the Court was not satisfied that the achievement of this objective required the suppression of all other languages on public signs and in firm names. Rather, the judges concluded that a law requiring the predominance of French on a sign, while still allowing other communities to use their language, would be more consistent with *Charter* rights.

Although the language rights guaranteed by sections 16 to 23 are not subject to the override, the "signs" law was found to violate freedom of expression. As described in chapter 5, the aftermath was that the Quebec government invoked section 33 of the *Charter* in new legislation limiting the use of English in public signs. This law was then the subject of a successful complaint to the United Nations Human Rights Committee under the *International Covenant on Civil and Polit-*

---

16   *Reference Re Language Rights under s. 23 of Manitoba Act, 1870 and s. 133 of Constitution Act, 1867*, [1985] 1 S.C.R. 721, (*sub nom Reference Re Manitoba Language Rights*) 19 D.L.R. (4th) 1 at 19 [*Reference Re Manitoba Language Rights*].

17   *Ford*, above note 15 at 604 (D.L.R.).

ical Rights. The Committee's reasons echo those of the Supreme Court in *Ford*, stating that the law was an unreasonable limitation on freedom of expression.[18] The Quebec government allowed the override to expire after five years.

E. INTERPRETING LANGUAGE RIGHTS

1) Institutional Bilingualism

The Supreme Court has not been entirely consistent in its approach to the interpretation of language rights. In early cases involving section 133 of the *Constitution Act, 1867*, the Court took an expansive view. In *Blaikie (No. 1)*,[19] the Court held that, in deciding which institutions were covered by section 133, the words of the constitution should be given a progressive interpretation, taking into account the changing nature of courts and government since 1867. Although section 133 required that "laws" be in both French and English, the Court found that the guarantee should encompass regulations and delegated legislation, not just statutes, given the proliferation of this type of law making today. In addition, the term "courts" was interpreted to include adjudicative tribunals, like labour relations boards or human rights tribunals, since many legal disputes are now determined by these bodies.

This generous view of language rights was evident again in *Reference Re Manitoba Language Rights*.[20] In an earlier decision, *Manitoba (A.G.) v. Forest*,[21] the Supreme Court had found that legislation enacted by Manitoba in 1890 purporting to repeal the bilingualism requirement in section 23 of the *Manitoba Act, 1870* was unconstitutional. A reference was then launched to determine the effect of almost one hundred years of non-compliance with section 23. The Court held that the requirement was mandatory, so that all laws passed only in English were invalid. If the Court had stopped here, a large component of Mani-

---

18 *Ballantyne, Davidson & McIntyre v. Canada*, Communications Nos. 359/1989 and 385/1989, UN Doc. CCPR/C/47/D/359/1989 and 385/1989/Rev. 1 (1993). In para. 11.4, the Committee stated: "A State may choose one or more official languages, but it may not exclude, outside the spheres of public life, the freedom to express oneself in a language of one's choice."

19 *Quebec (A.G.) v. Blaikie (No. 1)*, [1979] 2 S.C.R. 1016, 101 D.L.R. (3d) 394. In *Quebec (A.G.) v. Blaikie (No. 2)*, [1981] 1 S.C.R. 312, 123 D.L.R. (3d) 15, the Court expanded on the earlier holding. A more recent application of these cases is found in *Sinclair v. Quebec (A.G.)*, [1992] 1 S.C.R. 579, 89 D.L.R. (4th) 500.

20 *Reference Re Manitoba Language Rights*, above note 16.

21 (1979), 101 D.L.R. (3d) 385 (S.C.C.).

toba law would have been invalid and the legislature would have been improperly elected under an English-only law. Recognizing the need to prevent a "legislative vacuum" and to preserve the rule of law, the Supreme Court suspended the effect of its declaration of invalidity for a period that allowed Manitoba to translate and re-enact its laws—this time, in both official languages.

In contrast, the Supreme Court was initially unwilling to embrace an expansive view of language rights in relation to court proceedings. In cases decided under both section 133 of the *Constitution Act, 1867*, and section 19(2) of the *Charter*, a majority of the Court accepted the argument that the right to use French or English in proceedings of the courts entitles an individual to no more than that—a right to speak in either language. The individual cannot demand that the court proceedings be conducted in the language of his or her choice, nor that the judge understand that language. The right to use French or English in court proceedings extended not only to the litigant but also to the court staff and the judges. In *MacDonald v. Montreal (City)*,[22] the use of a unilingual French summons was found to be acceptable, while in *Société des Acadiens*, the Court held that a francophone litigant in New Brunswick could not demand a French-speaking judge.[23] In both cases, Beetz J., writing for the majority, emphasized that language rights were different from most others in the *Charter*. In his view, they were the result of a historic political compromise and should be interpreted more narrowly, with an attitude of judicial restraint.[24] In contrast, legal rights were described as "seminal in nature because they are rooted in principle."[25] It should be noted, however, that in *Société des Acadiens*, Beetz J. emphasized that the rules of natural justice or procedural fairness would require that any individual who did not understand proceedings be given access to an interpreter.

In contrast, the dissenting reasons of Dickson C.J.C. and Wilson J. emphasized that the right to use one's language included the notion of being understood. Neither stated definitively what this would mean. Dickson C.J.C. stated that this might encompass the use of interpreters or simultaneous translation, although on the facts of the case it had not been shown that the judges did not understand French. Wilson J. felt that section 19(2) of the *Charter* was evolving towards a requirement of a bilingual judiciary.

---

22 [1986] 1 S.C.R. 460 at 483–84, 27 D.L.R. (4th) 321 [*MacDonald*].

23 *Société des Acadiens du Nouveau-Brunswick v. Association of Parents for Fairness in Education*, [1986] 1 S.C.R. 549, 27 D.L.R. (4th) 406 [*Société des Acadiens*].

24 *MacDonald*, above note 22 at 496–97 (S.C.R.).

25 *Société des Acadiens*, above note 23 at 578 (S.C.R.).

The Supreme Court has now repudiated the narrow view of language rights that it took in *Société des Acadiens*. In *R. v. Beaulac*,[26] the Court interpreted the right to be tried in either English or French granted by section 530 of the *Criminal Code*. Although the case did not arise under the *Charter*, the Court explicitly stated that it would no longer be bound by the view that language rights should be interpreted more narrowly than other rights. Writing for the majority, Bastarache J. stated:

> Language rights must in all cases be interpreted purposively, in a manner consistent with the preservation and development of official language communities in Canada . . . . To the extent that *Société des Acadiens du Nouveau-Brunswick* stands for a restrictive interpretation of language rights, it is to be rejected.[27]

The Court now takes the position that the language rights in the *Charter* are meant to achieve substantive equality between linguistic groups, rather than formal equality.[28]

In an example of this expansive approach to language rights, the Supreme Court found that RCMP officers acting as a provincial police force in New Brunswick were obligated to provide services in both English and French.[29] The decision was based on section 20(2) of the *Charter*, which specifically provides that all services from a governmental body in New Brunswick shall be available in both official languages. The Court found that as the RCMP had contracted with the New Brunswick government to serve as a provincial police force, they were bound by that provision of the *Charter* which applied specifically to services of the New Brunswick government.

Where the *Charter* requires that government services be provided in both official languages, the services provided in each language must be of equal quality.[30] This requirement will not always be satisfied simply by ensuring that the services provided in each language are identical to each other. Depending on the nature of the services being provided, it may be necessary to provide services with distinct content in order to achieve substantive equality between the services offered to different linguistic groups.[31] For example, when the content of servi-

---

26   [1999] 1 S.C.R. 768, 173 D.L.R. (4th) 193.
27   *Ibid.* at para. 25.
28   *DesRochers v. Canada (Industry)*, [2009] S.C.R. 194 at para. 31 [*DesRochers*].
29   *Société des Acadiens et Acadiennes du Nouveau-Brunswick Inc. v. Canada*, [2008] 1 S.C.R. 383.
30   *DesRochers*, above note 28 at para. 3.
31   *Ibid.* at para. 51.

ces is determined through the input and participation of one linguistic group, and the services thus fail to benefit the other linguistic group to the same degree, there may be an onus on the government to consult with the second linguistic group and develop distinct content for the services offered to them.[32]

2) Minority Language Education Rights

Despite the hesitation to interpret language rights in relation to the courts in a liberal fashion, the Supreme Court of Canada has consistently given minority language education rights in section 23 of the *Charter* a generous interpretation. The first major section 23 case to come before the Supreme Court was *Mahé* from Alberta, which examined the degree to which minority language groups could demand management and control of their education system.[33] Dickson C.J.C., writing for the Court, emphasized that the minority language education guarantee had two purposes. First, education in one's language provides an important way to preserve and promote the minority group's language and culture. As well, educational institutions can provide a centre for the community, which helps promote the minority culture.[34] Dickson C.J.C. also noted the strong remedial component to section 23: the section was designed to protect the French and English minorities from assimilation and to give recognition and encouragement to the two official language groups in Canada.[35] In sum, section 23 represented, for him, the "linchpin in this nation's commitment to the values of bilingualism and biculturalism."[36]

In interpreting the scope of section 23(3), Dickson C.J.C. refused to set out a numerical formula whereby a certain number of students would entitle a group to minority language *instruction* while a larger

---

32 *Ibid.* at paras. 53-54.
33 *Mahé v. Alberta*, [1990] 1 S.C.R. 342, 68 D.L.R. (4th) 69 [*Mahé*]. An earlier case from Quebec, *Quebec (A.G.) v. Quebec Association of Protestant School Boards*, [1984] 2 S.C.R. 66, 10 D.L.R. (4th) 321 had struck down Quebec's attempts to narrow the group who could assert s. 23 rights. The Court described this as an attempt to abrogate s. 23 that could not be characterized as a "reasonable limitation" on rights under s. 1.
34 In a recent case, the Supreme Court recognized that "not only do minority schools provide basic language education, they also act as community centres where the members of the minority can meet to express their culture. Thus, the education rights provided by s. 23 form the cornerstone of minority language rights protection." *Solski*, above note 1 at para. 3.
35 *Mahé*, above note 33 at 362–63 (S.C.R.).
36 *Ibid.* at 350 (S.C.R.).

number would ensure that this instruction then be given in separate educational *facilities*. Rather, he concluded that the section imposed a "sliding scale requirement": "[S]ection 23 guarantees whatever type and level of rights and services is appropriate in order to provide minority language instruction for the particular number of students involved."[37]

With respect to section 23(3)(b) and the guarantee of separate educational facilities, Dickson C.J.C. concluded that this mandated a measure of management and control for the minority group. In some cases, this would require the establishment of an independent minority language school board; in other cases, guaranteed representation and certain exclusive authority within the majority board would be sufficient.[38] In deciding what level of service is required, a province should consider actual and potential numbers of students.

In *Arseneault-Cameron v. Prince Edward Island*,[39] the Supreme Court emphasized the importance of the remedial purpose of section 23 of the *Charter*, to redress past injustices and to provide "the official language minority with equal access to high quality education in its own language, in circumstances where community development will be enhanced."[40] The Minister of Education denied the request of a minority language school board for its own school in favour of a plan to bus the children to a French-language school in another community. The decision was successfully challenged on the ground that the Minister had "failed to give proper weight to the promotion and preservation of minority language culture and to the role of the French Language Board in balancing the pedagogical and cultural considerations."[41] The Court insisted that provinces have a positive duty to promote minority language educational services. Formal or supposedly objective comparison with the majority community was rejected in favour of a contextual approach that takes into account the unique history and the special needs of minority language communities.

When dealing with minority language education rights, the courts have to confront the question of how closely involved judges should become in the design and management of school facilities. In *Doucet-Boudreau v. Nova Scotia*,[42] the Supreme Court decided 5 to 4 that a judge

---

37 *Ibid.* at 366 (S.C.R.).

38 *Ibid.* at 371–73 (S.C.R.). Further discussion of s. 23 is found in *Reference Re Public Schools Act (Manitoba) s. 79(3), (4) and (7)*, [1993] 1 S.C.R. 839, 100 D.L.R. (4th) 723.

39 [2000] 1 S.C.R. 3.

40 *Ibid.* at para. 27.

41 *Ibid.* at para. 30.

42 *Doucet-Boudreau*, above note 3.

who had ordered Nova Scotia to make best efforts to build francophone schools could retain jurisdiction over the case and require the government to report back on its progress. The implications of this case for the remedial powers of courts will be discussed in chapter 17, but it is significant that such remedial activism arose in the context of the positive right to minority language educational facilities. Iacobucci and Arbour JJ. for the majority of the Court emphasized the remedial purposes of section 23 of the *Charter* in protecting linguistic minorities from assimilation and the reality that delay in fully implementing section 23 in Nova Scotia was hastening the assimilation of the francophone minority. They rejected an "in all deliberate speed" approach to remedies by observing that

> for every school year that governments do not meet their obligations under s. 23, there is an increased likelihood of assimilation which carries the risk that numbers might cease to "warrant." . . . If delay is tolerated, governments could potentially avoid the duties imposed upon them by s. 23 through their own failure to implement the rights vigilantly. The affirmative promise contained in s. 23 of the *Charter* and the critical need for timely compliance will sometimes require courts to order affirmative remedies to guarantee that language rights are meaningfully, and therefore necessarily promptly, protected.[43]

In *Gosselin (Tutor of) v. Quebec (Attorney General)*,[44] the Supreme Court denied a claim by francophone parents in Quebec that they had an equality right to have their children educated in the English language. The parents did not qualify under section 23 of the *Charter* because they did not receive their primary school instruction in Canada in English and their children were being schooled in French in Quebec. The Court concluded that the equality argument of the francophone parents in Quebec would destroy "the carefully crafted compromise contained in s. 23 of the Canadian *Charter of Rights and Freedoms*"[45] which allowed Quebec to take steps to protect the minority status of the French language within Canada and allowed anglophone minorities in Quebec, as well as francophone minorities outside Quebec, to manage and control their own minority language schools. The Court also approved of lower court cases that decided that anglophone parents outside of Quebec have no constitutional right to have their children educated in

---

43 *Ibid.* at para. 29.
44 2005 SCC 15.
45 *Ibid.* at para. 2.

French.[46] Minority language rights are tied to particular minority communities that exist in Canada and they cannot be overridden by more abstract claims of equality rights.

In *Solski (Tutor of) v. Quebec (Attorney General)*, the Supreme Court considered the different situation of families whose children had already received part of the primary education in Quebec in English. The right at issue was section 23(2) of the *Charter* which provides for continuity of language instruction by providing that "citizens of Canada of whom any child has received or is receiving primary or secondary school instruction in English or French in Canada, have the right to have all their children receive primary and secondary school instruction in the same language." Quebec had interpreted this right as providing a right to minority language education only where the child had received a mathematical majority of his or her instruction in English. The Supreme Court held that such a quantitative approach was too inflexible and too ungenerous in order to realize the purposes of section 23(2) in providing for continuity of minority language instruction even in cases where the family is not necessarily a part of the particular linguistic minority group. It stated that

> to purposefully assess the requirement for participation in s. 23(2), therefore, all the circumstances of the child must be considered including the time spent in each program, at what stage of education the choice of language of instruction was made, what programs are or were available, and whether learning disabilities or other difficulties exist. In this way, it is possible to determine whether a child's overall educational experience is sufficient to meet the requirements of s. 23(2).[47]

In the result, the Court read down Quebec's requirement that students had spent the majority of their time in minority language education to allow a more qualitative determination of whether students had spent a significant part of their time in such an environment. Although the Court recognized Quebec's need to protect the French language, it still defined the section 23(2) right in a broad and generous fashion. To this end, it suggested that if

> children are in a recognized education program regularly and legally, they will in most instances be able to continue their education in the same language . . . . Uprooting would not be in the interest of the

---

46   *Ibid.* at para. 30, approving of *Abbey v. Essex County Board of Education* (1999), 42 O.R. (3d) 481 at 488–89 (C.A.) and *Lavoie v. Nova Scotia (Attorney General)* (1989), 58 D.L.R. (4th) 293 at 313–15 (N.S.C.A.).

47   *Solski*, above note 1 at para. 33.

minority language community or of the child. Nevertheless, a qualitative assessment of the situation to determine whether there is evidence of a genuine commitment to a minority language educational experience is warranted, with each province exercising its discretion in light of its particular circumstances, obligation to respect the objectives of s. 23, and educational policies.[48]

F. CONCLUSION

Language rights have been a central and controversial feature of the Canadian constitution since Confederation. The recognition and protection of language rights was significantly enhanced under the *Charter of Rights and Freedoms* and the Supreme Court of Canada has, in recent years, given constitutionally protected language rights a generous interpretation, repudiating an earlier tendency to give them a narrow interpretation.

Minority language rights have at the same time an individual, a collective, and a remedial dimension. Courts will protect the language rights of individuals but also recognize that language rights are related to the collective interests and rights of minority language communities in Canada and are designed to resist the assimilation of such communities.

FURTHER READINGS

BASTARACHE, M., ed., *Language Rights in Canada*, 2d ed. (Toronto: Carswell, 2004)

BRAEN, A., P. FOUCHER, & Y. LE BOUTHHILLER, *Languages, Constitutionalism and Minorities* (Markham: LexisNexis, 2006)

GREEN, L.C., & D. RÉAUME, "Second-Class Rights? Principle and Compromise in the *Charter*" (1990) 13 Dal. L.J. 565

MAGNET, J.E., *Official Languages of Canada New Essays* (Markham: LexisNexis Canada, 2008, 1995)

NEWMAN, W., "Understanding Language Rights, Equality and the *Charter*" (2004) 15 N.J.C.L. 363

---

48   *Ibid.* at para. 47.

RÉAUME, D., & L.C. GREEN, "Education and Linguistic Security in the *Charter*" (1989) 34 McGill L.J. 777

RÉAUME, D., "Language Rights: Constitutional Misfits or Real Rights" (2006) 31 Sup. Ct. L. Rev. (2d) 201

ROULEAU, N., "Section 23 of the *Charter*: Minority-language Education Rights" (2008) 39 Sup. Ct. L. Rev. (2d) 261–345

SCHNEIDERMAN, D., ed., *Language and the State: The Law and Politics of Identity* (Cowansville, QC: Yvon Blais, 1991)

CHAPTER 17

REMEDIES

The *Charter of Rights and Freedoms* differs from the *Canadian Bill of Rights* in its emphasis on effective remedies. Section 24(1) of the *Charter* provides:

> Anyone whose rights or freedoms, as guaranteed by this *Charter*, have been infringed or denied may apply to a court of competent jurisdiction to obtain such remedy as the court considers appropriate and just in the circumstances.

In addition, section 52(1) of the *Constitution Act, 1982* provides:

> The Constitution of Canada is the supreme law of Canada, and any law that is inconsistent with the provisions of the Constitution is, to the extent of the inconsistency, of no force and effect.

As noted in chapters 3 and 4, the first stage in any *Charter* case is the consideration of whether a right or freedom has been infringed or denied. If the court finds that there has been a *Charter* violation, it then passes to the second stage to consider whether the violation can be justified as a reasonable limit under section 1. If a violation cannot be justified, the court must then decide what practical measures should be taken in view of the infringement. It has long been a principle of our law that there can be no right without an effective remedy. A remedy is the operative element of a court's order that translates the right into concrete form. There would be little point in claiming rights without effective and meaningful remedies for their violation.

There are a variety of possible remedial options. Section 24(1) of the *Charter* assures the individual whose rights have been violated that he or she will be given "such remedy as the court considers appropriate and just in the circumstances." The remedies of stays of proceeding and exclusion of evidence under section 24(2) in criminal cases have been considered in chapter 14. This chapter will review remedies available under section 24(1) as well as a variety of remedial responses that courts use to enforce the mandate in section 52(1) of the *Constitution Act, 1982* that any law that is inconsistent with the *Charter* is of no force and effect to the extent of the inconsistency. Before the availability of specific remedies is examined, some general considerations about the remedial role of the courts and remedial decision making will be examined.

A. GENERAL CONSIDERATIONS GOVERNING THE EXERCISE OF REMEDIAL DISCRETION

1) The Availability of Remedies under Section 24(1) of the *Charter* and Section 52(1) of the *Constitution Act, 1982*

The Supreme Court has stressed the different roles and purposes of constitutional remedies under section 24(1) of the *Charter* and section 52(1) of the *Constitution Act, 1982*. Chief Justice McLachlin has recently written in the 2008 case of *R. v. Ferguson* "that sections 52(1) and 24(1) serve different remedial purposes. Section 52(1) provides a remedy for *laws* that violate *Charter* rights either in purpose or in effect. Section 24(1), by contrast, provides a remedy for *government acts* that violate *Charter* rights."[1] Judges have an explicit grant of remedial discretion under section 24(1) and remedies can only be sought under that section by a person whose own rights have been violated. Section 52(1) is a more general statement of constitutional supremacy and it provides a mandatory rule that legislation that is inconsistent with the constitution is of no force and effect. Remedies under both section 24(1) and 52(1) can only rarely be combined,[2] for example, in cases where a law is declared invalid under section 52(1) but damages are justified under section 24(1) on the basis of governmental fault.[3]

---

1   *R. v. Ferguson*, [2008] 1 S.C.R. 96 at para. 61 [*Ferguson*].
2   *Schachter v. Canada*, [1992] 2 S.C.R. 679 [*Schachter*].
3   *Mackin v. New Brunswick*, [2002] 1 S.C.R. 405.

In *R. v. Ferguson*, the court held that the only remedy for an unconstitutional mandatory minimum sentence enacted by Parliament is to strike the law down in its entirety under section 52(1). The Court was concerned about the uncertainty that would be caused by crafting case-by-case exemptions from the law. At the same time, however, it would be a mistake to assume that striking down a law in its entirety is the only available remedy under section 52(1) to deal with a law that is an unjustified violation of the *Charter*. Although section 52(1) is framed in mandatory terms, judges still have remedial choices when determining remedies under that section. As will be seen, the remedies of reading in, reading down, and severance are alternatives to the complete striking down of a law under section 52(1). In addition, courts sometimes soften the remedy of striking down a law by suspending a declaration of invalidity for six to eighteen months in order to provide the legislature an opportunity to enact new legislation before the declaration of invalidity takes effect.

The jurisdiction of courts and tribunals was discussed in chapter 7. The provincial superior courts have constant concurrent jurisdiction to award constitutional remedies under both section 24(1) of the *Charter* and declarations of invalidity under section 52(1) of the *Constitution*. The jurisdiction of other courts and tribunals to award constitutional remedies depends on their statutory jurisdiction. In order to award a remedy under section 24(1) of the *Charter*, a court or tribunal must have jurisdiction, independent of section 24(1), over the parties, subject matter, and remedy requested. A tribunal that has jurisdiction to decide questions of law will be presumed to have jurisdiction to apply the *Charter* as the supreme law unless the legislature has clearly removed that power from the tribunal.[4]

2) The Judicial Role in Crafting Remedies

In *Doucet-Boudreau v. Nova Scotia*,[5] the Supreme Court outlined some general principles to govern the crafting of appropriate and just remedies under section 24(1) of the *Charter*. Section 24(1) should be given the same generous and purposive interpretation as applies to other parts of the *Charter*. Its purpose is to provide responsive and effective remedies.[6] Section 24(1) can require novel and creative remedies and "it is difficult to imagine language which could give the court a wider

---

4   *Nova Scotia (Workers Compensation Board) v. Martin*, [2003] 2 S.C.R. 504 at para. 36.

5   [2003] 3 S.C.R. 3 [*Doucet-Boudreau*].

6   *Ibid.* at para. 25.

and less fettered discretion."[7] The remedial discretion of the superior courts is not limited by statutes or common law, but only by constitutional principles which require

1) a meaningful remedy that responds to the circumstances of the violation and the claimant;
2) respect for the role of the legislature and the executive;
3) reliance on judicial functions and powers; and
4) fairness to the party against whom the remedy is directed.[8]

In the result, a majority of the Court upheld a trial judge's decision to retain jurisdiction over a complex minority language school case and to require the government to report back to the court on its progress on implementing rights. Four judges dissented and argued that the remedy was unfair to the government and exceeded the functions of the court by breaching procedural fairness and the separation of powers. Although the Court was divided on the extent to which constitutional principles restrained the exercise of judicial discretion, they were united in accepting that courts could make mandatory orders against governments under section 24(1) and that the remedial discretion under section 24(1) should only be constrained by constitutional principles.[9]

In *Schachter v. Canada*,[10] the Supreme Court outlined some general principles to govern the crafting of remedies under section 52(1) of the *Charter*. The Court held that courts were not limited to striking down unconstitutional laws in their entirety under that section. Courts could order less drastic remedies in the form of reading down or severance of unconstitutional parts of the legislation or even reading in words in order to cure a constitutional defect. The Court stated that these less drastic remedies may be appropriate in those cases where the law was only found to be unconstitutional because of concerns about the least restrictive means of the section 1 test as opposed to concerns about the importance of the legislative objective or whether the law was rationally connected to that legislation. In deciding the appropriate remedy under section 52(1), courts should be concerned with both the purposes of the legislation and the purposes of the *Charter*. One question in determining the purpose of the legislation is whether the legislature would enact the legislation as altered by the court. With respect to the purposes of the *Charter*, courts should consider whether the words they read in or read down were mandated with precision by the interaction of *Charter*

---

7   *Ibid.* at para. 50, citing *R. v. Mills*, [1986] 1 S.C.R. 863 at 965.
8   *Ibid.* at paras. 51–59.
9   *Ibid.* at para 105.
10   *Schachter*, above note 2.

analysis and the legislation. The courts should not make ad hoc choices best left to the legislature. In the result, the Court held that a reading in remedy that would add biological parents to a leave scheme made available to adoptive parents was not warranted either by the purposes of the legislation or the purposes of the *Charter*. In other cases, however, the Supreme Court has read in and added benefits for smaller groups such as gays and lesbians on the basis that such remedies were consistent with both the purposes of the legislation and the *Charter*.[11]

3) The Norm of Immediate and Retroactive Relief and Justifications for Prospective and Suspended Declarations of Invalidation

Another general consideration that governs remedies under section 52(1) of the *Charter* is the degree to which constitutional remedies should be immediate or retroactive, as opposed to delayed or prospective. In *Schachter v. Canada*,[12] the Supreme Court recognized that courts have an option of suspending or delaying a declaration of invalidation. Building on past cases, the Court stated that such delayed remedies may be appropriate in cases where an immediate declaration of invalidity would cause harm to the social order or rule of law, endanger public safety, or deprive a deserving person of a benefit simply because the benefit scheme was unconstitutionally under-inclusive. As will be discussed in greater detail below,[13] courts have frequently suspended declarations of invalidity for a variety of reasons with some commentators praising their actions for facilitating dialogue with the legislature and avoiding the disruptive effects of an immediate declaration of invalidity. Others have criticized such actions for depriving successful litigants of an immediate remedy and for sanctioning unnecessary delay in complying with the *Charter*.

In *Canada (Attorney General) v. Hislop*,[14] the Supreme Court dealt with the related issue of the degree to which departures from retroactive remedies could be justified by competing social interests. The Court recognized that the remedial norm was that courts provide fully retroactive remedies to benefit the successful litigant and to recognize that a legislature never had authority to enact an unconstitutional law. Nevertheless, the Court held that departures from this rule, and the

---

11   *Vriend v. Alberta*, [1998] 1 S.C.R. 493 [*Vriend*].
12   *Schachter*, above note 2.
13   See suspended declarations of invalidity in this chapter.
14   [2007] 1 S.C.R. 429 [*Hislop*].

granting of more limited prospective remedies, could be justified in cases where

1) the court made a substantial change in the law;
2) the government reasonably relied in good faith on the law as previously stated;
3) a retroactive remedy would unduly interfere with the role of the governments especially in allocating public resources; and
4) the departure from the retroactive norm would not be unfair to the successful *Charter* applicants.

In the result, the Court held that a retroactive repayment of spousal benefits to same-sex partners was not warranted given the substantial change in the law in recognizing same-sex relationships, the reasonable and good faith reliance of the government on previously judicially sanctioned exclusion of same-sex couples, the role of the government, and a conclusion that the successful litigants would still be left with more than a hollow victory even if they did not receive a fully retroactive remedy.

B. SPECIFIC REMEDIES

1) Declaratory Relief

In some cases, the rights claimant may seek no more than a declaration from the court of the *Charter* right at issue. In the common law tradition, courts tend to avoid making hollow pronouncements of law removed from any concrete order. There is, however, a well-established jurisdiction to award declarations of right in appropriate cases. In constitutional law, the declaration has proved to be an important remedy because of its flexibility. By declaring the right and going no further, the court defines the respective legal rights and obligations of the parties but leaves to them the task of implementing the demands of the constitution. From an institutional perspective, it may not be desirable for the court to become too involved in the details of implementation unless absolutely necessary. The alternative to a declaration is often a court order or injunction, which has to be articulated in clear terms because any violation of such an order may be punished as contempt of court. Although "declarations are often preferable to injunctive relief because they are more flexible, require less supervision, and are more deferential to the other branches of governments," they can be inadequate when *Charter* violations are the result of systemic inadequacies;

where "administrators have proven themselves unworthy of trust"; where subsequent litigation is likely; and where there is a need for remedial specificity and ongoing monitoring of compliance.[15]

Litigation involving minority language education rights serves as an example of the effective use of the remedy of declaration. As seen in chapter 16, section 23 of the *Charter* guarantees parents the right to have their children educated in English or French in certain circumstances. While the courts are able to determine when section 23 rights arise, it is quite another matter for them to determine the institutional arrangements appropriate to fulfil those rights. The demands of the *Charter* will be one important consideration in the design of a minority-language education facility, but there will be many other matters to be taken into account that have nothing to do with constitutional law. Furthermore, there may be a variety of ways to design a school system that respects the demands of section 23. Courts and judges are not experts in schools or education. Courts do not have the competence to raise resources or allocate public funds among competing claims and demands. In view of this, it may be in the public interest as well as in the interest of the litigants for the court simply to declare the right and leave it to the litigants and the appropriate public authorities to work out the practical arrangements. In *Mahé v. Alberta*,[16] the Supreme Court of Canada upheld the section 23 claim of a group of French-speaking parents and granted a declaration of their rights but stopped short of determining the details of school administration. Dickson C.J.C. explained:

> I think it best if the court restricts itself in this appeal to making a declaration in respect of the concrete rights which are due to the minority language parents in Edmonton under s. 23. Such a declaration will ensure that the appellant's rights are realized while, at the same time, leaving the government with the flexibility necessary to fashion a response which is suited to the circumstances . . . . [T]he government should have the widest possible discretion in selecting the institutional means by which its s. 23 obligations are to be met; the courts should be loath to interfere and impose what will be necessarily procrustean standards, unless that discretion is not exercised at all, or is exercised in such a way as to deny a constitutional right.[17]

---

15   *Little Sisters Book and Art Emporium v. Canada (Minister of Justice)*, [2000] 2 S.C.R. 1120 at paras. 258–61 [*Little Sisters*], Iacobucci J. in dissent, but not on this issue.

16   [1990] 1 S.C.R. 342.

17   *Ibid.* at 393.

The Supreme Court's preference for declatory relief rather than more specific injunctive relief has also been seen in some equality rights cases. In *Eldridge v. British Columbia*,[18] the Court interpreted section 15 of the *Charter* to require that those who are deaf or hearing impaired be provided with sign-language interpreters for medically required services. Justice La Forest stated for an unanimous court that a

> declaration, as opposed to some kind of injunctive relief, is the appropriate remedy in this case because there are myriad options available to the government that may rectify the unconstitutionality of the current system. It is not this Court's role to dictate how this is to be accomplished.[19]

A declaration differs from an injunction because it is not enforced through the court's contempt power. Because of this, declarations can be more general and vague than injunctions and can give the government more flexibility to decide how to comply with the court's declaration.

2) Injunctions

An injunction is an order of the court requiring a party to act in a manner specified by the order. In its usual form, the injunction is a negative order that forbids a party from doing something that infringes the rights of another. It is also possible, however, for the court to give a mandatory injunction that requires the wrongdoer to take positive steps required to respect the rights of the other party. In ordinary civil litigation, injunctions are seen as exceptional remedies, available only where damages are an inadequate remedy for the wrong. In constitutional litigation, as will be seen, damages are not commonly awarded, and while the courts still consider injunctions to be exceptional remedies, they may be given, where appropriate, to remedy a constitutional wrong.

The most difficult issue faced in connection with injunctions as a *Charter* remedy arises where the court is asked to grant an injunction that requires ongoing supervision or judicial involvement. *Charter* litigation often involves the operation of complex public institutions. Granting an injunction requiring that an institution take certain steps implies that the court is willing to enforce its order. If the public institution willingly complies, there is no problem. But what happens if there is resistance to the court's order?

---

18   [1997] 3 S.C.R. 624.
19   *Ibid.* at para. 96.

American experience with constitutional injunctions is instructive. In litigation involving desegregation of schools and conditions of prisons, American judges evolved what came to be known as the "structural" or "civil rights" injunction whereby courts became involved in the detailed management of a scheme required to bring the school system or prison into compliance with the constitution.[20] American judges did not rush into making these orders; they did so only when their directives respecting desegregation and improvement of prison conditions were not obeyed.

As noted in the above discussion of declarations as a *Charter* remedy, Canadian courts have been overtly conscious of the need for judicial restraint when making orders requiring complicated changes to public institutions. In the case of minority-language education rights, the courts' first step was to grant a declaratory order, stating the requirements of the *Charter*, but leaving the task of implementation to the school authorities. While it is to be hoped, and expected, that those authorities will comply, there is every indication that should they fail to do so, the courts will not sit idly by and fail to insist upon respect for the rights protected by the *Charter* as interpreted by the courts. In an Ontario case, a judge granted a mandatory order requiring a local school board "to provide the facilities and funding necessary to achieve . . . the provision of instruction and facilities equivalent to those provided to English language secondary schools."[21] In a subsequent ruling, the court reviewed the plans submitted by the school board to assess their adequacy.[22] Another Ontario judge declared that a long-delayed school construction project for a minority language facility should be exempted from a ministry moratorium on capital projects on the ground that "the open-ended delay in funding the construction after seven years of temporary and inadequate facilities does constitute an infringement of the applicant's rights under section 23 of the *Charter*."[23]

In *Little Sisters*,[24] the Supreme Court concluded "with some hesitation, that it is not practicable" to order a "more structured section 24(1) remedy" after finding that the free expression and equality rights of a

---

20   See O.M. Fiss, *The Civil Rights Injunction* (Bloomington: Indiana University Press, 1978).

21   *Marchand v. Simcoe County Board of Education* (1986), 29 D.L.R. (4th) 596 (Ont. H.C.).

22   *Marchand v. Simcoe County Board of Education (No. 2)* (1987), 44 D.L.R. (4th) 171 (Ont. H.C.).

23   *Conseil des écoles séparées catholique romaines de Dufferin & Peel v. Ontario (Ministre de l'education & de la formation)* (1996), 30 O.R. (3d) 681 at 685, Hawkins J.

24   *Little Sisters*, above note 15 at para. 157.

gay and lesbian bookstore had been denied by unconstitutional targeting of its imports by custom officials on the grounds of obscenity. The
Court's reasons for refusing to grant an injunction revolved around the
lack of information about what steps customs officials had taken in the
six years since trial to comply with the trial judge's finding of a *Charter*
violation and the fact that a general injunction requested by the applicant to obey the constitution "would scarcely advance the objectives of
either clarity or enforceability."[25] Any injunction issued under section
24(1) of the *Charter* would have to be clear and enforceable.

In *Doucet-Boudreau v. Nova Scotia (Minister of Education)*,[26] the Supreme Court decided in a 5 to 4 judgment that a trial judge had acted
within the bounds of his remedial discretion under section 24(1) of the
Charter when, after ordering provincial authorities to use their best
efforts to provide minority language school facilities, he retained jurisdiction over the case and required the province to report back to the
judge on its progress in building French language school facilities in
five regions of the province. Iacobucci and Arbour JJ. concluded:

> Section 24(1) of the *Charter* requires that courts issue effective, re-
> sponsive remedies that guarantee full and meaningful protection of
> *Charter* rights and freedoms. The meaningful protection of *Charter*
> rights, and in particular the enforcement of s. 23 rights, may in some
> cases require the introduction of novel remedies. A superior court may
> craft any remedy that it considers appropriate and just in the circum-
> stances. In doing so, courts should be mindful of their roles as consti-
> tutional arbiters and the limits of their institutional capacities.[27]

Iacobucci and Arbour JJ. stressed the breadth of the trial judge's remedial discretion. They also noted the context of positive rights to minority
language school facilities under section 23 of the *Charter* and a history
of delay in implementing those rights in Nova Scotia, combined with
assimilation of the francophone minority. The reporting requirements
were justified because they could prevent the francophone parents
"who had already waited too long and dedicated much energy to the
cause of realizing their s. 23 rights" from having to start fresh litigation
should there not be full and prompt provision of their rights. "Where
governments have failed to comply with their well-understood constitutional obligations to take positive action in support of the right in
s. 23, the assumption underlying a preference for declarations may be

---

25   *Ibid.* at para. 158.
26   *Doucet-Boudreau*, above note 5.
27   *Ibid.* at para. 87.

undermined."[28] With reference to the traditional powers of courts of equity, the Court also indicated that "constitutional remedies involving some degree of ongoing supervision do not represent a radical break with the past practices of courts."[29]

Four judges dissented on the basis that the trial judge's retention of jurisdiction and order were procedurally unfair because of their vagueness and because the remedy violated the separation of powers between courts and the executive. LeBel and Deschamps JJ. concluded that if the trial judge had made further orders after the reporting sessions, he would have violated the separation of powers by entering into the realm of "administrative supervision and decision making." They argued that such a managerial role did not accord with the institutional capabilities of the judiciary or with "the Canadian tradition of mutual respect between the judiciary and the institutions that are the repository of a democratic will."[30] They also suggested that the trial judge risked exerting "political or public pressure on the executive"[31] at the reporting sessions. In the view of the dissenting judges, the only appropriate manner for continued judicial involvement after a court issued an injunction that was consistent with procedural fairness and the separation of powers was to determine whether the government was guilty of contempt of the order.

The decision of all the judges in *Doucet-Boudreau* makes clear that courts can order injunctions under section 24(1) against governments when necessary to provide effective remedies for *Charter* violations. The majority's judgment also makes clear that judges can, when necessary, retain jurisdiction and require governments to report back on their progress in complying with the court order. Structural injunctions, as used in the United States, India, South Africa, and elsewhere[32]

---

28   *Ibid.* at paras. 61, 66.
29   *Ibid.* at para. 73.
30   *Ibid.* at para. 125.
31   *Ibid.* at para. 131.
32   After reviewing American, Indian, German, Canadian, and British law, the South African Constitutional Court has concluded:

> Where a breach of any right has taken place, including a socio-economic right, a Court is under a duty to ensure that effective relief is granted. The nature of the right infringed and the nature of the infringement will provide guidance as to the appropriate relief in a particular case. Where necessary this may include both the issuing of a *mandamus* and the exercise of supervisory jurisdiction.

Minister of Health v. Treatment Action Campaign (No. 2), 2002 5 SA 721 at 758. See K. Roach & G. Budlender, "Mandatory Relief and Supervisory Jurisdiction" (2005) 122 South African L.J. 325.

are now clearly available in Canada. The extent to which such remedies will be used in Canada, however, will depend on the context and how trial judges exercise their broad remedial discretion to order appropriate and just remedies.

Another less controversial form of injunction that may be used as a *Charter* remedy is the interlocutory injunction that is awarded pending a full trial on the merits. This remedy, which may also involve the temporary stay or suspension of legislation pending a full trial on its constitutionality, may be of great practical importance. In a series of cases, the Supreme Court has outlined the test for granting pre-trial or interlocutory relief in *Charter* cases.[33] First, the applicant must establish that he is raising a serious question under the *Charter* that is not frivolous or vexatious. There is no presumption that legislation is constitutional and there will be a serious question in cases in which the applicant demonstrates that the state must justify a violation under section 1 of the *Charter*. Second, the applicant must establish a risk of irreparable harm should the pre-trial relief not be granted. Again, this is not often an onerous requirement given that many *Charter* rights would not be adequately repaired by the award of damages after a full trial. The third and, in most cases, more difficult and crucial requirement is whether the balance of convenience favours granting the relief. Here it is important for the court to consider the public interest. Democratically enacted legislation is presumed to be in the public interest. A suspension of a law for all persons is presumed to be more harmful to the public interest than exempting some subset of the population from the law. The government, however, does not have a monopoly on representing the public interest and a *Charter* applicant can strengthen his case by establishing that his claim is also in the public interest.

3) Damages

In ordinary civil litigation, the most common remedy is damages, a money award designed to compensate the injured party for the wrong suffered. The aim of compensatory damages is, to the extent possible, to put the innocent party in the position he or she would have been in but for the wrong. A commercial case may lend itself readily to monetary assessment of the wrong, but in other cases damages are a less than perfect remedy. It can be extremely difficult to measure in money terms

---

33   *Metropolitan Stores (MTS) Ltd. v. Manitoba Food and Commercial Workers, Local 832*, [1987] 1 S.C.R. 110; *RJR Macdonald Inc. v. Canada*, [1994] 1 S.C.R. 311; *143471 Canada Inc. v. Quebec (Attorney General)*, [1994] 2 S.C.R. 339; *Harper v. Canada (Attorney General)*, [2000] 2 S.C.R. 764.

the amount appropriate to compensate the plaintiff for physical injuries or for damage to reputation, dignity, or privacy or simply for the violation of a *Charter* right. Translating into money the extent of the injury amounts to little more than sophisticated guesswork. In many cases, the damage suffered as a result of a *Charter* violation will fall into this intangible category. The rights and freedoms guaranteed by the *Charter* are abstract and intangible and thus assessment of the extent of the injury in monetary terms will often be difficult. Low awards for the violation of a *Charter* right may trivialize the right while high awards may create an unjustified windfall for the applicant.

On the other hand, there seems no reason in principle why compensatory damages should not be available where the injured party can establish a loss, capable of measurement in money terms, that was caused by the *Charter* breach.[34] In a few cases, damages have been awarded by the courts for *Charter* violations, typically in situations where the wrong is closely analogous to a recognized common law wrong such as assault or false imprisonment.[35] Some courts have also awarded more robust damages for *Charter* violations without proof of monetary damages.[36] The Supreme Court has not yet directly addressed how damages under section 24(1) of the *Charter* should be calculated. In *McKinney*, Wilson J. in dissent would have awarded damages for what she found was the unconstitutional imposition of mandatory retirement. She reasoned:

> [I]t is appropriate and just in these circumstances to award compensatory damages for the loss of income and benefits. Compensation for losses which flow as a direct result of the infringement of constitutional rights should generally be awarded. Impecuniosity and good faith are not a proper basis on which to deny an award of compensatory damages. Such damages are clearly part of the web of remedies that go to make the injured party whole.[37]

Recent developments suggest, however, that the Supreme Court might now take a more restrictive approach to the award of damages when the *Charter* violation was clearly authorized by legislation.

---

34 See the statement of Lamer C.J.C. in *R. v. Delaronde* (1997), 115 C.C.C. (3d) 355 at 371 (S.C.C.).

35 See, for example, *Crossman v. R.* (1984), 9 D.L.R. (4th) 588 (F.C.T.D.); *Persaud v. Ottawa (City) Police* (1995), 130 D.L.R. (4th) 701 (Ont. Ct. Gen. Div.); *Chrispen v. Kalinowski* (1997), 148 D.L.R. (4th) 720 (Sask. Q.B.).

36 *Auton (Guardian ad litem of) v. British Columbia* (2001), 197 D.L.R. (4th) 165 (B.C.S.C.), aff'd (2002), 220 D.L.R. (4th) 411 (B.C.C.A.), rev'd on merits [2004] 3 S.C.R. 657; *Delude v. Canada* (2000), 192 D.L.R. (4th) 714 (F.C.A.); *Ayangma v. Prince Edward Island* (2000), 194 Nfld. & P.E.I.R. 254 (P.E.I.S.C.).

37 *McKinney v. University of Guelph* (1990), 76 D.L.R. (4th) 545 at 623.

In a series of cases, the Supreme Court has indicated that damages under section 24(1) will usually not be appropriate to compensate for harm caused by legislation that is at the same time declared to be of no force and effect under section 52(1) of the *Constitution Act, 1982*. The Court has refused to award damages to those detained under an unconstitutional law providing for imprisonment for failing to pay fines[38] or the unconstitutional revocation of the semi-retired status of a sitting judge.[39] In the latter case, the Court noted that damages were not appropriate in the absence of evidence that the government "acted negligently, in bad faith or by abusing its powers." The reluctance to combine damages under section 24(1) of the *Charter* with a section 52(1) declaration of invalidity under the *Constitution Act, 1982* is based on "a general rule of public law" namely, that "absent conduct that is clearly wrong, in bad faith or an abuse of power, the courts will not award damages for the harm suffered as a result of the mere enactment or application of a law that is subsequently declared to be unconstitutional."[40] The rule creates a qualified or limited immunity from damages for governments that is designed to achieve a balance "between the protection of constitutional rights and the need for effective government."[41] The immunity is not absolute and the balance could tilt towards rights protection when the government acts in bad faith, abuses its powers, or even negligently enacts legislation that is clearly unconstitutional. In such relatively rare cases, it would be appropriate both to strike the legislation down under section 52(1) and award damages under section 24(1).

Damages may also be an appropriate and just remedy under section 24(1) of the *Charter* when an official violates *Charter* rights without any statutory authorization. As mentioned in chapter 4, such actions would not be "prescribed by law" and could not be justified under section 1 of the *Charter*. Thus the *Charter* analysis would move directly from rights violation to the determination of the appropriate and just remedy. The courts of appeal are divided on whether there is a requirement for proof of fault in addition to a *Charter* violation in order to justify the award of damages under section 24(1). The Ontario and New Brunswick Courts of Appeal have held that fault in the form of bad faith is necessary,[42]

---

38   *Guimond v. Quebec (Attorney General)*, [1996] 3 S.C.R. 347.

39   *Mackin v. New Brunswick*, [2002] 1 S.C.R. 405 at para. 82.

40   *Ibid.* at para. 77.

41   *Ibid.* at para. 79.

42   *Mammoliti v. Niagara Regional Police Service v. Niagara Regional Police Service*, 2007 ONCA 79; *McGillivary v. New Brunswick* (1994), 116 D.L.R. (4th) 104 (N.B.C.A.).

while the British Columbia Court of Appeal has upheld the award of damages for an unconstitutional strip search in the absence of proof of fault,[43] and the Nova Scotia Court of Appeal has stressed the importance of considering the need for appropriate and just remedies to affirm the importance of *Charter* rights apart from other common law actions such as false imprisonment and false arrest.[44]

It has been suggested that damages should be used as a means of controlling or disciplining inappropriate behaviour. There are, however, a number of hurdles in the way. Most *Charter* claims are advanced in criminal proceedings, and a criminal court lacks jurisdiction to make a damages award.[45] The result is that a separate civil proceeding is required. In civil proceedings, compensatory damages ordinarily must be proved to have been directly caused by the wrong. Fault must be brought home to an individual or organization capable of being sued. While the courts have removed the protection of common law immunity applicable to certain public officials, including crown prosecutors and police, it may still be necessary to prove malice or some other degree of fault in order to succeed.[46] That said, there is some danger that the purposes of providing appropriate and just remedies for *Charter* violations and the remedial discretion that is contemplated under section 24(1) will be lost if *Charter* damage claims are assimilated to existing common law actions. In the federalism context, the Court has also recently stated the importance of deciding remedial questions on the basis of constitutional principles as opposed to common law concepts. In that case the Court held that the appropriate remedy for an unconstitutional tax would be the repayment of money collected under the tax by the government regardless of common law principles that might limit the remedy.[47]

In certain cases, punitive damages are available in civil proceedings. An award of punitive damages serves to sanction wrongful behaviour and the amount awarded serves, in effect, as a penalty or fine rather than as an attempt to compensate. In a few cases, judges have found it appropriate to award punitive damages in addition to compensatory damages. The Quebec courts have made significant punitive or

---

43 *Ward v. British Columbia*, 2009 BCCA 23, leave to appeal to S.C.C. granted, [2004] S.C.C.A. No. 125.

44 *Bevis v. Burns* (2006), 269 D.L.R.(4th) 696 (N.S.C.A.).

45 *R. v. Mills*, [1986] 1 S.C.R. 863.

46 *Nelles v. Ontario*, [1989] 2 S.C.R. 170; *Proulx v. Quebec (A.G.)*, [2001] 3 S.C.R. 9; *Odhavji Estate v. Woodhouse*, [2003] 3 S.C.R. 263; *Hill v. Hamilton Wentworth Regional Police Services Board*, [2007] 3 S.C.R. 129.

47 *Kingstreet Investments Ltd. v. New Brunswick (Finance)*, [2007] 1 S.C.R. 3.

exemplary damage awards under the Quebec *Charter of Human Rights and Freedoms*. In *Patenaude v. Roy*,[48] the Quebec Court of Appeal found that there had been a "planned and deliberate violation of *Charter* provisions leading to a calamity."[49] A police SWAT team, acting without a warrant, had used a battering ram to enter a suspect's apartment and then fired twenty-five shots. The suspect died in the hail of bullets. The court awarded $100,000 in exemplary damages.[50] The Supreme Court has, however, reversed an award of $4,000 in exemplary damages in another fatal police shooting on the basis that the police officer did not intend to kill the victim and "using a weapon to keep a suspect under control at a distance is standard police practice."[51]

Despite the infrequency of damages as a *Charter* remedy, court orders in *Charter* cases often have significant financial consequences. A finding that procedural guarantees must be respected may require the state to create expensive administrative measures.[52] When necessary to ensure a fair trial, courts have not hesitated to order that counsel be appointed for a person who cannot afford a lawyer.[53] Rulings in equality cases that a benefit has been wrongfully denied will require the state to spend money.[54] An injunction requiring the state to take, or refrain from, certain actions may result in the expenditure of significant sums of public funds.[55] However, in each of these cases, while the remedy will have the effect of requiring money to be spent, the court is not quantifying the harm and requiring the wrongdoer to pay compensation to the party whose right was infringed.

4) Remedies Affecting Legislation

Remedies affecting unconstitutional legislation are largely dealt with under section 52(1) of the *Constitution Act, 1982*, sometimes known as the "supremacy clause" because it provides as follows:

---

48   (1994), 123 D.L.R. (4th) 78 (Que. C.A.).

49   *Ibid.* at 91, Tyndale J.A.

50   See also *Québec v. Syndicat National des Employés de l'Hôpital St. Ferdinand* (1996), 138 D.L.R. (4th) 577 (S.C.C.), awarding $200,000 in punitive damages to a group of mental patients denied essential services during an illegal strike.

51   *August v. Gosset*, [1996] 3 S.C.R. 268 at para. 121.

52   *Singh v. Canada (Minister of Employment and Immigration)*, [1985] 1 S.C.R. 177.

53   *New Brunswick (Minister of Health and Community Services) v. G.(J.)*, [1999] 3 S.C.R. 46. An alternative used in some criminal cases is to stop or stay proceedings until counsel has been appointed.

54   See, for example, *Eldridge v. British Columbia (A.G.)*, [1997] 3 S.C.R. 624, requiring hospitals to provide sign-language interpreters for deaf patients [*Eldridge*].

55   See above, section B(2).

> The Constitution of Canada is the supreme law of Canada, and any law that is inconsistent with the provisions of the Constitution is, to the extent of the inconsistency, of no force or effect.

The supremacy clause confirms the established doctrine of judicial review in Canadian constitutional law. The constitution is a law unlike all others, and its provisions, including the rights and freedoms guaranteed by the *Charter*, take priority over other laws. Should Parliament, a provincial legislature, or other law-making body enact a law that is inconsistent with the *Charter*, that law cannot stand.

The courts have evolved a variety of remedial techniques to carry out the mandate conferred by the supremacy clause and those techniques are considered below. As discussed above, the general principle that governs the choice between remedies is the need to respect the purpose of the *Charter* and the purpose of the legislation. In addition, the presumption in favour of immediate and retroactive remedies can in some cases be displaced if the government justifies a departure in favour of more limited prospective relief for reasons such as the need to respect the role of the legislature, the government's good faith reliance on prior law, and other matters of public interest.

a) Striking Down

Before the *Charter*, the most common constitutional remedy for legislation that did not respect the limits of the constitution was for the court to strike down, or nullify, the law in its entirety. When the constitutionality of a statute is challenged on the ground that the enacting body, Parliament or a legislature, has transgressed the limits of its authority under the division of powers between the federal and provincial governments, the emphasis is upon the essential purpose, or the "pith and substance," of the law. While the effects of a law may serve as a measure of the law's purpose, the established constitutional doctrine in federalism review is to concentrate upon purpose rather than effects. The result is that the courts tend to regard federalism review as an "all or nothing" proposition. As a general rule, the law either falls in its entirety or it is saved in its entirety. If it is upheld, incidental effects it may have in an area of jurisdiction reserved to the other level of government will be tolerated.

By contrast, under the *Charter of Rights and Freedoms*, the focus tends to be upon unconstitutional effects. It is, after all, uncommon for Parliament or a legislature to enact a law that has as its purpose the violation of some fundamental right or freedom.[56] More frequent is a law that, al-

---

56 Perhaps the leading example is the decision of the Supreme Court of Canada striking down the nineteenth-century *Lord's Day Act*, which required Sunday

though valid in its purpose, has in its operation an unacceptable impact or effect upon some fundamental freedom. For this reason, the range of constitutional remedies is much more varied and innovative in *Charter* cases than in federalism review. While nullification remains a frequently granted remedy in *Charter* cases, the courts have also developed a range of other remedies.[57] These remedies are designed to lessen the bluntness of an immediate declaration that an entire law is of no force and effect. They are guided by concerns for the purposes of the *Charter*, the purposes of the impugned legislation, and considerations of the proper institutional division of labour between courts and legislatures.

b) Severance and Partial Invalidity

The most common alternative to striking down an entire statute is severance and a declaration of partial invalidity. This results in the nullification of only the unconstitutional portion of the law. This technique is readily employed where the specific provision challenged represents a discrete and identifiable measure that can be excised without altering the overall structure or operation of the law in which it is contained. It had been used frequently, for example, to strike down provisions of the *Criminal Code*. It has never been suggested that the entire *Criminal Code* should be nullified because one of its provisions violates the *Charter*.

At times, however, the remedy of severance may approach judicial drafting of a statute and become more controversial. For example, one case[58] dealt with a provision of the *Criminal Code*, discussed in chapter 15, making it an offence for a male person to have sexual relations with a female person under the age of fourteen. The offence included the words "whether or not he believes that she is fourteen years of age or more." The Supreme Court found that Parliament was entitled to prohibit this conduct but that, as drafted, the section imposed criminal liability on a no-fault basis contrary to section 7 of the *Charter*. Rather than strike out the entire section and thereby leave unprotected a class of persons deemed by Parliament to be in need of protection, the Court "rewrote" the section by striking out the words "whether or not he believes that she is fourteen years of age or more."[59] The Supreme

---

observance. This measure was found to be in violation of the guarantee of freedom of religion and the law was struck down. See *R. v. Big M Drug Mart Ltd.*, [1985] 1 S.C.R. 295, discussed in detail in chapter 9.

57 The most comprehensive judicial discussion of these remedies is to be found in *Schachter*, above note 2.

58 *R. v. Hess*, [1990] 2 S.C.R. 906.

59 For another example, see *R. v. Lucas*, [1998] 1 S.C.R. 439, excising certain words from the *Criminal Code*'s defamatory libel section.

Court also severed the phrase "or any other just cause" from the tertiary grounds for the denial of bail on the basis that the severed phrase was excessively vague, but the remaining part of the statute referring to the need to maintain confidence in the administration of justice was not vague and constituted a just cause for the denial of bail.[60]

The technique of severance has also been employed in the case of "under-inclusive" laws. An under-inclusive law is one that is valid so far as it goes but constitutionally defective because it does not go far enough. Severance only works where the law is drafted to apply generally but then, in a specific exception provision, improperly excludes certain individuals or groups from the benefit. Where the exclusion of those individuals or class of individuals is contrary to a constitutional provision, the courts have held that the specific exclusion may be severed, thus leaving intact the provision granting the benefit to the larger class. An example is the decision that a provision excluding those over sixty-five years of age from entitlement to unemployment-insurance benefits should be severed and struck down as discriminatory, leaving unqualified the general provision conferring the entitlement to the general class of unemployed workers.[61] Severance in cases of this kind has the effect of extending a benefit and is discussed in greater detail below in section B(4)(d). In general, these types of remedies should only be used when consistent with both the purposes of the *Charter* and the impugned legislation.

c)   Reading Down

An "over-inclusive" law is one that has, at its core, a constitutional purpose and application but that, as drafted, casts too wide a net and infringes constitutional rights in some situations. In such cases, the Canadian courts have frequently resorted to the technique known as "reading down" or giving the law a sufficiently narrow interpretation to bring it into line with the demands of the constitution. A good example is the Supreme Court's decision in a case challenging Canada's obscenity law.[62] This provision of the *Criminal Code* was drafted in extremely broad terms that, if applied literally, would have had an unconstitutional effect upon freedom of expression. While the Court did not explicitly describe its judgment as an exercise of the power to "read down" the law, that was the effect. The Court held that the provision had to be interpreted more narrowly so as to catch only certain forms of pornography. The

---

60   *R. v. Hall*, [2002] 3 S.C.R. 309.

61   *Canada (Employment and Immigration Commission) v. Tétreault-Gadoury*, [1991] 2 S.C.R. 22.

62   *R. v. Butler*, [1992] 1 S.C.R. 452, discussed in detail in chapter 9.

Court's interpretation of the law reads like a statute, setting out point by point the elements to be established for a conviction and thereby significantly curtailing the reach of the general words enacted by Parliament. So interpreted, the obscenity law survived *Charter* scrutiny.[63]

The use of reading down in the above case is similar to the process of statutory interpretation in which judges, when faced with an ambiguity in the legislation, select the reading of the legislation that is more consistent with the constitution. In *R. v. Sharpe*,[64] however, the Supreme Court used a stronger form of the reading down remedy, which reduced the ambit of the offence of possession of child pornography even when it was clear that Parliament had intended the offence to cover such matters. A majority of the Court found that, while most of the new offence when properly interpreted in a manner consistent with the *Charter* was a reasonable limit on freedom of expression, the offence could not be justified as a reasonable limit when applied to material created by the accused for private use or private recordings of lawful sexual activity. The Court read in these exceptions to the legislation on the basis that it was honouring both the purposes of the statute and the *Charter*. Although the remedy may have altered the intent of Parliament, it also preserved as much of the new offence of possession of child pornography as was consistent with the *Charter*. It would have been more drastic for the Court to have struck down the offence of child pornography in its entirety simply because of its overbreadth when applied to a few cases.

Courts will employ reading down both as a device of statutory interpretation and as a stronger and more explicit remedy in order to save those parts of laws to the extent they are consistent with the *Charter*. Strong forms of the reading down remedy may seem to be a judicial assumption of the legislative role because the court reads in new limitations to legislation. As will be seen below, the judicial reading in of words to make legislation constitutional is also a controversial remedy. Nevertheless, both remedies can be justified on the basis that the court is respecting the broader purposes of the legislation insofar as they are consistent with the purposes of the *Charter*. In other words, the court

---

63   For other examples, see *Solski (Tutor of) v. Quebec (Attorney General)*, 2005 SCC 14, reading down a requirement that students receive a "major part" of their education in English to be entitled to minority language instruction to require instead a "significant part" as consistent with s. 23(2) of the *Charter; Canadian Foundation for Children, Youth and the Law v. Canada (Attorney General)*, [2004] 1 S.C.R. 76 (the child spanking case discussed in chapter 13), reading down s. 43 of the *Criminal Code*.

64   [2001] 1 S.C.R. 45 at para. 122.

is only invalidating the legislation "to the extent" of its inconsistency with the *Charter*, as contemplated in section 52(1) of the *Constitution Act, 1982*.

d)   Reading In and Extension of Benefits

A controversial remedy under the *Charter* is known as "reading in." Here, the problem is that the statute is under-inclusive and fails to extend its reach to those who have a constitutional claim to its protection. In such cases, nullification is unsatisfactory since it would deprive those who are otherwise entitled to the protection of the law and it would fail to satisfy the constitutional claim of those who ask to be included. On occasion, the courts have decided that the better course is to fill the gap by judicially "reading in" those who have a constitutional claim to the protection of the law, thereby adding to the list of those protected. Perhaps the best example is the decision of the Supreme Court of Canada dealing with Alberta's *Individual's Rights Protection Act*, a general anti-discrimination statute, which prohibits discrimination on certain specific prohibited grounds.[65] Sexual orientation was not a prohibited ground. The Court found that the Act was constitutionally defective in failing to extend the benefit of anti-discrimination protection to gays and lesbians, who were entitled to claim the benefit of the protection of the law pursuant to the *Charter* guarantee of equality. Rather than strike the law down and deprive the other specified groups of its protection, the Court found that the appropriate remedy was to add "sexual orientation" to the list of prohibited grounds.

Reading in is a controversial technique as the court appears to be exercising a legislative role. However, given the alternative of striking down the law in its entirety, it seems inevitable that reading in should be permitted in certain situations. To strike down an entire statute because it fails to extend its benefit to a group that is relatively small in relation to the overall purpose and application of the statute would seem to constitute an even more serious interference by the judiciary with legislative choice. Another alternative, examined below in section B(4)(f), is to strike down the under-inclusive benefit, but to suspend the effect of the declaration for six to eighteen months in order to give the legislature an opportunity to decide whether to extend or reduce the benefit or to repeal the benefit altogether.

---

65   *Vriend*, above note 11. The Ontario Court of Appeal came to the same conclusion with respect to the *Canadian Human Rights Code* six years earlier: *Haig v. Canada* (1992), 94 D.L.R. (4th) 1 (Ont. C.A.).

Probably the most controversial examples of reading in involve statutes that extend monetary benefits. In a Nova Scotia case, a single father
challenged a welfare statute that granted monetary benefits to single
mothers.[66] He argued that failure to extend the same benefits to single
fathers amounted to discrimination on grounds of sex contrary to the
Charter's section 15 guarantee of equal benefit of the law. A trial court
in Nova Scotia agreed with his substantive claim but stumbled on the
remedy. The court found that it was not possible for a judge to order
the legislature to expend the money and hence that the only available
remedy was to strike down the entire statute, thereby depriving single
mothers as well as single fathers of its benefit. The result was unsatisfactory to all. The single father would plainly be disappointed by the result.
He did not get the benefit for himself and he had no interest in denying
the benefit to single mothers. The legislature was clearly entitled to create the benefit scheme provided it acted with an even hand.

In *Schachter*,[67] the Supreme Court of Canada carefully considered,
in the context of extending benefits, the remedies of severance and reading in. The Court suggested that the Nova Scotia decision was wrong
in that, where the class of persons to be added is relatively small in
relation to those already in receipt of the benefit, a court may order that
monetary benefits be extended to those not originally contemplated by
the legislation.

Lamer C.J.C. outlined the approach courts are to take. The first
element to be considered is the extent of the inconsistency with the
Charter. The courts will not rewrite a law if the constitutional defect is
fundamental. In such cases, the law should be struck down. It is only
where the law is invalid because it fails to pass the minimal-impairment
test that reading in or severance should be considered. Second, severance or reading in will be available only where the legislative objective
is obvious, extending the reach of the law would be consistent with that
objective, and extension would constitute a lesser interference with that
objective than would striking down the law in its entirety. Third, these
remedies are appropriate only where the legislature's choice of means
is clear and severance or reading in would not intrude into the legislative domain. Particular care must be exercised where the remedy has
budgetary effects. Remedies that are so substantial as to alter the legislative scheme are to be avoided. Thus, in the *Schachter* case, the Court
would not have extended parental-leave benefits provided for adoptive

---

66   *Phillips v. Nova Scotia (Social Assistance Appeal Board)* (1986), 27 D.L.R. (4th)
     156 (N.S.S.C.T.D.), aff'd (1986), 34 D.L.R. (4th) 633 (C.A.) (*sub nom. Attorney
     General of Nova Scotia v. Phillips*).
67   *Schachter*, above note 2.

parents to biological parents. The group that would be added by extension was much larger than the group receiving the benefit, and extension would not be consistent with the legislative objective. If a section 15 violation of the rights of biological parents had been established (a matter about which the Court expressed some doubt), the appropriate remedy would have been to strike down the unconstitutionally under-inclusive benefit received by adoptive parents, subject to a temporary delay that would give Parliament an opportunity to enact a new law. Parliament could extend the benefit to all parents, repeal the benefit, or reduce the monetary value of the extended benefit.[68]

e)   Constitutional Exemptions

Another possible remedy is granting a "constitutional exemption." Here, the law remains valid for all purposes save that a particular individual is exempted from its application. A good example is a decision of the Yukon Territory Court of Appeal in a case dealing with an Aboriginal person convicted of a weapons offence.[69] The *Criminal Code* provided that, upon conviction for the offence, there was a mandatory order prohibiting the convicted party from possessing a weapon for five years. The convicted Aboriginal person established that it was necessary for him to possess a firearm to maintain his traditional lifestyle and to provide for himself and his family. The court found that to deprive him of the right to possess a weapon would, in the circumstances, constitute cruel and unusual treatment, contrary to section 12 of the *Charter*. However, the court also recognized that the law was valid in almost every other conceivable application and that it would therefore be undesirable to strike it down. The court's solution was to hold that the particular litigant before it was to be exempted from the application of the law. Parliament subsequently followed this approach by enacting a statute that provided for exemptions from firearm prohibition orders when use of a firearm would be necessary for the offender's sustenance or employment.[70]

The Supreme Court has been reluctant to use constitutional exemptions. The *Seaboyer* case[71] involved an attack on *Criminal Code*

---

68   In response to lower court decisions extending the benefit to all parents, Parliament in fact reduced the benefit from fifteen to ten weeks of leave for all parents. Adoptive parents subsequently challenged this reduction of their benefits as a violation of their s. 15 rights without success: *Schafer v. Canada (Attorney General)* (1998), 149 D.L.R. (4th) 705 (Ont. C.A.), leave refused 153 D.L.R. (4th) vii (S.C.C.).

69   *R. v. Chief* (1989), 51 C.C.C. (3d) 265 (Y.T.C.A.).

70   *Criminal Code*, s. 113.

71   *R. v. Seaboyer*, [1991] 2 S.C.R. 577.

provisions precluding an accused charged with sexual assault from cross-examining a complainant on prior sexual behaviour. Writing for the majority, McLachlin J. found that exempting those situations where the questioning was necessary to ensure the accused's right to a fair trial would be inappropriate, and that the section had to be struck down in its entirety. Granting an exemption would have the effect of giving the trial judge a discretion, the very result Parliament sought to avoid, and would also leave the law in an uncertain state. However, McLachlin J. specifically added that she did not foreclose the possibility that an exemption may be appropriate in some other case. Constitutional exemptions were also discussed in a dissenting judgment of the Supreme Court of Canada in *Rodriguez*, the assisted-suicide case mentioned in chapter 13.[72] There, a minority of the Court, led by Lamer C.J.C., found that the prohibition against assisted suicide did violate the constitutional rights of the terminally-ill plaintiff. However, Chief Justice Lamer hesitated to strike down the entire statute and ruled that the appropriate remedy would be a constitutional exemption permitting this particular individual, or others like her, to have the benefit of an assisted suicide, provided they could bring themselves within a narrowly defined set of criteria laid down in the judgment.

In *R. v. Ferguson*,[73] the Supreme Court ruled that constitutional exemptions were an inappropriate remedy for an unconstitutional mandatory minimum sentence. The Court stressed that such a remedy was inconsistent with the intent of mandatory sentences to exclude judicial discretion. The introduction of sentencing discretion that Parliament intended to preclude would, in the Court's view, be an inappropriate intrusion into the legislative sphere.[74] This conclusion can be reconciled with the courts' use of alternatives to striking down laws, such as reading in and severance, on the basis that the latter remedies do not fundamentally change the legislation whereas the introduction of exemptions would fundamentally change the nature of mandatory sentences. The Court also stressed that section 52(1) requires invalidation of unconstitutional laws and that "bad law, fixed on a case-by-case basis by the courts, does not accord with the role and responsibility of Parliament to enact constitutional laws for the people of Canada."[75] It remains to be seen whether *Ferguson* will prevent the use of constitutional exemptions in all other contexts. On the one hand, it can be argued that mandatory sentences signal a special form of legislative intent that clearly

---

72   *Rodriguez v. R.*, [1993] 3 S.C.R. 519 [*Rodriguez*].
73   *Ferguson*, above note 1.
74   *Ibid.* at para. 56.
75   *Ibid.* at para. 70.

rejects judicial discretion and constitutional exemptions or exceptions. The same concerns may not apply with respect to other laws that might have unconstitutional effects, for example if applied to certain minority groups. This would suggest that in non-sentencing cases, courts might still be able to order constitutional exemptions when consistent with the overall purposes of the legislation and the *Charter*. Constitutional exemptions may also have a role to play to exempt a successful litigant and perhaps others from the operation of a temporary suspended declaration of invalidity.

On the other hand, there is some language in *Ferguson* that suggests that courts should hesitate to order any constitutional exemptions. For example, the Court was concerned that any constitutional exemption creates undesirable uncertainty in the law and the use of constitutional exemptions outside of the sentencing context would still create uncertainty about when the statute would be applied. This may suggest that a court inclined to order a constitutional exemption in a single case might be better either to strike the law down in its entirety or perhaps to read the law down so that it does not apply to a foreseeable group of people whose *Charter* rights would be violated by the application of the law. In any event, if the law is a mandatory sentence, *Ferguson* makes it clear that the only remedy available to the judge is to strike down the law in its entirety as it applies in all cases.[76]

f) Temporary Suspension of Invalidity

In certain situations, the Supreme Court of Canada has used the technique of temporary suspension of invalidity. In these cases, the Court has found that, although a challenged law is unconstitutional, the immediate nullification of that law could lead to chaos or a serious threat to public safety. To avoid chaos or serious public harm, the Court has delayed the implementation of its order of invalidity to afford Parliament or the legislature the opportunity to repair the constitutional deficiency.

The leading example is the decision of the Supreme Court of Canada in *Reference Re Manitoba Language Rights*.[77] The Court held that the failure of the legislature of Manitoba to comply with a constitutional provision requiring it to enact all the laws of Manitoba in both English

---

76 For an example of the Court's use of such a remedy in striking down a mandatory minimum sentence of 7 years for importing narcotics see *R. v. Smith*, [1987] 1 S.C.R. 1045. The result was that a minimum sentence would not apply in any cases but a seven-year sentence could still be ordered in cases where a judge found that sentence to be a fit one.

77 *Reference Re Language Rights under s. 23 of Manitoba Act, 1870 and s. 133 of Constitution Act, 1867*, [1985] 1 S.C.R. 721 [*Reference Re Manitoba Language Rights*].

and French meant that all Manitoba legislation was invalid. Clearly, however, an immediate nullification of all the laws of Manitoba would lead to a situation of chaos, and the Court held that the overriding principle of the rule of law justified a temporary suspension of invalidity. The Court's order gave the legislature of Manitoba time to have its laws translated and re-enacted in both languages.

Temporary suspension of invalidity has been resorted to in less dramatic circumstances as well. When the Supreme Court held that provisions of the *Criminal Code* providing for the detention of those found not guilty by reason of insanity were invalid, it held that the immediate release of such individuals, most of whom had escaped convictions for murder because of their mental disorders, would result in a serious threat to public safety. Accordingly, the Court held that the declaration of invalidity should be suspended for a stated period of time to afford Parliament the opportunity to reconsider the matter and to enact a revised law in keeping with the requirements of the constitution.[78] The Supreme Court used a similar suspended declaration of invalidity in a case involving continued restrictions on the liberty of those found permanently unfit to stand trial because of a mental disorder. The Court split over the issue of whether a remedy for affected individuals under section 24(1) of the *Charter* could be ordered during the twelve-month suspension of the declaration of invalidity. The majority ruled that such section 24(1) remedies could only be ordered after the period of suspension while one judge in dissent would have used section 24(1) during the period of the suspended declaration to avoid the mischief of depriving someone of liberty under an unconstitutional law.[79]

In *Schachter*,[80] the Supreme Court indicated another situation where the remedy of temporary suspension of invalidity may be employed. As already noted, there are cases where laws are constitutionally defective because they are under-inclusive. In some cases, that defect can be repaired by having the court add the excluded class by using the techniques of reading in or severance. However, where the case does not permit extending the law to those not included, and the law is to be struck down, *Schachter* suggests that the court may temporarily suspend the declaration of invalidity to alleviate the harshness of denying the benefit of the law to deserving persons. This gives the legislature a stated period of time to reconsider the scheme in light of the dictates of

---

78   *R. v. Swain*, [1991] 1 S.C.R. 933.
79   *R. v. Demers*, [2004] 2 S.C.R. 489 at paras. 56–64 [*Demers*].
80   *Schachter*, above note 2 at 715–17.

the constitution without defeating the operation of the valid portion of the law in the interim.

In *M. v. H.*,[81] the Supreme Court did not read in same-sex couples to a provision providing for support after the breakup of a relationship because of concerns about the far-reaching implications of such a ruling. Instead, it struck down a provision providing for support orders between heterosexual couples as unconstitutionally under-inclusive, subject to a six-month period of delay. In that time, Ontario responded with new comprehensive legislation providing for the new category of "same-sex partners." Other provinces have responded to the ruling in different ways. The suspended declaration of invalidity can be an instrument of remedial dialogue, which invites the legislature to cure constitutional defects in a variety of constitutional ways and recognizes that the legislature can formulate more comprehensive remedies than the court could accomplish on its own. The suspended or delayed declaration of invalidity also allows governments to consult with the affected interests and debate the appropriate remedy in a democratic manner.

A suspended declaration of invalidity may have the effect of denying a successful *Charter* applicant an immediate remedy. In a few complex cases, the Supreme Court has sanctioned periods of delay of up to eighteen months in order to give the legislature time to consider the implications of its ruling and has not exempted the successful *Charter* applicant from the period of delay.[82] The Supreme Court has also indicated that courts cannot normally use a section 24(1) *Charter* remedy during a suspended declaration of invalidity ordered under section 52(1) of the *Constitution Act, 1982* and that any section 24(1) remedy for the individual can only take effect after the court-sanctioned delay has expired.[83] A delayed or suspended declaration of invalidity can be an instrument to promote dialogue between the courts and the legislatures, but it also allows an unconstitutional state of affairs to persist and may deny a successful *Charter* applicant an immediate remedy. It may also force a controversial issue back on the agenda of a legislature on an expedited timetable should the legislature wish to act before the six-to-eighteen-month period of suspension or delay expires.

---

81   [1999] 2 S.C.R. 3 [*M. v. H.*]. For a refusal to suspend a declaration see *Halpern v. Canada* (2003), 65 O.R. (3d) 161 (C.A.).

82   *Corbière v. Canada*, [1999] 2 S.C.R. 203; *Dunmore v. Ontario*, [2001] 3 S.C.R. 1016.

83   *Demers*, above note 79 at paras. 56–64.

g) Prospective Remedies and Refusals to Grant Retroactive Remedies

A temporary suspension of invalidity can mean that a successful *Charter* applicant will receive no immediate remedy. In some cases, the Court has also fashioned prospective remedies that will only apply at a stated time in the future in order to avoid the disruptive effects of immediate remedies. For example, the Court fashioned a thirty-day transition period in a case in which it declared that the right to counsel under section 10(b) of the *Charter* required detainees to be informed about the availability of legal aid. The Court justified this ruling on the basis that the police needed time to print new caution cards to discharge their new informational burden.[84] In an equality rights case, the Court gave the government of British Columbia six months to devise a system to provide sign language interpretation for deaf patients requiring essential medical services.[85] In cases that require the government to take positive action, an immediate remedy may simply be impossible.

In *Hislop v. Canada*,[86] the Court extended the above precedents and those relating to temporary suspensions of invalidity to hold in some cases it may be appropriate to provide no retroactive remedies and to ensure constitutional compliance in the future only. The case involved same-sex couples who argued that they should be entitled to survivor-benefit pension arrears retroactive to 17 April 1985, the day that the equality rights under section 15 of the *Charter* took effect. The Court recognized that this request for retroactive relief was supported by the traditional idea that an unconstitutional law, in this case a law denying same-sex couple pension benefits, was always invalid. The Court, however, ruled that departures from the traditional approach to retroactive remedies could be justified and were justified in this case in large part because the government had placed reasonable and good faith reliance on law which, until the 1999 *M. v. H.* decision,[87] had excluded same-sex couples from benefits provided to heterosexual couples. The Court was also influenced by its conclusions that the successful *Charter* applicants were not to be left without any remedies.

While the government was required to justify departures from the norm of retroactive remedies, the Court held that the recognition of same-sex partnerships in 1999 constituted a substantial change in the law. It distinguished a 1995 case recognizing common-law opposite-sex

---

84 *R. v. Brydges*, [1990] 1 S.C.R. 190.
85 *Eldridge* above note 54.
86 *Hislop*, above note 14.
87 *M. v. H.* above note 81.

partnerships as not constituting a substantial change in the law.[88] However, a substantial change in the law by itself will not justify the resort to only prospective remedies. In *Hislop*, the Court also found that the government reasonably relied in good faith on the law that had, until *M. v. H.*, excluded same-sex couples from benefits provided to opposite-sex couples.[89] The Court expressed concerns that in some cases a fully retroactive remedy would unduly interfere with the role of the governments especially in allocating public resources, though some would argue that such concerns should not have been pressing in this case which involved the self-funded *Canada Pension Plan* scheme. Finally, the Court also suggested that courts should consider the fairness of the departure from the norm of retroactive relief to the litigants. In this case, the Court concluded that the recognition of same-sex couples and the granting of some partial retroactive payments meant that the refusal to grant fully retroactive relief would not produce a "hollow victory"[90] for the successful applicants. In this case, the Court found that the government had justified the departure from retroactive relief, making it unnecessary to consider the applicant's challenge to a facially neutral provision that allowed applicants for a survivor's pension to claim only twelve months' pension-benefit arrears.

C. CONCLUSION

Some of the most difficult and controversial *Charter* issues concern remedies. Section 24 confers an express mandate on the courts to ensure that violations of *Charter* rights are remedied in an appropriate fashion. In determining remedial issues, the courts have drawn on existing principles but have also had to find new remedial techniques. As with other *Charter* issues, there is a delicate institutional balance to be struck. Remedial choice is governed in part by the need to ensure that indi-

---

88   *Ibid.* at 105 discussing *Miron v. Trudel*, [1995] 2 S.C.R. 418, and suggesting that a prospective remedy in the case of the exclusion of common law partnerships would not be justified because the government could not place good faith reliance on such an exclusion and because prospective relief would deny the successful applicants any remedy and retroactive relief would not interfere with the role of the legislature.

89   The Court argued that *M. v. H.*, was a clear shift from *Egan v. Canada*, [1995] 2 S.C.R. 513 in which four judges found no section 15 violation in the exclusion of same-sex couples with a fifth judge holding that there was a violation but that it was justified under s. 1 of the *Charter*

90   *Hislop* above note 14 at para 116

viduals receive an appropriate remedy and in part by consideration of the respective roles of courts and legislatures. In determining remedial measures to right particular wrongs, there is choice ranging from declaratory relief, which entails minimal judicial involvement, to injunctions, which may require ongoing judicial supervision. Similarly, with respect to the validity of legislation, the courts may strike down all or parts of a law, mandate affirmative changes to the law through reading in, and decide to strike the law down but suspend or delay its declaration of invalidity. There is also the rare option of the court finding that the government has justified a departure from the norm of retroactive remedies and that only prospective relief is required. As with other areas of *Charter* jurisprudence, the Supreme Court has not hesitated to break new ground, but at the same time it has attempted to proceed in a relatively cautious, incremental manner, conscious of the limits of the judicial function and the need to respect the role and responsibilities of the democratically elected representatives of the people.

FURTHER READINGS

CHOUDHRY, S., & K. ROACH, "Putting the Past Behind Us? Prospective Judicial and Legislative Constitutional Remedies" (2003) 21 Sup. Ct. L. Rev. (2d) 205

COOPER-STEPHENSON, K.D., *Charter Damage Claims* (Calgary: Carswell, 1990)

FITZGERALD, O.E., *Understanding Charter Remedies* (Scarborough, ON: Carswell, 1994)

GIBSON, D., "Enforcement of the *Canadian Charter of Rights and Freedoms*" in G.A. Beaudoin & E. Mendes, eds., *The Canadian Charter of Rights and Freedoms*, 4th ed. (Markham, ON: LexisNexis Butterworths, 2005)

PINARD, D., "A Plea for Conceptual Consistency in Constitutional Remedies" (2006) 18 N.J.C.L. 105

ROACH, K., *Constitutional Remedies in Canada* (Aurora, ON: Canada Law Book, 1994)

ROACH, K., "Remedial Consensus and Dialogue under the *Charter*: General Declarations and Delayed Declarations of Invalidity" (2002) 39 U.B.C. L. Rev. 211

ROACH, K., "Principled Remedial Decision-Making under the *Charter*" (2004) 25 Sup. Ct. L. Rev. (2d) 101

ROGERSON, C., "The Judicial Search for Appropriate Remedies under the *Charter*" in R.J. Sharpe, ed., *Charter Litigation* (Toronto: Butterworths, 1987)

ROULEAU, P., S. BHATTACHARJEE, & N. ROULEAU, "Revisiting *Doucet-Boudreau*: Perspectives on Remedies in Section 23 Cases" (2006) 32 Sup. Ct. L. Rev. (2d) 301

RYDER, B., "Suspending the *Charter*" (2003) 21 Sup. Ct. L. Rev. (2d) 267

SHANDAL, V., "Combining Remedies under Section 24 of the *Charter* and Section 52 of the *Constitution Act, 1982*: A Discretionary Approach" (2002) 61 U.T. Fac. L. Rev. 175

SHARPE, R.J., "Injunctions and the *Charter*" (1984) 22 Osgoode Hall L.J. 474

CONCLUSION

The *Charter of Rights and Freedoms* is a fundamental and defining element of the modern Canadian state. While it draws upon certain aspects of our democratic and parliamentary traditions, by entrenching certain rights and freedoms as fundamental, and by assigning an important law-making role to the courts, it also marks a break with the past. No longer are Parliament and the legislatures supreme.

We have suggested that this shift of institutional responsibility, subjecting the powers of elected bodies to review by the courts under the *Charter*, is supportive of Canada's traditional democratic values. Experience has shown that majorities, unchecked, may fail to respect the dignity of all individuals, tend to shut out annoying and unpopular views, and ignore or even make worse the plight of vulnerable minorities. The *Charter* protects the values of individual dignity, autonomy, and respect. These attributes of citizenship are essential to a healthy democracy and to free and open democratic debate. The *Charter* also protects the rights of those accused of crime, an otherwise unpopular group. It reflects the view that a healthy democracy cannot be defined in terms of crude majoritarianism. The *Charter* may be seen as Canada's commitment to the principle that the exercise of power by the many is conditional on respect for the rights of the few. The role of the *Charter*, we suggest, is to facilitate, not frustrate, democracy.

It is apparent that the difficult task of ensuring that *Charter* rights and freedoms are respected inevitably embroils the judiciary in difficult and contentious issues of public concern. The courts have been willing to exercise the power of judicial review with a certain vigour in many areas. Religious minorities have succeeded in attacking measures that required them to observe the religion of the majority. In some cases, freedom of expression has been defended against measures that limited open debate and dissemination of information. The right to "life, liberty and security of the person" has been found to impose significant constraints on the right of the state to criminalize abortion and to extradite or deport people to face the death penalty or torture. The *Charter* has had a major impact in the area of criminal justice where judges have not hesitated to subject police powers to close scrutiny. Individual rights of privacy and bodily integrity and the rights to counsel and fair trial have been expanded significantly. The equality guarantee has required legislatures to reassess the manner in which minorities are treated. The Supreme Court has insisted upon close scrutiny of virtually all measures that discriminate on the grounds enumerated in section 15 or on analogous grounds, even where the denial of equality is not intended. This radical departure from the disappointing judicial record under the *Canadian Bill of Rights* has been significant in a number of cases. The guarantee of minority-language education rights has also been interpreted in a generous fashion to encourage a dialogue between the legislatures and rights claimants about the design of school systems.

On the other hand, there are areas where the courts have demonstrated a marked deference to legislative judgment. To date, the courts have been very unsympathetic to claims of pure economic rights and have refused to become embroiled in most distributional issues. The courts have refused to imply a right of property from the language of section 7 and have similarly rejected overtures to protect contract rights. The refusal to permit the equality guarantee in section 15 to extend beyond substantive discrimination on prohibited or analogous grounds is, we suggest, also consistent with this general pattern of leaving matters of economic and social policy to the legislatures. An open-ended approach to equality would require the courts to review virtually every line drawn by legislation and would divert attention from, and perhaps dilute the protection accorded to, those groups that have been the subjects of particular disadvantage because of specified and analogous personal characteristics.

The Supreme Court's approach to determining acceptable limitations of *Charter* rights and freedoms under section 1 largely coincides with this pattern. The Supreme Court has not taken a uniform approach to section 1, and the level of scrutiny to which challenged legislation is subjected varies. The Court has seen section 1 as a recognition of the institutional role of Parliament and the legislatures to enhance and protect some of the same values that inform judicial review. Legislative initiatives to protect vulnerable groups have often been upheld when such initiatives have been challenged as violating the fundamental freedoms or equality rights of more powerful interests in society. Similarly, the Court has given legislatures considerable latitude where broad questions of social or economic policy are involved.

After almost three decades of *Charter* jurisprudence, certain broad outlines have been drawn, but we certainly do not yet have a fully completed picture. In recent years the Court has revisited a number of its prior precedents concerning matters such as extradition to face the death penalty, self-incrimination, equality rights and affirmative action, and the exclusion of unconstitutionally obtained evidence. It is often suggested, both by *Charter* "believers" and by *Charter* "sceptics," that the uncertainty of *Charter* jurisprudence reflects an inadequate and uncertain response from the Supreme Court. We suggest that an element of uncertainty is to be expected. First, a constitution is an expression of a society's most fundamental values. It is an enduring document that must allow our public institutions to address the issues of today but also offer the flexibility to meet the unknown challenges of the future. Definitive judicial pronouncements on every detail of the constitution or rigid adherence to what the words of the constitution may mean in one historical context could produce an institutional straightjacket inconsistent with this broader vision. The courts in the era of the *Charter* have quite appropriately remained faithful to the pre-*Charter* metaphor of the constitution as a "living tree" capable of growth and expansion within its natural limits. Second, there are inherent limits in the judicial process. The most obvious is that *Charter* issues are decided in the context of specific cases. The judicial method is necessarily responsive and incremental. While the Supreme Court has some control of the cases it hears through the leave-to-appeal process, it does not have the capacity to set its own agenda, but rather must deal with the issues that the litigants bring before it.

Much can be accomplished through litigation, but the democratically elected representatives of the people retain primary responsibility for social and economic policy and for resolving most of the ills that beset our society. While the *Charter* assigns an important role to the courts, it is but one aspect of a constitution that speaks to all who exercise power in our society. We continue to have a strong parliamentary tradition that has always imposed a moral and political duty upon our elected representatives to respect fundamental rights and freedoms. We also have traditions of respect for the rights of minorities, federalism, and constitutionalism and the rule of law, which pre-date the *Charter*. The enhanced power of the courts under the *Charter* should be seen as both a continuation and an enrichment of Canadian constitutional traditions. In this book, we have canvassed the way in which the *Charter* has altered the nature of public debate in Canada. We suggest that, on the whole, experience to date suggests that the *Charter* offers the promise of a stronger and more vibrant Canadian democracy.

GLOSSARY

Absolute liability: an offence for which the accused is guilty once it is proven that the prohibited act was committed and regardless of the existence of any fault, including negligence.

Adjudicative facts: facts relating to the immediate dispute between the parties, "who, what, where and how" (as distinguished from "legislative facts").

Affirmative action: positive measures intended to benefit a disadvantaged group.

Agency shop provision: a provision in a collective agreement compelling payment of dues to a union by non-member employees.

Appellate court: the court that hears appeals from judgments of the trial courts. There are provincial appellate courts to hear appeals from the provincial courts and the provincial superior courts, and a Federal Court of Appeal to hear appeals from the Federal Court, Trial Division.

Attorney general: the member of Cabinet who is the senior legal adviser to the government and who is ultimately accountable for prosecutions.

Civil law: a legal system in which private law is enacted by the legislature and is predominantly contained in a Civil Code. It is in contradistinction to the common law where the basis of private law is judge made. Quebec has a civil law tradition.

Closed shop provision: a provision in a collective agreement compelling membership in a union.

Commercial expression: expression conveyed for the purpose of earning money, usually in the form of advertising.

Common law: judge-made law, reflected by precedents established by the decisions of the courts, as distinct from statute-law passed by the legislature. In all provinces other than Quebec, the primary source of private law is the common law.

Constitutional convention: an unwritten rule, rather than formal laws, that is enforced through the political process rather than in the courts. The Canadian constitution consists of the written constitutional texts, judicial precedents, and constitutional conventions.

Constitutional exemption: the law remains valid for all purposes, save that the court exempts a particular individual or situation from its application.

Contextual analysis: assessing *Charter* issues in the light of the specific social, cultural, economic, and political factors that bear upon the right claimed or the basis asserted for limiting the right.

Damages: monetary award received by the injured party to compensate for the wrong suffered.

Declaratory proceedings: a suit in which the only relief sought is a statement by the court delineating the ambit of a right or stating that a statute or practice is contrary to the constitution, with no other concrete remedy provided.

Deference: the view that a court order is not the appropriate solution and that the matter should be left to the legislature.

Delayed declaration of invalidity: *see* suspended declaration of invalidity

Dialogue: the relationship of give and take between courts and legislatures resulting from judicial decisions striking down laws and fresh legislation enacted in response.

Disclosure: the obligation of the Crown to notify the accused prior to trial of any evidence it intends to use and any evidence that might assist the accused, even if the Crown does not intend to adduce such evidence at trial.

Division of powers: the constitutional allocation of authority between the federal and provincial governments to enact legislation.

Dualism: the conception of Canadian Confederation as being a historical compromise between the French- and English-speaking communities. Also refers to the traditional understanding of international and domestic law as distinct, with international not being enforced in domestic courts unless specifically adopted in domestic legislation.

Due process: principles of procedural fairness that have evolved through the common law.

Ex parte **injunction:** an injunction issued without notice to the defendant.

Expression: any activity that conveys or attempts to convey meaning.

Federalism: a governmental structure whereby the power to legislate is divided between various levels of government. In Canada, the division of powers is between the Parliament of Canada and the ten provincial legislatures.

Federalism review: judicial consideration of whether Parliament or a provincial legislature has the authority under the division of powers to enact legislation.

Freedom: ". . . embraces both the absence of coercion and constraint, and the right to manifest beliefs and practices." *R. v. Big M Drug Mart Ltd.* (1985), 18 D.L.R. (4th) 321 at 354 (S.C.C.).

Gerrymandering: a term connoting the exercise of self-interest on the part of political incumbents in control of the process of drawing electoral boundary lines.

Habeas corpus: a common law remedy, permitting anyone who is detained to require the person having custody to bring the detainee immediately before a court and to provide legal justification.

Injunction: an order of the court requiring a party to perform some act or refrain from some conduct so as to respect the rights of another.

Judicial activism: an inclination by the court to be fairly bold about striking down laws and policies that contravene the constitution.

Judicial Committee of the Privy Council: during the British Empire, the Privy Council was the final court of appeal for the colonies. The right of appeal from the Supreme Court of Canada to the Privy Council was abolished in 1949.

Judicial interim release: the release of an accused person pending trial, formerly referred to as bail.

Judicial restraint: an inclination by the court to be more cautious about overturning government laws and policies.

Judicial review: the power of the courts to determine the constitutionality of legislation enacted by the people's elected representatives. It is a consequence of having a written constitution that is the supreme law of the land.

Jurisdiction: legal authority to decide.

Legislative facts: facts relating to the causes and effects of the social, cultural, economic, and political issues that legislation addresses (as distinguished from "adjudicative facts").

Legislative override: section 33 of the *Charter of Rights and Freedoms* permits a legislature to declare, for a period of five years, that a law shall operate "notwithstanding a provision included in section 2 or sections 7 to 15" of the *Charter*.

Minimal impairment: the most important element of the section 1 proportionality test: does the challenged legislation infringe the right or freedom more than is necessary to attain the legislative objective?

Mootness: a case becomes "moot" when the immediate concrete dispute between the parties no longer exists, even though the legal or constitutional issue remains unresolved.

Natural justice: procedural rights evolved by the common law that apply when a decision affecting one's legal rights is taken, including the right to be heard by an impartial tribunal.

Negative right: a right to be left alone, therefore precluding Parliament or a legislature from interfering.

Notwithstanding clause: *see* "Legislative override."

***Oakes* test:** the method described by the Supreme Court of Canada for determining whether a law that violates a fundamental right or freedom should be saved as a reasonable limit under section 1 of the *Charter*.

Overbreadth: legislation that is drafted more broadly than is necessary or permissible to attain the legislative objective with the result that it impinges unduly upon a protected right or freedom.

Override: *see* "Legislative override."

Parliamentary supremacy: the principle that the elected representatives of the people, assembled in Parliament, have unlimited power to make the law, the one exception being that Parliament cannot bind its successors.

Positive right: a right to be accorded some privilege or benefit, therefore requiring action on the part of Parliament or a legislature.

Presumption of constitutionality: the presumption that evolved under federalism that legislation enacted by Parliament or a legislature does not violate the constitution.

Presumption of innocence: the principle, now protected by section 11(d) of the *Charter*, that everyone accused of a crime is presumed to be innocent until the Crown has proven the accused's guilt beyond a reasonable doubt to the satisfaction of a judge or jury.

***Prima facie*:** a case of sufficient weight presented by the party having the burden of proof to warrant judgment in that party's favour absent a response from the other side.

Private action: acts by individuals or corporations not subject to the direct control of government.

Proportionality: the central element of the *Oakes* test under section 1 of the *Charter*, weighing the breach of *Charter* rights against the government interest advanced by a challenged law. A law will be a proportionate limit on rights if it is rationally connected to an important objective, violates the rights as little as is reasonably possible to achieve the objective, and if there is an overall balance between the effects of the rights infringement and the advancement of the objective of the legislation.

Prospective relief: a remedy that only applies to future conduct and does not attempt to correct the effects of past Charter violations. See also suspended declaration of invalidity

Provincial court: a court consisting of judges appointed by a provincial government, which deals with criminal cases not tried by jury, family matters, and small civil claims.

Punitive damages: monetary award to an injured party designed to punish the wrongdoer and deter others from taking the same course of conduct, rather than merely to compensate the injured party.

Purposive approach: a method of interpretation based upon delving into the fundamental and underlying reason for a law or constitutional guarantee.

Rational connection: the first element of the section 1 proportionality test: does the challenged legislation further the legislative objective in a rational and non-arbitrary way?

Reading down: where a court gives an over-inclusive statute a sufficiently narrow interpretation to bring it into line with the demands of the constitution.

Reading in: where a court adds something to a statute to make it conform to the constitution.

Reference: the government may refer directly to the court questions of law or fact concerning the interpretation of the constitution, or the constitutionality of any legislation. A reference is an exception to the usual two-party, adversarial system.

Regulatory offences: offences that regulate risky behaviour that may cause harm but do not ordinarily involve truly criminal or morally reprehensible behaviour.

Retroactive Relief: a remedy that attempts to repair the effects of past *Charter* violations.

Rule of law: the ideal of the supremacy of law in the social order. There are three aspects to the rule of law: no one can be punished except for breach of a duly enacted law; everyone, from the highest official to the ordinary citizen, is subject to the ordinary law of the land; and the courts have ultimate responsibility for the protection of rights and respect for the legal order.

Search and seizure: a state activity that invades a reasonable expectation of privacy.

Severance: where a court excises a discreet and identifiable measure of a challenged law without altering the overall structure or operation of the law in which it is contained.

Standing: the requirement that an individual must show a specific legal right or interest before bringing an action to challenge the constitutional validity of a law.

Stare decisis: the principle by which decisions of a higher court are binding on and must be followed by lower courts.

Stay of proceedings: a disposition where a court does not allow a prosecution to proceed because of objectionable police or prosecutorial conduct or a violation of the accused's rights.

Superior court: the highest level of trial court in each province. The judges of the superior courts are appointed by the federal government. The superior courts have exercise over a broad jurisdiction in both civil and criminal cases and have the authority to apply both federal and provincial laws.

Suspended declaration of invalidity: a declaration of invalidity that does not take effect until some set period (usually 6, 12 or 18 months) after the court has issued its ruling finding legislation to be an unjustified violation of the *Charter.*

Temporary suspension of invalidity: where a court finds a law to be unconstitutional, but delays the implementation of its order of invalidity to afford Parliament or the legislature the opportunity to repair the constitutional deficiency.

Torts: non-contractual civil wrongs recognized at common law.

Under-inclusive law: a law that is found to be constitutionally defective in that it fails to extend its reach to those who have a constitutional claim to its protection.

Vagueness: an unacceptable lack of precision in legislation that leaves its meaning and application so uncertain as to unduly threaten a protected right or freedom.

CONSTITUTION ACT, 1982

SCHEDULE B

CONSTITUTION ACT, 1982

PART I
CANADIAN CHARTER OF RIGHTS AND FREEDOMS

Whereas Canada is founded upon principles that recognize the supremacy of God and the rule of law:

Guarantee of Rights and Freedoms

Rights and freedoms in Canada
1. The *Canadian Charter of Rights and Freedoms* guarantees the rights and freedoms set out in it subject only to such reasonable limits prescribed by law as can be demonstrably justified in a free and democratic society.

Fundamental Freedoms

Fundamental freedoms
2. Everyone has the following fundamental freedoms:
> (*a*) freedom of conscience and religion;
> (*b*) freedom of thought, belief, opinion and expression, including freedom of the press and other media of communication;
> (*c*) freedom of peaceful assembly; and

(d) freedom of association.

Democratic Rights

Democratic rights of citizens
3. Every citizen of Canada has the right to vote in an election of members of the House of Commons or of a legislative assembly and to be qualified for membership therein.

Maximum duration of legislative bodies
4. (1) No House of Commons and no legislative assembly shall continue for longer than five years from the date fixed for the return of the writs of a general election of its members.

Continuation in special circumstances
    (2) In time of real or apprehended war, invasion or insurrection, a House of Commons may be continued by Parliament and a legislative assembly may be continued by the legislature beyond five years if such continuation is not opposed by the votes of more than one-third of the members of the House of Commons or the legislative assembly, as the case may be.

Annual sitting of legislative bodies
5. There shall be a sitting of Parliament and of each legislature at least once every twelve months.

Mobility Rights

Mobility of citizens
6. (1) Every citizen of Canada has the right to enter, remain in and leave Canada.

Rights to move and gain livelihood
    (2) Every citizen of Canada and every person who has the status of a permanent resident of Canada has the right
    (a) to move to and take up residence in any province; and
    (b) to pursue the gaining of a livelihood in any province.

Limitation
    (3) The rights specified in subsection (2) are subject to
    (a) any laws or practices of general application in force in a province other than those that discriminate among persons primarily on the basis of province of present or previous residence; and
    (b) any laws providing for reasonable residency requirements as a qualification for the receipt of publicly provided social services.

Affirmative action programs
(4) Subsections (2) and (3) do not preclude any law, program or activity that has as its object the amelioration in a province of conditions of individuals in that province who are socially or economically disadvantaged if the rate of employment in that province is below the rate of employment in Canada.

Legal Rights

Life, liberty and security of person
7. Everyone has the right to life, liberty and security of the person and the right not to be deprived thereof except in accordance with the principles of fundamental justice.

Search or seizure
8. Everyone has the right to be secure against unreasonable search or seizure.

Detention or imprisonment
9. Everyone has the right not to be arbitrarily detained or imprisoned.

Arrest or detention
10. Everyone has the right on arrest or detention
    (*a*) to be informed promptly of the reasons therefor;
    (*b*) to retain and instruct counsel without delay and to be informed of that right; and
    (*c*) to have the validity of the detention determined by way of *habeas corpus* and to be released if the detention is not lawful.

Proceedings in criminal and penal matters
11. Any person charged with an offence has the right
    (*a*) to be informed without unreasonable delay of the specific offence;
    (*b*) to be tried within a reasonable time;
    (*c*) not to be compelled to be a witness in proceedings against that person in respect of the offence;
    (*d*) to be presumed innocent until proven guilty according to law in a fair and public hearing by an independent and impartial tribunal;
    (*e*) not to be denied reasonable bail without just cause;
    (*f*) except in the case of an offence under military law tried before a military tribunal, to the benefit of trial by jury where the maximum punishment for the offence is imprisonment for five years or a more severe punishment;

(g) not to be found guilty on account of any act or omission unless, at the time of the act or omission, it constituted an offence under Canadian or international law or was criminal according to the general principles of law recognized by the community of nations;

(h) if finally acquitted of the offence, not to be tried for it again and, if finally found guilty and punished for the offence, not to be tried or punished for it again; and

(i) if found guilty of the offence and if the punishment for the offence has been varied between the time of commission and the time of sentencing, to the benefit of the lesser punishment.

Treatment or punishment
12. Everyone has the right not to be subjected to any cruel and unusual treatment or punishment.

Self-crimination
13. A witness who testifies in any proceedings has the right not to have any incriminating evidence so given used to incriminate that witness in any other proceedings, except in a prosecution for perjury or for the giving of contradictory evidence.

Interpreter
14. A party or witness in any proceedings who does not understand or speak the language in which the proceedings are conducted or who is deaf has the right to the assistance of an interpreter.

Equality Rights

Equality before and under law and equal protection and benefit of law
15. (1) Every individual is equal before and under the law and has the right to the equal protection and equal benefit of the law without discrimination and, in particular, without discrimination based on race, national or ethnic origin, colour, religion, sex, age or mental or physical disability.

Affirmative action programs
(2) Subsection (1) does not preclude any law, program or activity that has as its object the amelioration of conditions of disadvantaged individuals or groups including those that are disadvantaged because of race, national or ethnic origin, colour, religion, sex, age or mental or physical disability.

Official Languages of Canada

Official languages of Canada
16. (1) English and French are the official languages of Canada and have equality of status and equal rights and privileges as to their use in all institutions of the Parliament and government of Canada.

Official languages of New Brunswick
(2) English and French are the official languages of New Brunswick and have equality of status and equal rights and privileges as to their use in all institutions of the legislature and government of New Brunswick.

Advancement of status and use
(3) Nothing in this Charter limits the authority of Parliament or a legislature to advance the equality of status or use of English and French.

English and French linguistic communities in New Brunswick
16.1 (1) The English linguistic community and the French linguistic community in New Brunswick have equality of status and equal rights and privileges, including the right to distinct educational institutions and such distinct cultural institutions as are necessary for the preservation and promotion of those communities.

Role of the legislature and government of New Brunswick
(2) The role of the legislature and government of New Brunswick to preserve and promote the status, rights and privileges referred to in subsection (1) is affirmed.

Proceedings of Parliament
17. (1) Everyone has the right to use English or French in any debates and other proceedings of Parliament.

Proceedings of New Brunswick legislature
(2) Everyone has the right to use English or French in any debates and other proceedings of the legislature of New Brunswick.

Parliamentary statutes and records
18. (1) The statutes, records and journals of Parliament shall be printed and published in English and French and both language versions are equally authoritative.

New Brunswick statutes and records
(2) The statutes, records and journals of the legislature of New Brunswick shall be printed and published in English and French and both language versions are equally authoritative.

Proceedings in courts established by Parliament
19. (1) Either English or French may be used by any person in, or in any pleading in or process issuing from, any court established by Parliament.

Proceedings in New Brunswick courts
(2) Either English or French may be used by any person in, or in any pleading in or process issuing from, any court of New Brunswick.

Communications by public with federal institutions
20. (1) Any member of the public in Canada has the right to communicate with, and to receive available services from, any head or central office of an institution of the Parliament or government of Canada in English or French, and has the same right with respect to any other office of any such institution where
  (*a*) there is a significant demand for communications with and services from that office in such language; or
  (*b*) due to the nature of the office, it is reasonable that communications with and services from that office be available in both English and French.

Communications by public with New Brunswick institutions
(2) Any member of the public in New Brunswick has the right to communicate with, and to receive available services from, any office of an institution of the legislature or government of New Brunswick in English or French.

Continuation of existing constitutional provisions
21. Nothing in sections 16 to 20 abrogates or derogates from any right, privilege or obligation with respect to the English and French languages, or either of them, that exists or is continued by virtue of any other provision of the Constitution of Canada.

Rights and privileges preserved
22. Nothing in sections 16 to 20 abrogates or derogates from any legal or customary right or privilege acquired or enjoyed either before or after the coming into force of this Charter with respect to any language that is not English or French.

Minority Language Educational Rights

Language of instruction
23. (1) Citizens of Canada
  (*a*) whose first language learned and still understood is that of the English or French linguistic minority population of the province in which they reside, or

(*b*) who have received their primary school instruction in Canada in English or French and reside in a province where the language in which they received that instruction is the language of the English or French linguistic minority population of the province,

have the right to have their children receive primary and secondary school instruction in that language in that province.[91]

Continuity of language instruction

(2) Citizens of Canada of whom any child has received or is receiving primary or secondary school instruction in English or French in Canada, have the right to have all their children receive primary and secondary school instruction in the same language.

Application where numbers warrant

(3) The right of citizens of Canada under subsections (1) and (2) to have their children receive primary and secondary school instruction in the language of the English or French linguistic minority population of a province

(*a*) applies wherever in the province the number of children of citizens who have such a right is sufficient to warrant the provision to them out of public funds of minority language instruction; and

(*b*) includes, where the number of those children so warrants, the right to have them receive that instruction in minority language educational facilities provided out of public funds.

Enforcement

Enforcement of guaranteed rights and freedoms

24. (1) Anyone whose rights or freedoms, as guaranteed by this Charter, have been infringed or denied may apply to a court of competent jurisdiction to obtain such remedy as the court considers appropriate and just in the circumstances.

Exclusion of evidence bringing administration of justice into disrepute

(2) Where, in proceedings under subsection (1), a court concludes that evidence was obtained in a manner that infringed or denied any rights or freedoms guaranteed by this Charter, the evidence shall be excluded if it is established that, having regard to all the circumstances, the admission of it in the proceedings would bring the administration of justice into disrepute.

General

Aboriginal rights and freedoms not affected by Charter
25. The guarantee in this Charter of certain rights and freedoms shall not be construed so as to abrogate or derogate from any aboriginal, treaty or other rights or freedoms that pertain to the aboriginal peoples of Canada including

    (a) any rights or freedoms that have been recognized by the Royal Proclamation of October 7, 1763; and

    (b) any rights or freedoms that now exist by way of land claims agreements or may be so acquired.[92]

Other rights and freedoms not affected by Charter
26. The guarantee in this Charter of certain rights and freedoms shall not be construed as denying the existence of any other rights or freedoms that exist in Canada.

Multicultural heritage
27. This Charter shall be interpreted in a manner consistent with the preservation and enhancement of the multicultural heritage of Canadians.

Rights guaranteed equally to both sexes
28. Notwithstanding anything in this Charter, the rights and freedoms referred to in it are guaranteed equally to male and female persons.

Rights respecting certain schools preserved
29. Nothing in this Charter abrogates or derogates from any rights or privileges guaranteed by or under the Constitution of Canada in respect of denominational, separate or dissentient schools.[93]

Application to territories and territorial authorities
30. A reference in this Charter to a Province or to the legislative assembly or legislature of a province shall be deemed to include a reference to the Yukon Territory and the Northwest Territories, or to the appropriate legislative authority thereof, as the case may be.

Legislative powers not extended
31. Nothing in this Charter extends the legislative powers of any body or authority.

Application of Charter

Application of Charter
32. (1) This Charter applies

    (a) to the Parliament and government of Canada in respect of all matters within the authority of Parliament including all matters relating to the Yukon Territory and Northwest Territories; and

(*b*) to the legislature and government of each province in respect of all matters within the authority of the legislature of each province.

Exception

(2) Notwithstanding subsection (1), section 15 shall not have effect until three years after this section comes into force.

Exception where express declaration

33. (1) Parliament or the legislature of a province may expressly declare in an Act of Parliament or of the legislature, as the case may be, that the Act or a provision thereof shall operate notwithstanding a provision included in section 2 or sections 7 to 15 of this Charter.

Operation of exception

(2) An Act or a provision of an Act in respect of which a declaration made under this section is in effect shall have such operation as it would have but for the provision of this Charter referred to in the declaration.

Five year limitation

(3) A declaration made under subsection (1) shall cease to have effect five years after it comes into force or on such earlier date as may be specified in the declaration.

Re-enactment

(4) Parliament or the legislature of a province may re-enact a declaration made under subsection (1).

Five year limitation

(5) Subsection (3) applies in respect of a re-enactment made under subsection (4).

Citation

Citation

34. This Part may be cited as the *Canadian Charter of Rights and Freedoms*.

TABLE OF CASES

INDEX

ABOUT THE AUTHORS

Robert Sharpe was formerly a professor at the Faculty of Law, University of Toronto, where he wrote and taught in the areas of constitutional law, remedies, civil procedure, and criminal law. From 1990 to 1995 he served as Dean of the Faculty. He has appeared as counsel in a number of *Charter* cases in courts at all levels, including the Supreme Court of Canada. From 1988 to 1990, he served as the Supreme Court's Executive Legal Officer. Robert Sharpe was elected a Fellow of the Royal Society of Canada in 1991. He was appointed to the Ontario Court of Justice (General Division) in 1995 and was appointed to the Ontario Court of Appeal in 1999. He was elected a Fellow of the Royal Society of Canada in 1991, awarded the Ontario Bar Association Distinguished Service Award in 2005, elected a Senior Fellow of Massey College in 2006, and received the Mundell Medal for Distinguished Contribution to Law and Letters in 2008. Justice Sharpe has published many scholarly articles and is the author of several award-winning books on law and legal history.

Kent Roach is a Professor of Law at the University of Toronto. He formerly served as Law Clerk to Madam Justice Bertha Wilson of the Supreme Court of Canada. He has been the editor-in-chief of the Criminal Law Quarterly since 1998 and has written extensively on constitutional law, criminal justice, and anti-terrorism law in both Canada and abroad, including a chapter on the criminal process in the *Oxford Handbook of Legal Studies* (2003). He is the author of *Constitutional Remedies in Canada* (1994), which was awarded the 1997 Walter Owen Book Prize as the best legal text in Canada, and (with Robert J. Sharpe) of *Brian Dickson: A Judge's Journey* (2003), which was awarded the 2004 Defoe Prize for best contribution to the understanding of Canada. Other books include *Due Process and Victims' Rights: The New Law and Politics of Crim-*

inal *Justice in Canada* (1999) and *The Supreme Court on Trial: Judicial Activism or Democratic Dialogue* (2001), which were both short-listed for the Donner Prize for best public policy book, and *September 11: Consequences for Canada* (2003). Professor Roach has appeared as counsel for Aboriginal Legal Services of Toronto and the Canadian Civil Liberties Association in cases in the Supreme Court of Canada, including *Stillman, Williams, Gladue,* and *Latimer.* He also acted as counsel for the Association in Aid of the Wrongfully Convicted in the systemic issues phase of the Kaufman inquiry into the wrongful conviction of Guy Paul Morin. Most recently he served as research director for the Goudge inquiry on forensic pediatric pathology and the inquiry into the bombing of Air India Flight 182.